THE
DONALD
RICHIE
READER

THE
DONALD
RICHIE
READER

50 Years of Writing on Japan

DONALD RICHIE

Compiled, edited, and
with an introdcution by
Arturo Silva

Stone Bridge Press • Berkeley, California

Published by
Stone Bridge Press, P. O. Box 8208, Berkeley, CA 94707
TEL 510-524-8732 • sbp@stonebridge.com • www.stonebridge.com

Donald Richie's *A Lateral View, The Inland Sea,* and *The Japan Journals* have been published by Stone Bridge Press. For information, go to www.stonebridge.com.

Some material in this book that originally appeared in the following publications is reproduced here by permission (Donald Richie is the author of record except where noted):

A Taste of Japan: Food, Fact, and Fable; What the People Eat; Customs and Etiquette (1984) and *Public People, Private People* (1996; orig. *Different People*, 1987). Tokyo and New York, Kodansha International.

Ozu (1974) and *The Films of Akira Kurosawa*, revised edition (1984). Berkeley: University of California Press. © The Regents of the University of California.

The Japanese Garden: An Approach to Nature. By Teiji Itoh. English version by Donald Richie. New Haven: Yale University Press. © 1972 Yale University Press.

A Lateral View: Essays on Contemporary Japan (1987) and *Partial Views: Essays on Contemporary Japan* (1995). Tokyo: The Japan Times.

Tokyo: A View of the City. London: Reaktion Books. © 1999 Reaktion Books.

Where Are the Victors? (1956), *Companions of the Holidays* (1968), *Tokyo Nights* (1988), *The Honorable Visitors* (1994), and *The Temples of Kyoto* (1995). Tokyo and Boston: Tuttle Publishing.

Zen Inklings: Some Stories, Fables, Parables, and Sermons. Tokyo: Weatherhill, 1982.

"Spring and All" by William Carlos Williams is from *Collected Poems, 1909–1939, Volume 1.* © 1938 New Directions Publishing Corp. Reprinted by permission of New Directions Publishing Corp.

All other text excerpts and photographs are used by permission of Donald Richie.

"The Great Mirror: An Introduction to Donald Richie" and "Bibliographical Note" © 2001 Arturo Silva.

Book design and layout by Linda Ronan.

Printed in the United States of America.

10   9   8   7   6   5   4   3   2   2010 2009 2008 2007 2006

LIBRARY OF CONGRESS CATALOGING-IN-PUBLICATION DATA
Richie, Donald.
    The Donald Richie reader: 50 years of writing on Japan / Donald Rich-
ie; compiled and edited by Arturo Silva.
        p. cm.
    Includes bibliographical references.
    ISBN 1-880656-58-2—ISBN 1-880656-61-2 (pbk)
        1. Japan—Civilization—1945– I. Silva, Arturo. II. Title.
DS822.5 R5 2001
952.04—dc21   2001020351

Contents

47 Japan: Film

91 Japan: People

The Gods

Miscellanea

119 Japan: Fiction

Miscellanea

The Japanese

The Foreigners   Miscellanea

The Great Mirror:
An Introduction to Donald Richie

ONE

Donald Richie is an amateur and a dilettante (in the best sense
of these words), a humanist and a romantic (as he calls himself,
so contrary to the contemporary tide), and an aesthete (as I also
think of him). He is also the best writer we have on Japan. This
statement requires two comments. First, while Richie's worldwide reputation rests specifically on Japanese film, he has also
written voluminously and variously on a wide array of Japanese
subjects—from gardens and Godzilla to temples and tattoos—
seemingly destined to be of interest only to so-called Japanophiles (except perhaps when tattooists or garden historians wish
to pursue their research further). But even within (and especially
beyond) the fairly specialized field of film studies, Richie has
much to tell us about Japanese culture, society, and character.
Second, in a very real—and aesthetic—way, it can also be said
that Richie has always had only a single subject: himself. Even as
he observes Japan, he also, as in a mirror, observes himself.

How romantic! Few have looked as "deeply" into the Japanese
mirror as Richie and seen not only Japan, but himself, reflected
back. And we, as we read him, are further thrust into a vertigo of
recognition: discovering Japan, Richie, and ourselves.

What we have before us then is Donald Richie's Japan, a

by Arturo Silva

ix

description and an interpretation that is recognizable certainly, and possible, but one that is also, in the best artistic sense, impossible, imagined. His is a Japan as interpreted and invented as was Lafcadio Hearn's. One may recall Oscar Wilde here: "The whole of Japan is a pure invention. There is no such country, there are no such people."* I am certainly not the first to be struck by the notion that Richie's view of Japan will serve for the twenty-first century as Hearn's did for the previous one. Nor is it coincidence that one of Richie's later works is a commentary on Hearn's Japan writings, the contemporary observer commenting on his most important predecessor.

But for all the work and decades spent on it, Richie's view of Japan seems still to belong only to the "happy few." One difficulty in "placing" him is that Richie is neither an academic nor a popular writer (that is, one who writes books meant to be popular). He lacks clout then in two areas that unfailingly gain respect (one for its "intelligence," the other for its profitability). Concerning his lack of academic affiliation, he comments, "I've never approved of the academic style, which seems to be obscurity. Nonetheless, I do do learned papers, but everybody complains that they're far too readable, and that they are far too lucid to be any good." As for the popularity end of writing, he cites a story about a piece on film director Akira Kurosawa that was commissioned by the *New York Times Magazine,* which turned it down no less than five times: "Richie, you just haven't got the drama inherent in the man," they complained. His response: "I said that I didn't know that drama was inherent in people. I thought people like you made it up."

Richie's interpretation of Japan is compellingly attractive, eminently full of common sense, almost too easy to subscribe to. But why do so few? The problem is its ironically perfect fit: it fits no one's Orientalist agendas, all of which require an *other* Japan. Indeed, Richie is doubly other: caught between two facing mirrors that no one bothers to look into. His view is that of the *gaijin,* the foreigner who will never fit in, a position necessarily to be accepted by all outsiders in Japan, though not all do, of course.[1] (And in his case, he is one who wouldn't want to: "I think if I didn't feel like a foreigner, I wouldn't be here. If I were Japanese, I wouldn't stay here ten minutes.") More importantly, Richie's views are "unofficial"; he is no academic nor affiliated with any major newspaper or governmental agency. The complete freelancer, Richie only observes; he has neither an agenda, paradigm, nor system to push, no "Us versus Them" policy to assert. As he

* See pages xxxvii–xxxviii for the sources of quotations cited in the main text of this section.

1 Richie speaks of "the tone of a lot of writers in Japan now" as being one of "violated innocence. 'Here I was, open like a flower, and look what you did to me,' they say about Japan. Of course, this is based upon the idea that Japan would ever return whatever affection they were lavishing upon it." The subject of the foreigner in Japan receives some of Richie's most scathing comments. For example, he also recounts this incident: "Can you imagine, I heard a man, who'd been here before [i.e., during the Occupation] and then came back, say, 'these people are getting uppity.' If you say a person's getting uppity . . . you're saying that their position was such that they should never have attempted equality. That's not a very democratic thought" (Interview, May 11, 1996).

EUGENE LANGSTON

At Engakuji, Kamakura, 1947.

says, "There are so many more resemblances between the Japanese and everybody else than there are differences—all this harping on difference really becomes irritating."

Refreshingly, there are no tired and offensive cliches about Japan to be found in his work, few statistics, and no financial forecasts.[2] While he is undoubtedly *the* expert on Japan, he has no pretense of being a "Japan expert." He takes no position: "I am not to be put on one side or the other. You can't get that bipolar grip on me." Richie has always happily acknowledged his status as outsider—he has never been a joiner—a position that allows him to observe dispassionately. "I didn't have to make the country coherent. All I had to do was describe things. I didn't have to have this superstructure that so many later writers about Japan thought they had to carry around. Particularly, I didn't have to construct models of the country. I could look at it and attempt to describe it."[3] For many an establishment or institution, he is neglected because no use can be made of him. ("Richie? Writes about films, doesn't he? Oh, and tattoos and gardens, eh? Good for him," one imagines editors and bureaucrats remarking.)

That, precisely, is the value and beauty of his work. What

2 And there is a good deal of (gratuitous?) debunking of many received notions. For example, Richie does not think that the Japanese are particularly hard-working nor especially devoted to cleanliness, arguable points, of course. For all of his descriptive abilities, Richie himself can also be faulted with the creation of a no-less-subjective set of peculiar views of the Japanese. While I largely agree with him, I also have to acknowledge that he does tend sometimes to wear the proverbial rose-tinted lenses. This is especially so, for example, regarding his notion of Japanese "innocence."

3 "I am at home in Japan precisely because I am an alien body. It is that I am no longer a member over there and cannot become a member over here—this defines my perfectly satisfactory position. One does not have to be a member of something" (*Journals*, March 21, 1992).

With a Gagaku dancer, 1947.

good is film criticism or a discussion of pachinko when it comes to international trade talks? None, certainly, to the academic's or the bureaucrat's mind-set. But a serious reading, of say, the opening chapter of Richie's book on the film director Yasujiro Ozu (included here), would provide any reader with a wealth of understanding of traditional Japanese family life. And a look at the essay on pachinko might provide some insight into the sense of loss, insularity, and insecurity of postwar Japanese (not irrelevant to trade talks). The use-value of Richie's eminently practical view of Japan is then immediately and ironically defeated by its beauty and charm—and yes, its real usefulness.[4]

Why then would one want to "subscribe" to Richie's view of Japan? Not because the establishment does not but simply because, it seems to me, his is a view one can live with. This is obvious, not in the views of big business or government but in terms of daily life, of mutual appreciation and comprehension, and of getting rid of that "Japan-equals-the-Other" mind-set. Generalizations about "the Japanese," or even "the Americans," "the Europeans" (or Italians, English, etc.) are in the end offensive. While Richie does make some generalizations—we all do—about "the Japanese," they are never held as unchanging truths. The truths lie in individuals, and of these, Japan has about 128 million.

* * *

4 His view might also be said to be self-defeating by being so varied: never having made the gesture of a single, all-encompassing history or, again, "interpretation" of Japan (which would be antithetical to his nature), Richie is thus (by this mode of thinking) not to be taken seriously. But taken together, his variety does possess an exceedingly impressive fullness—one that also resists "unity," systematicity. One of the obvious aims of this anthology is to display some of that variety; the reader, filling in the rest, will come halfway and perceive the fullness of Richie's view.

RICHARD LARSH

In the ruins of the Imperial Hotel, Tokyo, 1947.

For fifty years, Richie has observed, described, and commented upon the Japanese. One hesitates to say that he has also "interpreted" them as the term is usually understood; doing so would contradict the very core of his position, which is, that there is nothing to interpret, nothing to see through (no deeps to plumb, no essences to reach), no correlation to be made between some inner and outer worlds. At the most, one can say that, true to a rhetorical and aesthetic strategy holding, for example, that description itself is the strongest possible criticism (or even interpretation), so Richie's beautifully crafted descriptions of the Japanese must stand as his sole interpretation. One of the most important (and oft-repeated) themes of his view, his gaze, is that the ostensible is the real. What he observes is what he describes; what he describes is what we interpret.

* * *

Since he first arrived in Japan on the last day of 1946, in more than thirty books, scores of essays, and hundreds of book and film reviews, as well as dozens of lectures and presentations, not to mention a great miscellany of uncollected notes and articles, Richie has expostulated a view of Japan and the Japanese that is as "deep" or "true" as it is varied. He has not only written about Japanese film (perhaps a quarter of his work) but also the city of Tokyo (two books, many essays) as well as Japanese life in regard to nature and spirit (Zen, Shinto, gardens, etc.); such seeming abstracts as time and space as perceived by the Japanese; a host of Japanese arts, including traditional and contemporary theater; aspects of popular culture (Japanese comics, television, fashion); Japanese food, design, pornography, Japanese ghosts, and tattooing; not to mention scores of specific Japanese individuals. No one, to my knowledge, has ever written such a compendium on Japan in so thorough a form and with such style and erudition. The only comparable effort must be Basil Hall Chamberlain's perennial *Things Japanese* (1927), which, while somewhat outdated but nonetheless still enjoyable, is more of a collection of encyclopedic entries. Richie has even challenged that volume (see the bibliographical note). Also, one must consider the many genres and styles Richie has worked in. These include not only film history and criticism but also the historical as well as contemporary and experimental novel; short stories and drama; the biographical portrait (as well as autobiography in both memoirs and journals); the fable and satire; travel and garden and culinary writing; amateur or quasi-sociology, history, and anthropology (including religious anthropology), and semiology; art, theater, and music criticism; not to mention the journalistic grind of a book or film review written every week for almost five decades. His other roles include editor and lecturer, as well as composer and painter.

* * *

While this great variety is astounding, even more so is the consistency with which he approaches his subjects.[5] Somehow, early on, the subject and its writer formed a natural symbiosis, an immediate connection, and, as one might say, the texts simply came forth. What is astonishing about his first stay in Japan (1947–49) is the immediacy of connection Richie felt for this strange, new land. There is no easy explanation. Perhaps we can attribute the feeling to that most natural of occurrences, coincidence. Richie says he was simply ready. "I knew nothing about Japan. The reasons I liked it here were emotional. I was ready to fall in love with whatever fell in my lap. I'd come from an industrial town in the northwest corner of Ohio—I never liked it very much—and my earliest ambition was to leave. If you grow up having those feelings, and then when you finally get

[5] A keen reader will also, happily, find some inconsistencies and contradictions.

HOLLOWAY BROWN

to a place which is complicated and interesting and filled with promise, you're bound to have an emotional feeling. You've got all these feelings you haven't used. My roots descended, here, in this friendly loam."

Perhaps these lines from William Carlos Williams's "Spring and All" describe it best:

> *They enter the new world naked,*
> *cold, uncertain of all*
> *save that they enter.*
> . . . .
> *One by one objects are defined—*
> *It quickens: clarity, outline of leaf.*
>
> *But now the stark dignity of*
> *entrance—Still, the profound change*
> *has come upon them: rooted, they*
> *grip down and begin to awaken.*

*With Yasunari Kawabata,
Kamakura, 1948.*

TWO

Donald Richie was born in April 1924 in the town of Lima, Ohio, of Scottish and Swiss ancestry. There was nothing extraordinary about life in Lima (pronounced as the bean is), and that was the problem: "50,000 people, in the corner of the beet-growing fields of northwest Ohio." Precociously, at about the age of eight or nine years old, he became aware of language and its power to describe and order the world and his emotions. He was also sensitive to music—always classical—and listened to radio broadcasts. At the same time, during his weekly visits to the Sigma Theater, the local cinema, he discovered the magical world of film (at first merely an alternative to the reality of Lima). These three worlds of language, music, and film provided imaginative means of escape from Lima (as did a visit to the Chicago World's Fair in 1933), but he keenly felt the need for a real one. Around 1939 he read Frederick Prokosch's *The Asiatics*, which prophetically whetted his appetite for the Orient. At age seventeen, the revelation of film as another means of ordering and describing the world came when he saw Orson Welles's *Citizen Kane*. In the same year (1941), he read another book by Prokosch, *Night of the Poor*, in which a young man decides to leave home by hitchhiking. Richie did the same; he hitchhiked to New Orleans and stayed there for four months. Meanwhile, America had entered the World War, and Richie enlisted in the U.S. Maritime Service (the Merchant

Marines). He spent the next four years as an ensign and purser, positions allowing him a great deal of time to read deeply into modern and classic, European and American literature. It also gave him an opportunity to see much of the world: northern Africa, southern Europe, Shanghai, and other places.

On New Year's Eve, 1946, his ship was docked in Okinawa Bay. On the next day Donald Richie would enter Japan, and his *annus mirabilis* would begin.

After discharge from the Maritime Services, Richie joined the civil service as a typist for the U.S. Occupation forces in Japan. During that first year alone in Japan, he underwent a number of astonishing experiences. Not only did Richie see the air-raid-devastated Tokyo (and watch it come back to life), he could also see Mount Fuji everyday from the main Ginza crossing. Richie visited the shrine of Ise and the stone garden of Ryoanji; awoke on a beach to discover boys sleeping in the sand for the O-Bon (Festival of the Dead) holiday; took part in the all-male nude Festival of Darkness; and on Sundays visited Daisetsu Suzuki in Kamakura, where he attempted to "understand" Zen Buddhism. By the next year, he had moved over to a position as staff writer and film critic on the Army newspaper, the *Pacific Stars and*

6 In fact, Richie has continued to be very much the working writer. Despite the number of books in print and their steady sales, as well as the international film festival invitations, he continues to perform "regular jobs"—editing a newsletter, taking part on various film committees, subtitling films, etc. His "normal" day remains simple: early to rise, he takes care of his correspondence, then writes—always careful to have a variety of subjects at hand so as to keep inspiration fresh—then lunch, jobs, and in the evening, dinner with friends or social or cultural occasions. He is also, needless to say, the complete Tokyo *flâneur*.

7 "To see if I can find out how to do it. The process is everything, the result's nothing—and once I've decided that I know how to do it, then I don't have any reason for doing it anymore. I long ago made the decision that writing is the only thing that counts for me" (Interview, November 4, 1996). And: "The avocations are there because I am curious. And since I make my living as a critic, I think I should not criticize until I know how to do it myself. Once I learn how to do it, I lose interest" (from a letter, February 25, 1996).

Stripes. He also made a number of important and lifelong personal and professional friendships. By spring 1949, Richie knew that he had found his home. He had also decided that he needed a "proper" education and so returned to America, with no doubt that he would be returning to Japan. Richie enrolled at Columbia University in New York, majoring in English Literature and also taking part in the first academically sanctioned course in Film Studies, offered by Roger Tilton. It was during these Columbia years, too, that Richie made his first experimental films.

Graduated, he returned to Japan in 1954 and worked at a few jobs—teaching, editing, and writing film reviews for the *Japan Times*, an association that still continues to this day.[6] Richie took evening classes in spoken Japanese; continued earlier friendships and made new ones; and, in 1956, published his first book. Begun in 1949, the novel *This Scorching Earth* (later reissued under its original title, *Where Are the Victors?*) expressed his view of the Occupation and its varied personnel, "indigenous" and otherwise. Over the next few years, much of his energies would be devoted to educating himself about Japanese film. While doing so, he also wrote articles for international film magazines, thus making something of a reputation for himself abroad, which resulted in his meeting a number of distinguished visitors to Japan (Alberto Moravia, Igor Stravinsky, Stephen Spender). He also met another Japanese film researcher, Joseph L. Anderson, and together they would write *The Japanese Film: Art and Industry* (1959). This book secured his reputation and would shortly lead to his either assisting in or organizing director retrospectives at major European film festivals in the early 1960s.

Richie's activities increased significantly during that time. Living in a friend's traditional Japanese farmhouse (it had been moved to Tokyo's Roppongi district; this was before the area's neon pick-up days occurring a decade later), he set about writing about film (his book on Kurosawa appeared in 1965); making his own films; participating in the thriving theater scene (and becoming friends with such artists as Butoh founder Tatsumi Hijikata, playwright Shuji Terayama, composer Toru Takemitsu, and novelist Yukio Mishima); and writing some of his more important early essays (he had already become an aficionado on the Noh). Besides writing, Richie also composed music, painted, and made prints.[7] He also married the writer Mary Evans (they divorced in 1965). Intellectually and personally, Richie had also come to appreciate Existentialism (he calls the Kurosawa book a "hymn to Existentialism"), underwent analysis, and came again, not coinci-

HOLLOWAY BROWN

In Asakusa, Tokyo, 1948.

dentally, to be intrigued by Zen Buddhism ("Zen teaches one to be in harmony with one's own nature").

All of this came to a temporary halt in 1968 when he was invited to become curator of film at New York's Museum of Modern Art. Richie stayed four years, returning to Tokyo every summer for three months. ("The U.S.A. was just one big Ohio so far as I was concerned. OK for a visit but no place you'd want to live.") While there, he organized a hundred-film retrospective of Japanese cinema, as well as the first U.S. retrospectives of the films of Robert Bresson and Stan Brakhage.

Since the 1950s, and throughout the 1960s, Richie had taken extensive trips throughout Japan, especially to an area known as Seto Naikai, the Inland Sea, a body of water located between three of Japan's four major islands and itself containing hundreds of smaller ones. From the many notes taken on these journeys his masterpiece, *The Inland Sea* (1971), was formed.[8] In 1975, he would finish another masterpiece, *Ozu*, a study of the great Japanese film director.

The later 1970s, and the 1980s and 1990s, the second quarter-century of his life in Japan, saw Richie in the position of being a "Japan expert" (though not in the academic sense I referred to above) and now more free to write about whatever his attention and enthusiasm turned to.[9] In 1980 he moved to Shitamachi, the older quarter of Tokyo, parts of which had not been devastated by the war's air raids, and lived in what he called his "Ozu

8 Curiously, for all his extensive travels worldwide, apart from *The Inland Sea*, almost the only other travel pieces he has written are the few compiled in *Partial Views*. Interestingly, these all date from the early 1980s and are redolent of Richie's recurring nostalgia for a "lost Japan."

9 Or was distracted by. The early 1980s see him succumbing somewhat to a "French" semiological influence. But he says, "I have little respect for the French school. I want to put an imprimatur on sanity. I do believe strongly in the humanist approach—man is the measure of all things—no ideas, no systems" (Interview, September 1996). But it is also interesting to note that Roland Barthes, for whom Richie does have great respect, had hoped to meet him; alas, such an auspicious meeting never took place.

At Nikkatsu Film Studio, in front of a miniature set, 1956.

NIKKATSU

10 As a practical way to live, not out of some earnest nostalgia. After all, Shitamachi is still part of the greater capital. "I don't think I'd have stayed here if it hadn't been for Tokyo. Tokyo is, as you know, a world in itself. One of the things about Tokyo is that you can escape from Japan" (Interview, May 11, 1996). Though not much emphasized here, the city holds a position of absolute centrality to Richie's life in Japan. For a description of his final "Ozu apartment," see the last entry in this book, "New Year's 1999."

11 *Different People* was reissued in 1996 under the title *Public People, Private People.*

apartment."[10] During these years, he wrote prolifically on a variety of subjects (food, tattoos, temples, Tokyo, pop culture, etc.), despite all his public-work commitments (lectures, film festivals), publishing fifteen books in the 1980s and 1990s, and about a hundred essays. Among other notable prizes, Richie was awarded the prestigious Japan Prize in 1995. Especially important books include *Zen Inklings* (1982), a delightful retelling of Zen tales; *Different People: Pictures of Some Japanese* (1987), portraits of individual Japanese;[11] *Tokyo Nights* (1988), an experimental comic novel; *The Honorable Visitors* (1994), accounts of twelve illustrious post-Meiji Western visitors to Japan; *Tokyo* (1999), his *zuihitsu* ("follow the brush") meditation on the great city; and *Memoirs of the Warrior Kumagai* (1999), a historical novel-cum-intellectual autobiography. During these years too, he regularly served as a judge at major world film festivals; still tirelessly introduced Japanese film to the West; wrote a weekly newspaper book review column; took extensive travels to many countries around the world; and, needless to say, led a full, active, social life.

* * *

Donald Richie is now in his late seventies. He represents not only a generation of young men who came of age in postwar Japan—including well-known scholars such as Donald Keene and Edward G. Seidensticker and numerous business- and family men and women—"old hands," as the phrase once had it. But

In a bookstore, Kanda, Tokyo, 1958.

KYODO TSUSHIN

Richie represents more too. When he casts off this mortal coil, a whole world of irrecoverable experience and knowledge will pass with him. One need only take a look at a few of the hundreds of book reviews he has written over the past forty years for the *Japan Times*; one cannot help but be struck not only by the great learning he possesses in regard to "things Japanese" but also the intelligence and care with which he delivers it, the ease with which he dons it. His references to events, people, books, and films are encyclopedic (and more often than not based on experience), and as such, we feel, to our great loss but academia's gain, will never be so smartly worn again.

Richie has had the good fortune to have (in Frank O'Hara's words) the "grace / to be born and live as variously as possible."

THREE

Within the great variety of Richie's work, we also see everything that is human.[12] And within the human we see the artistic: the style is the man. For all the quasi history, sociology, and anthropology he has written, Richie is first of all a writer, an artist.[13] His Japan is, of course, his version, his own take on the place and the people, his "imaginative interpretation."[14] But it is also very real (or, being art, realistic). Indeed, his interpretation would seek to "redeem reality"—revealing it by describing it faithfully[15]—in the way that Ozu's films do or the way that the Japanese gardener does.[16]

12 Or almost everything: I cannot recall any births occurring in the oeuvre.

13 *Ozu* is great film criticism partly because it recreates the director's working method.

14 As it should go without saying, this essay is my "interpretation" of Richie; I am very aware that so many more are possible.

15 The faith being in that describing, that removal to language. (Richie also calls himself, rather modestly to my mind, a "descriptive journalist.")

16 The idea of a "redemption of reality" comes first from Sigfried Kracauer's and Andre Bazin's film writings, and later, Paul Schrader's study, *Transcendental Style in Film: Ozu, Bresson, Dreyer* (Berkeley: University of California Press, 1972).

17 Nor did he ever "go native," or equally as bad, become uncritical. Japan, or Tokyo, may be "home" but only to a limit: "I find anyone who is 'at home' in this universe a person seriously deluded. . . . Being at home means taking for granted, going blind and deaf, eventually not even thinking. It means only comfort. I would hate to be at home" (*Journals*, February 3, 1992). That said, one can also say that Richie can also wax nostalgic and even sentimental at times. "Cold comfort" (see the next note) can become cozy.

18 "The liberty of realizing that I am responsible for everything that I am and have been and will be. . . . That has remained, with its hard mindedness, its lack of sentimentality, its cold comfort" (*Journals*, January 20, 1960).

19 The only extensive use of musical reference that Richie has made of music in his Japan writings is in his "Notes on the Noh" in *A Lateral View*.

20 "The story is there entirely for its formal qualities. To read Henry Green is like listening to well done music" (Interview, November 4, 1996).

21 "Rereading Colette's *The Pure and the Impure*, her best book, or the one I like best. It is pure description, very pure. And she sits there alone with her subject and we see her describing. It is a tone that I admire. Much in *Different People* has been learned from her. But what she can always do and what I can only occasionally do is to forget self in pure description. She can keep the description pure and yet go deep, so deep" (*Journals*, February 8, 1992).

In terms of the specifically real and present Japan, his perception can be found in the spiritual/anti-spiritual notion that "yes, there might be a Paradise, but life here on Earth is a Paradise too." In other words, the transcendent is the here and now. Richie's film criticism exemplifies the idea that Japanese film reflected Japanese daily life, that "the people on the screen and the people in the theater were so much the same." But Japan never became any sort of art object for Richie;[17] instead, the country became the "friendly loam" in which he could discover and be true to his own nature (redeeming, again, that reality too). Japan is also the Great Mirror in which he sees himself reflected. Art and Nature, Self and Other are the terms behind Richie's work. On New Year's Day, 1947, one of the great recognition scenes took place.

Again, Richie is an artist first; he approaches his material through the literary lens (and not as, say, a sociologist in the field, gathering data). Among the ideas that form his thinking, I have already mentioned the influence of Existentialism,[18] and Zen, but these came later in his makeup. The earliest artistic influences—or at least sources of wonder—were, as also previously mentioned, music, film, and language (though not yet as literature). Though he has written some music and music criticism, music has remained for Richie something that has "enriched me, made me alert, made me more open."[19] Music, of course, offers a writer lessons in rhythm, weight, tone, and so on. From film he learned especially about narrative structure. "It taught us what to leave out. Films have a terseness about them that is very good for art." The most obvious evidence of such is in the fiction, but it can also be found in the portraits, in that specificity of gesture or word, which are so cinematically precise.

Richie is a widely read person, and at some undefined point, his taste in writing was formed (perhaps during youth when he was taught to be wary of display for its own sake, and to appreciate craftsmanship). The "Richie pantheon" is very select. Among writers, there are (supremely) Jane Austen, Henry Green,[20] Colette,[21] and Marguerite Yourcenar, with Proust, Gide, and Borges in the anteroom. In film, Ozu and Robert Bresson. In music, Haydn, late Beethoven, late Brahms, Hindemith. In the visual arts, Vermeer, Chardin, and Giorgio Morandi.[22] In one conversation alone, Richie drew on three different arts in describing what he has wanted to achieve in his own: "I would like to be as good a describer as Ingres is a pencil-drawer. [Later:] One of my goals was to become as good a classical novelist as Colette. [And later again:] If I could be somebody as assured and as much a

KAWAKITA MEMORIAL FILM INSTITUTE

craftsman as Mendelssohn, then I would be very pleased." Briefly, while I hope that the meaning of this list is apparent, I think we can recognize a few points about these writers: in all of them, the style is classical, restrained, and always charming. Too, character description is supreme and refined. And third—perhaps the most important point in the Richie aesthetic—structure is impeccable. That is, stories unfold with an inevitability that appears utterly natural. All art is concealed, but it is an art whose subject determines its form (see his introductory remarks in *Tokyo*), where things are only shown and never explained.[23]

* * *

Richie's art and character are one of continuity and change (terms he also uses to describe his fifty years in Japan). One cannot say "when" he decided (humanistically) that "man is the measure of all things" or (existentially) that "ideas are only emotions whose time has come" or that "it doesn't matter what was done to you, but what you do with what was done to you." Richie's earliest Japan writings (apart from the 1947 journal entries included here) come from the mid-1950s, by the time he was in his early thirties and by which time his ideas had had nearly a decade in which to develop. These are remarkably lucid. One can detect later developments. The writing of *The Inland Sea* (1971) represents a watershed in clarifying his idea of Japan (and, naturally, himself). The publication of *Ozu* (1975) is a further instance

22 Two further points might be made here. One, Richie's taste in art is not as overweening as it seems; indeed, he also sees a lot of "trash" films. In other words, his tastes run high and low, but never rest in the middle. As he says, "I like generals or privates; Bresson or King Kong" (Interview, November 4, 1996). Two, given this sort of taste, it should be no wonder then—as it long was to me—that Richie would never, apart from a few short essays, write a book-length study of Japan's other great filmmaker, Kenji Mizoguchi, simply because his films call such attention to their style. Likewise, Max Ophüls and Hitchcock are not to his liking.

23 "I gave an introduction to *Tokyo Story*, recounting how Ozu hated just this kind of introduction. The explanation is always unnecessary. If you use your eyes and ears properly you will understand; if you do not, no amount of explanation will inform you. The reason is that Ozu is interested in showing, not explaining. He implies; you infer. He builds his half of the bridge; you build yours. Each having made some effort, a real communication becomes possible. No effort, no communication. This is the only kind of art I admire" (*Journals*, May 23, 1978).

At an inn on the Inland Sea, 1962.

(especially as it takes him so outside of himself) and led inevitably to *Zen Inklings* (1982), a book he has called "a gift." Behind the first two books lies, to speculate for a moment, the early 1960s period of psychoanalysis as well as Richie's marriage and divorce. Behind the latter book lies the late 1940s weekends at Engakuji in Kamakura with Daisetsu Suzuki, and again the analysis.[24] *Different People* (1987) and the work of the decade to come represent on one hand a "unity of being" (the earlier lessons had been fully learned, and incorporated) and on the other a more intensely passionate period of freedom to write about whatever he wanted— *Tokyo Nights* (1988) and *Memoirs of the Warrior Kumagai* (1999) especially—while also having his "final say" on certain matters (some individuals, Japanese film). But these remarks are mere broad brushstrokes that deeper study could clarify.

* * *

The style is the man. The man is charming, open, witty, a cosmopolitan *flâneur*. The style, the prose, is as well. He is comfortable to read, smooth, steady, melodious. The art is disguised, remarks flow naturally. (And thereby he achieves his ideal of art.) Insight rests on common sense. Description is epiphanic, aphorism abounds. There are few extremes, few judgments. (These occasional latter come in when he derides Japan for having sold out to big money.) A kind person, his satire is never cruel (see his article here on the "sex industry"). The prose, given its seductive charms,

24 Richie sees a certain relationship between Existentialism, Zen, and Psychoanalysis in that all three are concerned with liberating the "self" from the idea of "itself" (while admitting the great differences too, of course).

MARY RICHIE

At Dogashima, 1964.

can be rather erotic (though never specific; the reader must read into his desires). A circumspect man, presentation being all, best face forward, Richie's deeper emotions are rarely laid bare, except in the *Journals*. (For erotic and emotional specifics, readers will have to wait for the *Journals'* posthumous publication.)

FOUR

Awash in this soup—of boredom in Lima, ideas, aesthetics, artistic influences, worldwide travels—we come back to Okinawa Bay, New Year's Eve, 1946.

Open-eyed, observing, accepting, and ready for transformation by an equally accepting and welcoming society, Richie landed in Japan, and, in a colorfully dramatic phrase he said to me once, "I felt my testicles descend to the earth."[25] What he saw was a nation in ruins and a people who were dealing with it most practically. He saw smiles on the defeated, facing and welcoming their just recent enemy. He saw what he would come to call a natural and innocent people who had accepted their lot. Though screened from full view by being a representative of the Occupation forces, he would soon meet individuals who would accept him as the person he was.[26]

He would come to see that these individuals (he didn't yet speak the language) were simply who they openly presented themselves to be. They in turn accepted him for whom he presented

25 The word choice is more than appropriate. As Richie has written, for most travelers, travel also entails sexual freedom and opportunity (see the excerpt from *The Inland Sea* in the "Foreigners" miscellany, page 155). The nature he would be true to in Japan would also entail his sexuality, as he did find a sexual paradise there.

26 "I'd grown up with a lot of the facades that one grew up with in the 30s and 40s in America. And then I suddenly came here. I'd never been to a poor country before, and Japan was what we'd now call a Third World country, it didn't have any money. And people were living somewhat naked lives, and so I didn't have to put up with the kind of hypocrisy that I was used to. I was able to see people, and I was able to approach people. They wanted to be approached because everybody needed help. And so I was able to achieve terms of intimacy with people that I had singularly failed to back where I came from" (Interview, May 11, 1996).

himself to be. The ostensible was the real; there were no "depths of character" to be trudged through, no "essence" to be reached after struggle. Life was lived on the surface (a much better term for this discussion than the loaded "superficial"); character was what was presented, what was done by a person. Japan had lost the war; America had won. OK, accept it, *shoganai*, nothing to be done.

The description above is mostly mine but encapsulates, I think, the essence (if I may) of what Richie perceived during his first two-year stay in Japan. The essence also contains what were to remain most of the central themes of his writings on Japan, which, intertwined, are not easily separated, the one leading to the other and back again.

* * *

Richie's ideas about Japan form a continuum; any attempted unraveling would be like taking a painting apart, separating its colors side by side, and saying, "There is your painting in its constituent parts" (or a poem and lining up the words, or a film and reediting it according to long, medium, and close-up shots). One can name them all as a single continuum or better, divide them into closely related groups. They can even be abstracted into a single and not unexpected familiar opposition: Nature versus Art. In what follows, I hope to do as Richie, not explain things away but rather only suggest or indicate salient points and ways to read him (and this volume).

The ostensible is the real is a phrase often found in Richie's work (or the variant, "appearances are the only reality"; compare Wilde's "Only shallow people do not judge by appearances"). Richie's phrase is perhaps so often repeated because it is the hardest lesson for most Westerners to learn. Existentialism might have told him that people were simply what they did and that "intentions are ashes," but his encounters with the Japanese demonstrated the truth to him. Here, the self was in fact its surface. Richie's Japanese are a sublunary people, facing facts, facing appearances.

Facing what is in front of one's self entails two further notions central to Richie's view of Japan: the ideas of presentation and acceptance. Whether it be a tattooed sushi chef or a family at a funeral, *people present themselves in the most appropriate manner* (even "privileged, emotional moments are no less staged"). None of this presentation is done in bad faith; on the contrary, and too, it bespeaks fine character. Time and again in

DAIEI

With Kon Ichikawa, 1965.

Richie's writings, characters are seen who put their best selves forward (telling phrase), who keep on in the midst of hardship for no other reason than that it is the best—indeed, the only—thing to do. None of this is to say that the Japanese do not possess "character" or "individuality"—a lingering Orientalist notion Richie detests, and, for example, *Different People* certainly demonstrates to be untrue—or that they do not have dreams and ideals. Look only at the Tanabata scene from *Companions of the Holiday* (included here): Sumiko has her somewhat silly dreams of marriage to an older, mustachioed man, but when she is kissed by Saburo, the local meat-shop delivery boy, she is very much in the present moment and those dreams vanish. She accepts the hitherto unrecognized real being presented to her and now finally revealed.[27] Daily life in Japan is such that people necessarily have to get along (for any number of reasons, e.g., because they are so crowded together or the government for centuries has so inculcated the idea into them). Richie's Japanese are not plagued by any sentimental depth psychology. Life is to be lived; work is its own reward, and nothing more.[28] The view may be a hard truth to many, but it becomes for Richie a real one.[29]

Acceptance—existential, Buddhist—*is all.* The idea may be attributed to the practical lot of Japanese life, that poverty from which they created so much, the oppression they have long had to endure. But it does not bespeak any sort of passivity.[30]

27 The scene is doubly poignant for being one whose possibility has fast faded in post-Bubble Japan.

28 Consider this also from *Companions of the Holiday.* The old housekeeper Setsu is doing the accounts and thinking to herself: "Laying down her pencil, she decided that she had learned one thing, and that this was all the philosophy that she contained: the meaning of work lay in the working, so the meaning of life lay only in the living; one added one day upon the next, and this was sufficient; whether one served oneself or served a master, it was the same; to fill the day was important; what filled it was of small importance."

29 But too, emotional expression and spiritual striving are equally real to him, and they occur in art, in that "redemption of reality." The crux is simply that there is no "essence" of character or "transcendent beyond"—because it is all here and now.

30 Nor, once more, does it imply any passivity on Richie's part. Yes, he has embraced life in Japan, but not uncritically, as many of his works testify. If I may be allowed a lengthy footnote, consider this entry from the *Journals* (September 16, 1990):

Thinking about Japan this rainy Sunday—about the increasing amount of social control. Though the Japanologists talk about "innate" Japanese need for consensus, for the search for the great *wa* [harmony], without which no one is happy,

With Hidetoshi Hirano and Clifton Harrington during the filming of Futari, *1967.*

the "work ethic" which is said to be inborn, all of these things dividing Japan from the rest of humanity and making it unique—though this is talked about, few observe that: consensus is forced and the dissenter is punished, the *wa* is applied, not discovered, the ethic is enforced and not chosen. Japan exhausts its citizens with forced work and it deadens them with the forced play of the tube, pachinko, drink, drugs such as tobacco, encouraging a pathological dependence upon what one would in other countries call the state. That we do not in Japan is because it is not visible as such. Indeed, little is visible. There seems to be no control—certainly not the government that holds up clean hands and denies repression.

What it is, is the rule of a bureaucratic elite, which determines how Japan is governed—this is an oligopoly which forces the citizens of Japan into their characteristic mold. This would be impossible without a pliable populace, hence the necessity of creating (through the hierarchy of schools, through popular prejudice, through fear—the fear of being left out, left behind) a pliable populace. This control is seen as "self-regulatory"—the limits are imprinted. One is expected to submit to *gyosei shido* (administrative guidance) and practice *jishaku* (self-restraint)—these are held

Again, quite the contrary: pragmatic acceptance has yielded great spiritual nourishment (or at least once did). To it also must be attributed that acceptance of Nothingness itself (the *mu* on Ozu's gravestone), the "Nourishing Void" as Richie calls it (and the title of another piece included here).

This acceptance, of what is presented, of one's lot, is active, trusting, curious. It reaches out. Without conscience, self-consciousness, cynicism, and irony, it is childlike. And thus *the Japanese are innocent*. At least they *once were* childlike (and too the source of many worse presuppositions).

In 1947, Richie landed in a Japan that he regarded as a Paradise. People were friendly, open, and naked. Mount Fuji could be viewed from the main Ginza crossing. Time had been conquered at Ise Shrine and space rendered mystic at the stone garden of Ryoanji. From the horrors of war, a whole nation had re-arisen, smiling and hard at work. There were no agonies of conscience to endure, only work to be done.

From about the early 1970s on, one begins to recognize a certain wariness in Richie's writing. He begins to remark that Japan is rapidly changing, and not for the good. The country is losing its "innocence" as the economic machine with its rapid develop-

SAZORIZA

With the cast of "Three Kyogen,"
Tokyo, 1969.

up as virtues. And none of this is new. Japan was governed in just this fashion in the Tokugawa period where a completely controlled society was under a totalitarian state and the rebels, the humanists, the dissenters were punished. Now they are merely ostracized, and have to go into the *mizu shobai* ["water trade," or hostessing and other red-light-district entertainments]. However, the press is still relatively uncontrolled, things are still made public, and so *jishaku* is not yet complete.

31 Also:

The virtues I have been describing have now vanished from the Japanese film as they are vanishing from Japanese life. Where there is no more *shomin* (the lower-middle class) there can be no more *shomin-geki* (films about the lower-middle class). In an affluent society, there is no more *mono no aware* [the transience of all earthly things]. In a land where little is forbidden, there can be none of the energy or power of restriction. Less still means more, but the Japanese no longer believe it. There are doubtless strong economic reasons for all of this, but the economic explanation, whatever its strength, is never sufficient. ("A Definition of the Japanese Film," in *A Lateral View*)

ment takes control. The earlier Japan had been predicated on an aesthetic of poverty, as Richie says in an interview session:

> What has gone missing? One, and of course it's irretrievable, is the beauty of the country. It was the most beautiful country I'd ever seen in my life, and now it's just about the ugliest. That and an attitude toward nature which was based upon penury. If you don't have furniture, then you pay a lot of attention to empty space. And if you have only mud, then you pay a lot of attention to pottery. This attitude based on want leads to all sorts of interesting things like *wabi* and so forth, has given way to a new sort of cultural carpetbaggery and nouveaux riches beyond anybody's wildest dreams of bad taste.[31]

And,

> One of the things that I prized most was a kind of creative innocence on the part of the Japanese. We think of innocence as being an empty vehicle, a thing that has to be filled. But that's not it. It's got its own proportions, and it is a thing in itself, and so it's a positive and not a negative thing. Innocence is a force, and this innocence leads to things like an open mind, an inquiring disposition, certainly trust.

No longer. From that period on—it is also the time of *The Inland Sea* and its search for the "real Japan"—Richie derides

32 A moment later in the same conversation, Richie says, "I know Roppongi gives me the creeps. If that's the future, I don't even want to look at it." And later in the *Journals*, he again derides Roppongi: "All of Roppongi growing like a poisonous fungi" (August 23, 1989). Richie had lived in the district in the 1960s, and the lifestyle enjoyed there then is lovingly recalled in the 1968 novel *Companions of the Holiday*.

33 This nostalgia becomes a regular refrain as the years go by. (Fifty years and Eden gone is certainly acceptable, but some might argue that Richie goes a bit far: tatami are still common, as are good manners.) On October 4, 1973, he meets a friend who hasn't been in Japan for thirty years and says,

> She still, however, speaks the pure pre-war Tokyo accent, now almost disappeared, a language free from Osaka vulgarisms.

Five years later (July 30, 1978), he takes a trip to Tachikawa, on the western side of Tokyo, observing:

> There was the Tokyo I remembered from a quarter century ago. . . . I had forgotten the trees of Tokyo—and empty lots graciously doing nothing at all. . . . Everything looking smaller and yes, more gracious.

And only a few days later (August 4) at an outdoor fair, he reflects:

> Japan in the summer is always more Japanese, and never more so than at this fair. . . . This is what Japan once looked like. And old attitudes as well. A sudden interest in nature. . . And a much slower tempo. And with it the old politeness.

Yet Richie has also stated:

what is happening to his lost paradise.[32] In fact, at one point, he even calls it such. On June 30, 1989, he sees Heinosuke Gosho's 1933 *Izu Dancer*:

> How astonishingly beautiful the Izu peninsula was half a century ago. It certainly isn't now. And so I gazed at this scratched, faded, black and white image and saw Eden.[33]

Can nature be reclaimed, can the Japanese original, innocent nature be found again? From the looks of it, no. But one can keep on looking, as Richie does. One can also at times make it reappear, and that is called art. Richie was never so naive (or Orientalist) as to believe in an unadulterated "natural Japanese." The aesthetic sensibility was just too strong, daily social life just too polite. And, nature just too right. Against the Western sentimentalism of a Japan somehow in perfect accord with nature, Richie was able to perceive that, yes, the Japanese did have a special relationship with nature, and the base of it was aesthetic (or animist). In Japan, nature is redeemed by being remade:[34] the flower is placed just so, the rock turned to reveal a certain outline, even the movie set furnished just right.[35]

* * *

This exposition can only offer an indication of Richie's thoughts about Japan. I do think that in the end one can discover an interesting opposition in them, between Art and Nature. Essentially, and paradoxically, on the side of Nature are the first four notions: the ostensible real, presentation, acceptance, and innocence. Paradoxical because one's first impulse is to consider them on the side of Art. But, to take only the most obvious example, presentation, while being a matter of making one's self up, has no sense of contrivance to it and comes from that lack of self-consciousness Richie also sees as characteristically Japanese. On the other hand then, and on the side of Art, is—what, but—Nature, or better, the Japanese attitude to Nature: that it must be remade. In a word then, *our nature is art:* to perceive what is made and to remake it, and so achieve that "clarity" and "outline" that Williams speaks of.

* * *

At the end of Ozu's *Tokyo Story*, Setsuko Hara presents the most compassionate and affirmative smile when her sister-in-law complains that "life is disappointing." It is the smile of Kannon, the same smile Richie speaks of Hearn speaking of, and the same

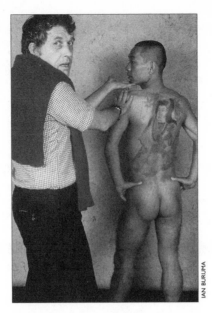

IAN BURUMA

But I don't want to think that I have turned into one of those old parties who are forever extolling the good old days—which, as a matter of fact, never were. I feel a sense of nostalgia if I go back to a place I've not seen for forty years—it strikes me like a blow. But on the other hand, where I usually go is where I've watched the change, which is so gradual that one can understand it if not approve it. (Interview, May 11, 1996)

34 Certainly, never "conquered" as in the West.

35 Wilde knew the same. From *The Importance of Being Earnest* (1895):

> Cecily: You dear romantic boy. I hope your hair curls naturally, does it?
>
> Algernon: Yes, darling, with a little help from others.

36 There are in fact a telling number of elderly women in the oeuvre, including the final characters of *The Inland Sea* and *The Honorable Visitors*. Richie speculates that they seem to represent potentially "threatening, yet caring and harmonious" figures (Interview, September 1996). The Ms. Watanabe character can also be criticized as having been written while wearing the rose-tinted lenses. After all, there are any number of Japanese who miss their train—and curse.

37 "I'm not very much like Hearn, but I do share this with almost

smile that Richie refers to somewhat frequently in his work, but never with more inquisitiveness and lucidity than in his portrait of Hanako Watanabe, an elderly lady[36] who rushes for but misses her train—and smiles. It is presentation, acceptance, surprised innocence all at once. And by surprising us, this ostensible real transforms our natures and redeems.

* * *

Japan is the Great Mirror in which Richie found himself reflected back.[37] Identification with his subject varies. In his early writing, one can read a strong desire to be liked by the people he encounters. In later works he simply wants to be liked (or laid). More importantly, in almost anything he describes, one catches glimpses of him. The most obvious example is *Different People*, where we are given portraits of a multitude of "Richie-selves" through the multitude of "Others," his friends and colleagues. Put the forty-eight characters together, and one has a forty-eight-part Richie as well. (Similarly, put the chapters of *Temples of Kyoto* together, and one has a twenty-one-part history of Japan.) Of course, "self" is a very slippery concept for Richie, but three extreme examples can be noted. The power of observation of *The*

everybody who's written at length on the country: one of the things you're doing is making it your own, you make it your subject, and you make it in a way a paradigm of yourself" (Interview, May 11, 1996).

38 Though he has never said so, to my reading, I believe Ozu to have been of monumental importance to Richie. To offer only a few reasons: In the director's work, he found not only the "redemption of reality" he believed to be film's especial art and mission but also a body of work that reflected his own ideas about art—inevitable, natural—and about Japan—natural, innocent, and so on. He also discovered significantly and unsentimentally truths about the life of the individual within life's chaos and disappointments (again, refer to the end of *Tokyo Story*), especially that life as it is reflected within the family structure. In Ozu's work too, he could observe emotion held back for the sake of social harmony; objective correlatives that could stand in for emotion (see the remarks on the vase at the end of *Late Spring*); and conversation itself as both real and art, and which he would so wonderfully capture in *Companions of the Holiday*, itself a "slice of Ozu" (whose screenplays are, incidentally, considered works of literature among the Japanese).

39 One must make mention too of what might be called "previous selves"—Richie's predecessors. For this, see the bibliographical note and its comments on *The Honorable Visitors*.

Inland Sea lies in the observer, Richie himself. The reader comes to know (and be fascinated by) the ostensible subject—Japan—as much as the real one—Richie. Identification is even. At the other end of the oeuvre is *Ozu*, a book in which it is almost impossible to discover the author. One is even tempted to wax Oedipal here. (Richie obviously "admired" Kurosawa, but he was "so devoted to the films of Ozu, and so cherished the man who made them.")[38] Finally, *Zen Inklings* can be read as a book about the "Non-self." Obviously, these are stories Richie wants to write (or wishes to have originally written); they are reflections of his desires but written dispassionately. He can be found inside them, while he is also outside: here, the self is not the subject. It simply does not matter.[39]

The Selections

This selection of Donald Richie's writings aims simply to present an idea of their fullness and many forms. (The exigencies of book publication—I've long felt that a CD-ROM would make the ideal Richie text—have determined that this book will be a sort of hybrid anthology.) Cinephiles know his work certainly. Most Japanophiles probably own one or two of his books, while also being aware that his name studs the various sections of any good Japan section of a bookstore or library. Few have delved into the variety: the fiction, essay collections, autobiography, specific commentaries (gardens, temples, Tokyo, etc.).[40] If they had, they would have noted not only the great range of his enthusiasms but the wholeness of the view and its deep attraction.

Any anthology is necessarily selective, and most anthologists somewhat defensively note why he or she has chosen to include certain articles and exclude others. I offer none such, and will only say that this book is (to use Borges's famous phrase) "a personal anthology." My position on Richie is stated throughout this introduction.

The Donald Richie Reader is divided into a number of thematic sections, drawing on a broad range of sources (including some rare or unpublished works).[41] These more formal set-pieces are themselves "punctuated" or remarked upon by other groups of writings placed as sidebars throughout. These are the Miscellanea, less than full-length essays or fictions. As my work on the book progressed, I kept placing into a separate envelope pieces

Portrait with Mount Fuji in the distance, 1985.

of text—from a few paragraphs to perhaps a few pages—that I thought worthy of inclusion, though I was not entirely sure how or where they might fit. When I later looked at these pieces all together, I saw that they did seem to fit into four separate categories of, well, miscellanea. These I called "The Body," "The Gods," "The Japanese," and "The Foreigners." An earlier assemblage had them grouped as individual, transitional chapters ("Miscellany I: The Gods," for example), but further discussion with my publisher persuaded me that they might be put to better use were they spread about the "main texts" (in a somewhat loose order), "commenting" on or "taking off" from them, thereby adding increased perspective.

"The Body" covers the sublime (a veritable prose poem on Japanese skin), the somewhat unexpected (a paragraph on Kurosawa's nose), some reflections on Japanese apparel (the kimono and men's traditional underwear), and a few other oddities. "The Gods" concerns Nature itself, shrines, gardens, and phallicism. (The latter is in reference to Richie's *The Erotic Gods*, a rare book now, and so I have chosen to include five passages from it.) "The Japanese" is a collection of short pieces that make further comments on those notions discussed above: presentation, innocence,

40 Why haven't they? Is it a cynical reluctance to seriously entertain the idea that one can write intelligently on such a variety of subjects? To take one example, Richie's fiction is some of his best work (artistically, and for the pictures it describes of Japan) but the most neglected. Is this because Orientalist policy would have it that Japanese fiction itself is "Other" enough, that "Western Japanese fiction"—artful, accurate—could only be dilettantism (in its worst sense) taken to an intolerable extreme?

41 Some minor housekeeping notes: The selections came from diverse sources, and I have not tried to make them all stylistically consistent, particularly in their treatment of Japanese words. However, most diacritical marks have been dropped and some obvious typographical errors in the originals have been discreetly corrected. In almost all cases throughout the selections, Japanese names appear in Western order, that is, family name last.

and so on. The final grouping is "The Foreigners": how they are regarded by the Japanese, the troubles they have in regarding the Japanese, and a couple of more beatific moments. I should add here that while it might seem an inordinate number of the Miscellanea come from *The Inland Sea*, they by no means exhaust the riches of that book. In fact, I believe that this book's selections, taken as a whole, offer a fair coverage of Richie's entire career and interests.

The groupings of the main texts reflect the main preoccupations of Richie's Japan writings.

The "Prologue" opens with a piece describing Richie's position in Japan, that is, "Intimacy and Distance," and is followed by one concerning his position before his arrival in Japan, that is, childhood and his longing to leave (his then) home. This latter piece, "Prose of Departure" is taken from a longer memoir wittily called "Watching Myself."

"Japan: Early" features two of his private journal accounts of events he experienced during his very first year in Japan (1947), appearing at the beginning and end, respectively, as well as another entry originally written in the *Journals* too but refashioned for his book of portraits, *Different People*. As well, there is one of his earliest (1962) and remarkably illuminating essays on some fundamentals about Japan, "Japanese Shapes."

Then we move on to "Japan: Film." The first piece is also taken from the *Japan Journals* and is a memoir of Richie's career as a film critic. Then comes a short piece (again from the journals) that acts as an amusing follow up. Then come several of Richie's tours de force, his preface and introduction to *Ozu*, and the conclusion to the first chapter, "Script." For all of Richie's vast writings on Japanese film—seven books, scores of articles, reviews, and lectures—I have chosen these brilliant pieces for two reasons: the light they shed on Ozu's (and Richie's) view of the Japanese family—hence, almost all of its society—and because they are certainly some of his most heartfelt pieces of writing. This section concludes with the notes of a 1993 lecture delivered at the Pacific Film Archive in Berkeley, California, "Buddhism and the Film." Richie lectures regularly in Japan, Europe, and America on Japanese film; notes such as these form the skeleton of his talks. They are particularly interesting for their quick, insightful wit and additional demonstration of Richie's interest in Buddhism.

"Japan: People" features five of Richie's portraits from *Different People*. Three are "commoners"—a senile man, a crazy

Portrait, 1995.

KAZUAKI KIYOTA

neighbor, the smiling woman who misses her train—and two are (relatively) famous. I could have chosen more famous people, e.g. Daisetsu Suzuki, Mishima, Kawabata, Kurosawa, etc., but these two portraits and people are for me more compelling. As for the semifamous, we have Ozu's selfless alter ego Chishu Ryu (forever clipping his toenails in the films and muttering an accepting "mmm"), and Toshiro Mifune, best known in the West certainly for his great samurai portrayals but here shown in an entirely new (and almost Borgesian) light. I have also included in this section one chapter from *The Honorable Visitors*, the one on Pierre Loti. (See also an extensive comment on this book and chapter in the bibliographical note.)

"Japan: Fiction" is the longest section, comprising as it does nine (actually fifteen) selections. (And even at that I have not included two of Richie's novels, his first, *Where Are the Victors?*, and his last, *Kumagai*, nor material from two important unpublished fictions.) Richie's fiction is probably the most neglected area of his work. And yet he displays as much (if not sometimes more) art in it as he does in any of his other work. Invention, humor—Richie is a very funny writer—wit, tenderness, and insight are all on display. The section opens with three stories from the series *A View from the Chuo Line* (previously published in small magazines but not yet as a collection). They are magical miniatures and completely believable (and the title piece is again Borgesian as it seems to describe an *aleph* in Japan). These are followed by a wonderfully tender scene from the novel *Companions of the Holiday*, which one could imagine appearing not so much in an Ozu film (though the dialogue could certainly fit), as in an MGM/Minnelli *Meet Me in Roppongi*. Then come five selections from *Zen Inklings*, retellings of Zen stories; in the last one, the sage is a wholly believable picture of life today in Japan. Next are the middle chapters of Richie's delightful novel *Tokyo Nights*. Finally, while *The Inland Sea* is known as a travel book, Richie considers it a novel. Certainly it has many of the trappings of being one, what with the hero's quest, the complication of a wife, his adventures (especially amatory), recurring characters, and "fantastic speculations" concerning the people he is traveling among. In any event, respecting Richie's view of the book, I include three amusing scenes.

"Japan: Later" includes a variety of pieces concerning contemporary (decidedly nontraditional) Japan. There are three pieces on Tokyo; one refreshingly un-solemn on Hiroshima; and two superb essays on what passes as Japanese culture today: the sex industry (a gentle satire), and television.

The "Epilogue" opens with "The Nourishing Void," an essay on a central (or pervading) Japanese concept (if that is the appropriate word). It closes with the reflective "Japan: A Half Century of Change," followed by two elegiac journal entries from New Year's 1999 echoing as far back as 1947 and earlier, and thus bringing the selections full circle.

A bibliographical note appears at the end of the book, written not so much conventionally but as a commentary on Richie's varied writings, including a list of what I consider to be his essential works.

"The Great Mirror"

In its early stages, *The Donald Richie Reader* was once known as *The Great Mirror*, a title I maintain a certain fondness for. After tossing forth and back a number of possible titles—bad puns and industrial and furniture references—I chanced upon a reference to a "great mirror" in the very last paragraph of *The Inland Sea*:

DAE-YUNG CHOI

At Tofukuji, Kyoto, 1997.

QUOTATION SOURCES

p. x. "The whole of Japan . . ." *The Decay of Lying*, 1891.

p. x. "I've never approved . . ." Interview, May 11, 1996.

p. x. "Richie, you just haven't . . ." Interview, May 11, 1996.

p. x. "I think if I didn't feel . . ." *Kyoto Journal*, no. 41, 1999.

p. xi. "There are so many . . ." Interview, May 11, 1996.

p. xi. "I am not to be put . . ." Interview, May 11, 1996.

p. xi. "I didn't have to . . ." Interview, May 11, 1996.

p. xiv. "I knew nothing . . ." Interview, May 11, 1996.

p. xv. "They enter the new world . . ." "Spring and All," *Collected Poems: 1909–1939, Volume 1*.

p. xvi. "50,000 people . . ." Interview, November 4, 1996.

p. xviii. "hymn to Existentialism . . ." Interview, February 26, 1997.

p. xix. "Zen teaches one . . ." *The Japanese Garden*, p. 167.

p. xix. "The U.S.A. was just . . ." *Journals*, 1960.

p. xxi. "grace / to be born and . . ." "In Memory of My Feelings," *The Collected Poems of Frank O'Hara*, 1971.

p. xxii. "the people on the . . ." *Journals*, 1960.

p. xxii. "enriched me, . . ." Interview, February 4, 1998.

"We must all remember that, as Helen Mears knew so well, for the Westerner Japan is a great mirror." I immediately took to it (as did Donald, initially). After all, the reference had ancient Japanese sanction: there was a tradition of writing "great mirrors" (of learning, of manly love, etc.), and within my furniture hunting it seemed not inappropriate. When I asked Donald who Helen Mears was, he sent me a short article that he'd written about her. Mears had been an American journalist in Japan and in 1948 written a book, *Mirror for America: Japan*, that was in fact critical of U.S. Occupation policy, not unlike his own later novel *Where Are the Victors?* What a perfect fit, I thought. The title was set—for a while, at least.

Amusingly, in an interview a few months later, Donald mentioned that this book was being compiled and said, "The mirror's not me, it's Japan. The idea is that you look at yourself in Japan as if in a mirror." "No, Donald," I had to remind him, "in this case, *you* are the mirror."

Donald also passed on this quotation from Percival Lowell: "It is because the Far East holds up the mirror to our civilization—a mirror that like all mirrors give us back left for right—because of her very oddities, as they strike us at first, we truly learn to criticize, examine, and realize our own way of doing things, that she is so interesting. It is in this that her great attraction lies. It is for this that men have gone to Japan intending to stay weeks, and have tarried years."

Portrait, 2001.

EVERETT K. BROWN

Acknowledgments

Lastly, it is always a happy task to make acknowledgments. First
and foremost, of course, I must give great thanks to Donald
Richie himself. Donald was enthusiastic and supportive of this
project from the first—and it went through many changes—and
afforded me every possible and patient assistance, from spending
hours of interview time together to generously loaning and copying rare works, especially numerous unpublished ones, including
his private *Japan Journals* and a copy of his unpublished novel,
A Divided View (a work he considers one of his best), as well as
responding to an unending tirade of questions. In these and all
other matters he was extraordinarily and utterly open and forthcoming with me.

I must also thank our mutual friend Leza Lowitz (who has
edited the *Journals*) for her unfailing encouragement and comments, and my publisher Peter Goodman for his patience and
belief in the project as well as his energetic staff, especially Linda
Ronan and Miki Terasawa.

Prologue

Intimacy and Distance:
On Being a Foreigner in Japan

As Edward Said has stated: "The more one is able to leave one's cultural home, the more easily is one able to judge it, and the whole world as well, with the spiritual detachment and generosity necessary for true vision. The more easily, too, does one assess oneself and alien cultures with the same combination of intimacy and distance."

I have lived for well over half my life in—from my original point of view—just such an alien culture; one, further, which is considered by both natives and visitors as more alien than most—Japan.

*　*　*

The visitor to mid-century Japan, particularly if he was an American romantic, was often accompanied by an urge to intimacy which was tempered by the fact of distance: his voyage was not only inner discovery of what he did not already know but escape from what he already did. These differences were rendered dramatic in that so much appeared Western but was revealed as Western only in appearance. He found in the shoe store something one did not know a foot could fit into, looking in the carpenter shop there were few tools one recognized, eating the Western meal he discovered it was mainly Japanese.

At the same time there was a new feeling of freedom. The visi-

From Partial Views, *1993*

3

tor was no longer controlled by his own mores and he could disregard Japan's. Exceptions were made for the *gaijin* who could be expected to know nothing. This freedom included the ultimate liberty of finding everything *other* than himself—walking down the street he enjoyed the freedom of being manifestly different.

And the lone person, the person who does not speak the language well, who never experienced a childhood in the culture—precisely this newcomer is most in need of the intimacy which is dangled before him, is always just around the corner.

In Japan the foreigner had been stared at for well over one hundred years. The early accounts all mention it and, until the massive foreigner influx in the 1980s, he still was. He became used to it and initial irritation turned to pleasure and then to need. No matter what the Japanese truly thought, he was treated in a special manner.

Shortly, however, the visitor discovered that Japan insisted that he keep his distance. It was suggested he live with his own kind: he was being edged toward ghettofication. The exceptions being made for the foreigner then began to be perceived as limitations. Though he desired intimacy, Japan was gently teaching him to keep his distance. (If he had been yellow or black instead of white—or pink—the lesson would have been much harsher and the distance greater.)

Another country, says Alastair Reid, an authority on the subject, is another self. One is regarded

as different and so one becomes different—two people at once. I was a native of Ohio who had known only the streets of little Lima, and I was also an expatriate who now knew best the streets of Tokyo, largest city in the world. Consequently I could compare them. And since the act of comparison is the act of creation, I was able to learn about both.

In the process I was absolved from Japanese prejudices of class and caste since I could not detect them and no one attempted to detect my own class and caste since my foreignness was difference enough. I remained in a state of continued surprise at all the differences and this led to heightened interest and hence perception. Like a child with a puzzle I was forever putting pieces together and saying: Oh. Or, *naruhodo*, since I was learning Japanese.

Learning a language does indeed create a different person since words determine facts. When I first arrived in Japan I was an intelligence-impaired person since I could not communicate and had, like a child or an animal, to intuit from gestures, from expressions. Language freed me from such elemental means of communication but it taught me a lesson I would not otherwise have known.

While it is humiliating to ideas of self to be reduced to what one says (nothing at all if one does not know Japanese), it teaches that there are other avenues than speech. Just as seeing a foreign film without subtitles may not impart much about the story but it does teach something about filmmaking, so being in Japan with no Japanese teaches much about the process of communicating.

What I am describing here is what any traveler, expatriate or otherwise, knows—but the degree and the difference depend upon the place and its culture. Japan tends to give a strong jolt because the space between the distance kept and the intimacy implied is greater than in some other countries. Japan is still openly (rather than covertly) xenophobic, but at the same time it experiences the need for the foreigner—or at least his goods. This creates an oscillating dialectic—one, which affects Japanese in regard to foreigners as much as it affects foreigners in regard to Japanese.

From the Japanese point of view, the ideal arrangement is for the visitor to come, do his business, and go home. For him who elects to live here, this fact is cause for interest and concern. How often it is implied that I would do better to go back. This is not unkind or even inhospitable. People are reacting as they would were they themselves in a foreign land. Many Japanese want to return to Japan, do not travel well, need miso soup, etc. They do not think of others behaving differently in a like situation. Where are you from? asks the taxi driver. Told, he asks: But you go home often don't you? Assured that I do, he is mollified.

Given the imposed distance, the intimacy promised by many Japanese becomes doubly attractive. The promise is, I think, not intended. It is occasioned merely by a real desire to give the guest pleasure, an inability to plainly say no, and a concern for gain.

This means that the foreigner is forever kept up in the air, be it a business deal or a love affair. The emotions are identical. I heard a frustrated merger specialist ironically complain about a failed deal with the metaphor: There I was open like a flower. . . .

And the lone person, the person who does not speak the language well, who never experienced a childhood in the culture—precisely this newcomer is most in need of the intimacy which is dangled before him, is always just around the corner.

That this need often takes sexual form is notorious. Travelers almost by definition screw more (or want to screw more) than other people. Part of it is the freedom ("no one knows me here") but most of it is the need to affirm self on

the most basic level, the emotional. Also sex is imperialistic since it always implies a top and a bottom, and one of the ways to encompass (and subject) the distant other is through what is often called the act of love but in this context should probably be called the act of sex.

When this urge meets the seemingly pliable "native" with her or his "different mores," the result is a kind of infatuation. It can work both ways and often does. But the major consideration is that the Japanese have to "live" in their country, and the foreigners cannot.

Foreigners, says Alastair Reid, are curable romantics. They retain an illusion from childhood that there might be someplace into which they can finally sink to rest: some magic land, some golden age, some significantly other self. Yet his own oddness keeps the foreigner separate from every encounter. Unless he regards this as something fruitful, he cannot be considered cured.

This is the great lesson of expatriation. In Japan I sit on the lonely heights of my own peculiarities and gaze back at the flat plains of Ohio, whose quaint folkways no longer have any power over me, and then turn and gaze at the islands of Japan, whose quaint folkways are equally powerless in that the folk insist that I am no part of them. This I regard as the best seat in the house because from here I can compare, and comparison is the first step toward understanding.

I have learned to regard freedom as more important than belonging—this is what my years of expatriation have taught me. I have not yet graduated but Japan with its rigorous combination of invitation and exclusion has promised me a degree. For it I have adopted as motto a paragraph quoted by Said from the *Didasclicon* of Hugo of St. Victor: "The man who finds his homeland sweet is still a tender beginner; he to whom every soil is as his native one is already strong, but he is perfect to whom the entire world is as a foreign land."

Prose of Departure: A Memoir

I wanted to leave. Looking past the catalpa tree, over the syringa bush, beyond the corner where the street ran straight south, past the park and into the future, I wanted to leave behind what I knew. What I wanted was what I didn't.

Familiar Ohio ran into imagined Kentucky and then spread into the unknown South, deep-dish black and opposite my pale North. Further off lay the blood-red Caribbean, so different from spit-colored Lake Erie—and then the whole world: Pacific and Indian oceans, deserts and jungles, pyramids and pagodas.

I had seen nothing of this and wondered if I ever would. But who could I ask about it? My parents didn't seem the right ones. He was working hard at Lima Radio Parts, and she was working hard at home. One of the reasons they were working so hard was to stay together to make a nice home for me, the only child. Asking when I could leave wouldn't be polite.

My relatives—grandparents, two uncles and an aunt on my mother's side—seemed to think it was OK for my parents to put up with each other so they could make a nice home for me. And it was nice enough as homes went in Lima, Ohio. I didn't so much want to run away from as I wanted to run toward.

That was why at the 1931 Allan Country Fair, I walked right past the prize bull and the biggest pumpkin, right up to Madame Olga and asked her. She looked down at me, wiped her rimless glasses, glanced at her crystal ball, and said: "Yeah, you'll go far."

Far—I carried the word carefully home and wouldn't answer

From Contemporary Authors: *Autobiography Series, volume 20, 1994*

when my mother asked if all those folks wouldn't think I wasn't well treated, when my father wondered what had gotten into me, a seven-year-old boy acting like that. I didn't answer because I knew they wouldn't understand. They had to spend all their time together because of having to make a nice home for me and they naturally resented it.

Instead of answering, I repeated that precious word to myself: F - a - r. It sounded like what it was: a fast start, a take-off, and then a soaring up and out. I wondered just how far I would go. I did not wonder why and I still don't. Even now when I know how it all turned out.

But if I was going to travel I needed a map. And just maybe I already had one, found two years back when I was five and my mother took me to the movies. There, in the cool, dark Sigma Theatre, I had had my first glimpse of the waiting world.

It was like the Market Street Episcopal Church. There were marble columns and murals, and high on the ceiling were floating figures which could have been angels except that they were all undressed ladies, and everyone was quiet and sat in the gloom until the matinee began, and there was an organ but Mr. Bouffer who rode it up from the basement didn't play hymns: he played "Melancholy Baby."

Then the curtain rustled up and there was the smell of stirred-up dust and a cold, backstage breeze. The world was about to appear, a better world, and the Sigma Theatre turned into the Pennsylvania Railroad Station with the Broadway Limited just pulling out. And there was Dorothy MacCail in back of the footlights, dancing her wonderful life away, and there was Warner Baxter, high up in a New York skyscraper, depressed by the Depression, getting ready to jump off. And there were coconut groves and the snow-covered Rockies, and earthquakes with untold dead, and floods with Mae Marsh going under. The movies were like that. I went in and

sat down and got carried away. These were my own coming attractions.

I could look past the people and see the places I wanted to be. Behind Clara was all New York and that thing that Dolores del Rio kept getting in the way of was a real volcano. There was the world awaiting me but I had to satisfy myself with my imagination. After seeing *The Lost World,* I lay in the bath, looked down the white peninsula of my body, and through the steam saw the head of the brontosaurus as it lazed in the turgid lake.

But the people in the movies were OK too. This was because they were so understandable. Milton Sills, for example, might be bad-tempered, but I knew him as I did not know my father; and I forgave Jack Holt things that I would have for weeks held against my parents; and Norma Shearer I loved like a mother and when she broke down my nose ran as it never did when the real one cried.

Being with movie stars was also educational. Gary Cooper would eventually teach me that being High-Minded wins out in the end, something I still believe despite proof to the contrary. Henry Fonda would tell me that Good Intentions are enough, and I still act as though that it is true. And Betty Grable taught me how to make Gas House Eggs. You butter a slice of bread on both sides, then cut a hole in the middle. Into this goes the yolk, and the white spreads over the bread as you fry it.

Movies were for getting away. So never did I look at the marquee to see what was playing. It didn't matter: movies were all the same. You were supposed to go out happy. Here was a place where people fought only to make up and no one was ever left-handed, like I was. In the dusty, dark of the Sigma I was content, at home as I never was at home. When the lights went down and the curtain went up and exhaled upon me its great stale breath, I was on my way.

Yet, though dazzled by the silver screen, I saw

through it. Movies might be fun but you couldn't trust them. Someone had imagined these patterns, created these shapes, and everything was not as it was, only as it ought to be. For example, travelling like they did in the movies—no sooner on a train than off it, boats used only to neck on, no one ever paying the taxi driver—I wouldn't get anywhere trying to get around like that.

But by that time I'd discovered another map, one I trusted more and one which over half a century later has still to let me down. I had found it when I was six—at the Horace Mann Grade School. It was a small room with an interesting smell since it was next to where they kept the creosote and the mops. There on the shelves was knowledge stretched—book after book, like travel folders. Or more like different sorts of people, all of them staring at me as people do when they know something you don't.

And I stared back. In the late afternoons after class I would run my fingers down their spines, wondering at what they knew. I'd already met some of them, like the Little Lame Prince who couldn't walk very well, being lame, but who had this magic cloak, like a small gray cloud, and it would nudge its way to his tower window, just like a car parking, and he would climb on and it would carry him away.

Just like me. Only with me it was books I climbed on as they flapped their pages and flew me off, carrying me to Oz, to Pellucidar, and to Omar and to Baghdad. All I had to do was follow the words as they led me over the mountains and across the seas. There the sun shone on the walls of the City of Brass as though a great fire had broken out, and the full moon flooded the leprous ruins of Omar; in the jungles of Paraguay the sloth eats twice its weight in fruit in one week, and red and blue in equal parts make purple. I was equally astonished. Spitting in my paint set, I rubbed together the salivated red and blue. It worked. I had a purple finger.

Words were as magic as the movies, but they always did what they promised, and they were more real. Maybe people imagined them too, but they didn't have to entertain a whole theatre sitting in the dark, they only had to entertain me, sitting there under the reading lamp.

If words can do that when someone else writes them, I thought, then they must be even more powerful if you write them yourself. I tried this out and on my yellow, lined tablet wrote: cake, dog, God. Even, daringly: pee-pee. But they just sat there.

Writing was hard. Though they looked alike, written words were not like words read. You probably had to go out and look for them and then you had to make them behave. Yet you could learn to do it. I found this out one spring Saturday when, eight or so, instead of reading my library book about a dumb boy named Penrod, I was looking out at the wet afternoon world. And feeling sad.

No, I decided. Not sad. It was more attentive than that. Being sad meant looking at the floor or at your hands. But I was looking out of the window and seeing the wet black of the tree trunks, the plain brown of the ground beneath them, the bare gray of the sky.

I wasn't feeling sad, yet that was the only word I knew to describe how I felt. So I stood on the armchair and pulled down Noah Webster, and he at once offered me sorrowful and mournful, melancholy and something called dolor. Also pensive, wistful, rueful, sombre. And, at the bottom—elegiac. The word with its two e's like sadly half-shut eyes looked attractive. I wrote it down: Elegiac. And, suddenly, I had captured what I was feeling. It was not the sadness of the trees or the earth or the sky, it was the sadness in me.

Elegiac became a title. Under it I wrote: The trees are wet and black. The ground is wet and brown. The sky is wet and grey. Then I stopped and thought and wrote: And there is the smell of the rain and the ground.

And as I wrote it I smelled it. Earth, water, a

waiting smell, cool but not cold, something alive but quiet. The smell of soil was there—it was only there on the tablet, yet I was smelling it as though it was real.

And it was real. It was real because I had written it. Sitting in the armchair, looking out through the storm window, I had made something just like the books did. And not only had I made it wet and fragrant, I had left something behind, for there it lay on my paper. Anyone could read it and I could make them feel the same. I had made an experience and in creating it I had been myself created, for I was now different from what I had been before.

I felt different. All you had to do was forget yourself. Just stop thinking and look outside, as though your eyes were windows. And then you drew what you saw as well as you could. And soon I was no longer there; I was outside—free. And what was left of me was sitting there, trying to describe. I sat up, felt brand new. I had my new map. Now all I needed was a way out. This I didn't yet have, though I was looking.

"Just where do you think you're going, young man?" asked my father. "Just down to the corner. Mama said I could."

And, as I was going through the kitchen, "Wherever are you going at this hour?" asked my mother, her hands full. "Just down to the corner. Daddy said I could."

Having received both their permissions, I took my blue bike out of the garage and peddled off into the October night, feeling the frost nibbling, for the air had, said the evening news, a bite in it.

Winter rushed by as I raced in the dark up Charles and down Hazel. Then, from far away, the sigh of the Broadway Express as it fled, and the distant smell of the last of the afternoon's bonfires, raked leaves curling and glowing, going up in smoke. I peddled through the public square, raced up Market, past the Lima Library—my new home once I was out of grade

school—and at a new, far corner, even, I straddled my bike in the and looked at the street lights v four directions, as though I were ter of all things. And in any of t future lie, I thought.

I could start right off, biking so was Elizabeth but then it turned Cable Road, and after that it was and after that it would be called s and then something else again. looping its way, ribbon-like, as it ra across a bridge, up a mountain, a going south—always south—wher and there was no frost. And if I we dling away, I would run straight int

The edge of town, a stand of tree under those brittle branches and breath white in the streetlight and beauty of being alone. A distant c freight train clanked and shuffled, a sand souls seemed already asleep town at the corner of the state, und grey lake, from where the Great Pl forever.

At the Catholic school on Nort at the sports field, looked at the bask and up at the ring dark against the ni as though surprised, with a mouthf was waiting for something: like me on the other side of that empty ci maybe.

Early religious impulses had been by my confusing him with Lon Chan four to see *The Phantom of the Opera* way carried screaming out. The pha ping someone by the ankles, had d from the eyes of man. My mother's that that was no phantom, only some Lon Chaney, made it even worse. Bo to move, Chained.

Thereafter my prayers, kneeling were made perilous by Lon, lurking

ed slats and ready to grab. And since I was deep in converse with God at the time (OK, please bless Mama and Daddy and me), he and Lon began to merge. Eventually they became identical—God with his pushed-up nose, awful teeth, and his fancy headgear like the feathered, felt mouring hat my grandmother used to wear when out in the Buick.

And so when I stopped being afraid of Lon, I stopped believing in God. And in all of his belongings—my immortal soul, for example. This I had heard of, if never seen, and the more I learned the more unlikely such a thing seemed. Eventually it became just one more of the grown-up lies, all of them to be detected and disposed of.

Why would anyone, I wondered, go to the trouble of inventing such things. The world was quite enough as it already was. The problem was that you couldn't get at it from my angle. It was

there all right but you couldn't see it very well from Lima, Ohio.

But I tried. Peddling back through the night I would look into lighted dining rooms where the natives were eating their ethnic food. Once returned to the syringa and the catalpa, I gazed into my own lighted dining room and watched my mother setting the table, my father reading the paper. The man of the house sat under the bridge lamp and perused *The Lima News,* I thought, while his wife in the kitchen prepared their evening meal. He is reading about the Depression, which is deepening, despite President Roosevelt. This evening they were having frankfurters and German pan-fried potatoes. Perhaps she has been crying again, her eyes seem red. He never cries but the wrinkles in his forehead indicate that he wouldn't mind.

There in the dark outside, an anthropologist, I tried to imagine that they in their lighted inte-

The Foreigners   *From* The Inland Sea, 1971

What they really wanted to know, I eventually learned, was whether or not Indians continued to roam the great West. Recently they had begun to doubt, and no amount of viewing American Westerns had eased his growing suspicion. I ended the fantasy forever by telling them about reservations and the poor mass-producing Zuni. To underline my explanation I said that the American Indian was just like the Japanese Ainu, once a proud and independent people living in the northern part of Honshu, now decimated and pushed into the wastes of Hokkaido in the far north and

reduced to carving wooden bears in department-store windows.

At the mention of something known, however, of something belonging to their own country, the boys lose interest. Instead, tell us about New York, tell us about the latest designs in automobiles, what about Jane Fonda, how did President Kennedy really die, and so on. I answer as best I can, aware—as one is always in Japan—that I have ceased being myself. Rather, I have become—once again—a Representative of My Country.

I cannot begin to describe

the sensation except to assure you that it is both tempting and disagreeable. I find myself, quite suddenly, a spokesman, and my every word seems accepted as literal truth. At the same time I realize that these boys are not looking at me as another person more or less like themselves, and that their friendly questions contain no friendship for solitary me. Like all Americans, like all romantics, I want to be loved—somehow—for my precious self alone. I don't want them to pay so much attention to what I say. I want them to pay more attention to me.

Under the strain I become

rior were black, or yellow, or red—something attractively different from what they were, white like me. And then in the light of that window I also darkly wondered if these unlikely natives were really my parents. Probably not. They had found me at some interesting place, or had been given secret charge of me. I was too different to be theirs.

And as I thought that, I felt the comfort of this vast difference and—at the same time—something like pity for them. There they were, every day the same for them, no escape from each other, nor from me. Maybe they had wanted more, or something different, and now they had forgotten all about it. There they were, up in the window, like up on the movie screen, going about their daily concerns, all unknowing.

But I was all packed and ready to go even though I still didn't know how. So I looked around at my elementary schoolmates. Maybe they knew. There was John, a sober little boy in a pressed shirt who read almost as well as I did. And there was Thelma who got excited and wet her pants and smelled like soda crackers with tea over them. And there was Betty, but she was bigger than I was and had knocked me down once and sat on me.

Then I looked at Manuel. He was as big as Betty but wore overalls while the rest of us boys were in knickerbockers, and he had scabs on his knuckles and smelled of funny things like garlic which we never had in our house. Maybe he didn't belong either; maybe he wanted out too.

My mother also wondered about him—wondered if he weren't Mexican and my father asked her what she was talking about: he was just some kind of half-breed. Manual began to sound better and better. Then I overheard a visiting mother ask—after a careless look around to assure that no one was listening—if Manuel wasn't a gypsy.

---

didactic, and eventually petulant. I know what it looks like, having seen the nicest and most well-intentioned foreigners turn themselves into nit-picking, narrow-minded pedants as they attempt to explain:

"Well, of course, I said that, but, actually, what I mean is that the Americans never—well, I can't say never, perhaps hardly ever would be better—hardly ever go to the extremes you suggest—you didn't suggest, of course, you implied, still, perhaps there is some truth, however, in what you seem to be saying, namely that . . ." And on and on and on, trapped in their doubts, asea amid their convictions, at a loss in this new, baggy, and completely unattractive role.

At such times I want to strike the table, stand up and bare my breast, strike attitudes, shout loudly that I am myself—take me or leave me. But I do nothing of the sort. I am patient, I pause, I consider. I become what every American longs to be—a teacher.

They nod, earnest, as I lay bare the secrets of the world, with particular emphasis upon the workings of American democracy and the love life of Jane Fonda. I try to be honest about both but soon lose impetus among the shards of my rhetoric.

They eventually tire of such concentration and, now that I have told them all about my country, are pleasantly anxious that I see something of theirs. Have I seen the famous beauty spots? The names are reeled off and I nod, pleased that I am widely traveled. Kyushu, Hokkaido, too? Yes, yes. Well, then, perhaps something more local. Have I seen the Ritsurin Koen? No, I don't even know what it is—a park of some kind? So it is, and one of them, the largest, wearing the touring cap and the red and tan shirt, the darkest sunglasses, seems to know all about it. Such being the custom of the country, he offers to take me. Not the next day. He, being a butcher-shop employee, must work that day. But the one after that, Sunday.

Miss Williams said not at all and that ended that. Her reply may have convinced the prejudiced mother, but not me. I became bigoted at once—in the gypsy's favor.

I knew what a gypsy was. There were still some around and I had once seen a caravan pulled by a dejected horse clanking and tinkling its way down a country road. Also, children heard a lot about them. They were used to make us behave, or else the gypsies would get us. I had thus acquired an amount of attractive information: gypsies roamed by definition; they had no proper home; they were known to steal non-gypsy children and bring them up as their own. So I had a chance. They would spirit me away. There I went, clanking and tinkling down country roads with a big brown family, eating nothing but garlic, and always on the lookout for pale but attractive orphans by the wayside.

Sitting in the armchair, looking out through the storm window, I had made something just like the books did. And not only had I made it wet and fragrant, I had left something behind, for there it lay on my paper.

With this I became deeply interested in Manuel. I savored our variances: me fair, him dark; me small, him big; me smart, him dumb. He seemed to wear his gypsyhood like a crown, and I followed him around, his loyal subject. I wanted to sit next to him, to feel the gypsy warmth, to smell the garlic.

I followed him about but kept such distance that he did not detect his admirer. I even fol-lowed him into the toilet to ascertain further dif-ferences. Discretely I dropped my eyes and there it was, rich and golden brown while mine was merely pink. His hung there in all of its naked difference, so divergent from the suddenly some-how spurious mine.

I even found where he lived and in the twi-light of early winter bicycled among the tar paper shacks then, hidden by the growing dark, stared into the bare little room where Manuel, suddenly a child like any other, sat small between his large mother who sliced potatoes and his big father who sat looking at his hands.

For them I felt none of the easy pity I had for my parents, though they too were going about their daily concerns, all unknowing. No, I was feeling the power of the watcher in the dark: hid-den, different, stronger. Standing there in the frost I felt the strength given me by my invis-ible gaze. Once home I took out the pad and described what I had seen. She put the potatoes in the boiling water, and there was no meat at all. While his father looked at his work-worn hands, their son stared at his plate, hungry for his sup-per. This I wrote—and he and his whole family became mine.

Bike flights aside, I got out only with my par-ents and that was not like escaping at all. Sunday afternoon drives in the Dodge, even a trip down to Russell's Point on Indian Lake, was like being on a leash. I gazed at the Cyclone, a roller coaster that creaked like a ship at sea, but was not allowed on it—dangerous. I consequently spurned the safely wheezing merry-go-round with its cosmet-ic horses going always, just like me, in a circle. Together we stood at the fence of the Avalon Dance Palace and watched the 1932 Marathon Dancers within, swaying couples asleep on each other's shoulders, the man sometimes drooling down the lady's neck. And I would look across the stale sweet water at the tree-lined outline of ordinary Orchard Island and tell myself it was the Gardens of Hesperides where the golden apples came from. I was almost there, a boat was all I needed, but then one of my parents would turn from the dead dancers, swaying there like trees, and we would go home.

And here I was stuck with ten more years of being young—a whole decade of childhood. But I whined, complained, pleaded. Eventually, my parents grew weary of this and I was from time to time allowed out. There I was, bicycling to the nearby Columbus Grove where Aunt Mae, my mother's sister, lived. Starting early in the morning when the ground mist was still rising, I pedaled away from home and family and smiled at the foggy road stretching before me. Past the cemetery, past the old abandoned Irish homestead, ghosts in the one, doubloons in the other, I followed the back road and two hours later was ten miles away.

Though this venture into the unknown ended at the ordinary front door of my aunt's house, she was young enough to remember what it was like to be curious, and since I was not her child I did not have to conform to her ideas. So I could go by myself to the magical mulberry tree and eat as much as I wanted, or I could walk to the quarry—submerged cathedral—and gaze into its solemn depths, or wade in the creek and grab crawdads as though it was Africa.

And when I returned, my young Aunt Mae would have cake and real coffee ready and I would tell her what I had seen—not at all a late child explaining, but a returned explorer divulging.

"Is that what you want to be when you grow up?" she asked. "An explorer?" Yes, it was. I wanted to go to Africa and to Asia. Then she would sometimes get down the Rand McNally atlas and we would look at the maps and find far-away places with names like Samarkand and Nairobi and Tokyo.

And sometimes I would get out by going over to where my uncles—my mother's brothers—lived with their parents, over nearer the railway tracks. It was my wild Uncle Kenneth I

wanted to see. He was making my grandmother grey-haired, said my mother, and since she was quite gray already, it looked like he was doing a good job of it. And he wasn't like anyone else in the family, though he looked a lot like Manuel grown-up, I thought.

But it was always the other one, Uncle Ralph, who was there. He was quiet, well behaved, wore glasses, and never gave anyone grey hair. Looking at him reading his book in the light of the gooseneck lamp, the grandfather clock ticking forever in the dark parlor, I asked: "What are you reading?" looking at his green book while a big, full autumn moon slowly sidled over to the window.

"It's by Willa Cather. She's a good writer," he said.

"Is she as good as Edgar Rice Burroughs?" I wanted to know.

"Well, she's different," said Ralph.

Then he put down his book and we talked about reading. I said that it was a good way of getting out, that you just sat down and opened the page and weren't there any more. He agreed, then said: "For a while."

I looked at him. Maybe he wanted out too. So I told him that writing was an even better way to escape. He turned and looked at me. "You think words are real," he said.

"Aren't they?"

"Yes, but what's real isn't only words," he said.

The moon turned to stare and there was silence for a while.

Then I asked: "When is Uncle Kenny going to come home anyway?"

Uncle Ralph looked at me and his glasses shone like the moon: "Sometimes, he doesn't come home until late. And sometimes," he lowered his voice, though his parents were both upstairs, "sometimes not at all."

Not at all? He'd gotten out, all right. But what could he be doing?—my wild and different uncle. Out there all night under the full moon

like an animal himself. I saw him running along under the dark trees of Faurot Park, past the cage where lived an unhappy cinnamon bear, up the hill to the lake where the Civil War cannon guarded, stopping, still as a wolf, silvered by the moon. When I got home I would write about it. Silvered by the moon, Kenneth, half-man, half-animal, raised his beautiful muzzle to the sky and . . .

That very summer, when I was nine, I did for a time escape. A thoughtful remark to rich Nella, a cousin of my father's, that I wanted to see the Magic Mountain, ride the Sky Ride, view the Sinclair Oil Dinosaurs, led to her offering the money for my mother and myself to go to Chicago.

I was soon gazing at the whirling beet fields from the window of the Broadway Express—going in the wrong direction but still heading someplace—and stared at passing grain elevators in anticipation of the Tribune Tower, the Wrigley Building, and the wonders of the 1933 Exposition: A Century of Progress.

Set by a neutrally green lake, this exhibition of our progress was just like the amusement park at Russell's Point on Indian Lake made big. And instead of the Cyclone there was the Sky Ride inching along its cabled length over the wide lagoon, an attraction I merely observed since my mother would not let me actually ride—it was too dangerous, what if it got stuck, what if it fell down?

Instead, holding her hand, I stood on the moving sidewalk and was—mouth open—carried past the rubber Sinclair brontosauri, waving their necks to the sound of grinding gears; I observed our progress in the Hall of Transportation where they hid the toilet so securely that we never did find it; I climbed the Magic Mountain and slid down the chute through its plaster interior while my mother, vigilance relaxed, was sitting next door listening to Paul Whiteman for Kraft Cheese, Ted Weems for Johnson's Wax, and Ben Bernie for Pabst's Blue Ribbon Beer.

A glass of the latter was in front of her, and she was nodding her head to "The Isle of Capri," smiling, looking so young, so different from the way she looked around the house. Over her beer she leaned toward me and said, with that look I associated with Christmas and birthdays: "How would you like a little brother or sister?"

Never! But as I thought about it, I also saw the advantages of a small ally, a little confederate. It all depended, though. So I asked her which it was going to be: a little brother or a little sister. When she told me she did not know, I was surprised. Something that important and still adults didn't know. When? Oh, in eight or nine months. She had only just learned about it from Dr. Johnson. Only just learned? I frowned. Telephone? Letter?

She, feeling perhaps that the frown was occasioned by news of the small arrival, or by a memory of when fat, false Dr. Johnson had spoken of a candy bar and then held me down, poured out the ether, and snatched my adenoids, cheered me up by taking me up in the big ferris wheel from where I had the whole progressive century laid under me like a map with the Shedd Aquarium at one end, and the Art Institute with its bronze lions tiny in the middle. Then, once down, she bought me a rootbeer float and we stared at the Algerian Village with its painted people and their wailing airs. Then, whatever lingering thoughts of tonsils and new babies I had were forgotten when I saw right next door something familiar to me from the inside pages of the Sunday *Chicago Tribune*.

Sally Rand—the Fan Dance. Oh, Mama, let's go. The idea of someone dancing with ostrich feather fans was attractive to me, though I did not know that Sally did so only to cloak an apparent nudity. My mother did. She hurried me past the packed pavilion but I managed to see one of the pictures out front, and there Sally had turned around, fan dropped, and was showing me her big peach-colored bottom. I felt I had seen something of importance, something not ordinarily glimpsed, at least not in public. It was part of the century of progress and I was happy to be a part of it too, to have seen the future in Sally's bare bottom.

My mother, perhaps still thinking of my coming sibling, of her having to carry it around, said that I looked tired, that I mustn't get exhausted, and that we ought to go home. And so we did. The Broadway Express on its way to New York—site of my next ambition—dropped us off at that small station in the suddenly narrower town of the state which, I had heard, had more people out of it than any other. But I carried, balanced in the hands of my mind, the sights, sounds, and smells of the outside and under the covers that night I smiled into the dark at the waiting world.

Once back I had to go and thank my generous second cousin. Nella had married the owner of the *Lima News* and lived on Market Street and had a lawn, people said, like a pool table. Her home was like another country. It smelled rich and funny, like the inside of our closed-up china closet, and there were flowers in vases, as if she wanted to show people how well she could keep house. There was a black cook, too, and a maid, and an old grey-haired chauffeur named Charles, and as I sat in the big leather chair in the sunlight I was given a glassful of something I had never before seen.

This, I was told, was ginger ale. The sunlight caught the pale bubbles as they wobbled up through the tall glass. I swallowed and my mouth was filled with a fizzy taste that stung my tongue and made my eyes water. The pedigreed bull terrier panted and drooled and I looked at the cut-glass animals catching the sun and felt the expensive bubbles in my mouth and turned to stare at the roses. This was what it was like to be rich.

That was what Nella and Roy were, my father had said: rich. I had already compared Manuel's boiled potatoes with our sausages, and this meant that we had more money and were therefore better people. But here was cousin Nella and Roy and they had steaks every day for all I knew. So, maybe they were better than us. They went to Florida. And further too. They had gone to Egypt to see the pyramids, and Nella had had a bad headache and stayed in the hotel the whole time. They were that rich.

And to the surface swims a statement: You think words are real just because you find your reality in words. And with this— and I can hear the neutral tone, the flat Ohio accent—the suggestion that words are not real, not really real.

And she was affected, a new word for me with its stiff double *f* and the curt and final *ed*. "Real affected she was," said my father, and then gave an example. "But it looks very pretty," said my mother, gazing at the embossed page, a letter, all distinctive peaks and hooks. "But can you read it?" he asked. "No, of course not. She only does things for effect."

My mother turned the letter over. "I can make out Donald's name," she said, as though defending. "Here, she seems to be asking about him. Yes: I do hope the dear little boy is well."

I liked that—dear little boy—but wondered about people going to Egypt and missing the Sphinx, then writing in a way that no one could read. I knew already you only wrote because you wanted to make people feel the same way you did. But maybe being illegible was one of the things

rich people were. Maybe that was why my poor father did not like his wealthy cousin and resented it when she sent Charles over with little things for me. Never anything I much wanted, nothing to read, but always something curious, something which made my mother shake her head in wonder as she put it in the china closet: a little buddha made of amber, a bone owl with brilliants for eyes, a Chinese box with dragons on it.

I approved of the attention, however, and decided that I must have somehow deserved Nella's interest. To have someone notoriously wealthy send you things meant that you were a fine person and not nearly so insignificant as some people—your own father, for example—seemed to find you.

But as I was one day idly wondering, a self-congratulatory mood upon me, why Auntie Nod (a name the woman herself had suggested) was so fond of me, hoping to hear my mother agree that I was a serious, studious, charming, and deserving ten-year-old, she instead said: "Oh, because when you were a baby you reminded her so much of Edna."

Edna was my father's sister, and he had not even been born when she died. She died that young. There was a picture of her in lace looking out on the world she wasn't going to see for very long. Not having liked her before, I liked her less now. I went to the bureau drawer and took out the picture of the small usurper.

Under it I found another picture. A smaller person in a high chair, even more wan than the sainted Edna. It was my father. He had come apparently in answer to his parent's prayers for a replacement. And if I was to be singled out for a fancied resemblance to the dead child, what must my baby father have endured, since he did not look like her at all.

He sat there, wearing a polka-dotted pinafore, in his slatted high chair, as though in a cage. I had heard that he was sickly, that he had been given ice cold baths when a baby in order to perk him

up. I imagined his mother bending over him, as mine bent over me, trying to undo his father's severity. I gazed at that sickly little polka-dotted body, which would eventually make mine. Maybe he too had wanted to be an orphan, maybe he had wanted out.

As I looked at the sepia photo I felt cool understanding slowly seeping into me. He had been like me once. Just look at him, miserable. And looking at his childhood from the viewpoint of my own, I thought of how like he was to Milton Sills and then how I was like him.

But prejudice is seductive. It feels so warm, so snug, like the bed when you don't want to get up. So, I turned from the thought that my father and I were much alike to the belief that we were different and plunged once more into the drama of difference.

I did not, however, allow my disappointment with my wealthy cousin to disturb my relations with this person who sent the checks. I told her what a good time I had had in Chicago, though I did not mention Sally, and then turned to her magical surroundings.

"Oh, what nice things you have, Auntie Nod," I would say, while I held the Chinese bowl up to the afternoon light or peered at the sun shining through the swath of Japanese silk.

She loved her possessions, liked them to be admired. We were two children together as, like a little girl, finger to lips already older than my mother's, she would open the wall safe behind the sliding panel to show me where they kept the icy diamond and the bloody ruby. I would clasp my little hands together, an amazed Ali Baba in the cave, truly amazed at actually looking at a diamond.

She too knew how to charm and we were shortly casting mock reproachful glances, surrendering to little bursts of mutual enthusiasm, gazing into each other's eyes like lovers, this older woman and myself.

"Oh, you," she would say, just as though I

were her age. And we would go upstairs to look at her furs and I would bathe my face in fox and slide my hands along the belly of a lynx.

Lying on her bed with its matching spread, the same brocaded cloth as the curtains, I would hug the bull dog all the long, sunny afternoon in that far foreign land that was her bedroom, and she would sit by her enormous vanity and hold up various scents. I could smell them from where I lay in the dog's embrace. "And this," she said, "is Evening in Paris. It is very expensive."

I freed myself from the animal and pattered over to be splashed. She looked at me and arched her eyebrows that said: Now you are the only little boy in all of Lima who smells like this.

When I got home my father, already in the armchair, thought so too. "What you got on?" he called to my mother. "I can smell it way in here." Leaving the frying pan, she looked at me, sniffed, and apologetically laughed: "Oh, it's just him. He's been over to see Auntie Nod."

He told her that the woman's name was Nella and she need not make it any more foolish by calling her Auntie Nod, and that here I come home smelling like the perfume counter at Newbury's and all she could think of was laughing. It was no laughing matter. You women are turning him into a real sissy.

I now knew what a sissy was. It was a boy who acted like a girl. He acted that way because his mother made him. Along with the book about the Little Lame Prince, I had read the one about Little Lord Fauntleroy, and there he was with his long hair, his velvet suit, and his beaming mother—a real sissy.

I knew something about this. Johnny Morgan, who was three years older than I, had come over to where I was sitting in the Sigma and, after Mr. Bouffer had played and the lights went down and Ginger Rogers had come on, he took my hand and put it between his legs and he already had it out. He told me to move my hand up and down while he gazed at Ginger. This I did because I had never done that before, not even with myself, and it was something new and different. Then he started to have a fit and I pulled my hand away just in time. I thought I had broken it but, as he wiped himself off with his handkerchief, Johnny told me it was usual. But even so I mustn't tell anyone or they would know I was a sissy.

So now I knew what Little Lord Fauntleroy had been doing when his mother was not around, and I also understood—standing there between my parents while the potatoes burned—that this was something my father did not like and per-

---

From The Honorable Visitors, *1994*   *The Foreigners*

[Henry] Adams' attitude was not original. Many others, before and after, have been pleased to note a childlike quality, and Victor Hugo, a writer who never went to Japan, seems to have said that this country was the "child of the world's old age." He doubtless did not intend his remark in any literal sense, but nineteenth-century travelers usually agreed in finding the country childish. Toward the end of the century, there appeared a spate of travel books in which Japan, driven even deeper into the nursery, became the "wee country," the "land of topsy-turvy," and the like.

The condescension is apparent. What is not so obvious is the political purposes to which the picturesque is put. Prattling, playful Japanese were also, it was assumed, pliable Japanese. To condescend is to have the power to do so. Americans and Europeans visiting Japan brought with them, in their mental luggage, this assumption of superiority. They still often do.

haps even feared. This new knowledge I tucked away for future reference.

The future—it hung there like Orchard Island, still impossible, yet I could tell that it was getting nearer. When I was little the days took forever but now—ten years old, eleven, twelve—time, having dawdled for so long, was finally stepping out. The reason was that I had gotten busy, in junior high, studying.

Making birdhouses in industrial arts would not much help me on the road, but history could because things as they were were probably like things as they are. Mr. Steiner told us all about Ancient Rome and what Nero did to the Christians. Thelma got sick but I thought about what I would get to see—well, maybe not ravening lions but the Colosseum was still there. Mr. Curtis taught all about H_2SO_4 and Miss Brown made us conjugate our verbs—*j'ai, tu as, il est, nous avons*—no, no, no! I struggled along, pulling the load behind me: you never knew what might come in handy on a long trip.

But here we all were in high school already and I was the only one who was going to go away. Oh, no, said John when I asked if he was going to. Then: Well, maybe down to the lake once in a while. But I'm going to work in the store. My father said I could Take Over. And Thelma was going to go to the Lima Business School, and Johnny was looking forward to a lifetime of self-abuse and the Locomotive Works.

Mr. Steiner said that with us human beings it was either fight or flee and I could tell that my body was getting ready. I was thirteen and I was getting hair and my knees and elbows hurt, and now I had fits just like Johnny had. Growing pains, that is what these were. I had heard about them and here they were. Well, I would just have to get over them. I knew already that I was not going to be one of those who fought and I had known from as far back as I could remember that I was one of those who would flee. And I

looked at my little sister as she sat at the kitchen table and drew pictures of the cat with crayons that smelled just like bacon. She was going on five now, about the age when I had found out about books. Already she had a way of looking at our parents as though she maybe didn't believe them and that was a good thing. But, promising though this was, she was still not much company. Yet she distracted my parents. They had much less time to get in my way. Now my mother would say: "No, I am busy right now. Why don't you go out and ride your bike?"

Ride the bike, go to the library, or to the movies if I had the money. Or go to Hunter's Drug Store near school and order a cherry coke. This was what you did. And you did it because everyone else did it. And though I did it too, I didn't enjoy it. A cherry coke was, unlike ginger ale, an interesting beverage only once. And if you had to drink it, because everyone else did, it turned to tap water in the mouth.

Here I was—me, who had never willingly once done anything my parents told me to—willingly doing everything everyone else did. And here my life was almost half over—for I would die painlessly before thirty—and I was still stuck in Lima. Joyce who wore tight sweaters thought it was swell I was going to get out of this burg. I told her about my favorite Uncle Kenneth and how he had just up and left, but I didn't admit that it was just down to Indian Lake, and then only because he had to get married because a baby was on the way—and I now thought of my beautiful uncle with a leash around his neck, caged for life like the unhappy cinnamon bear. But I didn't tell her this. I told about how I might just go out to LA, after NY, that was, and she liked that because she knew Hollywood was in LA. The boys called her Lana on account of the sweaters and she used to spend a lot of time on the stool at the soda fountain at Hunter's with her chest pushed out.

Since I was still stuck, I tried other ways to

get away. I smoked in the men's until I was ready to throw up, and I drank Sloe gin fizzes until I did throw up. Also, during the hayride Joyce let me have what I guessed was my way with her, but it took me away from myself for only a little. Most of the time, except for the fit at the end, I thought about how tempting that pale road looked, glowing under the moon as the haywagon, filled with burrowing couples, bumped and clanked through the sleeping fields.

Sleeping fields—I liked that—and us wandering o'er the lea, too. I had discovered that poetry, no matter what, lent a permanence and an importance to whatever I was feeling. The surrounding beet fields turned transparent under the moon of literature and became the land of the future, toward which I was heading.

At the same time, I was discovering that what I read in books and what I saw at the movies was pushing attractively away what I saw around me. Having seen on the screen the bleak mid-West farmscapes of John Ford, I could now see the elegiac (nice word) beauty of the old houses and rusted windmills in Allan Country, Ohio. After I saw reproductions of Grant Wood, the groves around Lima turned into tamed gardens, symmetrical renderings of the banks of the far Potomac. And when I saw silos and barns shining in the paintings of Charles Sheeler, I looked at Lima Fertilizer with respect because it too was an emblem of modern America, whatever that was.

And, since I had read Sinclair Lewis, I was now writing a novel about this talented and attractive youth who was too fine for his surroundings—a small town in Ohio. I described my hero desolate in the Lima Public Square and loitering solitary but handsome near the bear in the Faurot City Park. All you had to do to lose yourself was look out and try to draw what you saw. My mother, finding it, had read part. Her comment was: "That boy doesn't seem very happy."

Nor was I—taller now, tormented by my glands, always looking at where I wasn't, forever dissatisfied, hanging around the house because I did not know where else to hang. And, besides, there was the state of the world. It was 1937 and things were beginning to look pretty bad over there—over there being just where I wanted to go. Germany was flexing its muscles, said my father, and Italy was a mess, France was caving in, and the Japanese were being sneaky again. And here I was, merely reading, only writing, and still trying to find the shape of my life.

Trying to find it without having made it. That is not surprising when I consider that even now that it is made I am still looking. The real world is now my memory. Yet, peering from my second childhood into my first, I still stand in the known dark and stare as though into a lighted window. Clutching this strand of years—seven to seventeen—I turn them this way and that, like Madame Olga at her glass ball. How to make any sense of these beginnings? Yet, I am interested in the way I was because of whatever connection it has with what I did.

And to the surface swims a statement: You think words are real just because you find your reality in words. And with this—and I can hear the neutral tone, the flat Ohio accent—the suggestion that words are not real, not really real.

Now who could have said that to me? Maybe Uncle Ralph, putting down his Willa Cather sixty years ago. He's right but it has taken me half a century to see that he is. And even more time to see it makes no difference—seven or seventy—reality is just too much: all you can do is decide in which partial way you want to define it.

Ah, that pebble offered the abyss has elicited another echo from the past. A voice that has the ring of common sense. "Do you really think you can run away from yourself?" it asks. Who could that be? Then I recognize the tone. It is myself just before the take-off. It is the voice of fear which common sense, as always, is trying to

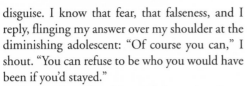

disguise. I know that fear, that falseness, and I reply, flinging my answer over my shoulder at the diminishing adolescent: "Of course you can," I shout. "You can refuse to be who you would have been if you'd stayed."

I remember when I learned that, when I saw that there was no one shape but a lot of them, and that one could only choose. Like so many things in my life, it occurred at the Sigma.

Though now just turned seventeen, I still did not look up at the marquee but bought my ticket in the dark and sat there, not even curious to know what I was going to see. There was no more Mr. Bouffer at the mighty Wurlizer, he had died long before. Nonetheless, I simply assumed that, as always, some sort of pleasing pattern would appear.

Hence my impatience when I found my pleasure compromised by an incompetent projectionist. He started all right, some old guy dying in a castle, but then he picked up the wrong can and began the newsreel. By the time he had noticed his mistake, all the reels were mixed up and they stayed that way.

But as I watched, indignation faded into incomprehension and was then transformed into intimation, for as the film unfolded I saw that it was itself a search for a shape, for a pattern, for the reality of someone. And this exploration was so dazzling and so right, so beautiful and so true, that I sat in the Sigma with my mouth open and tears in my eyes, stayed to see the movie again, missed my supper, and came out a man.

As for so many of my generation, this first viewing of *Citizen Kane*—May, 1941—had shown me not only what film was capable of, but what art could do and what life was like. When I walked out of the Sigma into the bright lights of small-town Saturday night, my wide-open irises could now stare straight at that horizon for so long only imagined.

My maps firmly in hand I need now only wait for my departure: the day after Lima Central High let me go, a graduate. My parents had been told of my resolve and there was some reluctance and a few tears but not much nor many. Living with me was, I think, an experience with few rewards.

My goal was set and the means established. Since money was still a problem I would hitchhike, and such were the times in that distant past that this seemed to my parents a safe and economical way to travel. I would step out on Highway 7 and raise a thumb.

Waiting, those last few weeks, I again saw Manuel. While still in grade school I had hoped that Manuel might somehow come along with me. With his strength and my cunning we would be invincible. But he had long dropped out and gone to work. Biking to high school I sometimes saw him. I was out of knickers and into long pants now, but he was into a real uniform with buttons all the way down the front and a cap with a bill on it, and he stood big and handsome and manhandled the cars at Standard Oil. Sometimes I went out of my way to go past the gas stand and pretended to be fixing my chain just so I could gaze at him. And once I spoke—Hi, Manuel—and he just stared. He had forgotten who I was.

Now I went up and I asked if indeed, going out into the world as I was, Route 7 was the right road. And he, not knowing who I was nor how I had stood outside the window of his life, looking in, said: "Well, yes, sir, if you're wanting to go East that's probably the best bet." And then he smiled.

So I took the best bet and one June morning there I was standing on Route 7 with Manuel's helping hand on my back and with my parents looking at me from the wings as I put out my thumb.

JAPAN
Early

August 14, 1947:
Festival of the Dead

The sun was not up and the eastern sky was still dark, and the sleeping sea was still. Walking toward the silent surf where I had walked the afternoon before, I stopped and looked, for something had changed. It was not like yesterday. The beach now held mounds of sand, it was pocked with large holes.

There was a faint light now, the eastern horizon a hazy grey and I saw that there were many of these strange holes, as though an army had dug in during the night. Each seemed occupied, as though the invasion had been that of turtles, come to lay eggs. Slowly I walked through the growing light to the nearest and looked in.

There, like a chick in its shell, lay a small boy. In the next hole too, another was curled, and in the next. The beach was pitted with holes and in each a sleeping child.

What were they doing, why were they here, I wondered, standing over this small, sleeping army. I was curious but I had already learned not to be surprised. This was, after all, despite everything, still a mysterious land—the way the world had once been.

Just the day before, on arrival from Tokyo, we had walked along this beach—Kujikurihama in Chiba—and had stopped in surprise at the sight of the fishermen.

Young or old they were all naked as they worked at their nets,

From Japan Journals, *1947*

helped by half-clad wives and sisters. Each of the men wore only a headband and a narrow red ribbon around the penis. They saw us and smiled, nodded. Not at all self-conscious, they went on with their work.

—Maybe it has something to do with not offending the sea goddess.

—Going naked like that?

—No, wearing the ribbon.

—I wonder if she's Benten?

—No, this is the Garden of Eden.

* * *

And so, now, on next day, I was prepared for innocent magic as I stood above the sleeping children in the promised dawn of a midsummer morning.

Then as the great orb rose, higher and higher, like some radiant balloon, the mysterious children stood and yawned, shook off the sand, became themselves again.

And as the darkness drained from the sky I wondered what had happened. The beach now seemed a battlefield—for the war was only a year or two behind and thoughts came easily of bodies rolling in the surf.

Then one of the bodies stirred and a hand was thrown across the eyes. The light was now that dim grey that precedes dawn and I heard the surf, as though it too was just awakening.

The grey turned white and I walked across the still cold sand, looking into the holes. The children were very young, five, eight, ten. They were still curled in their sandy nests but now in the

early light they were awakening like the newly hatched.

The surf splashed and a head appeared over the rim of sand. What were they doing, this small, sleeping army? Then a wave slapped and a child sat up, dark against the brightening east. Then another, and another, as though responding to a signal I could not see. Soon, they were all awake, looking eastward, waiting.

I thought I knew what they were waiting for. The sky shone as though in a like expectation, and there, in the wings of the ocean, was the sun itself. As it appeared each child shifted, now sitting formally, legs beneath him—and slowly, they turned a solid black as the sun rose beyond them.

Then as the great orb rose, higher and higher, like some radiant balloon, the mysterious children stood and yawned, shook off the sand, became themselves again. Off they wandered down the beach, back to their lives.

Later I discovered what had occurred. It was the beginning of Obon, the feast of the dead. The departed are welcomed into the land of the living, into their former families, where they stay until they must return to their silent land beyond the sea, three days later.

There are round dances, the altars hold flowers, dumplings, fruit. The fathers all wear proper clothing—shirts and pants or summer yukata— and were now waiting, facing the rising sun, waiting for their sons. The children had gone to spend the night, to await these barges of the dead. When the sun appeared they went home, their invisible guests following them.

There they went, these small escorts, while the new sun shone as though for the first time. They turned and ran, like a flock of plovers, all instant accord, as they flew down the beach along the shouting sea, back to family, to home.

And I, my shadow black behind me, turned to look at these sandy nests which the approaching tide was filling in, one by one.

1947: Fuji from Ginza

1947—It was winter—cold, crisp, clear—and Mount Fuji stood sharp on the horizon, growing purple, then indigo in the fading light. I was standing at the main crossing on the Ginza.

It was clear because there was no smoke, few factories, no fumes because the few cars were charcoal-burning. Fuji looked much as it must have for Hokusai and Hiroshige.

I stood and watched the mountain fade. From this crossing it had not been seen since Edo times but now all the buildings in between were cinders. Between me and Fuji was a burned waste-land, a vast and blackened plain where a city had once stood.

At this crossing there were only two large buildings standing. The Ginza branch of the Mitsukoshi Department Store stood but it was gutted, hit by a firebomb and even the window frames had been twisted by the heat. Across the street was the other, the white stone Hattori Building with its clock tower: much as it had been with its cornices and pediments.

There was not much else left: the ruins of the burned-out Kabukiza, the round, red, drum-like Nichigeki, undamaged. At Yurakucho, on the edge of the Ginza, were a few office buildings and the Tokyo Takarazuka Theater, renamed by the Eighth Army the Ernie Pyle, and the Hibiya and Yurakuza motion-picture the-atres, these last now also destroyed, as has been so much else, by peace, affluence and the high price of land.

Otherwise block after block of rubble, stretching to the hori-zon. Wooden buildings had not survived the firestorms of the

From Japan Journals, *1947*

American bombers. Those that stood were made of stone or brick. Yet, already, among these there was the yellow sheen of new wood. People were returning to the city. During its destruction many had left and now they were still returning.

During my cold, late-afternoon Ginza stroll, walking down to view Fuji in the five-thirty twilight of mid-winter, I saw them shuffling along the pavements, all those who had returned. One somehow expected festivity—there were so many people shambling along or lounging about. But there was no laughter and little conversation. And it was dark, this Ginza which had once been a fountain of light, the wonder of the Orient. Now it was lit only by the acetylene torches in the night stalls, and by the passing headlights of Occupation jeeps and trucks.

It was clear because there was no smoke, few factories, no fumes because the few cars were charcoal-burning. Fuji looked much as it must have for Hokusai and Hiroshige.

Here everything was being sold—the products of a dead civilization. There were wartime medals and egret feather tiaras and top hats and beaded handbags. There were bridles and bits and damascene cufflinks. There were old brocades and pieces of calligraphy, battered woodblock prints and old framed photographs. Everything was for sale—or for barter.

Stopping looking, handling, passing, were the people. Uniforms were still everywhere—black student uniforms, army uniforms, young men wearing their forage caps, or their army boots, or

their winter-issue overcoats; others were in padded kimono, draped with scarves. Women still wore kimono or those *mompe* trousers used for farm work, which in the cities had served as wartime dress. And many wore face masks because of winter colds. Also, everyone was out of fashion: in peacetime they were still dressed for war.

How quiet the crowd was. The only sounds were the scufflings of boots, shoes, and wooden sandals. These and the noises of the merchandise being picked up, turned over, put down. The merchants made no attempt to sell. They sat and looked, perhaps smoking a pinch of tobacco in a long-stemmed brass pipe, staring at the black throng passing the darkness of an early evening.

I remember faces from those winter nights, an old woman illuminated by a passing truck, the white profile of a young student in the acetylene glare. But I do not remember anyone talking— just the quiet and the glances. Over a year had passed since the unthinkable had occurred and the unendurable was still being endured. I was regarding a populace yet in shock. There was an uncomprehending look in the eyes. It was a look one sometimes still sees in the eyes of children or the very ill.

And in the eyes of convalescents as well. People recuperating are people keeping quiet. Yet, compared to the clatter and chatter of forty-five years later—today—Tokyo was a city of the dead. So many had been killed, so many had been burned or boiled in the firebomb raids. The survivors remembered.

But at the same time the dead were being forgotten, as they must be if we are to go on living. Everyday the crowd grew larger and the eyes got brighter. I remember a small stand on the Ginza run by a tough, smiling countrywoman. A Japanese army helmet was displayed and under it a similar-looking pot. Her sign said: "We Will Turn Your Old Helmet into a New Cooking Pot for Only Seven Yen."

I still have a photograph taken earlier in the subway corridors of Ueno Station. There, sitting or lying down, are some of the thousands of the hungry homeless. Men, women, a few children, on straw mats or on the bare concrete.

They are being inspected by two bespectacled policemen wearing mouth-masks. Many of the people are dirty, and all wear remnants of what they had owned during the war: cracked shoes, torn blouses, battered hats, buttonless shirts. But no one looks sad.

Everyone is smiling—everyone except the policemen, and maybe they are as well beneath their masks. Smiling for the camera, making a good impression, best foot forward. Even in the depths of national poverty everyone remembered this.

Up above, on the plaza, around the statue of Takamori Saigo, there were many more, sitting on benches and embankments, some with a newspaper, some with nothing at all—all of them waiting. Waiting, it seemed, for this too to pass so that they could get on with their lives.

Many had been and gone. The pedestal of Saigo's statue was plastered with hand-written notices: "Noriko Watanabe—Your Mother Waits Here Every Day from One to Five; Grandmother Kumagai—Shiro and Tetsuko Have Gone to Uncle Sato's in Aomori—Please Come; Tetsuro Suzuki—Your father is Sitting on the Staircase to the Left—If You See this Please Come."

The snows and rains have washed the older notices away and new ones are put up. They are like the votive messages left at shrines, invoking supernatural aid. Answered or not, they are left there until rained away or covered by notices of later misfortunes.

Tokyo back then was poor. Poverty gave it the Asian look, an appearance that prewar Japan had been at some pains to avoid. But then Asia had

---

From The Japanese Garden, 1972   *The Gods*

Occasionally, however, Japan too feels the need for a better world than this. This attitude was particularly strong during the closing years of the Heian era. It was a period of bitter civil war, of disillusion and destruction. Social order, even life itself, became less and less secure. Human life was like a snowflake which "melted, thawed, resolved itself into a drop of dew"; life was as short, as fleeting as a floating bubble—an image used by a man of that period, Kamo no Chomei, in his essay, *Hojoki.* Mutability, constant change—this was a native feeling acknowledged as the very essence of our life in this world, and a view which the times forced and which Buddhism upheld.

To the Japanese, eternity was, and remains, a pattern of change, and to the Japanese artist, the garden with its variously changing aspects was a symbol of this eternity. The garden, like life, was mutable. A geometric garden, or one which disregarded nature's quality of change—this concept did not occur to the Japanese. Immutability was death itself; only the changing was alive.

At the same time, however, the appeal of an earthly paradise was very strong. Mutability is the way things are, but how nice if there were also a paradise. This was a feeling experienced by these early Japanese, one encouraged by Esoteric Buddhism which was full of such concepts of *enri odo* ("to leave this detestable world") and *gongu jodo* ("to seek for paradise"). After death all desired to live in this better world, to be saved by Amitabha, the lord of paradise himself. Which, of course, is one of the reasons for the growth of the paradise garden itself during this period. If one owned a replica of paradise in one's backyard, as it were, the real one was that much closer.

moved closer. And with it a kind of natural nudity once the weather got warm enough.

By summer, many were unclothed. There were no more laws against going naked and so people naturally did—in hot weather being naked is more comfortable than being clothed. Bare breasts in the suburbs were not uncommon and in Asakusa I once saw a man returning from his bath wearing his towel on his head, and nothing else. Children were often naked in midsummer and the fisherfolk of the further coasts of Chiba traditionally worked nude with only a small red ribbon tied around the member lest the goddess Benten, deity of the sea, be offended.

I used to stand on the street corners—not perhaps those of Ginza, but certainly those of Ueno and Asakusa—and gaze at the shapely limbs, the curves and angles of all this beautiful bare skin. And some not so beautiful. Malnutrition is no beauty aid.

When you look at naked people one of two things can occur. You become excited, feel sexy, view the nude as desirable. Or, you see the human race, finally, as it is: innocent, vulnerable, unknowing and beautiful in that general way which discourages possessiveness. Standing on those street corners I felt both, alternately—one at a time, since one cannot experience such disparities simultaneously.

I remember Tokyo moving slowly in front of me, fittingly undressed in the hot summer night, showing a beauty and an innocence and a naturalness by which I, from the rigid West, was alternately ravished and enlightened.

Another Asian-seeming quality was the usual means of locomotion. By the end of the war the rickshaws were gone but the pedicab bicycled rickshaw, introduced late into Japan, were as many as they still are in Chiangmai. These were like large tricycles. In front was a man or a boy astride his bike. In the back was the two-wheeled double seat in which one reclined while being pedaled about.

Or lolled. This was a favorite means of getting about by enlisted men who had no jeeps and did not want to wait for the Army bus. The spec-

 *The Foreigners*   *From* Where Are the Victors?, 1956

She drew a deep breath of the cool autumnal morning air and, for no reason, felt better. She breathed and smiled, realizing that, absurdly enough, she felt happy.

It was being in Japan that did it, she guessed. Here she seemed to weigh less, her body had a suppleness and dexterity that surprised her. The sun shone directly into her face, and she felt tall, beautiful, and altogether different from what she knew herself to be.

Often she had seen other Americans here smile for no apparent reason as they walked in the sunlight. Was it because they were conquerors? She doubted it. It was because they were free. Free from their families, their homes, their culture—free even from themselves. They had left one way of living behind them and did not find it necessary to learn another. Nothing they'd ever been taught could be used in understanding the Japanese, and most of them didn't want to anyway. It was too much fun being away from home, in a country famed for exoticism, in a city where every day was an adventure and you never knew what was going to happen tomorrow.

Actually, thought Gloria, there was something paradoxically reassuring about being in this country where the ground might shake at any moment, where the distant, snow-covered mountain might, for all one knew, blow the whole island to pieces. You could almost feel yourself living. At any moment the ground might crack beneath your feet and you'd find

tacle, however, was so obviously illustrative as to who had won the war that we civilians, already anti-Army, rarely used them. That we might have helped the economy had we done so did not occur to us.

Instead we used taxies, prewar models with large round tanks at the rear that in the cold of winter emitted clouds of smoke and steam. They ran on charcoal and the arrangement was apparently complicated because they need much stoking and never went very fast nor very far since they were always breaking down.

There were Japanese buses, some of these also charcoal run, and after electricity was again general in the city, streetcars. There was also a variety of buggies, more often pulled by cows than horses. I remember seeing braces of oxen on the Ginza.

We occupiers had to watch how we traveled. In the local trains we had to ride the Allied Cars with their broad white stripes painted on their sides. From one of these, seated in comfort, we could see into the other cars and look at the peo-

ple crammed flat against the glass. The subway (just one line: Shibuya to Asakusa) was off-limits to Occupation personnel, as were the buses. Only the streetcars were, for some reason, allowed us. There, occupiers and occupied were permitted to promiscuously mingle.

This was rare because attempts were truly made to keep the two of us apart. We were often so informed. "No Fraternization with the Indigenous Personnel"—this is what the signs said. They meant it too. Occupiers could not eat in any of the restaurants still operating in those days of food rationing. Nor could they go to any of the local entertainments. No movie theaters, no all-girl dance shows, much less the Kabuki—showing at one of the department stores until its own home was rebuilt.

Instead, there were special nights when the occupiers and only the occupiers were invited. Thus, one by one, we got to see the Noh, the Bunraku, the Kabuki, the Takarazuka All-Girl Opera, the Kokusai Gekijo All-Girl Dance Theatre and other examples of Japanese culture.

yourself face to face with eternity. It was quite different from safe, dull Muncie where habit very soon cut you from life, and Gloria was inclined to prefer Japan.

The gold-spotted leaves fell at her feet, and the cool air brushed her ankles. There was a clarity here—so different from the foggy, rainy island she had expected—a dryness, a precision in the atmosphere which made the most ordinary occurrence—a walk to the station for example—something joyous, as though a carnival were just around the corner.

There was another kind of clarity too. She felt herself a part of something larger, something benevolent, like god, engaged in kind works and noble edifices. And she could see enormous distances. Her own country—the United States, Indiana, Muncie—like an arranged vista, fell perfectly into place. She understood it; she understood her place in it and even that of her parents. It was as adorable as an illuminated Easter egg.

And here, all around her, was freedom, even license. The ruins were one huge playground where everything forbidden was

now allowed and clandestine meetings were held under the noonday sun. The destruction, evident everywhere she looked, contributed to or perhaps caused this. She felt like a looter, outside society. Society no longer existed.

Here she was free, here in this destructive country where autos collided as though by clockwork, where sudden death was always a possibility, and where dogs went mad in the sun, casting their long, barking shadows behind them. More than at any other place she had been in her life, Gloria felt alive in Japan.

The effect of such segregation was to make one want to flaunt integration. And this most of us did, though penalties were enforced. For Japanese who tried to enter forbidden occupied zones the punishment was extreme: they were handed over to zealous Japanese police, anxious to placate outraged Army authorities. For the occupiers caught in a bar or all-girl opera or Kabuki, the penalty was severe enough. The culprit received a D.R. (Delinquency Report) and if a certain number of these was acquired he was, it was said, sent home.

Nonetheless, the occupiers nightly flocked where they were not supposed to be. The most popular of these off-limit places was not the Kabuki but the red-light districts. These were, discreetly, just everywhere. The largest, the most famous and most lucrative, was out of town in Funabashi, which you had to have a jeep or a truck to reach. There were two establishments, side by side, one for officers, the other for enlisted men. Here the MPs were never seen, except of course as customers.

Another place where fraternization was permitted was the Mimatsu Night Club, located in a large building directly behind the Mitsukoshi Department Store on the Ginza. In the afternoon the occupied went; in the evening the occupiers. At five the doors were closed and the Japanese customers were turned out; at six the doors open and the Allied customers were ushered in. At nine the doors closed for good.

Dancing was permitted. That was the extent of it. MPs patrolled the premises. Under orders from a General Swing they also carried with them a rule just six inches long. This they would from time to time insert between the bodies of a dancing GI and his indigenous partner to make certain that fraternization was not taking place.

The six-inch rule did not apply when the GI went to Yurakucho Station, directly behind the Dai-Ichi Building—GHQ Headquarters—and there took his pick of all that was parading there.

The girls wore dirndl skirts, then a rage from the U.S., with limp cotton tops and lots of wooden jewelry, bracelets, necklaces, all painted a cherry red. The hair was piled up or else frizzled in the popular 'cannibal' fashion of the day. On the feet were platform shoes with cork soles, and silk stockings were often painted on—very strong tea was used—with a perfectly drawn back seam on each leg.

The proper present was a pair of real silk stockings, straight from the PX. But equally welcome was food from the commissary—cocktail sausages, canned stew, Ritz, Kraft Velveeta. Goods were safer than money, and though the PX and the Commissary rationed some items, most of us could buy what we wanted. There were, for example, no rations on Almond Crunches, a favorite confection of my Japanese friends.

Many Japanese, however, sold their goods. Particularly popular were American cigarettes and whiskey, light-flints and Spam. All became symbols of status among the Japanese—until they became common enough that everyone had them. But for a time lighting a Lucky was like driving a Rolls.

Despite the MPs there was an amount of fraternization. Even an amount of unofficial fellow feeling. One notorious example was the hot-dog and hamburger stand, run by the Eighth Army, which stood right on the Ginza corner, in the clock-towered Hattori Building where the windows of Wako now beckon.

It was for Occupation Forces only. The occupier, G.I. or civilian like myself, could stand on the Japanese street and yet consume dogs and shakes from the States. He did so, however, surrounded by a still hungry populace. Particularly, hungry children. These did not beg. No matter what had happened to them they were still Japanese. They did, however, stand and stare.

Food was handed over. The Allied person, however, was not permitted to simply purchase and offer intact. He could, however, give the hungry child a bitten burger, a sipped Coke, a licked Eskimo Pie. I do not know whose idea it was that the food had to be partially consumed in such token fashion. Perhaps it was the whim of some now nameless monster of a quartermaster-corps lieutenant, perhaps it was an order in triplicate issued from the Eighth Army Headquarters itself.

When I now pass that corner I still think of the outdoor PX bar. I stood right by it, though I ostentatiously refused to patronize it, when I Fuji-viewed. Now I recalled it because at the same place where there used to be a "No Japanese" sign there is now another.

It says: "Please Do Not Bring Food and Drink into the Store Premises." It says this in two languages and has been posted by the expensive Wako Department Store, which now occupies the old PX location. It is not, however, directed to old occupiers and their descendants, the tourists. Rather, it is addressed to the young, Japanese or otherwise, who have been down the street to McDonald's or Dunkin' Donuts or the Dairy Queen and who are biting and sipping as they walk. Thus American eating habits—now fully Japan-franchised—continue to harass the indigenous personnel.

So I sometimes pause on that corner, look at all the tall buildings, all that glass and marble and steel and remember what it was like before—the soft shuffle of the crowd, the smell of charcoal burning. Then the sky would darken and the stars appear—bright, near. The horizon stayed white in the winter light after the sun had vanished and Fuji turned a solid black.

From The Japanese Garden, 1972   *The Gods*

To accept yourself completely you must also accept your own mortality, and this is what, somehow, and admittedly at an enormous expense, some Asians have been able to do. They can celebrate the changes of the seasons and still not feel that April is the cruelest month: they may contemplate the truly permanent with a dignity, which does not allow easy if ironic thought of Ozymandias. Though sometimes sentimental and unusually given to the pathetic fallacy, the Japanese rarely allows the merely anthropomorphic to cloud his perhaps unique vision of the timeless.

This is because by sacrificing an urge to immortality, and through a knowing acceptance of himself and his world, he stops time. He has found a way to freeze it, to suspend it, to make it permanent. He does this, not through pyramids and ziggurats, but by letting it have its own way.

This is seen no better than in the Japanese garden where the seasons may change nature's skin, but the bones—rocks, water—are always visible, always unchanged. The Japanese garden is like a still picture—a frozen moment which is also all eternity. It remains the same no matter the season because the seasons are acknowledged, and this acknowledgment is spiritual, a combination of idea and emotion. As an old saying has it: ". . . gazing upon the mountain one's knowledge is widened: looking upon the water one's feelings are increased."

A mountain for intelligence, a lake for feelings; solid stone and fluid water. These are the antipodes of Asia. Its mountains and its seas are its only realities. Rocks to make mountains, waters to make oceans—the everyday stone and the commonplace pool allowed to express their natures, allowed to whisper their meaning. This is what the Japanese garden has been about from the beginning. It is a celebration of the elementals, a glimpse of nature bare, an analysis of the world in which we live.

Tadashi Nakajima:
Festival of Darkness

Slowly, as the summer light faded, they came, singly, in pairs, in groups, the young men of Fuchu. They came from the lanes and country roads leading into town, joined others at streets and avenues, then marched abreast, past the high school and the town hall. Like rivulets trickling into creeks, then merging to form a river, the young men of Fuchu streamed into the center of the town, where the shrine was.

The setting sun cast their shadows far ahead. The men were barefoot, wore only loincloths and sometimes a towel twisted around the head to keep the sweat from falling in their eyes. For this was a Shinto ritual toward which they were moving, a ritual that purified, and here one must be naked.

This was the famous Yami Matsuri of Fuchu, the Festival of Darkness, and it occurred once a year late in the summer. All the young men from this town outside Tokyo and the surrounding countryside came walking through the dying light, making for the central shrine where the great *kami,* deity of darkness, waited.

I too had wanted to join in, curious—had read about it, asked around, and now, having parked the jeep just outside town, was following the naked men, their numbers growing as street turned into avenue. Soon we were too many for the sidewalks, were walking down the middle of the asphalt toward the shrine, somewhere ahead of us.

From Different People, *1987*

The shops, the homes were already lit and people stood and stared at all these men and me, the only one in clothes, while we paraded past. As our numbers swelled, they retreated to watch from open doorways, windows. And I, among the crowd, became aware of the odor of those around me: a clean smell—of rice, and skin.

They in turn were aware of me, a foreign object in their midst. But they were also busy, intent upon the coming rite, and so a glance or two was all I received—no words at all, no questions as to what I was doing there.

I was there because I wanted to see, to experience, for myself. This was why I had driven far into the countryside and found the place, and why I was now one of them, walking through the dusk as though I knew where I was going.

But I did not need to know. The press was now so great that I was going wherever it went. There was no stepping aside, much less turning back. I was caught in this flowing river, surrounded by men who knew where they were going. Our shoulders touched as we walked, our hands collided as we swung our arms.

The sky had deepened, and all at once it was completely dark. Nine o'clock, and someone had pulled the main switch at the power station. This was the signal, the ritual had begun.

Even with eyes closed I would have known. With the instant black there was a sudden tension, like the stopped-short intake of a breath. No sooner had this jolted, body to body, throughout these hundreds than the march became a jostle.

Pushed, I lurched to one side, then the other. Those behind pressed with their hands to move me faster, and I found my palms against the bare flesh of those in front. The walk turned into a ragged trot and from blindness I returned to sight—a partial night sight, with the white of loincloths in front and, farther off, glimpsed through black trotting bodies, others as though

phosphorescent in the night, and above and beyond them the summer stars.

All else was sound and smell. I saw nothing of the sudden hand that struck my side, the bare foot that heedless trod on mine. I felt flesh now close, and smelled it and heard its slap as all of us ran forward, blind, into the night. My shod foot came down, hard if innocent, and I heard the jerk of breath, the exclamation choked, cut off.

There was then a sudden tightening of all these limbs, as torsos crushed together like cattle roaring through a gorge, and I looked up and saw against the sky the great black beam passing overhead. It was a *torii,* a shrine gateway we were passing through. Then, a blacker darkness, overhanging on either side like cliffs—perhaps rows of cypress, cedar, or the outskirts of the shrine.

And now a sound was growing. Jostled, hands before me, palms out, fearing collision, fearing falling, I heard it as a growling coming nearer as we raced along. But I was wrong—it was us.

It was the festival chant, heard when pulling the great-wheeled float or shouldering the *omikoshi,* but now—no longer redolent of effort—it was pure sound, like surf, like wind in the pines. *Yu-sha, yu-sha, yu-sha*—repeated endlessly, a chain of sound on which we moved, our steps running to its beat. It was all around, filling my eyes and nose as well as ears. And then I heard it deep inside me. It was coming from myself as well.

Possession. We were all possessed by this deity toward whom we were rushing. Chanting, I recalled what I had heard. A Shinto deity and thus without features, name, or disposition— simply a *kami* like the myriad others—this one, however, retained a quality. He—the gender seemed inevitable—liked darkness. Just as the sequestered *kami* in the carried *omikoshi* loved to be jostled and jerked about, tossed and turned, so this god adored the dark and all that happened there.

Abruptly, there was a sharp wrench, a fracture

(continues on page 39)

Just to Be Safe

I know of no people more lack-ing the religious sense than they. They love the rituals of reli-gion in the same way they love the ritual of the tea ceremony, the etiquette of an intricately choreographed wedding. They admire the panoply, the art, the architecture, the ostentation that religion produces. They love belonging to an obviously successful and powerful organi-zation. But the spirituality behind these concrete manifes-tations—it does not exist for them.

Not only have they never been religious, they have also never felt the need to be. Shinto shrines, Buddhist temples, Christian churches—all are attended, but the same man will sometimes attend all three—apparently just to be safe—and not find the tenets of any one antithetical to the others. The Japanese choose to believe in the surface of things and do not welcome the probing or the hopefully profound. They live on the surface of life and rarely seem to feel the need for deeper meaning. Granted that the more esoteric types of Bud-dhism have, or had, a vogue in Japan. Still, I do not think that it was their profundities that appealed, nor their deeper meanings that were believed. The appeal lay on the surface and the meaning was the osten-sible meaning.

The Lure and Promise

Seven in the evening found me standing in a chill wind surround-ed by the blinking bulbs of Hiroshima's considerable night-town. It stretched into the distance in all directions, very large, seemingly as big as that of Tokyo's Shinjuku, certainly as lively.

Just as lively for everyone but me, I thought. Being in one of these exciting warrens of plea-sure always brings out the most morose in the white man. He feels neglected and incapacitat-ed; at the same time—and this is one of the greatest of Japan's many attractions—he is sensible of a permissive atmosphere, the very lure of promise. Just now, just around this corner, just on the other side of that door, surely awaits the one for whom you have been searching so long, throughout all your life. There, just there—only turn and smile and you will have happiness forever.

This marvelous illusion is based, in part, on the people who throng the streets, eager for a good time and almost fre-netically happy; in part it is due to those others who will serve this mood: the sandwichboard man who winks and smiles, the kimonoed girls who stand just inside the big plate-glass door and open it invitingly and seduc-tively as you pass, the uniformed doorman who grins and wants to shake hands, the dressed-up

hostesses who are lined in the entryway, smiling, shifting their feet and dabbing at their make-up, casting glances the while.

And it is an illusion, though one wonderfully sustained. These people belong to the world of *mizu shobai*. This is an interesting phrase, perhaps a poetical one. The *mizu* is "water" and *shobai* is "business." But there are other connotations, particularly in the water aspect, which not only suggest the unstable world in which entertainers have to make their living, but also the stream along which we all drift, the *ukiyo*, the floating world. All these people, from the lowest bobbing barboy to the grandest geisha left, are united by a com-mon skill: the art of pleasing. Jap-anese, particularly women, lend themselves well to this. It means that even if you are right and the customer wrong, you apologize prettily; it means greeting joyfully customers you particularly dis-like; it means using heightened pronouns for the visiting farmer and lowly pronouns for yourself; it means pleading prettily and politely when the oaf is messing your best kimono; it means an almost complete abnegation of self; and it means utter hypocrisy.

I have watched *mizu-shobai* girls by the hour, wondering at their strength, at their ability to endure and continue. Then, eventually, I understood that, in its way the art of pleasing is sin-cere. I thought of the probably apocryphal story of the great tea master who, having prac-ticed for an hour an aestheti-cism so great it seems almost self-indulgence, stopped on the way home to urinate in the street. It is not the incongruity that should claim our attention, but rather the fact that each of these seemingly disparate acts is what we would, with our limited vocabulary in these matters, term as sincere. He means this artful discipline and he means this gratifying voiding.

When with the customer, the geisha or the bargirl means every thing she says, even the most extravagant flattery. The reason is that sincerity comes with the role. This she puts on as she puts on a kimono. It may bind a bit but it is both pretty and proper. It does not, however, follow that she means it forever. No one means anything forever, but this is something only Asians seem to admit.

It all becomes very clear, standing there in the cold, windy, lighted streets. The Japanese are a people who have managed to retain, right into the latter half of the dehumanized twentieth century, a very human, even primitive, quality: their inno-cence. While this does not pre-vent great subtlety and a degree of sophistication, this mighty innocence—one that the Japa-nese share with those the white man elsewhere calls natives—rests upon an uncompromising acceptance of the world as it is. The innocent does not look for reasons behind reasons. He, secure in the animal nature that all of us have and only half of us admit, is able to see that all reality is what the West finds merely ostensible reality. Real-

ity is skin deep because there is only skin. The ostensible is the truth. There is no crack between the mask and the face because the mask is the only face anyone ever has—that crack, which contains irony and wit as well as cynicism, does not exist.

It is not perhaps, then, the contrast between the old and the new that so attracts in Japan as it is the contrast between innocence and experience. What I flee from in the cities is the beginnings of something new: cynicism, that big-city vice, and with it that great and final breakdown—occurring here, finally—between man and his own nature; that neurosis which creates great cities and occa-sionally great art.

This native innocence results in ignorance on the one hand, mere knowledgeability on the other. It accounts for the almost absurd atrocity of the Japanese at war, the Japanese at business. At the same time it allows the Japanese to live in peace with himself.

They are not perhaps natural in the sense of Rousseau's noble savage, but they are neverthe-less natural beings in their own way. They know what all natural men know: that life is here and now, not in any further state, either theological or financial; they know that death is certain and this they accept with a grace almost shocking to the strug-gling West, which must retaliate by calling them suicide prone or death oriented; and they know perfectly well that reality is that which is apprehended and noth-ing more. This does not make

them pragmatic, because no one would think of constructing a rationale to support such a natural observation, but it does make them empirical. And we of the West find it difficult to live in a land of one dimension such as this. We must always have the further lure and promise of something more, something better, whether it be heaven or a yet higher standard of living, because we must think of our-selves as somehow more, some-how better.

But I am speaking of the people of the Inland Sea; I am speaking of old Japan. Already the change is upon us—already the innocence is fading, going, gone. It lingers here, in these islands that I have so recently visited, but only for a time. I'm fortunate to have seen it.

Feeling much better after such thoughts—it is always surprising what a tonic mere thinking is—I decide to go and have a drink on it.

 ## It Sounds Sordid

It seems coarse to say customer. That was, of course, what he was, just as a whore was what she was. But it sounds sordid, and sordid is one thing a Japanese cannot be. He can be a number of unpleasant things, he can even be some unpleasant things that we cannot, but he is, I think, incapable of sordidness. Rarely looking further than the surface, usually unmindful of consequences and implications, he retains good will and innocence. The whores of Japan remain pure, their customers innocent.

One Way to Eat

The food is southern in Hiroshima. I met *unagi-domburi*. In Tokyo this would be grilled eel over rice. Here it is eel grilled and sweetened and covered with rice to which a vinegar sauce has been added. It tastes Chinese, like sweet-and-sour pork. Also Chinese in appearance are the great butterfly prawns I next order. They are so large that I pick them up with my fingers to eat them.

This excites the interest of the waitresses, who talk among themselves and eventually call the manager. He stares at me for a time and then politely approaches my table.

Is this then, he asks, the proper way to eat prawns? His manner is properly respectful, he intends no irony, he really wants to know. Perhaps the Japanese, using their chopsticks, have been eating prawns wrong over these hundreds of years.

"Not really," I say, "but it is *one* of the ways to eat them."

Are there then several ways of eating them? He wants to know. Perhaps the Japanese might avail themselves of these new ways.

"Yes," I answer, though I had not thought much about the problem. "There is this way, with the fingers, and the other way, with chopsticks, which is also correct."

He is not convinced, lingers. Maybe, he suggests, with a diffident smile, it is merely a provincial custom, something that occurs only in my esteemed home-country but is not to be seen in the world at large.

I put down my bitten prawn. Service is so uniformly exemplary and at the same time so impersonal that, though I have on many occasions interrupted waiters in their work to talk to them, this is one of the few times that anyone has interrupted my eating in order to talk with me. Delighted, and not yet detecting the faint animosity in him that later became more apparent, I said I did not know much about the proper way of eating prawns but that I had been surprised at Hiroshima, had not expected such a bustling and business-like city, and had not expected so strong a Chinese influence.

"Chinese?" he asked, smile fading at the corners.

"Yes," I continued, dilating on the subject. I compared Hiroshima with Nagasaki in this regard, mentioned the fact that before the war there were many Chinese businessmen and sailors, spoke of the way my eel had been done, glanced around, and added, "That painting there, for example."

All Japanese restaurants of this order have murals, just as all public bathhouses have murals. They are all done by the same man. He has a very oily brush, uses very bright color, and always does the same scene: lake or sea, islands, pines, boats, little people, big clouds—occasionally a railway train, more often a steamboat. They look Chinese to me because they are so garish, like pictures in Chinese restaurants.

He looks at the painting, then back at me, face blank—the expression of a polite Japanese disagreeing. Then, this being south and the people more open: "You're wrong" (*chigaimasu*). "It's Japanese—not Chinese at all."

I meant that it was so loud (*hade*) that it looked Chinese to me; Japanese art is much more nicely subdued (*jimi*).

He was not mollified by my explanation, but continued to stand there, began to bite his underlip. Finally he surprised me with a cold "*Do itashimashite.*" This one of the more unsatisfactory polite phrases in Japanese. It is used to mean something like "You are welcome," but a more literal translation might be "What makes you say so?" I am never certain whether it is being used literally or figuratively. Consequently I didn't know what he meant. I suspected, however, that rarest of commodities—irony.

Perhaps it was the Chinese reference that had irritated him. Most Japanese dislike Chinese. They also hate Koreans. The majority here is convinced that these neighboring peoples are hopelessly inferior. To be sure, so, in a way, is everyone else in the rest of the world, but these two are more so.

The belief is surprisingly widespread. Good friends inform me that the Chinese are untrustworthy and the Koreans naturally have a bad smell. We find this shocking, remembering all too well the now hopefully-vanished attitudes of our own that were prevalent in the era of the Kike and the Nigger. But we—remembering—should also find it, however lamentable, natural.

Actually, the Japanese go further than most peoples in discrimination of this sort. Anyone not Japanese is, naturally, in some way inferior. Those who maintain that the Japanese themselves are victims of what they call an inferiority complex are themselves victims of an elaborately sustained illusion. Actually, like the Germans and the Americans, the Japanese suffer from a very advanced superiority complex. This being so, anything not Japanese is so different that it may, in various ways, be discounted.

The commonest way to discount is to dismiss. The Japanese dismisses the entire remainder of Asia, for example. He has no real interest in India, China, Korea, Southeast Asia, though he may take advantage of these countries. During the Pacific War he simply took those lands he wanted; now, after the war, he simply takes the money he wants out of those lands. His attitude is shown in his apparent disinterest. Japan, civilized, will bring its civilization to these inferior peoples who do not enjoy and perhaps indeed are incapable of enjoying the higher life that Japan represents.

One may also, however, discount by appropriation. Europe, America—these lands are also inferior, but their ideas and products may be put to good use if they are first run through the Japanese mill and emerge unrecognizable and therefore very Japanese. This results sometimes in a watch or a camera that is, in all but a few, if telling, ways, identical with some Occidental original; it also results, however, in such fascinatingly monstrous transmutations as the Japanese idea of Humanism, or Democracy.

It follows that all foreigners are stigmatized, but some are stigmatized more than others. At the bottom of the heap are the poor Koreans. Even those born in this country, whose families have been here for generations, are denied citizenship. I knew a Korean man, born and raised in Japan, who, weary of life here, went to America. There, running foul of America's law against aliens working in the country, he was told to leave. But he could not return to Japan, his own country, because he was not a citizen, and the Japanese would not have him. He was sent to Korea, a country to which he had never been, the language of which he did not know, and where he knew no one. I never heard from him again.

Americans are near the top of the pile. Nonetheless, I have found it expedient to tell curious strangers, inquisitive tradespeople, and cab drivers that I come from such safely neutral lands as Sweden, Switzerland, Canada. This is because I do not

want to defend (indeed, cannot defend) America's policies, both domestic and foreign. And I would be expected to. I am not actually myself—not to the taxi driver, nor even to acquaintances who should know better. I am, instead, a typical representative of my land and my people. No matter my protesting that if indeed I were, I would still be there among my own kind; still I am forced into first explaining and then defending "my" country. Since the Japanese do not truly believe themselves to be individuals, they refuse to allow anyone else to be.

Sitting here in this restaurant in Hiroshima, under the eye of a piqued manager who guesses my nationality, I refuse to give in to that easy and sentimental feeling of guilt in which Americans specialize and, at the same time, I refuse the equally easy thought that the disapproving manager is not after all representative, but merely a single man among millions. I can, it is true, attempt to be myself, attempt that divorce from country, but few indeed are the people who attempt this and fewer indeed are those who succeed.

At the same time my journey, my quest, strikes me as quixotic. I want to find the place where the real Japanese live. But are there any?—any other than those I already know? Is not what I really want a place where I can find my own individuality? Is not that what the search is about? And is it likely that there is such a place among these lovely islands?

I am looking for a land where people will accept me: I am not looking, as I had thought, for a land where I could accept them.

Turning to stare at the mural again, I find that it appears now very Japanese—it is an unlikely country, a strange place in which I am engaged in such a venture.

Finished, I stand up, pay, tell the tight-lipped manager that the food was good.

"*Do itashimashite.*"

I Wanted to Be Unhappy

A long and eventually tiresome train ride from Imabari all the way to Matsuyama. It begins well, however. I go to the end of the last car and stand hanging out the doorway, enjoying the wind. Even on the smallest American railways you cannot do this anymore, I should guess. There you are well taken care of. You cannot even open a window. You enjoy the air conditioning until it breaks and you roast. Here, however, off the main lines you can still open windows. Anyone who wants to may lean from the door of a moving train. Anyone who cares to may fall.

Back in the car some children stare at me. I stare back and eat the grass-green caramels I bought at the last station, bought mainly in order to enjoy the delights of a transaction through an open window. The caramels taste like the waxen penny candy I bought when young—a sickly peach-pink taste. Japan is the land where penny candy should come from, even if it doesn't.

I watch a train boy on the platform house across the track. He is drinking tea, staring straight ahead. He does not see me. He is thinking. The train jerks. I hope he will see me. He does not.

Travel in Japan is pleasant because of the sense of accomplishment it gives. I look at my map and discover that if I had gone the same distance in another direction I would be in Korea. Japan is not small. It is a full-sized country with more variety than most. Japan is thought to be small mainly because the Japanese want it to be thought small, just as they themselves want to be known as a small people. They feel that it is gross to be large. Actually, Japan does not feel large or small. It feels just right. It is the ideal size for human habitation.

The train passes a small boy playing with his dog in a field. The train goes through a long tunnel. It comes out. And there is another boy playing with another dog in another field. The two will never meet. A mountain lies between.

Later, however, after Miyawaki, the land turns flat and the weather turns rainy—and I have run out of things to read, having given my much-read copy of *Emma* to the old man at Kinoe, who thought he would like it since it was about a girl, even though it had no pictures and he knew no English. So I spend the rest of the day looking out of the window of the slow and dirty local train, sweating in the wet heat, and watching the raindrops course down the pane.

At such times one becomes lonely. Usually I make a distinction between being alone and being lonesome—a distinction that Japan both fosters and observes. Today, however, I welcome loneliness and would probably have resented a book. It would have distracted me from my indulgence.

At such times one feels very much the foreigner in Japan. I could have spoken to any number of people and been again assured of my being equally alive. Rather, however, I was silent, would not answer the friendly stares, gave way to my emotions. I wanted to be unhappy and so, naturally, I was.

Yet, if there is one thing that Japan teaches, it is to distrust the emotions. They are, after all, only ideas, like any other. You can change your mood as you can change your mind. I see people doing this every day. Japanese have a particularly taking way of doing so. After an emotional excess of some sort, they will shake their heads as though just waking up and say, well, that's enough of that now, and turn their minds to other things. It is not a question of ability—anyone is able to do this—it is a question of volition. Today I have decided to be unhappy just as I might have decided to spend the day in bed.

in our chant as though a windpipe had been seized, and the crush was suddenly so great that I was lifted off my feet. We were passing through a narrower gate, I guessed, and into the compound of the shrine itself.

Then there were cries from up ahead and the sound of scuffles, and the chant was broken off; the bodies about me pressed hard into mine, and our whole enormous mass rolled to a halt.

We were in the shrine and from its other gates had pushed in gangs as large as ours; we had collided as we had for generations past, and those left outside were still pushing, pushing their way inside.

I had, I now realized, lost both shoes. My shirt was open, buttons torn away, and I was so flattened against someone's back that we seemed fused together.

At the same time I suddenly heard the silence. It was as startling as any noise. Utter darkness; complete silence. I moved my head away from it as one moves back from a too bright light. But it was not the silence of solitude, though just as complete. It was vastly peopled, and in it I was slowly being crushed by all these bodies. And the pressure became greater and greater as those outside forced their way in, fighting to join the swarm, to become one with it.

While I could still see in the phosphorescent dark, while I too could chant and run with the rest, then I had been exhilarated. But now in the sudden grip of alien skin and muscle, beginning to feel the sweat seeping out of me, sensing the seams of my clothing pulling, then giving with the strain, I became afraid.

What was I doing here in the midst of all these strangers?—a different race, animated by different thoughts and different feelings. Perhaps they could tolerate such barbarous ceremonies as this, but not I. I must escape. There must be some way out of this solid multitude. I thought of Tokyo, of the jeep. And in a few hours I was thinking of home, America.

For in these hours there had been no movement, none was possible. The only sensation was the gradually steadying pressure which now made even breathing hard. That and the few small shifts that occur when water freezes, when a plant expands. The body next to mine had suddenly found a way to turn, a movement as sudden and as meaningless as a bubble of trapped air rising swiftly to the surface.

My imprisoned hands were now a part of someone else. Moving my fingers, I felt warm, damp flesh—someone's back perhaps. Behind me a thigh shifted. Then a weight on my shoulder, the quick fall of a head—the man beside me—as though it had been severed, or as though the man had died, crushed to death, upright.

There we stood, rooted like trees. And I was terrified, seeing myself trapped here forever. There was no pushing my way free, no climbing over heads and shoulders or crawling between legs to find a way out. To sink to the ground could only mean a final, hopeless fall.

Thus my imagination gripped me. But since there was truly no escape, I just stood there and, with the other trees, endured. Then, as the hours passed, I felt rather than heard a new chant—low, soft, rhythmic, a measured breathing. With it came, at first almost indiscernibly, a gentle movement, as though this packed and standing forest was being swayed by a distant breeze.

As the chant gained, the swaying grew. Damp, hard limbs, a hip perhaps or a shoulder, rubbed me like a branch. And as the night deepened, we chanted—*yu-sha, yu-sha, yu-sha.*

I felt my fear depart. It lifted slowly and I thought no more about our differences. We were now a single mass crammed into this narrow vessel, and there was no telling us apart.

Cradled, we were slowly merging. This I knew, looking up at the dusty stars, losing all feeling in arms, in legs, smelling the hot rice odor which was now mine as well. I, the man I thought I

knew, was gone, become a thousand others. I let my head drop.

It fell across a shoulder or a neck and I realized that I was floating. My feet were no longer on the ground. The pressure had pushed me up, and I was being held aloft by this tight network of bodies, swaying but supporting.

---

*What had terrified me
now consoled me.*

There was no more fear of falling. For the first time I no longer fought for my inch of earth. I lay back and with this came support as more and more of those swaying bodies accepted more and more of me. Or so I felt. But at the same time I knew, an ear suddenly against my cheek, that I was in turn supporting them. And then . . .

And then, I suppose, I must have slept. The deity had had his way with us. His darkness had made us one. Perhaps we all slept, slung in the air, soles off the ground—whole thousands levitating.

I remember only, after a long, long time, raising my head and seeing that pale glow which is earliest morning. Seeing also the breathing profile of the boy asleep beside me, turning and looking deep into his armpit, for his arm was flung about my neck. And I shut my eyes again, not wanting to move, to wake up. I shut my eyes as one pulls the covers over one's head, unwilling to rise.

What had terrified me now consoled me. How secure, how safe, how warm, those bodies molding mine, those several near, those hundreds farther off. This was as it should have been. Like cells we were within a single form, all breathing, all feeling together. And now it was being alone I dreaded—once more, exposed.

Yet, one by one, all of us were waking up.

And those at the farthest ends, whole miles away it seemed, were now stumbling off; slowly the pressure was growing less. I was standing on the ground, the earth strange against my soles, and shortly I could turn and even stoop to retrieve parts of my trampled clothing, the jeep keys still there in the pocket, safe.

The man in front whose back I knew so well stirred and turned. The man behind released me, his flesh becoming separate. The boy whose armpit I had studied was now a plain farmhand who gave a sleepy smile, turned to look for his lost loincloth, searched, gave up.

Then, completely naked, or with dirty loincloths newly tied, or, in my case, the rags of a shirt and most of a pair of trousers, we moved slowly away from each other and out into the brightening day.

We walked, stumbled, streaked with sweat, with dirt, as though newborn and unsure on our feet, as though our eyes, blinded by the dark so long, were not fully open. There was no smell—except for that of urine, pungent, but not unclean. And now I could see, revealed in the gaps in the thinning crowd, that we were making for the font, the great stone urn in front of every shrine, where we could drink.

When my turn came I pushed my whole head into that cold, holy water, taking great gulps as though I were breathing it. I came up dripping and the farmboy led me off to a veranda.

There, on the edge of this large but ordinary shrine, we sat, uncovered in the morning light, and watched the others, our comrades, ourselves, vanish into the empty streets, each alone, silent, surrounded now only by space.

I felt lost, as though my family were deserting me, as though the world were ending, and when an old priest in his high lacquered hat came by, saw the white foreigner, stopped, surprised, then smiled, I asked: And is the *kami* happy?

He nodded, affirmed. The *kami* was happy.

It did not occur to me to ask, as it certainly

would have twelve hours before, just what this ceremony was all about anyway and why we should stand there all night and why nothing had happened, or had it?

And so we sat there, recovering, and the priest with his little acolytes, either up early or up all night, brought us small cups of milky ceremonial sake and the farmer's son, whose raw young body I knew as well as I knew my own, turned with a smile, not at all surprised that I spoke, and asked me my name.

I told him, then asked his. He told me. What was it? Tadao . . . Tadashi? Nakajima . . . Nakamura?

But before long the sun was up, the streets were emptying. Cleansed, tired, staggering, satisfied young men were going off by the hundred, their shadows long behind them. And I found the jeep just as I had left it, and was surprised that the engine turned over—that the gasoline had not evaporated during my century asleep—and drove back to Tokyo, disheveled, content, at peace.

Over the following year I often thought of this experience. And of the single person it had somehow become: Tadashi Nakajima . . . was that his name? Somehow it now seemed to belong to the whole experience, it was the name of everything, of everybody.

And a year later I went back, not because of young Tadashi, whose face I had quite forgotten, whose very name was blurred. No, because of this experience and what it had meant to me.

But now it was 1947, and already the local authorities were cleaning things up. Such relics as the Yami Matsuri did not look right in this new and modern age. Barbaric they seemed, and it couldn't have been good for the health of those poor boys jammed together in the shrine all night long.

So hundreds of years of history were brought to an end, the chain of generations severed. The Festival of Darkness was stopped—I had attended, become a part of, the very last.

Oh, Fuchu still has a Yami Matsuri of sorts—even now, forty years later—but it is not the real one and the *kami* is not, I believe, happy. This god is happy only when people return to their real state, when humans again become human, when we are as we truly are. And this can occur only in darkness and in trust.

From The Temples of Kyoto, *1995*

The Gods

The verandahs, for example, are deeper than usual in order to accentuate the picture that nature makes: the round bushes on the gravel assert their nature by turning pink in the spring for these nearly abstract shapes are really azaleas; the small man-made waterfall asserts its timeless natural voice, punctuated by the rustic clatter of the *sozu*.

The latter is an ingenious contraption in which a section of cut bamboo fills with water from a streamlet until, full, it turns upon its pivot, dumps the water, and drops back upon the waiting rock with a resounding clack. Its use was originally that of an aural scarecrow—deer and boar, both destructive to gardens, were thought dispersed by the sound. At the Shisen-do, however, its role was from the first aesthetic.

It was this sound that Tanizaki Junichiro's grandfather heard and so admired that he had a *sozu* made to reverberate among the storehouses and factories of Tokyo. Even now it is redolent of unspoiled forest, of pure, running water, of a natural ideal of where men actually lived which has never existed, but after which they have always hankered. The sound cleaves, the air closes, and the silence is the more deep from having been rent. Like an articulated emptiness, a space is formed by its confines.

Japanese Shapes

Man is the only one among the animals to make patterns, and among men, the Japanese are probably the foremost pattern makers. They are a patterned people who live in a patterned country, a land where habit is exalted to rite; where the exemplar still exists; where there is a model for everything and the ideal is actively sought, where the shape of an idea or an action may be as important as its content; where the configuration of parts depends upon recognized form, and the profile of the country depends upon the shape of living.

The profile is visible—to think of Japan is to think of form. But beneath this, a social pattern also exists. There is a way to pay calls, a way to go shopping, a way to drink tea, a way to arrange flowers, a way to owe money. A formal absolute exists and is aspired to: social form must be satisfied if social chaos is to be avoided. Though other countries also have certain rituals that give the disordered flux of life a kind of order, here these become an art of behavior. It is reflected in the language, a tongue where the cliché is expected; there are formal phrases not only for meeting and for parting but also for begging pardon, for expressing sorrow, for showing anger, surprise, love itself.

This attachment to pattern is expressed in other ways: Japan is one of the last countries to wear costumes. Not only the fireman and the policeman, but also the student and the laborer. There is a suit for hiking, a costume for striking; there is the unmistakable fashion for the gangster and the indubitable ensemble of the

From A Lateral View, 1962

fallen woman. In old Japan, the pattern was even more apparent: a fishmonger wore this, a vegetable seller, that; a samurai had his uniform as surely as a geisha had hers. The country should have resembled one of those picture scrolls of famous gatherings in which everyone is plainly labeled; or one of those formal games—the chess-like *shogi*—in which each piece is marked, moving in a predetermined way, recognized, each capable of just so much power.

More than the Arabs, more than the Chinese, the Japanese have felt the need for pattern and, hence, impose it. Confucius with his code of behavior lives on in Japan, not in China; the Japanese would probably have embraced the rigorous Koran had they known about it.

The triumph of form remains, however, mainly visual. Ritual is disturbed by the human; spontaneity ruins ethics. Japan thus makes patterns for the eyes and names are remembered only if read. Hearing is fallible; the eye is sure.

Japan is the country of calling cards and forests of advertising: it is the land of the amateur artist and the camera. Everyone can draw, everyone can take pictures. The visual is not taught, it is known—it is like having perfect pitch.

To make a pattern is to discover one and copy it; a created form presumes an archetype. In Japan one suffers none of the claustrophobia of the Arab countries (geometrical wildernesses) and none of the dizzying multiplicity of America (every man his own creation) because the original model for the patterns of Japan was nature itself.

One still sees this from the air, a good introduction to the patterns of a country. Cultivated Japan is all paddies winding in free-form serpentine between the mountains, a quilt of checks and triangles on the lowlands—very different from the neat squares of Germany, or that vast and regular checkerboard of the United States. The Japanese pattern is drawn from nature. The paddy fields assume their shape because moun-

From Where Are the Victors?, 1956 **The Foreigners**

There, across the moat, was the land he knew. It was a land beautiful in rain and fog—the only country on earth that was—yet even more beautiful when the smallest pebble was seen with a photographic clarity, a clarity that Michael's American background had never attained in his eyes. There was an abruptness of contour, a sharpness of line, which was as invigorating as sea air. Against a brilliant blue sky, cloudless and enameled, Fuji stood, the single most preposterous object in this impossible landscape.

No, nothing was really incongruous in Japan. Temple boys in full costume on motor-scooters and neon signs by the Kamakura Buddha were not somehow incompatible with Fuji at sunset. The face of Greer Garson here might be that of the great Daibutsu itself. There was a cohesiveness here, a wholeness which might have been satisfying for someone other than Michael; it did not allow one to pick and choose, to like this or that. One must accept it all, for it was all necessarily both part and whole at the same time.

But this freedom from choice, this simple security fostered by the logic of inevitability, which had once so invigorated Michael, now merely depressed him. He wondered if this weren't perhaps the way the Japanese felt about their own country. Then his new depression created by his former enthusiasm, this new state of mind which so saddened him, was perhaps the perpetual outlook of, say, Haruko. Her choice meant that she was merely bowing to an inevitability, which came from living in Japan. Would she have married him in Persia, in Iceland, in America?

tains are observed and valleys followed, because this is the country where the house was once made to fit into the curve of the landscape and where the farmer used to cut a hole in the roof rather than cut down the tree.

The natural was once seen as the beautiful and even now lip service is still given this thought. However, both then and now, the merely natural was never beautiful enough. That nature is grand only when it is natural—Byron's thought—would never have occurred to a Japanese. No, this ideal is closer to the ordered landscape of Byron's grandfather: forests become parks, trees are dwarfed, flowers are arranged. One does not go against nature but one takes advantage of it: one smoothes, one embellishes. Nature is only the potential—man gives it its shape and meaning.

Since it is the natural forms that are traditionally most admired—the single rock, the spray of bamboo—it is these, which are seen more frequently in Japanese art, delivered from the chaotic context of nature and given meaning through their isolation. There are canons but they derive from nature. Purple and red do not clash because, since they occur often enough in nature, no law of color can suggest that their proximity is unsatisfying. A single branch set at one side of the nichelike *tokonoma* and balanced by nothing is not ill-composed because there is a rule that insists that formal balance is not necessarily good. The Japanese garden is not the French: symmetry is something imposed upon nature, not drawn from it; asymmetry is a compromise between regularity and chaos.

To think of Japan is to think of form, because

The Foreigners

From a work in progress, 1953, unpublished

1948 Tokyo.
Tex and I attended an exhibition one fine October day of Bugaku at the Ueno Gardens. The frail, dissonant sound of the sho, floating through the overhanging trees, the curious duple beat of the drum, the deep cutting sound of the koto, sound like no other music I have ever heard as they rise to the blue autumn sky. After the simple opening prelude, unchanged for a thousand years, a dancer with a halbard walked forward, kneeling in the most natural attitude then, art replacing—or, perhaps, reintensifying—nature, just as the music made me conscious of the trees and the sky, he slowly turns his head to the right, poses for a

second, then swiftly moves it to the left, his profile again against the sky.

The very artificiality of the movements, the gravity of the ritual, seemed to make his body, muscular beneath the stiff orange silk, the floating gauze of his sleeves, the lacquered wire of his head-dress, more than ordinarily natural and made me think not of an art, elaborated over a millennium, but of a mythological animal. He was joined by four other dancers who, one after the other, repeated his gestures, his steps, in the manner of a fugue—or, more precisely, a four-part canon. The music was not aware of this and continued, as mysterious as the

sound of the sea in a shell, the timeless immutability of an art over which the transient patterns of the dance for a moment were traced.

Later I met the first dancer, his name was Ono, his coat—for he now wore Western clothes—was too small and his shirt was frayed. In his lapel was one of the tiny red feathers, which mean the wearer has contributed to the Community Chest drive. He bows and smiles and I learn he is also a violinist. Later yet Tex asks me if I was disappointed in Ono. He seems slightly surprised when I say of course not. But, indeed, how could I be for I scarcely noticed the red feather. Instead, I saw these patterns are repeated often and faithfully. Wherever the eye rests they occur. They give the look of the land a consistency, as though a set of rules had been rigorously followed.

It is these patterns, these shapes, these forms, these designs endlessly occurring, which mark the country. Chaos is vanquished; pattern prevails. They make the view more consistent than would otherwise have been possible—they create what often identifies art: style.

A pattern exists for everything: for temples, kimono, carpenters' saws, and the new is often in the shape of the old. There is only one way to build a shrine, to sew an *obi*. This traditional rigidity is in the outlines, the profile, and is based upon a geometry of stress and repose. In the decoration is individual variation: endless, myriad, protean invention. The shape of a temple bell remains but the patterned surface varies. Dressed stone, planed wood, decorated cloth or pottery, now the gleaming facets of plastic, chrome, glass—the surface is made visible by its own texture. The profile, austere and timeless, is metamorphosed into the unique, the individual.

Japanese design surprises, both in its extent and in its rightness. It is found in the castle and in the kitchen, and the combination of a nearly unvarying outline and a completely varying surface—a decoration which is all form—creates the kind of design that is weakly called "good."

Not however until recently by the Japanese themselves. Traditional design was never noticed. We, the curious foreigners, are in a better position. On the other hand, if we had never seen and did not know the use of some of our own more lovely objects—the light bulb, the toilet bowl, the

only the Heian era recaptured, the undistinguished head above salmon brocades and stiffened gauzes, the blank eyes surmounted by lacquered wire and by the feathers from birds which had not lived for a thousand years.

Most of the guests at the Bugaku exhibition were American and apparently the list had been compiled by leafing through the phone-book and picking out only captains and higher.

The Genroku picnic turned rapidly into a Westchester garden party. Behind me were two young ladies with feather hats who found the dance uncontrollably funny. When one became quiet the other would dig a sharp elbow into her side and off they would go again. With each new absurdity on the platform before them they became more hysterical and ended by laughing through the entire hour-long performance. A major beside me after having listened for a time with the pained expression of someone who knows what he likes, solemnly decided that "this Japan music is sure confused," though by comparison with what he didn't stipulate. I even heard my favorite euphemism for the Japanese from the mouth of a lovely blonde child, hardly more than a baby, who lisped to her striking mother, "Mama, what all those gooks doin'?" Her mother smiled at her fondly and then called her husband's attention to their child with a little wrinkle of her nose and a smile of sheer pride.

All this time cameras were clicking and buzzing for Bugaku is probably the most photographed, and most photogenic, of the arts. Despite their obvious dislike and confusion the Americans were not going to let go a good chance for immortalizing something with their box Brownies or their imported Leicas. All were pleased with the last dance, however, when four warriors in gorgeous azure brocade performed a stunning martial quartet. In this dance they suddenly disengaged their swords and with a motion, blinding in the sun, held them aloft for a second before dropping. So swift had been the act, so unanimous their precision that not one of the amateur photographers captured it.

spoon—we would possibly find them beautiful. But habit blinds and practical knowledge usually deprives of vision. Japan is still distant enough from us that essence is perceived. Disassociated from function, the object become formal rather than practical; it becomes a complete entity, and its visual character is all there is.

Though other countries also have certain rituals that give the disordered flux of life a kind of order, here these become an art of behavior.

Design is a matter of economics, and an unchanging economy creates an unchanging design. Usually this design is the conjunction of the nature of the material plus the least possible effort. Japanese design is inseparable from art in that it is rarely the least effort but the most. Consequently, Japanese craftsmen are paid almost as much as artists would be, as anyone now wishing to construct a real Japanese-style house soon discovers. In Tokugawa Japan, as in eighteenth-century England, one is continually surprised that the gentry spent its money so well.

This economy not only produced the audience for craft, it also maintained it, and the standards of the craftsmanship itself. So long as the economy remained undisturbed there could be no question of fashion. For two and a half centuries the country was closed and even before that there was—except, of course, for the massive cultural importations from China and Korea—little foreign (Western) influence, that great fashionmaker. From the age of Shakespeare to the time of Tennyson, through all the French Louis and all the British Georges, Japan isolated itself. Until

Meiji, the latter half of the nineteenth century, Japan had no arches, corner stones, fireplaces, armchairs or farthingales.

Thus, Japan had never had to contend with the old-fashioned. It had never seen an entire style wane and then wax again. Since old things continued to be used, except for the minor surface variations there was no concept of the structurally old. There were no antique stores, only second-hand stores. Precious, old objects existed but always in the context of the present.

These old things showed the same "perfect" shape. They accommodated themselves both to their desired use and also to the natural laws of stress and repose. Design followed the Confucian standard in all things: uniformity and authority. It followed that Japan is thus the home of the module unit, the first of the pre-fab lands. At the same time, though the profile is standard, individuality is allowed, insisted upon, on the surface itself. One might say of Japanese art as Aldous Huxley said of the Mayan: ". . . it is florid but invariably austere, a more chaste luxuriance was never imagined."

Although the distinction between outline profile and surface decoration is as artificial and as arbitrary as that between form and content, it is possible to say that Japanese design not only permits but insists upon archetypal patterns and all such patterns show a like division, a like propensity.

This natural affinity everywhere remains. Lewis Mumford has observed that the airplane is called beautiful because it looks like a seagull. In Japan this affinity is more acknowledged, more displayed, than elsewhere. Thus, one of the reasons for the beauty of Japanese design, its rightness, its fitness, and one of the reasons for the proliferation of Japanese forms, their economy, their enormous presence, is that the Japanese man and woman, artist or not, is among the last to forget the earliest lesson which nature teaches all makers.

JAPAN *Film*

1960: Becoming a Film Critic

The movie theatre was packed and I was wedged against the back wall looking at the naked screen, waiting for the movie to start—as I had so often in my life.

As for so many of my generation—who, like me, had profitably spent their youth in the dark—it was a moment of promise, the last of the ordinary before the projector's beam focused on the empty screen and a better, truer, more manageable world unreeled.

But this beloved anticipation which I so well knew from long childhood afternoons at the Sigma in far Ohio was now touched with concern as well. For I was no longer a child, twenty-three, this was the Gekijo Tokyo Kurabu in Asakusa, and I was transgressing.

The people standing pressed against me knew this—waiting for the dark, their gazes moved across me, eyes carefully unfocused. No one wanted to acknowledge a foreigner at the movies: we were forbidden.

There were still signs in place: "No Fraternization with the Indigenous Personnel." If the MPs caught any of us occupiers—at Kabuki or coffee shop, dance hall, brothel or cinema—we would be punished, sent back home.

I did not want this—not Ohio again. Yet I risked it because, though I could well imagine a life without Kabuki or brothel, I could not conceive one without movies. They had been my childhood, had made the world seem a simpler and more com-

From Japan Journals, 1960

forting place than it was; Norma Shearer and Johnny Weismuller were my mother and father, and Charles Foster Kane had only just begun to educate me.

So I had been brave, looked along the Asakusa Rokko, seen no MPs, and slipped into the theatre. Though I had no money to buy a ticket—the Occupation used military scrip, not Japanese yen—no one was going to stop an occupier.

And now I was standing, wedged at the back, smelling the rice odor sweat of the people back then, mixed with the fragrance of the camellia oil pomade the men used to use on their hair, and beyond these, the beloved odor of the vast, cold, dusty expectant emptiness in back of the screen. Then the lights went down.

. . . it was a moment of promise, the last of the ordinary before the projector's beam focused on the empty screen and a better, truer, more manageable world unreeled.

What, I wonder, did I see? I remember a sports car in front of Fuji, a pert and modern young woman in wedgies who smoked a lot, and two comedians, one of whom fell in a pond. It was a comedy, apparently, but beyond that I knew little. I did not understand the language, knew nothing about stars or directors, indeed knew nothing about Japan. I had only come in January and it was still cold March.

Later, after I knew a bit more, I searched through the images in my memory. Probably a Toho film, I decided, since they specialized in comedy in that period. But, wait, the Tokyo Club was even then a Shochiku theatre. If so,

then maybe one of the two men, the one with the penciled moustache who fell in the pond, was Tony Tani, forgotten Shochiku comedian. As for the pretty girl in wedgies, I have poured through old stills of films from 1947 but I never saw her again.

From such beginnings knowledge of the Japanese film could only grow. And so it did, slowly. While I later bravely sneaked into motion picture theaters all over the city—Asakusa having originally been chosen because it was remote from the trodden paths (Ginza, Yurakucho) of prowling MPs—I still did not know how to speak or read. I was forever getting sisters confused with wives and mistresses with mothers, and I was instantly lost in the labyrinths of the period film.

I dumbly absorbed reel after reel sitting in the winter-cold of the Yurakuza, or the summer-heat of the Hibiya Gekijo. Yet, in these uncomprehending viewings of one opaque picture after another, however, I was also being aided by my ignorance. Undistracted by dialogue, undisturbed by story, I was able to attend to the intentions of the director, to notice his assumptions and to observe how he contrived his effects.

Though I understood little about cinema, I had seen a lot of it, and now I began to realize that space was used differently in Japanese films. There was a careful flatness, a reliance upon two dimensions, which I knew from the Japanese prints. And emptiness was distributed differently. Composition seemed bottom-heavy, but then I realized that—like in the hanging scrolls I had seen—the empty space was there to define what was below: it had its own weight.

And there were also many less close-ups than I was accustomed to in American films. The camera seemed always further away from the actors—as though to show the space in between. A character was to be explained in long shot, his environment speaking for him. Sometimes I could not even make out his face but I knew who he was by what surrounded him.

I also noticed the pace of the films of the period: slow, very slow. Time—lots of it: long scenes, long sequences—was necessary. Feelings flowed and flowered to what Ohio would have thought extravagant lengths. The screen was awash with undammed emotion. Yet, though decidedly allergic to the displays of Joan Crawford and Bette Davis, I did not mind the emotionality of women I later discovered to be Kinuyo Tanaka and Hideko Takamine.

Wondering why I so willingly wept along with them, I decided that the very fact that they were so far away, and crying for such a long time, compelled my moving nearer, and hence feeling more. So different from the big and demanding close-up of Joan, with nostrils large enough to drive a truck into. Being apparently asked for nothing I gave more. And so, sitting there, smelling the pomade, I was learning my first lesson in Japanese art.

* * *

And now I wonder which films taught me. 1947—one could have been Ozu's *Record of a Tenement Gentlemen* released that May; another could have been Mizoguchi's *The Loves of Sumako* (with Kinuyo Tanaka), released that August. Whatever I saw, I have forgotten, if I ever knew. I later looked at both the Ozu and the Mizoguchi but not a memory budged.

Despite my general ignorance I was learning. And I wanted to learn more. In this I was hindered by my occupation. I was a CAF-2, a typist in the Office of Cultural Reparations, and though I had been a champion typist at Lima Central High School I was not fond of my talent. Here I was in Japan wasting my time typing out forms in triplicate.

So I presented myself to the Army newspaper in Tokyo, *The Pacific Stars and Stripes,* and informed them that they had no film critic. They agreed, I was hired, and though restricted largely to reviewing Hollywood for the troops, I now,

if caught, had some excuse for being in a local motion picture theater.

The first Japanese film scene that I can now identify was one I recognize only because I had seen it being made. In early 1948 I was taken to the Toho Studios. This was not because of my new critical position but because I had made friends with the composer Fumio Hayakawa.

Relations on fraternization with the indigenous personnel having been relaxed, I asked him to my billet to hear the Berg *Violin Concerto,* newly recorded and inexplicably on sale in the P.X. He responded by taking me to Toho to watch a movie he was doing the score for being filmed.

The open set was a large sump surrounded by ruined buildings, a scene much like those I had seen in ruined Asakusa when I first arrived. At work was the main actor, a young man in a Hawaiian-shirt, and the director, an older man in a floppy hat. Though I was introduced, there was nothing I was able to say to them nor they to me, and so I watched the action—the young man being noisy with another older man with a beard.

In April Hayakawa took me to the Toho screening room to see the finished picture and I realized that the young man in the shirt was Toshiro Mifune, the man with the beard was Takeshi Shimura, the man in the floppy hat was Akira Kurosawa and the film was *Drunken Angel.* Whenever I now see this film and we reach that scene by the sump, I look to the right of the screen—there I am, just a few feet off the edge, twenty-four now, mouth open, watching a movie being made.

Thanks to Hayakawa it became known that this occupier was interested in Japanese movies—not in censoring them, there was a whole office full of occupiers who were doing that—but in studying them.

Meeting people, I was able to understand more about the movies I was seeing. Told about Ozu and Naruse, about interesting younger directors

like Kinoshita and Yoshimura, and new directors such as Ichikawa Kon, I was able to detect styles. Though I tended still to get their films mixed up, I was finding my way around, slowly devising a map.

And getting to see many more movies as well. Officially, I would go to the Army screening room and see for review the new Grable, the latest Lana. Unofficially, I would then run off to Japanese movie houses and hope it was the just released Mizoguchi or Shiro Toyoda or Tadashi Imasi. By 1949 the MPs had stopped prowling and though theaters were still off-limits no one paid much attention any more. I walked right in—Ginza, Yurakucho, Shinjuku—with never a wary glance. Nor did people bother to ignore me any more. Instead I was stared at along with the people on the screen. And I stared back, impressed that the people on the screen and the people in the theater were so much the same.

This had not been true in Ohio. We in the audience looked up at Fred and Ginger in top hat and fox fur, or at Cary Grant in tails and Jean Harlow in ermine. All very different they were, and their difference was their attraction.

But here I saw on the screen the same family around its sparse table that I would see through the windows of houses I passed on the way back from the movies. And in watching these film families I was joined by those families (they were all around me) who seemed in no way different.

This surprised me. I had not really known—being American—that movies were not always about differences and emulation, that they could also be about similarities and agreement. The Japanese audience standing around me—in 1949 movies were so popular it was still standing room only—was willingly looking at and learning from people in no way different from themselves.

I thus learned something about realism as a style. All of those identical dining rooms had been crafted from life by the art department, the originals of those beaten fathers and hope-

ful mothers had been observed and imitated by the actors, those domestic spaces, that everyday time, were created and controlled by the director. What looked just like life was really art.

All of this discovery was exhilarating. And yet I still knew little about the nature of film itself, though I had made some guesses. Norma Shearer and Charles Foster Kane were not really enough—I needed an education.

*   *   *

In the fall of 1949, I entered Columbia University in New York. I went there because that institution was among the first to be convinced that cinema was more than entertainment. So, I enrolled in their first film studies course. My teacher was Roger Tilton and under him I read Eisenstein, Arnheim, Kracauer, learned about montage and could finally see films I had only heard about: *The Cabinet of Dr. Caligari, Intolerance, Potemkin.*

Studying with my teacher, I began to realize that there was a lot more to the movies than I thought. Under the entertainment I began to sense the art—that film could present experience in patterns that themselves recreated emotions, created understanding.

Searching, wanting to find out more, and more, I went to the Museum of Modern Art and—not knowing for what I was looking—saw films which created what I felt and enlarged what I knew—*La Passion de Jeanne d'Arc, Zéro de conduite, Ménilmontant.* These black and white images on the big square screen no longer built a world that I could better manage. Rather, they opened one I could not have imagined, one through which I could understand a pattern I recognized, feel inside me an emotion I at once knew. A murder became the arc of itself, a succession of violent fragments; a mock procession in slow motion became a real celebration of an innocence I had forgotten, and the great mocked face, pocked as the moon, turned to me and the tear-filled eyes no longer demanded—rather, they saw me, sitting there in the future.

Looking, I was learning. It was a new language. Soon I was thinking of sentences and paragraphs, pondering over the grammar of pictures. The linguistic parallel was not precise, but cinema offered a distinct way of showing and the language paradigm seemed one way through which this could be understood. It also, as I soon learned, offered a kind of respectability to the study of cinema.

Roger Tilton had experienced the greatest difficulty in persuading Columbia University that film was a proper, academic discipline, one for which credits for graduation were allowed, one which could accommodate scholarships, theses and M.A., Ph.D. degrees. Universities were, in 1949, still skeptical.

One way to convince them was to prove that cinema was serious, and one of the ways to do this was to demonstrate that film had its own standing as a discipline which could, like any other, be reduced to its moving parts. If something like an exact science could be approximated, then academe would allow the cinema as a discipline.

I was present at this elevation and I enthusiastically supported its academic ascension. Though I did not much care about whether the movies were respectable or not, I very much cared about whether underlying rules could or could not be discovered, indicating that the movies as a kind of language could be codified, learned. I found in Jean Debrix—who thought they could—a prophet bearing the good news of a possible analysis, which would disclose structure revealed.

When this actually occurred, however, I was no longer at school and Debrix had had little do with the revelation. The advent of a completely structural model based on considerations largely linguistic occurred when I was back in Japan, a place quite open to new imports, including movies, but hermetically sealed against new ideas.

Thus I remained in ignorance of what was occurring in film studies until it was far too late for me to learn the required new vocabulary.

Undistracted by dialogue, undisturbed by story, I was able to attend to the intentions of the director, to notice his assumptions and to observe how he contrived his effects.

In the meantime, undisturbed by the growing discipline, I was devouring all the actual film that I could. Particularly I sought out those films that Japanese directors had told me were important to them: *The Wedding Circle, Stagecoach, Poil de Carotte.* Having seen Lubitsch I could look at Ozu with a more informed eye, viewing Ford I could understood more about Kurosawa, and after having looked at Duvivier I was able to see how reality was recreated in a Naruse film.

But there were no Japanese films to be seen—*Rashomon* would not appear in New York until late 1951—and I was, despite the cinematic banquet, hungry for Japan. I found the one Japanese restaurant in the city and went there to eat bad sukiyaki and improve my equally bad Japanese. *Eiga wa dai suki,* I love films, I said. *Doshite?* asked the counterman—why? I didn't really know why, but I knew that films had made some sense of my life, and that they would make sense of Japan too.

It was not until late 1953—many movies later, Columbia behind me—that I, now as educated as that institution could make me, returned to Japan, anxious to look at more Japanese films. This time, however, it took some ingenuity to get back in.

(continues on page 60)

Space Is Spread

I landed at Inokuchi and took the bus to the other side of the island. Here at Oyamazumi on Omishima is one of the three oldest shrines in Japan. It must be old indeed. The most important shrine, that at Ise, built by the emperor Suinin in honor of the Sun Goddess Amaterasu Omikami and still functioning, was completed, if the records are to believed, fully twenty-two years before, on the opposite side of the globe, Pontius Pilate washed his hands of that other religious matter. I am also assured by the priest that this Omishima shrine remains one of the three most important in the land, on a par with those at Ise and Izumo.

Of great antiquity and so remote that it remains largely unvisited, this shrine contains an atmosphere long vanished from sacred but tourist-filled Ise, from well-tended Izumo. Distance alone, however, does not explain its neglect. Perhaps it is that the Japanese no longer expect shrines on islands. (Even Kompira-san, that great shrine near Takamatsu dedicated to seafarers, is surprisingly located in the mountains and has no view of the sea.) Perhaps it is that, in this new age of mass tourism, little Setoda drains away the potential visitors. Or perhaps it is that Japanese like their religion humanized just as they like their nature domesticated. Oyamazumi is too rigorous, too near the gods.

It is a series of low buildings among trees. Space in a shrine is horizontal and not, as in a cathedral, vertical. In a church, space is confined. It must struggle upward, having no place else to go. In a shrine, space is spread. There are no high walls, no tight enclosures. The space is a grove and this grove seems so endless that it might be the world itself.

The sky seems low, near. There are long expanses of lawn or grove among the buildings. One is not enclosed, nor is one directed. One is liberated, and almost always alone.

Shrine prayer, as I have said, is not communal prayer. It is solitary prayer. It is not a state—it is a function. It lasts only a minute or so and it is spontaneous. One does not enter, as in churches, or descend, as in mosques. The way to the shrine is through a grove, along a walk, through nature itself, nature intensified. Through these trees, over this moss, one wanders to shrines.

This casual, unremarked acceptance of nature speaks to something very deep within us. It speaks directly to our own nature, more and more buried in this artificial and inhuman century. Shinto speaks to us, to something in us which is deep, and permanent.

Certainly we feel—which is to say, recognize—more here than in smiling Buddhism with its hopeful despair, more than in fierce manmade Islam with its heavenly palaces on earth, more than in the strange and worldly tabernacles of the Hebrews or in the confident, vaunting, expectant Christian churches.

This religion, Shinto, is the only one that neither teaches nor attempts to convert. It simply exists, and if the pious come, that is good, and if they do not, then that too is good, for this is a natural religion and nature is profoundly indifferent

There is no personification. The gods have neither shapes nor forms. They are simple *kami-sama,* whose numbers are unknown but vast—so vast that they meet together only once a year, far away in Izumo.

How to Stop Time

Climbing slowly down the shadowed stones I thought of Ise, the greatest shrine of all, the mother shrine, home of the Sun Goddess herself. A visit to any shrine, as humble and forgotten a one as this, leads one to consider such imponderables as life, death. Thoughts of ancient Ise led me to consider another—time.

Time for the West is a river. Down its changing yet forever unchanging length we float. In the East, however, the river is more a symbol for life, our earthly span, the *ukiyo,* than it is for time itself.

Time has no symbol in this Asia where almost everyone, at least formerly, lived in a continuous and unvarying present. If it had one, it might be a symbol as startlingly up-to-date as the oscillating current. The reason this occurs is Ise—not only one of the great religious complexes of the world but the only answer yet discovered to man's universal wish either to invent the perfect perpetual-motion machine or, else, to stop time entirely.

The way to stop time, the Japanese discovered, is by letting it have its own way. Just as the shape of nature is observed, revered, so is the contour of time. Every twenty years—and for over a thousand years—the shrine at Ise is razed and a new one is erected on an adjacent plot reserved for that purpose. After only two decades, the beam-ends barely weathered, the copper turned to palest green, the shrine is destroyed. Only twenty generations of spiders have spun their webs, only four or five generations of swallows have built their nests, not even a single blink has covered the great staring eye of eternity—yet down come the great cross-beams, off come the reed roofs, and the pillars are carted off to be reused in other parts of the shrine grounds.

On the adjacent plot is constructed a shrine that is in all ways similar to the one just dismantled. More, it is identical. Something dies, something is born, and the two things are the same. This ceremony, the *sengushiki*, is a living exemplar of the greatest of religious mysteries, the most profound of human truths.

And time at last comes to a stop. Forever old, forever new, the shrines stand there for all eternity. This—and not the building of pyramids or ziggurats, not the erection of Empire State Buildings or Tokyo Towers—is the way to stop time and thus make immortal that mortality which we cherish.

 ## Swept Her off Her Feet

But what, I now safely wondered, if I had swept her off her feet, had smothered her protestations with kisses, had—No, I'm not the type, and this she knew.

Becoming rapidly soberer in the growing light, I still fantasized on. I imagined taking her—what was her name? but we hadn't told each other our names—with me through, let us say, Europe. There she was in her gray-and-rose kimono standing shyly in the Piazza San Marco.

But when I looked more closely I saw that she had changed, that she was no longer herself. The Japanese are like that. They do not travel well. The men are embarrassed, shy, sad, or else—the obverse—so miserable that they become rude; and the women—they turn more and more into themselves until they close completely.

The Japanese is all Japanese and he must be seen in his own context because his mountains, his forests, his seas are also him. It is not that he does not have individuality, for he does. It is that he has more than individuality, he has his context—and he has never been taught to foster a strong personality, has never been told that each and every person must be, somehow, different, unique, only himself. He has never found that necessary because his strength comes from his land and from his people. This is why the Japanese are most themselves among others of their own kind. The Japanese-I stopped.

 ## Sad but Never Tragic

Coca-Cola long finished, its remains attracting bluebottles, I walk slowly back through the pleasant city and continue my ruminations.

The Japanese always think us younger than we are. That is because they are all so young. The reason they are so young is that they have no conscience, maybe, certainly that there is no cynicism and no corollary of disillusion. No one ever taught them to expect more of life than life can in fact offer. Appearances are reality, the mask is literally the face, and the cynic can find no telltale gap because none exists. The result is a kind of innocence, in our eyes at any rate.

And we know all about this. We moaned its lack all during the nineteenth century and now the new romanticism in manners and clothes, in novels and movies, continues to indicate the extent of the loss we still feel. Since we can still find this quality in children, we call it childlike.

Actually children are destructive and amoral little savages, rendered safe only by their small size. A six-foot two-year-old would be very dangerous. Such observations, however, do not occur to those who moan most loudly over lost innocence. They always like children.

What one finds in Japan is something different. It is a grown-up, very civilized nation that has, somehow, managed to retain this quality that we so prize and that they never think about. To be sure, not all of us like it. Then we find the country vacuous, filled at most with a frenetic gaiety and a morose bathos that all but mock our own earnest and adult endeavors. (Such a feeling was certainly behind General MacArthur's patronizing and ill-judged remark that the Japanese are a nation of twelve-year-olds. Actually, of course, they are a nation of eighteen-year-olds, that excellent age when innocence and experience are as nicely balanced as they ever will be.) But those of us who prize the quality gratefully discover a land where one may be serious but seldom earnest—except when writing books about it—where one can be sad but never tragic.

The Japanese may occasionally be childlike. He is never childish. He knows who he is (alienation is a very recent urban phenomenon in Japan) and what he can do. Perhaps that is why he is so standoffish when alienated expatriates come moping to his shores. He welcomes them for what they bring—money, English,

a breath of fresh air, reflections of foreign lands in those strange blue eyes—but he doesn't bring them home. He puts them up in a hotel.

So considering, I saw that I had reached my own—a perfectly adequate city-type inn with a tiled roof, a dwarf pine or two, and new tatami—smelling like freshly cut grass—on which I lay down and took a nap.

Faintly Translucent

Japanese skin—why has no one ever properly celebrated it? One would not expect the Japanese themselves to. They, after all, live in it. But we the coarse, the hairy, the heavy-pored—we might have been expected to make much of this finely spun, hairless covering, reminding of some half-forgotten childhood friend.

That is what the skin is like, the skin of children. Faintly translucent, which is why the Japanese get red when they drink; lightly perfumed, the odor of rice, because of the diet; and smooth—not smooth as leather is smooth, but smooth as some fabled Asiatic cloth is smooth to the touch.

The skin of children, the skin of animals. To us in the West who revere anything more innocent than ourselves, this is what the Japanese skin is like. To run the hand along not a leg but a flank, to raise the wondrous and silken texture of a haunch, a forearm—there is in this skin

a natural perfection that seems untouched, as though we are the first to touch it.

Such perfect covering makes it seem as though we can feel deeper than the skin itself. The skin is not a barrier. It is yielding, it invites.

It is possible, says the skin, to know more, to enter more fully, to understand more deeply.

There is no hair on this skin—just the blackly shining hair of the head, the eyebrows. Under the arm is not a bush but a small shrub. Japanese girls do not show the triangle. Rather, something like a cornice and two pillars, a small torii, a holy gateway. Japanese men do not have that inverted tree the roots of which clutch the navel. Low, like a hip-hugging belt, the hair stops straight, as though shaved. It is the pattern of the ideal, seen in early Greek statues.

The bodies, too, are early Greek. The breast is small, comely. The thigh is short, lowering the body. It destroys our Renaissance ideas of human beauty. It restores that of the Cretans. We remember these proportions and respond to them. The long legs of the Hellenic era, of all Western culture afterwards, are forgotten. These short thighs, the texture of this skin—they retain the matrix in our memories. To cup a hand over a breast we would call immature, run a hand along a thigh we would name adolescent—these erase experience and recall innocence. It makes the Japanese seem sometimes childlike. It makes us, once again, for a blessed and horizontal moment, children.

The Japanese Toilet

In Matsuyama it continued to rain. I did not again visit the castle; did not go to Dogo, city of hot springs; did not have any adventures. Instead, to punish myself, to make myself feel more badly still, I picked the cheapest and most unprepossessing inn I could find. It was so cheap that, as I soon discovered, there was no toilet paper in the lavatory, or else they had forgotten to replenish the stock—at any rate there was none. I never remember to carry a stock around with me—really a necessity in Japan, where it is but rarely found in public conveniences—and always have to ask for it.

I asked for it here in the cheap inn and at once the two silly maids set up a merry noise. The thought of a foreigner coping with the Japanese toilet is a happy one, and to be thus informed in advance seemed to double their enjoyment. With my simple request, squeals of merriment began and continued for an hour or two, fresh bursts of delighted laughter echoing from corridor and kitchen.

To be sure, it doubtless *is* amusing. The Japanese toilet is notoriously difficult for the uninitiated. One squats over this enameled hole in the floor that—if there is no plumbing, and there seemed to be none in this inn—leads directly into the noisome pit itself. One hangs there, legs aching, awaiting deliverance. It is strange that a people who have without a murmur relinquished their own architecture in favor of plastics and prefabs, who have cheerfully cut down their forests, leveled their hills, and dirtied their seas, who have turned their entire country over to that modern juggernaut, the automobile—that these same people should with such stubborn tenacity cling to such a medieval, even barbaric, device.

Yet they have, and the two maids all but loitered in front of the door hoping to hear if not actually view my exertions. It had obviously made their day, and I went to bed grumpy and sour and fell instantly asleep.

Accidental Beauty

The entire prospect was superbly beautiful, even if one remembered gossip about its presiding goddess. The scene was made of so little—the horizon of the sea, some rocks piled high, a pine or two, the little shrine, the sky. Views are rarely this simple. This one was so right, so appropriate, that it seemed ideal. And like all ideal things it did not seem real, but more like a mirage floating on the surface of the sea.

If I had seen a picture of it, I would have said it was pretty—a postcard view, typical Japan. But coming upon it in a boat under a summer morning sky, I was startled into beholding its simplicity. It was accidental, this beauty. And it is difficult for us to believe or remember or admit that the greatest beauty is always accidental.

And this accidental quality is to be captured only if the full context is shown. Japanese scenery is like Japanese poetry. Both its beauty and meaning depend upon a context of things perhaps incongruous. One observes a relationship that had always hitherto escaped notice but which, once seen, becomes inevitable.

Such an island as this exists, but its beauty exists in the morning sky, in the endless expanse of sea, in the light that hovers and bathes. Japanese scenic beauty is a whole beauty because it requires this context before it can be recognized. Since it is whole, it creates in the viewer a sense of wholeness, however fugitive. Travelers from our fragmented West are ravished by the vision of such wholeness, such natural inclusion of everything in the world. I gaze. The beauty lies not in the single lovely object standing alone. It is in this combination that slides into and out of its background. The shrine is not beautiful, nor are these pines. It is their being so much a part of the sea and the sky that makes them beautiful.

Nature and Artifice

Viewed from a height—from the top of Chikami-yama on Shikoku, or from this terrace of Washu-zan—the islands spread out as though on a table. They remind one of a scattered jig-saw puzzle or a mighty game of checkers. A calm sea reflecting each low shape, these convo-luted and somehow decorative islands stretch into invisibility. They remind one of something man-made. One thinks of Sesshu, of Claude Lorrain, of Seison, of Poussin.

To look at a Japanese land-scape is, often, to think of art. To look over the middle Inland Sea is, for me, to think of the rock garden at the Ryoan-ji in Kyoto—a rectangle of white sand from which rises a number of large stones—and to real-ize what this amazing piece of landscaping is about. It is not about a mother tiger and her young crossing a river, nor about geometry, nor music, nor astronomy, nor mathemat-ics—proffered explanations all. It is about islands in the sea.

Others, looking at the Inland Sea, have thought of tray land-scapes, those common and artfully constructed dishes of miniature seas and mountains that have been called imaginary landscapes made for the plea-sure of artists to whom reality is, perhaps, a disappointment. Not at all—tray landscapes are like photographs: no imagination

needed, no fancy necessary. You take a tray, some stones, some sand; you bring them to a height, sit down, and faithfully copy.

To the Western eye a landscape this artful-appearing does not seem quite real. It is so beautiful it seems ideal. It seems, literally, too good to be true. To the Jap-anese eye, however, such per-fection seems real enough but unwelcome. Tray landscapes are not considered a major art and, with the exception of a few cele-brated heights, the beauty of the Inland Sea is little noticed. We of the West, however, are ravished by such scenes, no matter how unreal they seem. And at the same time we are intrigued with a sense of the familiar.

Then we recognize where we have seen similar views. When Gozzoli or Paolo Uccello want-ed an imaginary backdrop, when Giovanni Bellini or Piero di Cosimo needed an exotic land-scape in the distance, when Puvis de Chavannes or Max-field Parrish required an ideal land—then all of these painters created a painted paradise that closely resembled the humped and humanized country of the Inland Sea.

It is not to the taste of all trav-elers. Perhaps the eighteenth-century wanderer, with his sense of the ordered and the ideal, would have most loved it. This is where Rasselas and Vathek should have come, where Haydn ought to have placed his unin-habited island, where Paul and Virginie belonged. Consequently, perhaps, the succeeding century would have found here little to

please. The Japanese continue to regard unfinished nature with the delight early evidenced by Chateaubriand and are to this extent still nineteenth-century—or else the romantic sensibility as it is known in Europe is Japanese. In any event, Byron, with his taste for crags and tarns, would have passed through the Seto Naikai without a glance. Great ravines, gorges, waterfalls, the startled deer, Wordsworth country—this is Shikoku, not the islands of the Inland Sea.

The attitude of celebrated travelers would have varied. Charles Waterton, Kinglake, Norman Douglas—no matter their other differences—would have agreed that civilization was pressing disconcertingly close. Doughty would certainly have demanded more discomfort than these hospitable islands can afford. But Beckford would have loved them. If one expects nature and artifice, extensive woods and a distant pagoda, or the green roof of an ancient shrine seen floating above a grove centuries old—then one comes to the Inland Sea.

Borrow might best have liked this sea, these islands, because he liked his landscape peopled. The wilderness meant little to him. There always had to be a house in the middle distance; there always had to be someone to look at, someone to listen to. Late-nineteenth-century travelers delighted in the pic-turesque fisherman, the quaint costume, the amusing woman, the adorable child. They made them part of the genre scene, an undifferentiated grouping, family balancing both nearby grove and distant prospect. Borrow, who understood both landscape and people, would have seen through the picturesque. He would have suspected legend, myth, a people different from other peoples. And he would have been right.

Waiting by the Boat

There was another silence. We were waiting by the boat. It showed no sign of leaving.

Such moments always embarrass a Westerner. He is in between: something has ended, something else is beginning, but neither is yet accomplished. He grows gruff, blows his nose, looks in the direction in which he hopes shortly to be moving. Not the Japanese. This is one of the great moments, one of those when the eternal flow is nearest the surface. Hence, I supposed, those painfully prolonged scenes of departure in railway stations all over the country. Hence the good-bye songs over loudspeakers at piers and wharfs. Hence all the colored streamers on a boat that, after all, is only going to the next island. Such a moment is relished, prolonged, and—to the Westerner— stretched out until embarrassment becomes its own anesthetic.

She was silent. The boat was silent. I was silent.

This Small Puffing Engine

It is, to be sure, very easy for the foreigner to give way in this fashion. If he thinks about it at all, he cannot but realize that he is regarded as unreal by the Japanese. He is too curious, too strange, to be taken seriously. His sorrows are not theirs, nor his pleasures—at least, so their attitude suggests. The friendliness is real but it rests upon simple curiosity. Most Japanese will go out of their way to help a foreigner in some kind of trouble, but this does not mean that he is any more authentic to them, nor that they find him emotionally understandable. And if a foreigner gets into a kind of trouble that the Japanese think is bad, then heaven help him, because they won't.

One lives with that knowledge, however, just as one lives with the knowledge of gray hair, wrinkles, and never becoming rich enough. It is not an important consideration and not one truly responsible for the funks in which foreigners find themselves in Japan occasionally, like that I have made for myself today.

Why am I on this train, creeping through the rain, on this dismal island? I asked myself. What possessed me to forgo what civilized qualities Tokyo offers—books, friends, food— and exchange them for this misery? What do I want, where am I going?

Such went the funk, and, as always, the malaise of being alive was diminished to this small puffing engine and its toy cars with me in one of them creeping along a dank seacoast. I didn't see, refused to see that it was the voyage of life I was questioning and not the voyage through the Inland Sea. It is always so much easier to blame the more apparent, the lesser.

Then there was no food on the train, and since it was raining, they were not selling any at the small stations where we stopped for long periods before sighing and puffing onward. Certainly, I told myself, this is redolent enough of old Japan to suit me—I who have this argument with the new, this quarrel with my times. If I don't like the speedways and hamburger stands, the pizza parlors and parking lots, if I do not agree with the hordes now covering the face of the earth, surely then, poking along an absolutely deserted stretch of coast in a coach possibly constructed in 1900, saved from hamburgers, pizzas, anything edible at all—surely, this might please me.

Such are the vagaries of the romantic temperament, however, that it is never satisfied. While believing that such a temperament—mine, for example—is the only thing that can save the world, I was nonetheless morose, bored, and unpleasant with myself.

At this point, however, tired of my emotions, I fall asleep.

Before, I had been a Shinchugen, a member of the New Advancing Forces, an occupier. I'd merely walked into the country. Now, however, the Occupation was two years over, and I was just another carpetbagger wanting a job. Finally I got in by arranging for a fictitious position on the staff of *The Reader's Digest,* a magazine which I had never read. Once in Tokyo, I prevailed upon acquaintances on my old paper (still publishing, though with its military circulation much curtailed) to recommend me to *The Japan Times.*

Under the entertainment I began to sense the art—that film could present experience in patterns that themselves recreated emotions, created understanding.

By the beginning of 1954, just seven years after I had first come, I was finally back in Japan, and—this time—learning Japanese. This occurred twice a week, night classes, at the Naganuma Language School in Shibuya. After my evening lesson I would walk down Dogenzaka to the station, stopping at several of the small drinking places which lined the slope, talking with whoever would, and by the time the bottom was reached I had my homework, and lots of sake, under my belt.

I also now had a fitting job—film critic for *The Japan Times*—and I was actually beginning to understand some of the films that I saw. I comprehended enough to see and review Kinoshita's *A Japanese Tragedy,* and Ichikawa's *Mr. Poo.* I was hoping to get to do *Seven Samurai*—but the senior critic, the otherwise supportive Fumi

Saisho, wanted it. I did, however, get to go to the premiere of this Kurosawa film.

It occurred on April 26th, at the big Nichigeki, Toho's best house. Kurosawa had so gone over the budget that the company decided it must exploit the picture and this included a big star-filled gala premiere and—later—cutting the picture from nearly two hundred minutes down to much less for other local screenings. I was thus a member of that favored audience who saw the complete picture—everyone else had to wait thirty years until further commercial considerations persuaded Toho to reinsert the cuts and make new prints.

It is probably just as well that I was prevented from reviewing it. My Japanese was not nearly good enough to handle period-language. Even a year later I was still hopeless. Attending a screening of Mizoguchi's *New Tales of the Taira Clan* I was baffled by the many stately injunctions to go to the toilet. The toilet? asked the Daiei man, incredulous. Yes, I quoted—*Benjo e mairo.* No, no, no, he said: Not *benjo* but (a term for the old imperial palace) *denjo.*

Even though I could not entirely follow the language of *Seven Samurai* it made little difference to my appreciation (as separate from my understanding) of the film. I had seen Dovshenko now, and John Ford, and I was able to understand the accomplishment of Kurosawa and to recognize in that final reel one of the great feats of film editing and to see in the final scene one of the great moral statements.

And there, as though in long shot on the Nichigeki stage, was Kurosawa, without the floppy hat, and Mifune, his hair slicked back, and my friend Hayakawa, to die only a year later, solemn in his round horn-rimmed glasses but shyly smiling.

Now that I was a critic who reviewed only Japanese films (never again did I touch Betty Grable), I also had a modest place in the Japanese film scene. I had my credentials and—more important—I was in a position to help get Japanese films abroad, an attractive option after *Rashomon, Ugetsu,* and *Gate of Hell* started earning prizes at film festivals.

Having to write more about Japanese film, I had to learn more about it. Posing as an expert, I had to become one. And since there was nothing in any language I could read, I began making lists of directors and their films, taking notes on their styles. In this way I could create some coherence and begin a system of categorization without which any criticism would be meaningless.

In January, 1956, I saw my first Ozu film, *Early Spring (Tokyo Story* I had missed, being still in New York when it was released) and saw everything come together—my earlier thoughts on Japanese time and space, my recognition of the meticulous artifices of Japanese realism, my seeing in my Japanese neighbor, right there in the next seat, the person on the screen. My list on Ozu became my longest and my notes on him the most.

I was not alone in making lists and taking notes. Another Tokyo Ohioan, Joseph Anderson, was also studying film and we met because we were both invited to write something about our subject in the *Eiga Hyoron,* then the most progressive film journal, edited by Tokutaro Osawa, a smiling, enthusiastic, helpful man who felt much about Japanese film as we did.

Originally Joe and I were going merely to write an article for *Films in Review,* an American publication where he knew someone. Then this original article grew into a longer piece, then into a pamphlet, and eventually into our big, long book, *The Japanese Film: Art and Industry.*

Our collaboration was ideal in that we complemented each other. I could not read Japanese but Joe could, and what he couldn't his wife could. On the other hand my spoken Japanese was better than his. So he did most of the historical research and I did most of the legwork, talking to directors and the like. Each of us kept full notes and showed them to each other, talking our eventual book into shape.

When we decided we had enough, we took the notes and spread them all over the floor. I was living in a large house in Roppongi at the time and these took up the entire living room. Our work laid out before us, we began to shape it. Since there had been no book on the subject (Ichiro Tanaka's multi-volume history was just then coming out) we had no Japanese map, but we both admired Lewis Jacob's *The Rise of the American Film* and decided to use it as our model.

Walking around, being careful not to step on our spread-out notes, we began to shape our book. Where is 1918 to 1921? Oh, there, by the couch. Shouldn't we start the *benshi* a little earlier? OK, where are the notes? By the chair. Let's put them in after Matsunosuke.

When we finally had the mess on the floor laid out in some order (we wanted an order not only chronological but one through which themes and genres could also be seen evolving) we pasted these hundreds of notes one by one onto a great roll of brown butcher-paper. Our book was now three feet high and over a foot thick, standing there in my living room like a stack of film cans. It was done. Now all we had to do was write it.

It was I who wrote it—that had always been the understanding, that I was the writer and Joe was the scholar/investigator, and in any event he and his family at this point went back to America.

So, unrolling the massive scroll, I began. A copy of the day's work—on onionskin paper to save on postage—was sent off to Columbus where Joe read, added to, edited, and mailed it back. In this way, over the days, the weeks, the months, our book grew. And in 1959 it was published.

Book out, I discovered that I was considered an authority—so was Joe but he was no longer in Japan and was hence unable to take advantage of

his new position. Film companies, having heard of our work, became more helpful, directors who had not been forthcoming now wanted to talk. Though the book was not translated into Japanese (indeed, it never was, since about this time Japanese scholars began putting out their own versions), the new book about Japan became, no matter the language, soon known about if little read. Japan is the most knowledgeable country in Asia.

So it became easier to gather information now. This I kept on doing because, though the book was out, Japanese film, art and industry was continuing, and so was I—in *The Japan Times*.

And other places—for I found that having a book out was like being given a passport. You got asked abroad. I helped the Kawakitas at the 1961 Mizoguchi Retrospective at Cannes Film Festival, and I myself did the 1963 Ozu Retrospective at Berlin.

Also I wanted to write another book on Japanese film, this one about a director. Having organized the Kurosawa Retrospective at the 1961 Berlin Festival, I had an opportunity to see those films I had not seen and to re-see those I had. Also I now knew Kurosawa better than I had in 1947 when we had not understood a word the other said.

Joe and I had been in 1957 asked to an open set of *The Throne of Blood* in the mountains of Izu. We had joined the Kurosawa group, chatted with Asakazu Nakai, the cameraman, taken a bath with Mifune. We had also talked with Kurosawa and though he is not a director who likes to talk about any of his works except the next one, in both these and later talks I gathered enough material so that I finally thought I could say something.

Taking my notes and my portable typewriter, I went to a hot springs resort in Kagoshima—the Ibusuki Kanko, then just a small country inn alongside its enormous baths. I would work every morning until lunch, eat and take a bath,

then go back and work until dinner, then eat and take another bath before falling asleep. In this way I could, quickly and easily, write a chapter a day.

The Films of Akira Kurosawa was written in less than a month. Each morning as I began on another chapter, I noted with satisfaction the growing pile of finished first-draft ms. It might have been the good Kyushu food, the hot water, the fact that I was far from home without a phone, but never have I written with greater ease. After much polishing in Tokyo, this painless delivery resulted in the finished book, published in 1965. The process was very different from both the trials of the first book with Joe and the tribulations of the next—about Yasujiro Ozu.

As I had for the Kurosawa book, I looked at all the Ozu films as often as I could—and in the days before cassettes this meant persuading the producers to arrange screenings—and I had translated everything I could find that he had said about his films. In addition, I got into the early scripts and went over his notes and paid particular attention to those story-board-like sequences he had sketched. But I had met the director only a few times, most notably on the open set of *Late Autumn*, and had not much talked with him about his work.

Originally, I thought that the form of the Ozu book would be chronological, as it had been for the Kurosawa. But the more I went over my material, the more I saw that this would not work. It would imply a narrative and this was not important for Ozu, though it had been for Kurosawa. Consequently I spent a lot of time searching for some kind of paradigm.

I knew that this could be not any of those I already knew about. The social-humanist model of my book with Anderson might suit a country but it would never fit an individual. And the chronological creation of an individual voice, the model for the Kurosawa book, did not suit Ozu.

I strongly felt (still do) that the nature of the

subject determines the model. Just as I believe that all clinical analysis should be eclectic, tailored to the patient, so all extended film criticism should be fitted to the subject. Many of the analyzed do not respond to a therapy all-Freudian or all-Jungian; many film directors do not respond to an analysis all structural or all psychoanalytical. One must find the model that best approximates the achievement.

The only way to do this, I finally decided, was to make a book in the shape of an Ozu film. I would in my process reflect his. Just as he began with dialogue, so would I; just as he only later decided upon person and place, so would I—in the form of a book attempting to reflect the logic which both compelled and enabled Ozu to create his own consistency.

Ozu took years to write—there were many false starts, much rewriting. The last chapter took as long to write as had the whole Kurosawa book. Writing away, I wondered why this should be and finally decided that it was not because of the differences between the men and their work, but because of differences in me.

I admired Kurosawa's films; I could examine and describe them. But I was so devoted to the films of Ozu, and so cherished the man who made them, that I could only wait in front of the typewriter and hope that from these emotions something encompassing his work might eventually appear on the page. Eventually it did. The book was finally, after ten years of work, finished and published in 1974.

* * *

Now when I saw Japanese movies it was in the screening rooms of the companies concerned. I was invited to these private showings by card or by call. Viewing films in 1967 was very different from 1947. Twenty years had passed—no longer was I transgressing. And no longer was I pressed among the populace—often I was grandly alone in the screening room, a grown-up, a forty-three-year-old film scholar, no longer a film fan suffering a long delayed adolescence.

Grandly alone as this film critic for *The Japan Times* occasionally felt himself to be, he was shortly to become even more so. Willard Van Dyke, head of the film department at the New York Museum of Modern Art had decided upon a rotating curatorship and chose me for the first. I, who had educated myself in the MoMA auditorium, was now—as in some Biograph rags-to-riches saga—to be in charge of it. This meant leaving Japan, to be sure, but the position was rotating and soon the revolving door would sweep me home again. Thinking of Charles Foster Kane and the biggest toy train a boy ever had, I accepted.

But I was so devoted to the films of Ozu, and so cherished the man who made them, that I could only wait in front of the typewriter and hope that from these emotions something encompassing his work might eventually appear on the page.

In New York not only could I now see any movie I wanted to, I could also show anything I wanted. And, since one of the reasons I had been chosen was for my knowledge of Japanese cinema, I was expected to impart it. This resulted in "The Japanese Film," a retrospective of over a hundred prints.

In this I was much helped by Nagamasa and Kashiko Kawakita. I had met her very early—we had sat next to each other at a vocal concert, selections sung by students of the old German

music teacher who gave the recital in her house. I was much impressed by this lovely lady in a lavender kimono who knew so much about movies, and was even more impressed when I later learned that she was in her own house. She had loaned the dwelling to the impecunious music teacher who would otherwise have had no place to live.

Such generosity was, I discovered, quite typical of both Kawakitas. He ran a big film import house, Towa Films, and was on the Toho board, and so long as the company made some money on popular pictures he was quite ready to lose money on good films—in this way the works of Rene Clair, Pabst, Vigo, and later of Bresson, Bergman, and Godard came to Japan.

It was they who had helped Japanese film get abroad as well—he had himself taken a Mizoguchi picture to Berlin in the late 1920s. And it was they who so encouraged Joe and me. More, it was Kashiko who made it possible for me to remain in Japan forever—she became my sponsor when I eventually qualified as candidate for *eijuken*—permanent residence.

So, the Kawakitas made my showing of Japanese film at MoMA possible, as did the Japanese National Film Center, and other friends I had made in my twenty-five years in the country. Across the Pacific bridge came all those films I had seen in my quarter-century—or all those of which I could get ambulatory prints: *Souls on the Road, Crossroads, The Neighbor's Wife and Mine, I Was Born, But, Wife, Be like a Rose, Humanity and Paper Balloons*—one hundred of them.

Every day I went and stood at the back of old silver and black MoMA auditorium and looked at Kinuyo Tanaka and Hideko Takamine and Toshiro Mifune and seemed to again smell the sweet scene of rice sweat, the reek of camellia pomade, and the cool, pregnant air of the Asakusa Tokyo Kurabu Gekijo.

And as I looked again at those scenes I had first seen a quarter-century before, I saw, vibrant

on the MoMA screen, a whole culture—Japan seeing itself through its pictures. Just as the movies I had first seen at the Sigma seemed to form a whole, to suggest some kind of working model, a paradigm of America, so now in these seasons of afternoons and evenings at MoMA, the whole of Japan in miniature was unreeling, a replica of the real.

As the person responsible for this upturned Oriental cornucopia I found that I was being regarded as an authority on Japanese movies, being asked things such as what it felt like to have been a pioneer. I liked the idea—slashing with my critical machete through the coils of film history like Neil Hamilton in the vine-filled jungles of Tarzan. But I had never before thought of myself as a pioneer.

I was rather a kind of translator who carried things back and forth across the Pacific. The Japanese themselves always referred to me not only as a *gakusha,* a scholar, but as someone who performed the much important (to them) task of the *shokai suru,* the introduction. Introductions led to more important things—for the film industry this meant international prizes and foreign sales. If I am pioneer, I thought, then I'm just the person who—a better Perry—opened the door. And there was a nice symmetry too: it was my love of movies that brought me to Japanese film, and it was Japanese film that had taken me back to show Japanese movies in America.

Except I didn't want to stay there. The U.S.A. was just one big Ohio so far as I was concerned—OK for a visit but no place you'd want to live. And that was what MoMA wanted—that I live there. The rotating curatorship did not turn even once. It stuck, and there I was standing in the stationary revolving door.

Five years I was in New York. The work was wonderful, the city was awful, and I terribly missed my hometown—Tokyo. Though I managed to escape every summer to go back home I always had to return to New York (back to school after vacation) in the fall. The only things I could look forward to were good friends at MoMA and all the work I could do.

Nagisa Oshima, then a brilliantly polemic director and a great concern to the Japanese film industry, I invited. He came and showed his films and talked. He pointed out that the future of Japanese cinema lay in the independent production. With all big studio films for the first time losing money—the menace of television was now in almost every home—the age where a company head would protect a Mizoguchi or an Ozu was over. Rather, the producers with their ideas of what the remaining public wanted had taken over from the directors.

The public, they said, no longer wanted to see themselves on the screen. Just like the Americans—they wanted to see themselves as they wanted to be seen: rich, pretty, powerful. Since it is difficult to make serious cinema of such ambitions, making non-serious cinema was the only solution. Consequently any writer or director of any originality was out of a job.

Making your films yourself, independent production, this was the only answer. And Oshima indicated this in a brilliant series of pictures the funding for which he himself found. With much help from such new production centers as The Art Theatre Guild, a project began by the Kawakitas, which was responsible for almost any good Japanese film during the 1960s and 70s—including those of Oshima, Hiroshi Teshigahara, Susumu Hani, and Masahiro Shinoda, all of whom I invited to show at MoMA.

Working there gave me a view of the Japanese film I might not otherwise have had. I was, being in New York, always seeing my subject in long-shot, as it were, surrounded by the social and political context I might otherwise have been too close to notice. Thus, I could see the changes that were creating a different kind of film.

The advent of a powerful bureaucracy made a

From Ozu, 1975   *The Japanese*

Any task can become a performance. In *The Only Son,* the mother has been given a new pillow, and we watch her as she puts into place the paper wrapper that will prevent its being soiled, a long and intricate business. In *Early Summer* we watch the father feed his mynah bird, an almost equally lengthy occupation. The most celebrated such scene is at the end of *Late Spring,* where the father, now alone, begins to peel a summer pear while we watch. To be sure, a desire for character delineation may play some part in determining the length of such scenes. Yet

many of them come at a point when we know the characters so well that a prolonged observation of such activities can offer little new information. Rather, Ozu would have us share his respect for a task, any task that is done for itself alone.

One is reminded of a Zen aphorism: "When I eat, I eat; when I sleep, I sleep." When one does something one does nothing else; one immerses self entirely in the task at hand, and appreciates it while completing it. A corollary is that in this fashion the present instant, the *now* that all of us are continually

and notoriously forgetting, is preserved. The present moment is immortalized in the father's peeling of his fruit. As we watch the skin fall away, it is the concentration on the present we appreciate and, if we are like Ozu, admire. It is when the hands stop moving, the knife remains poised, the peeling remains unfinished, it is when the father looks up with vacant eyes, that we know he is, after all, like us—that the present is now lost in the future with its hopes and its fears, that he is feeling his loneliness.

new *Ikiru* irrelevant. The consolidation of power politics made a new *Bad Sleep Well* impossible. The rapid erosion of family values, foretold in *Tokyo Story*, made the affectionate acceptance of *An Autumn Afternoon* illegible to new viewers. Ozu had died in 1963—just as well, a friend said, for Shochiku would not have allowed him to go on making his kind of film.

. . . in these seasons of afternoons and evenings at MoMA, the whole of Japan in miniature was unreeling, a replica of the real.

From abroad I watched the monolithic Japanese film industry collapse and saw its place taken by the small precarious but wildly diversified companies devoted to independent production. In this the Japanese industry was no different from that of other countries. It was just that it took longer to die. Indeed, Toho, Shochiku, Toei, were still shifting about in the deepening tar pits.

Though I had a good balcony seat for the spectacle, I wanted to get closer. This ambition was facilitated when I was told that I was going to be the new director of the Film Department at MoMA, Willard having been retired. Since I had seen what my beloved mentor had had to go through—going around on bended knee after funding, attending countless useless meetings, never getting to see any films—I refused, but said I would stay on as curator—if I could have the summers off. Told that they were collapsing my position and so I would have to be the new director, I said: OK, I quit.

* * *

Thirty years after my first sneaking into my first Japanese movie I was finally back in Tokyo again The city was, as always, different and Japanese film was different too.

Now it was known abroad, it had won prizes, had books written about it. There was a new generation of film scholars—soon to include Audie Bock, Noël Burch, Keiko McDonald, Max Tessier, David Desser, Joan Mellen, Robert Cohen, Gregory Barrett, Joanne Bernardi, Arthur Noletti, Jr., Lucia Nagib, Mark Le Fanu, and others—some of whom studied with me.

But Japanese film was no longer the major reflection of Japanese reality that it had been. What passed for reality was now not in film but on television, and its vehicle was not the screen but the tube.

In this, Japan was no different from anywhere else—but it coped less well. Europe, the United States still had some small place for the honest filmmaker. They could borrow money—from the bank for example—and find a place to show what they had made. In Japan, however, the banks did not gamble for such low stakes as the movies and a cartel insured that the major companies owned the major theaters so the independents had no place to show.

I saw fine directors lost: Kon Ichikawa turned into a company hack simply to have a chance to work; Yasushi Nakahira went off to Taiwan to do action programs rather than remain idle. The Japanese film as I had known it, taught it, was now not only history but even something like archeology.

Yet, at the same time, something new was occurring. During the 1970s and 80s there grew a large youthful interest in the experimental film—pictures you could make yourself on super-8 with no studio behind you. These were called avant-garde or personal or *jikken* but they were all made because the director wanted to make them. And, having made them, wanted to show them.

At first there was no place to do so, but shortly Image Forum was conceived. Founded and funded entirely by the very determined Katsue Tomiyama, it offered a small hall, and some kind of organization—and real commitment. When Kazuo Hara finished his self-financed documentary, *The Emperor's Naked Army Marches On,* there was no company, club, theatre, group, brave enough to show a film this honest. It was Image Forum, which offered its hall, put up with rightist threats and "official" investigations, and saw that the film got seen.

An archive was begun, a festival was held, modest prizes awarded—Image Forum was training a whole new generation: for it was from these filmmaking students that new directors were coming.

They jammed the hall to see Stan Brakhage, they formed long lines when the National Film Center showed an Ozu picture. They had no other place to study—Japan had no film schools—and so they studied the films themselves. In the old studio days they would have became assistant directors at one of the studios and often wait a long time to direct the debut film—Naruse was well into his thirties, but he did learn filmmaking. Now, apart from the porn studios, which always needed cheap labor, no one would hire an untrained student. The only real way to go it was to look at good movies and emulate.

There are certainly worse ways. Though these young directors mostly had no theoretical or practical knowledge, the new filmmakers had seen good movies—they'd all looked at Ozu and Bresson, they'd seen Kurosawa and Scorsese, Oshima and Godard, Imamura and Cassavetes.

One of the students, Kohei Oguri borrowed money from a factory-owner film-buff and made *Muddy River;* another, Mitsuo Yanagimachi, borrowed from his parents, and made the documentary, *God Speed You, Black Emperor;* an actor, Juzo

Itami, mortgaged everything he owned and made *The Funeral.*

Oguri showed his film in civic halls until it started to win prizes abroad, then it was acquired by one of the studios, given theatrical release and went on to win most of that year's film prizes; Yanagimachi managed to pay back his parents and have something left over for the next film—in this way, he continued until his *Fire Festival* won the Locarno Prize; Itami's film was a critical and financial success—with the proceeds he made *Tampopo* and moved into the neighborhood art houses.

He could do so because, with new independent films appearing, unaffiliated theaters were also opening. These were shortly commanding a small but loyal audience and since the films had cost nothing like what a studio production would have (all that overhead, all those people on the payroll) there was no need for great profit.

To be sure many of the new directors sold out to television, or got stuck in making music-spots, or just stayed in porn. But enough persevered and made the kind of film they wanted that a new kind of Japanese cinema began to be visible—one, which in the 1990s reflected reality as the movies had back in the 1940s.

This was where I had come in. But now no longer would I stand crammed in crowded cinemas nor sit in state in screening rooms, beckoned there by call or card. Instead I would go to offices with a 16 mm machine, or schoolrooms on holidays, or small houses in the suburbs. I saw Kaizo Hayashi's *To Sleep so as to Dream* projected on a bed sheet.

In this way 1995 is like 1947. I set off into Tokyo, find my way through back alleys, wander about neighborhoods until I finally locate the director's apartment, where he has his film and his projector set up. I sit there, looking at the wall on which the movie will appear, enjoying that moment of promise, waiting for the movie to start.

January 11, 1960:
The Film Book Party

I am given a testimonial (or, to be precise, the book *The Japanese Film: Art and Industry*) by film people on the top floor of a big restaurant. I arrive first and wait nervously for my hosts—the Kawakitas. Both of them (Nagamasa and Kashiko) so helped us (Richie and Joseph Anderson) in writing our book. They have also managed, in the midst of running a successful motion picture import firm, to retain their love of film and the knowledge of what is good and what isn't. They are in a corrupt industry triumphantly uncorrupted.

One by one the guests appear and as they assemble a curious dreamlike atmosphere grows. They are gathered for the ritual of congratulation and it is like certain dreams which begin with homage to the dreamer—all of one's friends from babyhood brought together.

Kozaburo Yoshimura, big and bulky, well-intentioned as an elephant, willing, anxious to speak of film theory, never tired of the subject which so consumes him; Susumu Hani, stuttering, slightly, pale, smiling, behaving with that quick courtesy of his; Zenzo Matsuyama, more darkly handsome, more ambivalent than ever, wearing charm as he wears his Italian suit; Hideko Takamine, his wife, in a black felt cloche, the very picture of herself in the films.

There are speeches. Takamine, always straightforward, held up

From Japan Journals, *1960*

a copy and said she couldn't read it but it sure felt heavy enough to be important. Then I make a speech hoping I get it right. In Japan, more maybe than elsewhere, one can observe the ballet of ritual, the casting of which is arranged by the invitation, the steps of which everyone knows. In this microcosm one sees the entire dance: people whose life is other people, being them, acting them, ruling them. Observing the ritual imposed from above, I see what Versailles must have been like.

Then the leave-taking: I am led from group to group to say goodbye. I bow, they bow, but I do not quite understand what is happening. After the last group there is nowhere for me to go. They are not going and I understand finally. It is I who am leaving. And since I am guest of honor I am royalty for a day and no one can leave until I do.

From the hall no place to go but the vestibule where my coat is held out for me. I must put it on; it won't do not to put it on. Then the elevator door is held open; I glimpse into the hall where they all stand, talking, drinking, just as though I am still there. I step into the elevator. The door closes.

This must be what death is like: a leave-taking under the impression that the rest are going, that one oneself is staying. The sudden flurry of understanding, the thought—well, all right, but just to the hall. Then the shroud and the coffin.

One by one the guests appear and as they assemble a curious dreamlike atmosphere grows. They are gathered for the ritual of congratulation and it is like certain dreams which begin with homage to the dreamer—all of one's friends from babyhood brought together.

Mr. Kawakita comes with me, he too is bundled up, he too is dead. At least I have a companion. But then he stops on the streetcorner. Virgil is leaving; he has business elsewhere. I thank him, we shake hands. He is gone—maybe back to the party and I in the cold, outside the building look up and see the lights and the backs of my friends far above me.

From The Films of Akira Kurosawa, 1965   *The Body*

His physical features do not reveal much. He is tall, very tall for a Japanese, and his face centers around his nose. Flanked by large, generous ears, supported by a full, sensuous mouth, this nose—Kyoto-looking, traditionally aristocratic—indicates a sensitivity that is not suggested by the tall, lanky body and the big, capable, workman-like hands. Like many creators, he is not of a piece. He has a divided look: the face of a mystic, the body of a carpenter. Standing in the set, wearing the hat that is his single personal affectation, amid the ordinary furor and occasional chaos of moviemaking, he is calm, patient, ruminative, sometimes softly smiling, or quietly indicating how things should be done—the personification of intellect. One might ascribe his demeanor to Oriental impassivity, were there any such thing. Rather, it is the knowing tranquility of a man under control. He already knows what he is going to do, and he knows how to do it. At the same time, however, his hands are always busy.

Ozu

Preface

The Japanese continue, ten years after his death, to think of Yasu-jiro Ozu as the most Japanese of all their directors. This does not mean he is their favorite, though he has been given more offi-cial honor than any other. It means that he is regarded as a kind of spokesman; Ozu, one is told, "had the real Japanese flavor." This "Japanese flavor" has a more definite meaning than, say, "the American way" or "the French touch" if only because Japan remains so intensely conscious of its own Japaneseness. Modern civilization, only a century old, remains a Western veneer over an Asian culture that has endured for two millennia.

The uneasy juxtaposition of the two cultures has created the familiar contrasts of the country, and has given the Japanese his often near-schizoid intensity and made him extremely conscious of his differences from the Westerner. The careers of many men of letters, and some not so lettered (politicians, for example), show a familiar pattern: a period of early exploration among things Western followed by a slow and gradual return to things purely Japanese. The career of Ozu followed this pattern. After an early enthusiasm for American films, particularly the works of Ernst Lubitsch, he consolidated these influences into his mature

From Ozu, 1975; includes the preface, introduction and concluding portion of the chapter "Script"

and fully "Japanese" style—and indeed this pattern is one of the things celebrated in the Ozu films. Their tension derives from confrontations between men and women who are in different sections of the pattern, between, for example, parents who have returned to Japaneseness and children who are on their way out.

There is never any doubt where Ozu's essential sympathies lie in these confrontations, though as a moralist he is scrupulously fair, and for this reason some young Japanese have disliked his work, calling him old-fashioned, bourgeois, reactionary. And so he would appear, since he so continually celebrates those very qualities, the traditional virtues of their country, against which young Japanese must revolt. That these virtues are mainly theoretical in no way falsifies Ozu's position. Though everyday Japan is not a country noted for its restraint, simplicity, or near-Buddhist serenity, these qualities remain ideals, and Ozu's insistence upon them and the public feeling for or against them make these ideals more than empty hypotheses.

Take, for example, the quality of restraint. In even a strictly technical sense, Ozu's films are among the most restrained, the most limited, controlled, and restricted. From early in his career, for example, Ozu used only one kind of shot: a shot taken from the level of a person seated in traditional fashion on the *tatami*. Whether indoors or out, the Ozu camera is always about three feet above the ground, and is rarely moved. In the early films, though there were numerous dolly shots, there were few pan shots. Likewise there were some fades in and out, but dissolves were rare. In the later films the camera is almost invariably immobile, and the only punctuation is the straight cut.

This traditional view is the view in repose, commanding a very limited field of vision. It is the attitude for listening, for watching. It is the same as the position from which one watches the Noh or the rising moon, from which one partakes of the tea ceremony or a cup of hot sake. It is the aesthetic attitude; it is the passive attitude. Less poetically, it also represents the viewpoint of a then-majority of Japanese. They spent their life on the floor and "any attempt to view such a life through a camera high up on a tripod was nonsense; the eye level of Japanese sitting on the tatami becomes, of necessity, the eye level through which they view what is going on around them."

Finally, it also resembles the attitude of the haiku master who sits in silence and observes, reaching essence through an extreme simplification. Inextricable from Buddhist precepts, it puts the world at a distance and leaves the spectator physically uninvolved.

Ozu's method, like all poetic methods, is oblique. He does not confront emotion, he surprises it. Precisely, he restricts his vision in order to see more; he limits his world in order to transcend these limitations. His cinema is formal and the formality is that of poetry, the creation of an ordered context that destroys habit and familiarity, returning to each word, to each image, its original freshness and urgency. In all of this Ozu is close to the *sumi-e* ink drawing masters of Japan, to the masters of the haiku and the *waka*. It is this quality to which the Japanese refer when they speak of Ozu as being "most Japanese," when they speak of his "real Japanese flavor."

More is implied in this description, however, than restraint in the service of art. The unique art of Ozu is very evident, but so is his common humanity. The Ozu character is among the most lifelike in cinema. Since character for its own sake is always a major subject in the Ozu film and since it is but rarely that a character must work to forward the ends of the story the director is determined to tell us, we are often given that rare spectacle of a character existing for himself alone. This we observe with the delight that precise verisimilitude always brings, and with a

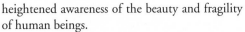

heightened awareness of the beauty and fragility of human beings.

The unexpected humanity of the Ozu film is made possible by the rigor of its construction. In an Ozu film, as in Japanese architecture, one sees all the supports, and all of them are equally essential. Like the carpenter, the director uses neither paint nor wallpaper; he uses, as it were, natural wood. The finished object one may measure, one may inspect, one may compare. But within this object, this film, as within the house, lives the human, the immeasurable, the nonfunctional. It is this combination of the static and the living, of the expected and the surprising, that makes the films of Ozu the memorable emotional experiences they are. Without the rigorous frame that is the director's technique, the intense humanity of the character could not be so completely revealed. Without the useless and lovable humanity of the Ozu character, the film's structure would degenerate (as indeed it sometimes does) into mere formalism.

A similar duality occurs with respect to the sense of time in an Ozu film. His pictures are longer than most and at the same time have less "story" than most. What story there is, moreover, often seems more anecdote (which is why a précis of an Ozu film fails even more completely than usual to convey what the picture is like as an experience). Since the story is presented over a long period of time, and since there is little overt action to sustain the time values, unsympathetic critics complain about a pace that to them seems slow. They would have real grounds for complaint if this pace existed by and for itself. Yet Ozu's films are not slow. They create their own time and for the audience, drawn into Ozu's world, into a realm of purely psychological time, clock time ceases to exist. And what at first seems a world of stillness, of total inaction, is revealed as appearance. Beneath this seeming stillness one finds the potential violence present in any Japanese family, and also the quiet heroism of the

Japanese faced with his own family. One finds drama enough to justify the length of the Ozu picture, but the point is that one *finds* it, it is not deployed before one. It is their potential for action that gives Ozu's films their vigor, and that makes his use of time meaningful.

Thus, just as technique restricted comes to make us see more, so tempo slowed comes to make us feel more. The effect of both is the same: characters come alive in a manner rare in film. And both means are the same: the spectator is led into the film, is invited to infer and to deduce. He gives of himself and of his time, and in so doing he learns to appreciate. What remains after an Ozu film is the feeling that, if only for an hour or two, you have seen the goodness and beauty of everyday things and everyday people; you have had experiences you cannot describe because only film, not words, can describe them; you have seen a few small, unforgettable actions, beautiful because real. You are left with a feeling of sadness, too, because you will see them no more. They are already gone. In the feeling of transience, of the mutability and beauty of all life, Ozu joins the greatest Japanese artists. It is here that we taste, undiluted and authentic, the Japanese flavor.

Introduction

Yasujiro Ozu, the man whom his kinsmen consider the most Japanese of all film directors, had but one major subject, the Japanese family, and but one major theme, its dissolution. The Japanese family in dissolution figures in every one of his fifty-three feature films. In his later pictures, the whole world exists in one family, the characters are family members rather than members of a society, and the ends of the earth seem no more distant than the outside of the house.

The Japanese family, in the films of Ozu as

in life, has two main extensions: the school and the office. Both are almost foster homes, traditionally far less impersonal than their analogues elsewhere. The Japanese student finds a second home in his school and keeps close contact with his classmates throughout his life; the Japanese white-collar worker finds in the office a third home, and will identify himself with his company in a way rare in the West. The Ozu character, like the Japanese himself, tends to move among the three: the house, the schoolroom, the office.

Thus Ozu's films are a kind of home drama, a genre that in the West rarely attains the standard of art and that even now is generally perceived as somehow second-rate. In Asia, however, where the family remains the social unit, the home drama has been refined far beyond the examples found, say, on American radio or television. Ozu's home drama, however, is of a special sort. He neither affirms the family as, for example, Keisuke Kinoshita does in his later films, nor condemns it, as Mikio Naruse does in many of his pictures. Rather, though Ozu creates a world that is the family in one or another of its varied aspects, his focus is on its dissolution. There are few happy families in Ozu's films. Though the earlier pictures sometimes show difficulties overcome, almost all the mature films show the family members moving apart. Most of Ozu's characters are noticeably content with their lives, but there are always indications that the family will shortly cease to be what it has been. The daughter gets married and leaves the father or mother alone; the parents go off to live with one of the children; a mother or father dies, etc.

The dissolution of the family is a catastrophe because in Japan—as contrasted with the United States, where leaving the family is considered proof of maturity—one's sense of self depends to an important extent upon those with whom one lives, studies, or works. An identification with family (or with clan, nation, school, or company) is necessary for a complete identification of self.

Even in the West the remnants of such a need are strong enough for us to regard the plight of the Ozu character, and the predicament of the contemporary Japanese, with sympathy. The father or mother sitting alone in the now empty house is an image common enough in Ozu's films to serve as an epitome. These people are no longer themselves. We know they will somehow survive, but we also know at what cost. They are not bitter, they know this is the way of their world, but they are bereft. The reason they impel our sympathy is that they are neither victims of their own flaws, nor the prey of a badly organized society; they are the casualties of things as they are, the way that life is. And here we are, all of us, similar casualties.

Though the majority of all Ozu's films are about the dissolution of the family (as are a large number of Japanese novels and of Western novels too, for that matter) his emphasis changed during his nearly forty years of filmmaking. In his first important films the director emphasized the external social conditions impinging upon his characters: the strain in a family occasioned by the father's joblessness in difficult times, the children's inability to understand that their father must be subservient to his employer to keep his job, etc. It was only in later films that the director found more important the constraints on the human condition imposed from within.

This change has been held against the director: "Ozu used to have an open-minded view of society; he tried to capture the complicated aspects of its day-to-day existence. . . . He always had a burning fury against social injustice, but his realism began to degenerate and to decay. . . . I remember that when *Passing Fancy* and *A Story of Floating Weeds* were released, many of us were deeply disappointed to find that Ozu had abandoned serious social themes." Though Ozu's "pioneering achievements" in creating a realism new to the Japanese cinema are credited, and though *I Was Born, But* . . . is found to be "the first work of social realism in Japanese film," the pictures after 1933 are found wanting: "Young critics who have seen only Ozu's postwar films know but one side of the director. . . . His craftsmanship and taste are, of course, impeccable; and his deep, mature understanding of the life that scintillates within is profound. Nonetheless, the sorry truth is that Ozu's greatest virtues those which made him what he was in his earliest days, can no longer be found."

The criticism is cogent and one may argue only with its basic assumptions: that realism must be social, and that proletarian reality is somehow more real than bourgeois reality. Ozu did not, of course, abandon realism. He did, however, abandon the idea that unhappiness is caused solely by social wrongs; he came to recognize that unhappiness is caused by our being human and consequently aspiring to a state impossible to attain. He also abandoned the naturalism of his earlier pictures. This was in part due to his changing families, as it were. The struggling middle-class or lower-class family, prey to every social current, disappears from his films. From the mid-1930s on the family was, with exceptions, of the professional class, and in the postwar years it became, again with exceptions, upper-middle-class. Ozu's sense of reality, however, did not change. One still hears the complaint that the interiors in the later Ozu pictures are too pretty, too neat. But an attempt at neatness and prettiness is, after all, one of the attributes of bourgeois life everywhere. Bourgeois life is no less real for being more pleasant

The Japanese

From Japan Journals, *1989*

October 27, 1989.
On the jury once again for the Competition for Cultural Films on Japan. Cannot say no, though it is a great waste of time. Cannot say no because Mr. Kuroda, its organizer, years ago came and rescued me when I broke my back, carried me out of my house on *his* back, and down to the waiting taxi and into the hospital of his choice, at which he had made a down-payment out of his own money for my care. I would consequently do anything Mr. Kuroda asked. And he only asks for me to be a jury member.

I don't know what he has on the others, but we all assemble. People high up in the Foreign Ministry, in the *Asahi* and *Mainichi* papers, we all agree to waste a number of days looking at films intended to "introduce" Japan.

However, we have done this so often that we are now cynical and take full advantage of our prerogative of removing the film from the screen. A small degree of unrest is felt after ten minutes or so. Then wavelets of remarks: "Not very good." "Who do they think this is for." "Not again!" etc. These grow into a tsunami of comment and then our chairman formally asks what we think. It is unanimous. "Take it off." "Ugh." "Away, away." etc. Another film disposed of. In our first session we only looked at two complete: one about Bunraku and one about fishing, both of which interested us.

There are worse ways of judging. We cut right through the cant. Shown yet another mendacious travelogue about "beautiful Japan," the *Asahi* man says: "There's nothing like that around any more." And the *Mainichi* man says, "Any tourist is going to be mighty disappointed after seeing this." And the Foreign Ministry man says: "It must be made by the Foreign Ministry." And a picture all about temple bells and lovely singing crickets called "The Sounds of Japan" brings forth the comment: "They forget the sound most Japanese really like best—the sound of pachinko."

During our box lunch we talk of other things. We discuss the relative merits of alligators

than proletarian life—a fact that Ozu's critics, quite unfairly, hold against him.

If anything, Ozu's later films gain in a feeling of reality, and, more important to his art, transcend it. He is concerned not with quintessential family. He achieves the transcendental from a base in the mundane, in the bourgeois family—undisturbed by social upheavals, undismayed by financial misfortunes—where a sense of the dailiness of life is perhaps most readily to be discovered. It is precisely "day-to-day existence" that Ozu so realistically and hence so movingly captured.

The life with which Ozu is concerned in so many of his films, then, is traditional Japanese bourgeois life. It is a life singularly lacking in the more dramatic heights and depths found in

a society less conspicuously restrained. This does not imply, however, that such a traditional life is less affected by the universal human verities; on the contrary, birth, love, marriage, companionship, loneliness, death, all loom particularly large in a traditional society because so much else is ruled out.

A traditional life also means a life based upon an assumed continuum. As Chesterton somewhere remarks: "Tradition means giving votes to that obscurest of classes, our ancestors. It is the democracy of the dead. Tradition refuses to surrender to the arrogant oligarchy of those who merely happen to be walking around." Traditional life assumes that one is a part of something larger: a community in time encompassing the dead and the yet unborn. It assumes one is a part

and crocodiles. I am asked the difference and since I happen to know, I tell them. Then the *Asahi* man informs us that the meat tastes like chicken which is not odd because all our avians came from ancient saurians, from which these two reptiles are also descendants. Then on to other odd foods. Puppy is admitted by one to be delicious but the *Mainichi* man admits to having had trouble with horse testicles.

Those who maintain that Japanese are not individual, do not criticize, are creatures of a single accord, should be at occasions like this. But then such critics would have to know the culture and speak the language, something which they notoriously do not.

On the other hand, the ingrained formality, the ritual quality of such meetings can eas-

ily give the wrong impression. For example, I have known Mr. Kuroda for well over twenty years. We have eaten and drunk and told dirty jokes many, many times. And yet so strong is a sense of occasion that at the beginning of the meal, he asked (in English) "You do eat sashimi, don't you, Mr. Richie?" And, as though that were not enough, "Chopsticks are all right, aren't they?"

But for me to have seen this as exclusive callousness would have been to miss the point entirely. I was a part of the ritual. And this was ritual language. If there is a foreigner present, even one so suspicious as myself, then accord is ensured by such noddings in the direction of convention as this. Americans with their passion for the real, the sincere, etc., cannot tolerate things like

this—the placing of ritual over feeling. To them it seems inhuman. To the Japanese there is no better way of being human.

Such differences represent the shoals, which catch at the keel of the international bark. What is not generally apprehended in the West is that such language, such treatment is a visible way of making me a member of the group. Invisibly I am already a member. I know it. They know it. And if I had said: "Come on, Mr. Kuroda, give me a break. You know I like sashimi and use chopsticks better than you do." If I had said this it would have been accepted and chuckled over. But I would have put myself i n the position of a guest who tells his host that the steak is burned and the brandy lousy.

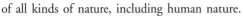

of all kinds of nature, including human nature.

Traditional life gives rise to an attitude that is as common in Japanese daily life as it is in the films of Ozu. Though there is a useful Japanese phrase for it, *mono no aware,* a term that will be examined later, the attitude was best described in English by W. H. Auden, when (in another context) he wrote: "There is joy in the fact that we are all in the same boat, that there are no exceptions made. On the other hand, we cannot help wishing that we had no problems—let us say, that either we were in a way unthinking like the animals or that we were disembodied angels. But this is impossible; so we laugh because we simultaneously protest and accept." Perhaps the Japanese, in accepting the conflicts of being human, would sigh rather than laugh, would celebrate this transient and unsatisfactory world rather than merely find it absurd. But the underlying, profoundly conservative attitude remains the same, and it animates all but the very young in the Ozu family.

If the family is Ozu's almost invariable subject, the situations in which we see it are surprisingly few. The majority of the films are about relations between generations. Often a parent is missing, dead or absconded, and the one remaining must rear the children. The dissolution of the family, already begun, is completed by the marriage of the only or the eldest child or the death of the remaining parent. In other films the family members move away from one another; the children attempt, sometimes with success, to reconcile themselves to their married state. Or again, the child finds the restrictions of traditional family life stifling and must, albeit against his will, defy them. There are perhaps a few more variations on the theme, but not many.

Just as Ozu's illustrations of his theme are few, so his stories, compared to the majority of those found in full-length films, are slight. A précis of an Ozu film (e.g., daughter lives with father and does not want to marry; she later discovers that

his plan to marry again was but a ruse, accomplished for the sake of her future happiness) sounds like too little upon which to base a two-hour film. Any Ozu story, however, is in a way a pretext. It is not the story that Ozu wants to show so much as the way his characters react to what happens in the story, and what patterns these relations create. Ozu used progressively simpler stories with each succeeding film, and he rarely availed himself of plot. In the later films the story is little more than anecdote. Some of the reasons for this will be discussed later. For the present it suffices to observe that Ozu was perhaps primarily interested in pattern, in the design that Henry James called "the figure in the carpet."

Ozu's patterns are reflected in his stories. A character moves from security to insecurity; he moves from being with many to being alone; or, a group shifts, loses members, accommodates; or, conversely, a younger character moves into a new sphere with mixed emotions; or a person moves from his accustomed sphere and then returns with a new understanding. These patterns are stacked, as it were, one upon the other; it is the rare Ozu film that has only one pattern and one story. Through the similarities and differences of the patterns and stories with their parallels and perpendiculars, Ozu constructs his film, the sum of his thoughts on the world and the people living in it.

Ozu's pictures, then, are made of very little. One theme, several stories, a few patterns. The technique, too, as mentioned earlier, is highly restricted: invariable camera angle, no camera movement, a restricted use of cinematic punctuation. Similarly, the structure of the film (to be examined later) is nearly invariable. Given the determined limitations of the Ozu style, it is not surprising that his films should all resemble one another. Indeed, there can have been few artists whose *oeuvre* is so completely consistent. In film, Ozu is unique. Some of the noteworthy recurrences in his pictures are described below.

Many of the titles are similar (*Early Spring, Late Spring, Early Summer, Late Autumn,* etc.), and the general structure is, in the later films at any rate, invariable. The titles remind one of the novels of Henry Green, and both the titles and the general structure of the novels of Ivy Compton-Burnett. Ozu was obviously not the kind of director who said all he wanted on one subject and then turned to another. He never said all he had to say about the Japanese family. He was like a close contemporary, Giorgio Morandi, the artist who spent his life drawing, etching, and painting mainly vases, glasses, and bottles. As Ozu himself said, during the publicity campaign for his last film, *An Autumn Afternoon,* "I always tell people that I don't make anything besides *tofu* (white bean curd, a common and essential ingredient in Japanese food), and that is because I am strictly a *tofu*-dealer."

Not only did Ozu often use the same actor in the same kind of role, playing, generally, the same kind of character (Setsuko Hara and Chishu Ryu are notable examples), he also used the same story line in various films. *A Story of Floating Weeds* is the same as *Floating Weeds, Late Spring* is very similar to *Late Autumn,* which in turn resembles *An Autumn Afternoon.* The secondary story of *Early Summer* (children running away from home) becomes the main story of *Good Morning,* etc.

Character, too, is recurrent. The daughters in *Late Spring, Early Summer, Equinox Flower, Late Autumn,* and *An Autumn Afternoon* are, though played by different actresses, essentially the same character involved with the same problem—whether or not to get married and leave home. Minor characters, too, are often near identical. The unfeeling sister of *The Brothers and Sisters of the Toda Family* becomes the unfeeling sister of *Tokyo Story,* and shows her insensitivity in the same way (asking for something after her parent's funeral). There is often (*Late Spring, The Flavor of Green Tea over Rice, Tokyo Story, Early Spring,*

Good Morning) an old salaried man due to retire who, drunk, thinks back over his life and questions it. There is, from *The Brothers and Sisters of the Toda Family* on (including *Equinox Flower, Late Autumn, Tokyo Story, An Autumn Afternoon*) the gently ridiculed lady proprietor of a Japanese-style restaurant. Characters also tend to keep the same names. In some cases they are as invariable as the burlap backing that Ozu consistently used for the main titles of all his sound films. The father is usually named Shu something-or-other, a favorite being Shukichi, with Shuhei a close second. The traditional daughter is often named Noriko (as in *Late Spring, Early Summer, Tokyo Story, The End of Summer*), whereas the more modern friend or sister is named Mariko (*The Munekata Sisters, Late Autumn*). The younger brother is usually named Isamu (*The Brothers and Sisters of the Toda Family, Early Summer, Good Morning*), and so on. This is not primarily because the names carry special connotations (though Shukichi sounds old-fashioned and Mariko rather modern to the Japanese), but rather because Ozu was arbitrarily consistent with what he had already created.

The activities of Ozu's characters are also consistent. They almost all admire the civilized nature that they view in their gardens or in Kyoto or Nikko, they all are acutely aware of the weather and mention it more often than any other characters in films, and they all like to talk. They also like bars and coffeehouses. The former, in film after film, are named Wakamatsu or Luna, the latter Bow and Aoi and Bar Accacia. Here Ozu characters sometimes get drunk, though they are more likely to do so in nameless small Japanese restaurants and drinking stalls. More usually they sit and enjoy the slightly foreign flavor so gratifying to city Japanese. (There are many foreign references in Ozu's pictures, mostly from the movies: characters speak of Gary Cooper in *Late Spring,* of Jean Marais in *The Flavor of Green Tea over Rice,* of Audrey Hepburn in *Early Summer.*

In the background of *That Night's Wife* is a large poster for *Broadway Scandals;* Marlene Dietrich has a poster in *What Did the Lady Forget?,* as does Joan Crawford in *The Only Son* and Shirley Temple in *A Hen in the Wind.*) They also eat, more often than most film characters, and seem to favor Japanese food, though they handle knives and forks as easily as chopsticks, just as they are equally at home on chairs and tatami matting. This ease, however, is one they share with other Japanese film characters and with most Japanese themselves. Western critics who believe that Ozu is commenting on Western influence in his country are mistaken; he is simply reflecting Japanese life as it now is.

The father or brother in an Ozu film is typically shown sitting in his office (we almost never see him doing any actual work), and the mother or sister doing the housework (hanging out towels to dry is a favorite occupation, but there are others; *The Brothers and Sisters of the Toda Family* and *Early Summer* have identical scenes in which the women fix the *futon* bedding) or serving tea to guests who are always appearing in the Ozu household. The children often study English (*What Did the Lady Forget?, There was a Father, Tokyo Story, Good Morning*), and the daughter of the house can type in English (*Late Spring, Early Summer*).

The family (and its extension in the office) likes games (go in *A Story of Floating Weeds* and *Floating Weeds,* mah-jongg in *A Hen in the Wind and Early Spring*), riddles (*I Was Born, But . . ., Passing Fancy*), puzzles, and jokes. Another pastime to which the Ozu family is addicted is toenail cutting, an activity worth mentioning because it occurs possibly more often in Ozu's pictures (*Late Spring, Early Summer, Late Autumn*) than in Japanese life.

Outdoor activities are also few, including only hiking or bicycling (*Late Spring, Early Spring, Late Autumn*), fishing (*A Story of Floating Weeds, There Was a Father, Floating Weeds*), and golfing (*What Did the Lady Forget?, An Autumn After-*

The Body

From A Hundred More Things Japanese, 1980

Hé.
The fart.
Though the fart is, obviously, not a phenomenon to be observed uniquely in Japan, the Japanese attitude toward it is, I think, unique. Among indications of this attitude is that both *he* and its slightly more common variant, *onara,* are accepted. Both, for example, are found in Japanese dictionaries; one usually searches in vain, however, for "fart" in English dictionaries. In addition, the terms are heard in conversation with a frequency much greater than that with which

(until recently) one encountered the like words in the West. Also, these are not considered dirty words and no euphemism ("break wind") is found necessary.

Many also are the proverbs—indications of a general acceptance. "*Aitsu wa furo no naka de he o hitta yo na yatsu da,*" for the translation of which Kenkyusha priggishly offers only: "He is a wishy-washy sort of fellow." Or, more philosophically: "*Hyaku nichi no seppo—he hitotsu,*" "An hour may destroy what took an age to build," advises Ken-

kyusha. English must content itself with, I believe, just one: "That is not worth a fart in hell." It is noted that both cultures use the fart in a derogative manner, but how much more the Japanese have to be disparaging with.

Finally, there is the common incidence of the fart in Japanese literature and the arts. While we in the West had had to content ourselves with but one celebrated fart (that of the frivolous seducer in Chaucer*), the Japanese have long had the widest choice.

noon). The outdoor activity, though no sport, most often depicted is train-riding. To be sure, movies have from their inception featured trains, and Lumière, Gance Kinoshita, Hitchcock, and Kurosawa have all been fascinated by them. Ozu, however, probably holds the record. Almost all his films include scenes with trains, and in many of them the final sequence is either in or near a train. *A Story of Floating Weeds, There Was a Father, Equinox Flower, Floating Weeds,* and others all end in trains; *Tokyo Story, Early Spring,* and others all have trains in their final scenes. One reason for all the trains is simply Ozu's liking for them. Another is that for the Japanese, if no longer for us, the train remains a vehicle of mystery and change. The mournful sound of a train in the distance, the idea of all those people being carried away to begin life anew elsewhere, the longing or nostalgia for travel—all these are still emotionally potent for the Japanese.

In some Ozu films the nostalgia for a once visited place is stated directly. In *The Munekata Sisters* there is a scene in which the two sisters sit on the steps of Yakushiji. The elder is very subdued. Later she returns with the man she loves, and we learn that they had met there before when their love was new. Her feelings during the scene with her sister are thus explained without our seeing the event that prompted them. Sometimes an occurrence in one film is mentioned in another, even though all the characters are different. In *Late Autumn* the mother is reminded while traveling of a pond of carp at Shuzenji; these are the same carp that appear in *The Flavor of Green Tea over Rice,* a film made eight years before. The same line of dialogue expressing a sense of life passing will recur in a number of films. One such recurring line is "*Owarika?*" (Is this the end?), an utterance typical of Ozu in its simplicity, clarity, and use of familiar vernacular. It is used by the father in *Tokyo Story* when he learns his wife is dying; it was used, we are told, by the father as he lay dying in *The End of Summer,* and it is also used by the father when he learns that the girls

---

From the celebrated farting-contest scroll and the early illustrated *He Gassen* (The Fart Battle), up to such recent representations as the delightful farting games in Ozu Yasujiro's *Ohayo* (1959), Japan's culture is filled with vivid examples. To choose from poetry one need turn only to the *senryu,* that accepting form that, as R. H. Blyth so finely phrased it, is opposed to haiku in that "senryu are expressions of moments of vision into, not the nature of things, but the nature of man."

Farting is certainly included in the nature of man and there are a number of moments that capture this very human vision.

One is:
"'And what may you all / Be laughing at, may I ask?' / The retired master's fart." Another is: "Four or five people, / Inconvenienced / By the horse farting / On the ferryboat." Concerning this last, Blyth, (whose translations the above are) says "... an extremely vulgar affair ... the senryu writer, however, will and must have it and keep it, and bring it out again. Such things are among the miseries of life, and should be recorded as such."

Just here, I think, is the difference in attitude between Japan and the West. That a thing *is* sufficient to warrant its notice, even its celebration. The hypocrisy of the idealistic (where some things, often those most intimately human, are to be denied) has not until recently infected Japan.

In both cultures the fart is funny but only in Japan, I think, is its humanity acknowledged. This entails a full acceptance of the human state. There is even a rubric for such matters. This is known as the *ningen-kusai* (literally, "smelling of humanity") and within it the he takes an honorable place.

Editor's note: Richie, apparently, has forgotten the famous "bugle" that concludes Canto XXI of Dante's Inferno.

will have to close the Bar Accacia coffeehouse in *The Munekata Sisters*.

Ozu's most potent device for nostalgia, however, is the photograph. Even though family pictures, class pictures, company pictures, remain in Japan something of the institution they once were in the West, there is a surprising amount of formal portrait-taking going on in Ozu's films. There is the group picture, of students and teacher, for example, in front of the Kamakura Buddha in *There Was a Father;* there is the wedding portrait, as in *Late Autumn;* there is the family portrait, as in *The Brothers and Sisters of the Toda Family, Early Summer, The Record of a Tenement Gentleman.* Except in the first example cited above, we do not see the finished picture. No one drags out the portrait of his dead mother and gazes fondly at it. Rather, we see the family gathered (invariably for the last time), smiling bravely into an uncertain future. Nostalgia lies not in later reflections, but in the very effort to preserve the image itself. Although Ozu's characters occasionally lament that they have no photos of a missing loved one, the actual use of photos is restricted to prospective brides and grooms. Death, in the films of Ozu as in life, is simple absence.

A person's past has done its work,
but it is not interesting.

All these similarities (and there are many more) among the films of Ozu came about partly because he saw each film as either a continuation of the preceding picture or a reaction to it. The notes written by Kogo Noda, the well-known scenarist and collaborator in more than half (twenty-seven) of Ozu's films, in the joint diary

the two men kept at Tateshina are indicative: "FEB. 1, 1962. As preparation for our work [on *An Autumn Afternoon*] we read some of our old scenarios. FEB. 3. We talk [about the new film]; . . . it will be in the genre of *Equinox Flower* and *Late Autumn*. We consider some story about a [widowed] man and his child, and a woman trying to find a bride for him. . . .

JUNE 10. For reference we reread *Late Autumn*. . . . JUNE 11. For reference we reread *Equinox Flower.*" Such a method of construction (more common for the later pictures than the earlier ones) inevitably meant strong similarities from picture to picture, particularly since Ozu and Noda apparently defined genres in terms of their own earlier work.

Similarities, then, are many, and differences few in the extraordinarily limited world of the Ozu film. It is a small world, closed, governed by rules apparently inflexible, controlled by laws that are only to be deduced. Yet, unlike Naruse's narrow family-centered world, Ozu's does not provoke claustrophobia, nor do its apparently inflexible governing rules give rise to the romantic idea of destiny seen in the apparently wider world of Mizoguchi. What keeps Ozu's films from these extremes are Ozu's characters, the kind of people they are and the way they react to their life. The simple and real humanity of these characters, their individuality within their similarity, makes it difficult and ultimately misleading to categorize as I have been doing for these past several pages. Although Ozu's stories certainly are few, the pictures do not seem repetitious; though a précis of the anecdote is thin, the film never is; though the roles are similar, the characters are not.

Human nature in all its diversity and variation—this is what the Ozu film is essentially about. It must be added, however, that as a traditional and conservative Asian, Ozu did not believe in any such essence as the term "human nature" may suggest to us. Each of his characters is unique and individual, based on known types though they all may be; one never finds "representative types" in his films. Just as there is no such thing as Nature, only individual trees, rocks, streams, etc., so there is no such thing as Human Nature, only individual men and women. This is something that Asians know better than Occidentals, or at least act as if they do, and this knowledge is responsible, in part, for the individuality of the Ozu character; his entity is never sacrificed to a presumed essence. By so restricting our view and confining our interest, Ozu allows us to comprehend the greatest single aesthetic paradox: less always means more. To put it another way, the several invariably indicates the many; restriction results in amplification; endless variety is found within the single entity.

Ozu never said this, and for all I know never thought it. He did not question his interest in character or his ability to create it. Yet that interest never failed. When he sat down to write a script, his store of themes firmly in the back of his mind, he rarely asked what the story was to be about. He asked, rather, what kind of people were to be in his film.

Script (Conclusion)

We have in this chapter been discussing how Ozu and his collaborator constructed their scripts: how they relied, initially at least, entirely upon dialogue; how the joke or light comment became a motif; how this in turn often became a parallel; how the main theme was elaborated; and how the characters were formed. In actuality, of course, all this happened at the same time. Here the method has been schematized, to make it easier to apprehend. Ozu and his collaborating scriptwriter obviously did not think in terms of motifs or parallels any more than they pondered

mono no aware and *mu*. And, as we have seen, the end result of this work was not story but character.

Any artist this interested in character, and this adept at creating it, is inevitably, I think, a moralist. This is certainly true of artists who long ago created characters so strong we still believe in them—Jane Austen, Tolstoy, Dickens, Chekhov. Along with this interest and ability comes a concern for excellence in anything pertaining to practice or conduct, a concern for what is proper and what is ethical. The moralist in Dickens is immediately apparent because he takes up questions of right and wrong; in Ozu's case it is less a question of what is right and what is wrong than a question of what is and what isn't. The message of an Ozu film—to the extent that one can be sorted out from the sum experience of the film itself—is, perhaps, that one is happiest living in accord with one's own imperfections and those of one's friends and loved ones; that these imperfections include aging, dying, and other calamities; that man's simple humanity must, in the end, be recognized and obeyed.

Seen in this light, Ozu was a truly moral man, a profound moralist who wanted the greatest good for the greatest number of people. As a realistic, even pragmatic man, he knew that this was an impossible aim, but considered the hope itself important. He was also an artist, and thus expressed his moral views only indirectly. To assemble moral comments from various films and then present them as a coherent moral statement, as I shall do below, does Ozu disservice as an artist, and obscures the strength and, to the West, the originality of his moral viewpoint. It does, however, offer some approximation of the moral effect of an Ozu picture.

Though Ozu, particularly in Japan, is often thought of as affirming traditional values, particularly in his later films, this is not quite true. He accepts these values, and he occasionally criticizes them—though to be sure, it all depends on what

you mean by tradition. I take it to mean a series of assumptions about life that have been handed down from ancestors to posterity, an inheritance largely unremarked, a body of assumptions largely unspoken. When a society becomes self-conscious about its traditions, it means they are losing their viability.

One object of Ozu's criticism throughout his career, beginning with such early pictures as *The Life of an Office Worker* and *Tokyo Chorus,* has been the texture of Japanese urban life, traditional in that it has been unthinkingly passed on from generation to generation for over a century. In *Early Spring* the young office clerk who is the leading character is in a bar with an older customer, Hattori. He and Kawai, a fellow worker, are talking with him. The latter asks, "How many years have you been working there, then?" Hattori answers, "Just thirty-one years." "Well," says Kawai, "then you'll get your retirement pay." "Hardly," answers Hattori, "that's just the point. I had hoped after retiring to open a small stationery shop near a school someplace. I thought I would have a happy life. But the retirement allowance isn't large enough. And that's the way it goes. I've known only loneliness and disillusion. And I've worked thirty-one years to find that life is just an empty dream." This sentiment

is later echoed by another older friend, Onodera: "A company can be a cold thing; . . . at my age I feel it more and more." In *Good Morning* the father of the two boys is talking to an older next-door neighbor, Tomizawa:

TOMIZAWA: Reaching retirement age—that's an ugly word. It's like being told you're half-dead. The company seems to think that a man no longer has to eat after he reaches retirement age. But he does—and drink, too. My wife says that I have to go out looking for a job, but at my age that's hopeless. Life is an empty dream. FATHER: But surely your retirement allowance—TOMIZAWA: No use. They calculate these things. They don't give you that much. Thirty years of work. Rainy days, windy days, pushed around in crowded trains. A dream—nothing but an empty dream.

Later in the film the boy's mother says, "We'll have to start thinking, too." "About what?" asks the father. "About when you retire." He nods. "Probably so."

Life is a dream. This is a familiar Buddhist concept, radically updated. Originally the observation that the world is a mirage was meant to console the sufferer, but in Ozu's universe there is no afterlife. That life is a dream means one has had no life at all. We may feel that Ozu over-

 The Japanese   From A Lateral View, "A Definition of the Japanese Film," 1970

There are various ways for the director to restrict, and consequently amplify, his film. He may limit his locale, his theme, or his method of description. Kenji Mizoguchi's method of creating atmosphere depends entirely on two limits: he puts the action far from the camera and continues the scene for a long time. These two restrictions are seen, for example, in the lawn scene

from *Ugetsu*. Machiko Kyo and Masayuki Mori are in the far distance playing on the grass by the shores of Lake Biwa. Nothing happens, yet the scene continues for some time. The result is that we slowly absorb the beauty of the scene and, consequently, apprehend what the surroundings mean to the two in the far distance. We feel the

atmosphere much as they themselves feel it. By giving us almost nothing to look at, Mizoguchi has led us to see.

Although the film no longer exists, Eizo Tanaka's 1917 version of Tolstoy's *The Living Corpse (Ikeru Shikabane)* was an example of the use of atmosphere as limitation. In this film, nature becomes a generalized

states the case, but he does so with compassion and even restraint.

The inequalities of Japanese urban life—and of life in general, to be sure—are soon recognized by Ozu's characters. In *I Was Born, But . . .* the two little boys reproach their father: "Why do you have to bow to Taro's father?" demands one of them. "Because his father is a director of my company." The child then asks, "Why don't you become a director, then?" The father answers that it isn't that easy. "I'm only an employee. He pays me my salary." "Don't let him," says the boy. "No," says his younger brother: "You pay *him*." The father tries to reason. "If I didn't let him pay me, you couldn't go to school, you couldn't eat." The boys see neither justice nor sense in such an arrangement. In the following scene the father admits to the mother: "I know how they feel. . . . It is a problem they'll have to live with for the rest of their lives. . . . But will they lead the same sorry kind of lives that we have?" At the conclusion of the film, Ozu leaves no doubt that they will.

Ozu's view of life is not, indeed, a comforting one. In *Early Summer* a character observes that life is like a game of chance: "Happiness is only a hope—hope more like a dream, like hoping you are going to win at the racetrack." In *The Flavor of Green Tea over Rice* this concept is elaborated. A character is complaining about pachinko, the ever-popular pinball game. "It's bad that a game like this should be so popular—I'm sorry I opened this place. . . . It will invite decay, it will ruin the national morale." Its attractions are later explained by a friend: "Pachinko develops into a passion. . . . It allows you to feel isolated while in a crowd and to enjoy a kind of solitude. Just you and the ball become one and so you are completely alone. Blissful solitude. And then you realize that this ball is in itself a kind of cycle. And the whole game becomes an epitome of life itself."

If life is a dream, a hope, a game, then we, the players, cannot do much about it. One reason is that this is the way it is; another is that human beings are simply not the special creatures they think they are. In *Floating Weeds* one of the actors denounces a plan to steal the funds and abandon the troupe: "Never. . . . the only difference between us humans and animals is that we aren't ungrateful," a distinction he himself erases when he steals from the others and runs away. In *The Flavor of Green Tea over Rice* one of the characters says angrily to another: "Look, Setsuko, we aren't dogs or chickens, it's true . . . ; and you may think that we are higher beings or something, but

substitute for specific emotion. When the director used the closeup, he did not use it, as Western directors almost invariably do, to illustrate an emotional climax: he used it directly before that climax. At the emotional zenith—the heroine receives some bad news—he pulled back and showed her alone in a field, leaning against a tree. In other words, just where the West would have called for a closeup to show emotion, the Japanese director made the barren field, the lonely tree, the cloudy sky comment upon the emotional state of the heroine. This is the Japanese way of seeing, of showing things. Forty years later, in *The Throne of Blood (Kumo no Su-jo)*, Kurosawa again deliberately pulled back his camera at the emotional height of the story. When Toshiro Mifune finally realizes the worst, when Isuzu Yamada feels most strongly, the camera retreats. We see their emotion from a proper distance, framed by clouded skies and an encroaching castle.

The later films of Yasujiro Ozu offer particularly good examples of the Japanese genius for meaningful restriction. The camera is stationary, and there is virtually no punctuation save that of the straight cut. In Ozu's pictures it becomes impossible not to bring oneself into his milieu; the spectator is totally involved in

in the eyes of god we are mere animals." Though Ozu does not linger on such heights (the very next line is, "You like these noodles?"), we know what he thinks.

Another reason we cannot change the world is that the world itself changes all of the time. In *The End of Summer* Manbei is speaking with his mistress: "And we wouldn't have met that day if I'd taken the first streetcar." "That's right," she agrees. "Fated to meet." "And then we didn't meet for nineteen years." "And to meet at a place like that." He remembers: "A bicycle race. Well, life is a running stream, forever changing." "Our world has really changed," she agrees. "It's disturbing," he says, to which she adds: "I do miss the old days. Remember the tea shop?" "And the night we went snow viewing, and the firefly hunt—that moonlit night." "I remember that all right," she says. "That was the night you turned me from a girl into a woman." The theme of the world in change is sounded again and again in the films of Ozu. In *Tokyo Story*, for example, the mother says when she sees her child: "I'm so glad I lived to see this day. The world has changed so." To which the children reply: "But you haven't changed at all."

This is the way of the world, the old no longer change, the young continue to change, as the parents in this picture discover. Yet the parents never cease to hope that their lives will find some vindication in those of their children. The happiness they seek is a mirage. Most of Ozu's films are about parents and children, all of whom suffer a degree of disappointment. As Shuichi says in *Late Spring:* "Raise them and then off they go. If they don't get married you worry, and if they do you feel disappointed." In *An Autumn Afternoon,* Hirayama and Kawai are talking. "You know," says the former, "when you come down to it, a son is best. Girls are no use." Kawai answers: "Boy or girl, it's all the same. They all go off sooner or later." As the father says in *Tokyo Story,* talking about a son lost in the war: "To lose one's children is hard; but living with them isn't easy either." This disappointment is built into the human condition, as many an Ozu character learns during the course of the picture. They begin by hoping that all will be well, that things will turn out as they wish; they often end by consoling themselves that at least they have suffered less than others they know.

In *Tokyo Story* the mother finally turns to the father and says: "Some grandparents seem to like their grandchildren more than their own children—what about you?" "I like my children better, but I'm surprised at how they change," he

a carefully controlled vision of house and family. Such involvement is virtually unavoidable in his films, not only because Ozu creates a totally credible atmosphere, but also because he understands the basic nature of film. The cinema's greatest strength is that it is able to record perfectly the surface of life, nothing more. Since this is so, we should expect no more than a reflection of surface reality; the first films were newsreels and every film remains, in essence, a newsreel. Those great closeups of emotionally contorted faces in Western cinema and in some Japanese films as well do not usually make us feel grief, pain, or happiness; what those images really convey are skin pores, mascara, and nostril hair.

Since cinematic art, however, is symbolic, we accept this cosmeticized monster face as a representation of human emotion; we accept it even though we are not necessarily convinced by it.

But when Ozu shows us Setsuko Hara at the end of *Late Autumn (Akibiyori)* sitting alone in the middle distance, hands folded, eyes downcast, we move nearer and nearer to a genuine feeling of sadness. One of the reasons is that Ozu does not demand our emotions and, paradoxically, we more freely give them. But the most important reason is that by showing in the way he does, by respecting the surface appearance of life, he succeeds in suggesting the depths

answers. A bit later she ventures, "Children don't live up to one's expectations." "Let's think," he says, "that ours have turned out better than most. They're certainly better than average." "We are fortunate," she says. "Yes, I think so," he concludes. In *Early Summer* a similar conclusion is reached. One of the characters says: "Our family is every which way, but we've done better than the average—why, we've done lots of things together. We shouldn't ask for too much. We've been really happy." Of course they have not been happy in the way he implies; he himself had already seen the breakup of the family as inevitable.

Ozu shows in his films both the natural reluctance of the old to let go of the young and the natural impatience of the young to be rid of the old. He is not, however, interested in comparing the virtues of the one with the shortcomings of the other. What Ozu chronicles, rather, is the impossibility of accord. Those critics—mainly young Japanese critics of a decade or so ago—who found Ozu old-fashioned and reactionary were obviously misreading his films. And those other critics who complain that Ozu lost interest in social problems obviously restrict their definition to political problems, since there are no social problems greater than the unavoidable

misunderstandings between the generations, the indubitable unfairnesses of any society, and man's yearning for security in a world susceptible only to change.

And the end is always there, staring us in the face. When asked why he seems so sad, Kawai in *An Autumn Afternoon* says, "Solitary, sad—after all, man is alone." Man is alone, and as one of the characters toward the end of *The End of Summer* remarks, "Life *is* very short, isn't it?" The conclusions of many Ozu films—*Late Spring, Tokyo Story, Late Autumn* among them—underline this common fate. It is so common, indeed, that its appearance in films as in literature always surprises. Loneliness and death are in a sense such banal facts of human experience that only a great artist, a Tolstoy, a Dickens, an Ozu, can restore to them something of the urgency and sadness that we all someday experience. Ozu does this through a deliberate description of the facts, a full display of them, and—surprisingly in one so often described as an apologist for the traditional—by confrontation. Ozu is one of the very few artists whose characters are aware of the great immutable laws that govern their lives.

The son in *I Was Born, But . . .* says that if all adult life is like his father's, then he won't grow up. In *Late Autumn* one of the girls is dis-

beneath the surface. He allows us to apprehend the emotional quality of life which its surface—that portion captured by the camera—can only suggest. The less he shows, the more we feel. In doing this he respects not only us and himself, he respects the very nature of cinema.

The Japanese director could not respect the nature of cinema unless he also respected the nature of life itself. His aim, like that of all film directors,

is complete credibility, but the Japanese director is better equipped than most to achieve this end. We have already seen that he uses the atmosphere of a place to ensure our belief in it, that he purposely restricts what he shows and how he shows it to ensure our participation. Now we shall see the respect that the Japanese has for life, and consequently for cinema.

Several years ago I watched some workmen building a new

wall where I lived in Azabu. Nearby was a tree with low-hanging branches. The workmen continued to build the wall and it rose closer and closer to the lowest branch. They stopped, talked, then continued building. They built a hole in the wall to accommodate the branch. They did not cut off the branch as the Westerner would, as the Japanese probably would today; they enriched their wall with it.

appointed that their friend did not wave. "And we were such good friends, too," she says. "Yes," answers the other, "but time passes and friends part." The first girl is struck by this remark. "Is that all friends are? Are men that way, too? Well, if that's all friendship means, then I think it's just disgusting." Later in the film, the daughter is complaining about her problems. "But that's how life is," says her mother, a remark heard again and again in Ozu's pictures, a statement neither condemning nor condoning. The mother adds, "Grown-up life isn't as pretty as you might think. So you can just stop being a child." In the very beautiful and moving scene at the end of *Tokyo Story*, Noriko, the daughter-in-law, is speaking with Kyoko, the younger sister. The latter is crying. "Even strangers would have been more considerate," she says of her brothers and sisters. "Look, Kyoko," says Noriko: "At your age I thought so, too, but children begin to drift away from their parents . . . ; everyone has to look after his own life." Kyoko looks up: "Really? Well, I won't be like that. That would be too cruel." "And so it is," agrees Noriko. "But children become like that—gradually. And, then, you too . . ." "I may become like that?" asks Kyoko. "In spite of myself?" She stops, then says, "Isn't life disappointing?" Noriko smiles, a beautiful, gracious, accepting smile, and replies, "Yes, it is."

If Ozu's characters can accept life as a hope, or a game, or a disappointment, it is *because* they are aware they see life that way. Even the foolish men and women in Ozu's films are unusually canny about their own character, and the wise are often profoundly knowing about themselves; they know what kind of person they are, what their limitations are, to what ambitions they may aspire. It is this unusual degree of self-knowledge, which of course does not preclude blind spots and illogic that enables the Ozu character to take an ironic view of life. He is concerned but not enmeshed. This self-knowledge leads neither to

cynicism (as it does among the characters of Ivy Compton-Burnett, who display a preternatural degree of self-knowledge) nor to sentimentality (as it sometimes does in Chekhov, whose people's self-knowledge usually extends only to limitations). Rather, as in Jane Austen, self-knowledge leads to a balanced sense of life and self, an understanding of the world and one's place in it, and an unexalted but nonetheless accepting opinion of one's own capabilities. In this sense Noriko, and so many of Ozu's young women, are like Emma. Having come to know themselves, they may hope for contentment.

It is here that morality enters into the Ozu film. What Ozu is saying is not that the old way is the best way, or that youth must have its fling, or that you come into the world and leave it all alone—though all these thoughts have their places in the Ozu universe. Ozu is saying, rather, that within the given constraints, one forms one's own character by consciously deciding upon this course or that. One does not delve into oneself, find there a character already formed, then recognize it as one's own. Rather, out of the inchoate material of human nature one forms a single human being, inconsistencies and all.

Morality exists that one may have a guide through the labyrinth. Ozu's morality, like that of most Asians, is simple. You act in a way that is consistent with nature, for you observe your kinship with other beings and perceive that you are a part of the nature around you, neither its slave nor its overlord. You observe the laws of your civilization until the point at which they seriously interfere with your own well being, and then you make a compromise. You behave like the guest in this world you truly are.

You are a transient in a transitory world. With a feeling that goes far beyond the demands of good breeding, you gently celebrate (*mono no aware*) those very qualities which threaten (and eventually extinguish) your personal entity. You do so because you are part of this world and you know its rules, and you accept them. They are right because they are.

To achieve this relationship with the world, you learn to choose. We watch the people in an Ozu film choosing and deliberating over and over again, usually in the knowledge that in choosing one forms one's character. You are what you do, and nothing more nor less; the sum total of your choices, your actions, is the sum total of yourself. In choosing, you not only create self, you transcend it. You are, in a way, the self you always were, but the awareness of alternatives brings awareness of the most important fact of human life: there is no immutable inner reality, no inner person, no soul. You choose what you will become.

Here, perhaps, is the reason why Ozu's characters have, as has been mentioned, no past. They may refer to times past, but we never see them. Ozu is one of the very few directors who never once in his entire career used a flashback. A person's past has done its work, but it is not interesting. Of his people you may truly say what is important is not what life has done to them, but what they do with what life has done to them.

One understands, then, Ozu's dislike and distrust of plot. Plot is possible only if it is agreed that a character is a certain kind of person with a certain kind of past who will therefore predictably do certain kinds of things and not others—that he is, in short, limited in a way people never are, before death. One understands also why inconsistency of character is so important to Ozu: it is a sign of life because it is a sign of choice. Choice is important to all of Ozu's people, as it is to all of us, which is one of the things that makes them so lifelike. What is involved, one must add, is nothing so sweeping as absolute free will. The freedom of Ozu's characters is, from the first, restricted. They are after all, human, which implies certain constraints; they must live together, another constraint; and they are part of a larger society, yet another constraint. They are offered not the *à la*
carte menu, but the *table d'hôte*. Limitless choice exists no more for them than it does for anyone, but the range of choice is wide enough to be meaningful, to let Ozu's people form their own character.

And this, finally, is what the Ozu film shows us—character being formed through choice. We have seen the various ways in which this is done; we may now more fully appreciate the enormous difficulty of the task. Ozu and his collaborator had to work as their finished characters have to work: pondering, deciding, choosing. The Ozu character has only his own concerns, director and writer had the concerns of all their dramatis personae. No wonder Noda said that even after forty years of writing scripts, each new one constituted a tremendous problem. "What should this one be like, and how should we go about it—this was something that made us both sweat."

Yet the picture would stand or fall with the script. Ozu consequently was always much relieved when it was finally finished. Chishu Ryu remembers:

> Ozu always looked most pleased when the scenario was completed . . . ; by the time he had finished writing it—about four months of work—he had already made up every image in every shot so that he never changed the script after we went on the set. And the dialogue was so polished that he would not allow even a single mistake. . . . He told me how happy he was when the script was done, but he also told me, though jokingly, that he was often disappointed to find how his images came apart when he started working with the actors. [Still,] once the film was completed, even if the acting was poor, he never complained. Even when we were certain that he was disappointed in us, he took all of the responsibility as his own and never spoke of it to others. This alone gives you some idea of his character.

Buddhism and the Film

There are various ways in which to regard a Buddhist cinema. From the simplest to the more complicated:

1. Films about the historical Buddha
2. Films about Buddhist belief
3. Films on Buddhist themes
4. Films which incorporate Buddhist beliefs

These and their implications will inform this talk.

1. Films about the historical Buddha are few, though not so few as those on the historical Mohammed since there is no proscription; yet there are many less than those on the Hindu pantheon and those on the historical Christ. Explain.

    a. Reasons might include the fact that the Buddha story is simply not dramatic. He laid down and died—certainly less sensational than being nailed on a cross.

    b. Equally important is that Buddhism is not originally at any rate, a proselytizing religion, though certain sects (Soka Gakkai) have certainly become so. Christianity on the other hand is. Buddhism does not have the propaganda needs that Christianity does. *The Ten Commandments, The Robe, The Greatest Story Ever Told*—all of these to an extent are intended to spread the good news.

Notes for a speech given at the Pacific Film Archive, Berkeley, 1993, unpublished

Compared to the various lives of Christ there have been very few lives of Buddha. Those countries which might be inclined to make them (Little Vehicle countries) do not have the money—historical spectaculars are expensive; those countries which have the money (Japan) are not inclined to make them (though they did make one, the Daiei *Life of Buddha*). That the life of Buddha can be regarded as material for a spectacular can be seen in the forthcoming film of Bertolucci. That it need be relevant to nothing at all may be seen in the choice of Keanu Reeves to play the title role.

2. Again, films about Buddhist belief are relatively few when compared with the many films about Joan of Arc, Joanna of the Angels, St. Sebastian, and various nuns, monks, priests, and so on. And when they are made, the emphasis is often different from the films about Christian beliefs.

   a. In the various Korean films about Buddhist monks the emphasis is not upon exemplary lives but upon the *do*, the way itself.

   b. In the Sri Lankan films about Buddhist monks and nuns the emphasis is not upon martyrdom but about some more peaceful manner of joining the elemental.

   c. In the Japanese (and some Korean) films about Buddhist nuns, the link between religion and sexual expression is candidly acknowledged (something which would never occur in a Christian picture) and no penalties are paid.

3. Films on Buddhist themes themselves (i.e. pictures which animate known liturgical beliefs) are much more rare than like films concerning Christian themes. In the West, in the earlier days, there were many Christian propaganda pictures the burden of which could be reduced to: Love Thy Neighbor; Do Not Commit Adultery, and the like. In the East the Buddhist theme-film often attaches itself to the religious-bio.

   Thus the various Japanese movies about the militant Nichiren are theme-pix: Give Your All for Buddha. The film about Shinran (being about Pure Land doctrine) is theme-reducible to: Speak Up for Buddha.

4. Films which incorporate Buddhist elements are, of course, everywhere since Buddhism is a part of Asian culture as a whole. Such elements are included along with chopsticks, saris, kung fu, etc., with no one being the wiser—and no one intending to be Buddhist in the first place.

   As an example, let us look at the work of the Japanese film director, Yasujiro Ozu. A completely secular man, he would doubtless be startled to find himself an exhibit in a talk on Buddhism, yet he belongs here.

   a. The camera gaze, the paradigm is Zen Buddhism

   b. The camera shot height: person on cushion—not only *zazen* but also tea master, haiku master, host-and-guest

   c. The shot length—paradigm is religious concentration

   d. The mundane—one of the qualities of the transcendental

5. Finally, there is a more important matter: the fact that film itself can be seen as a kind of paradigm of Buddhism since it shares so many of its properties. In a sense the cinema might be seen as a Buddhist vehicle (though a strange one) in that so many of its observations are therein inculcated.

   a. First, and not so frivolously, it might seem, film is an illusion. There are only shadows on the screen. Like the mere

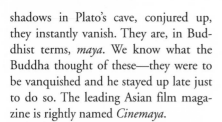

shadows in Plato's cave, conjured up, they instantly vanish. They are, in Buddhist terms, *maya*. We know what the Buddha thought of these—they were to be vanquished and he stayed up late just to do so. The leading Asian film magazine is rightly named *Cinemaya*.

b. The Buddha observed that all life is flux, transience (*antiya/mujo*), and what are the movies but just this. And in a double sense: each of the images only lasts 1/24th of a second, and film itself (both nitrate and safety) only lasts a number of decades before it chemically combusts. (Tape is no less transient, though the time needed for the dispersement of magnetic traces is not yet agreed upon.) Since such films are reflections of life they reflect life's own modes, and the major mode is flux. Again we know what the Buddha thought of this. Not much.

c. The Buddha also held that all life is suffering (*dunkha*) and that the root of this suffering is illusion. We desire that which is transient and illusionary. Therefore the root of suffering is desire. We must learn not to want. However, wanting is the stuff of life. This the movies amply and historically show. They are about nothing but desire and suffering. In this sense Douglas Sirk is a Buddhist sage and Lana Turner a bodhisattva. In a larger sense a conversion to the Buddha would mean the end of cinema since this is itself a compound of desire, suffering, and illusion, and all of these are bad things.

d. In the Buddhist limbo the deluded are forced to endlessly repeat those actions which led to their being put there in the first place. Again a parallel suggests itself.

As anyone knows who has endured the same film twice, the film experience is (except in rare cases) unduplicatable as experience (though not for study purposes, nor for the emotional—the need to cry, for example). The person who willingly saw *The Sound of Music* some dozens of times was, in my opinion, either undergoing a purgative or enduring something approximate to the Buddhist hell. One of the ideas behind that of the *dharma* is that of *karma*—the repetition of life. And it takes many forms. In its infernal form, one of the finest and most thoroughly Buddhist films ever made was *Groundhog Day*.

6. *Dharma* comes from an Indian word the original means of which is: law, custom, duty, justice, etc. Its contemporary meanings are double: (1) the teachings of the Buddha and (2) those various elements that combine to make the physical world, including us.

This is not very helpful but it is clear that Buddha did not go to the movies and would not have approved of them if he had. They are distracting, illusionary, transient, and they inculcate desire. Also, they encourage opinion and self-expression, while one of the tenets of original Buddhism is *atman*, the impossibility of just this self. There are no film critics in the Buddhist pantheon.

In that sense then a retrospective about *dharma* and the film is anathema and a lecture entitled "Buddhism and the Film" adds insult to injury.

On the other hand, we are here today practicing Buddhists because we are in the position of praying to Kannon the Bodhisattva to forgive us these trespasses and to bless our endeavor—this film series.

Thank you.

JAPAN
People

Pierre Loti

Chishu Ryu

Toshiro Mifune

Shozo Kuroda

Hisako Shiraishi

Hanako Watanabe

Pierre Loti

When he first came to Japan in 1885, Pierre Loti was a thirty-five-year-old French naval officer whose real name was Louis Marie Julien Viaud. After novelistic fame had struck, however, he was generally known by the pseudonym that he took from the eponymous hero of his best-selling *Le mariage de Loti.*

This book, a sensation in France, had chronicled the author's exotic romance in Tahiti, and an earlier volume, *Aziyadé,* also enjoying wide readership, had been about another affair of the heart, this time in Istanbul. Consequently, Loti's readers had the highest expectations of Japan. His reputation as a lover was almost as great as his fame as a writer and, in addition, Japan was fast becoming the place to have romances.

Indeed, the "immorality" of the Japanese in this regard had long attracted attention. Three hundred years before, Francesco Carletti, speaking of the "rampant immorality," said that one could get hold of "a pretty little girl" for very little money, and "with no other responsibility beyond that of sending her back home when done with." In 1860 the Right Reverend Bishop George Smith of Hong Kong was "outraged at how many of the foreign residents live," referring to domestic arrangements with local women.

The Japanese themselves were aware of the mixed nature of this foreign interest. Writing in *The Tokyo Press* in 1898, Yukichi Fukusawa remembered that the late ex-president Grant had been forced to sit and watch geisha. "It is fortunate that [he] did not

From The Honorable Visitors,
1994

know the language and was not well acquainted with Japanese life." Otherwise, he would have understood that "they performed illicit acts for money. . . ." and "if General Grant had realized that, he would have stood up in the midst of the dancing and walked out."

Perhaps this was because Loti's motivation seems to have been his desire to have had a romance, something he could then write about. This being so, the reality about him did not impress. He was much like the modern tourist to whom the picture taken is more important than the sight photographed.

Well, perhaps, if Julia had been along. Otherwise, however, he would probably have shared the pleasantly scandalized prurience that contributed so much to the enjoyment of being in Japan. Word had indeed gotten around concerning the excellence of Japanese women. Charles MacFarlane, an otherwise staid Englishman, had said that they "are the most fascinating, elegant ladies that I ever saw in any country in the world." One may then imagine that Loti, given his lucrative Turkish and Tahitian conquests, was ready to entertain the softest feelings for the women of far Nippon.

Once in Nagasaki, he set about attempting to acquire one. This was, at the time, possible. John Luther Long's Madame Butterfly was

obtained as the result of such a business transaction. So was Clive Holland's. The latter wrote in his once-popular book, *My Japanese Wife,* that his was "a butterfly . . . playing at life . . . with the dainty grace of Japan . . . that idealized doll's-house land." Plainly, if Japan was thought a land of dollhouses, then one must have one's own doll.

This Loti attempted, but he initially seems not to have done so properly. His go-between was his laundry man, a part of whose motivation seems to have been his mere desire to launder the dirty linen of Loti and his comrades. In any event, no maiden appeared.

Despite his having initially gone about it the wrong way, a young woman was eventually found for the famous Frenchman. But it was then *his* turn to be difficult. As Loti later told it, while still on the ship he had said, "Yes, I shall choose a little yellow-skinned woman with black hair and cat's eyes . . . not much bigger than a doll." Presented with such, however, he complained that the proffered woman was much too white, "too much like our own women. I wish for a yellow one just for a change." To which the procurer explained: "That is only the paint they put on her, sir. Beneath it, I assure you, she is yellow."

So, the deal was struck. Twenty dollars, a farcical "wedding ceremony" at the local police station, and Loti had his own *musume,* a word that was being picked up by gallivanting foreigners. Though it means merely "daughter" and, by extension, "girl," the new users were giving it any meaning they pleased. Loti was quite taken by it. "It is one of the prettiest in the Nipponese language . . . *mousme* [sic] . . . It seems almost as if there were a little *moue* in the sound, as if a pert physiognomy were described by it."

Pleasant as all this sounded, reality was something else. The liaison did not turn into the grand passion that Loti's readers, and maybe even Loti himself, expected. There were, to be sure, some things he liked about her. He liked her name—Okiku-san, Miss Chrysanthemum—and he liked her when she was asleep. He thought she looked like "a dead fairy" with her kimono spread all about. "What a pity," he reflected, "this little chrysanthemum cannot always be asleep; she is really extremely decorative seen in this manner—and like this, at least, she does not bore me."

Otherwise, she did. He did not pause to consider that boredom is an admission of inadequacy in those entertaining this emotion. Rather, he found fault with her and with her country.

She was not fascinating and she was not elegant; rather, she was "a soul which more than ever appears to me of a different species to my own; I feel my thought to be as far removed . . . as from the flitting conceptions of a bird." Indeed, [italics his] ". . . *we have absolutely nothing in common with these people.*"

Given this attitude, it is not surprising that Loti understood little of the country and its inhabitants. Not, to be sure, that he wanted to. Just the opposite. As he had demonstrated in his books on Turkey and Tahiti, he needed a sense of the *ailleurs,* a quality of "otherness," to create the

opaque exoticism upon which his forays into the picturesque depended. And, as he was now going to sit down and write *Madame Chrysanthéme,* he had to cultivate this attitude.

But in Turkey and the South Seas, Loti had liked what he had seen and had reveled in his lack of understanding. In Japan, he complained about it. Perhaps the reason was that he himself had changed since the ardent days of earlier years. Lafcadio Hearn noticed the change. Writing to his friend Basil Hall Chamberlain in 1893, he said that the earlier work of Loti might be read in preference to the later since this "was written before his nerves became dull," though, of course, "as for the moral side, you will find him much worse than in *Madame Chrysanthème.*" And as Leslie Blanch writes in her biography of Loti, "Impatience and an amused detachment sound behind all he wrote [while in Japan]."

Of the country, Loti penned that he "knew it all, long ago, from scenes painted on the bottom of tea cups," and these standardized views were all he now found to write about. He did not observe, did not look around him. "Some magic had vanished," says Blanch. "Life as he had once

---

From A Lateral View, *"The Tongue of Fashion," 1981*　　*The Body*

What is moulded, however, are not the breasts, the hips, the behind, those areas emphasized in the West, but the human form itself, the torso. The result is a costume so tight that it hobbles the wearer and prevents any actions other than walking, standing, sitting, kneeling, a repertoire of movements which, given the possibilities of the human body, is quite limited. The inescapable suggestion is that something this tight and constricting must therefore enclose—like the lobster's shell—something soft and fluid.

In this sense the kimono can be seen as a metaphor for the idea that the Japanese has of himself—and is hence presenting. We are a people whose social consciousness is at least as strong as our individual consciousness; we live in a rigid conforming society and both

our strong social self and the strong social rules we obey are necessary because we would otherwise not know who we were. Like the lobster we are defined not by an inner core but by an outward armor—which may be social or sartorial. These—our ideas, our clothes— are informed from the outside. We so express our social self because, to an extent, that is all there is.

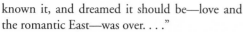

known it, and dreamed it should be—love and the romantic East—was over. . . ."

Perhaps Japan was here a bit at fault, if fault it be. It no longer looked exotic. Gazing out over Nagasaki harbor, Loti turned to a friend and wondered: "Where are we in reality? In the United States?" This familiar initial disappointment, echoing still a century later, was complicated by many further signs of civilization and enlightenment in the capital. Loti found that the all-brick Ginza had about it *une laide americaine,* and that the Rokumeikan, that grand Meiji edifice, resembled a casino at a second-rate French spa.

Invited there to a ball for the emperor's birthday, he found that the bustled women were correct but wooden. "They dance quite properly, my Japanese in Parisian gowns," he wrote. "But one senses that it is something *drilled* into them, that they perform like automatons, without any personal initiative. If by chance they lose the beat,

they have to be stopped and started over again. Left on their own, they would never get back in step."

One wonders what he wanted. When he came upon a sight not yet modernized, he was no more pleased. Of one such he wrote, "Some Japanese Watteau must have mapped [it] out . . . for it has rather an affected air of rurality, though very pretty."

Perhaps what he wanted more than anything else was some setting that would show him off to what he considered his advantage, and this was something Japan could not often provide. Jean Cocteau, himself later to make a highly personal appearance in Japan, remembered meeting Loti years later. Apparently, the urge to self-dramatization was still strong. He looked like "a painted china goat. With his tight corsets, his little high-heeled shoes, his little painted face, his large moustache, his staring eyes, I can hardly see him meeting some Aziyadé. . . ."

The Japanese   *From* The Japanese Tattoo, *1980*

**Tattooing
as Definition.**
To be human is to be amorphous, unformed. Thus one of the main businesses of life is to make some sense out of the chaos of simply being human. In the West this often results in a set of opinions and character traits chosen by the individual himself. He decides he likes this and does not like that, that this is true and that is false, and thus builds up a coherent structure that he calls himself. Strong characters with strong personalities are thought well of in the West. This means

that the man has successfully arranged his disorder and has imposed a proper and individualistic character upon himself.

In other countries, and Japan is one of them, a strong character is not well thought of. A man solving his own problems in this fashion creates problems for others. If he is so certain of what he likes and what he doesn't like, he will then not be able to adapt and compromise in the manner his culture finds both necessary and attractive. In Japan, therefore, people put themselves together differently.

They do not structure any presumed inner man. Rather, they structure the outer.

The difference is often expressed collectively—hence all the *nakama* manifestations visible in Japan. These outward marks, all the badges and costumes, do not indicate any inner conviction, nor are they intended to. All necessary decisions are displayed on the surface; all the structuring that the West devotes to the inside is visible in Japan on the outside. Order is thus achieved in a way quite different, even opposite, from that

However, Loti did have at least one experience when he seems to have found himself in properly flattering surroundings. This was his outing with the imperial court, an event to which he had been invited as a naval officer rather than as a famous author.

It was a chrysanthemum viewing in Tokyo (which the romantic Loti insisted upon calling Yedo), and the empress was there with her suite. She wore her full court costume, wig and all, and carried a violet parasol. In the background a band played, unlikely as it seems, the Berlioz *Symphonie Fantastique,* and the scene was fraught with *ailleurs.*

Loti, all eyes, fancied that as the empress passed him she carried a faint smile, "The remote smile of an idol." Already on a first-name basis (he calls her Harou-Ko), he recounts that she allowed her shadow (as he tells it in the 1889 *Japoneries d'automne*) to fall across his path and he longed to snatch this *ombre imperiale,* to take it home and treasure it. There is at this chrysanthemum viewing no talk, one notices, of his own little chrysanthemum girl back in Nagasaki. The author affects an interest in distant royalty, but he truly has none for nearer reality.

Perhaps this was because Loti's motivation seems to have been his desire to have *had* a romance, something he could then write about. This being so, the reality about him did not impress. He was much like the modern tourist to whom the picture taken is more important than the sight photographed.

He could not, however, but occasionally notice Japan as it was. "All the vases are of bronze but the designs varied as according to each changing fancy . . . of a simplicity so studied and exquisite that to our eyes they seem the revelation of an unknown art, the subversion of all acquired notions of forms."

The Parisian "Japanese" drawing room was overcrowded with curios and knickknacks, but

---

common in Europe and North America.

At the same time there is the purely human urge to make the amorphous self into something certain, strong, unchanging. In the West this results in persons with strong and unvarying opinions who draw solace from their very consistency. They are able to reduce the world to a firmly opposed series of rights and wrongs.

In Japan a person with such a need has neither the training nor the example to be so opinionated. Rather, and often with equal rigor, he arranges his surface, his façade, in a manner he considers set, fixed, indubitable. Hence all the costume wearing, hence all the wearing of badges and other identifying emblems, and hence also, and in this sense, tattoos.

A man who is fully tattooed is stable, unchanging. He has solidified his own skin and become that solid object, that permanent identity that all men in fear of the amorphous become. Indelibly dyed, unchanging, his skin supports him. Specifically, it defines him.

This means that his life is much less open to alternatives. This is a state toward which all men aspire. Alternatives—alternate ways of thought, for example—threaten the equilibrium of the structured man. In Japan tattoos remain as socially unrespectable as they once were in the West; there are many (a majority of) professions and avocations not open to a tattooed man. This means that his life is much simplified—it becomes manageable.

The tattooed man is thus one who needs this simplification. It does not follow that his thinking is codified to the extent common to the Western man of strong character and set opinions. Rather, it means that he need *not* codify his mind because his body has become codified. In both East and West, these various attempts at definition are based, further, upon a fear of the undefined.

"the true Japanese manner of understanding luxury consists in a scrupulous and indeed almost excessive cleanliness, white mats and white woodwork; an appearance of extreme simplicity and an incredible nicety in the most infinitesimal details."

"But for all that," he wrote about some large temple he had seen, "let the sanctuary be ever so immense and imposing in its somber gloom, the idols ever so superb, all seems in Japan but a mere semblance of grandeur. A hopeless pettiness. . . ." And so, "it is all very paltry . . . I feel as if I were acting for my own benefit some wretchedly trivial and third-rate comedy." Expecting *grandeur* and other bolsterings to *l'amour propre,* Loti made little attempt to understand anything.

Even when he did, he got it wrong. He noticed that his little Chrysanthème was always arrayed in dark colors. "This," he added hopefully, "is a sign here of aristocratic distinction." No, she had subdued her wardrobe because, unfortunate woman, she thought that she was really married.

But she wasn't, and six months later it was time to part. Loti wrote, "Well, little *mousmée* [sic], let us part good friends; one last kiss even, if you like. I took you to amuse me; you have not perhaps succeeded very well, but after all you have done what you could . . . you have been pleasant enough in your Japanese way."

An odiousness this extreme is now apparent, but when *Madame Chrysanthème* appeared in 1887, few thought any less of the author. Indeed, this book and a later one, fruit of a second trip in 1900, *La troisième jeunesse de Madame Prune,* were enormously popular and set something of a vogue in regards to Japan and its *musume.* After all, as Edward Said has well observed, "oriental women" in the writing of visitors "are usually creatures of a male power-fantasy. They express unlimited sensuality, they are more or less stupid, and above all they are willing."

They were also there to be deserted. This was the import of not only Loti's novels, but also *Madame Butterfly:* the story, the stage play, and the opera; as well as a spate of melodramatic entertainments with titles such as *A Japanese Nightingale, The Darling of the Gods, The Lady of the Weeping Willow Tree,* and so on.

And what, one wonders, did Okiku think of her little French "husband"? Probably as a way to get by in the brave new world of Meiji. There is small evidence that his leaving unduly upset her. In the celebrated final scene of *Madame Chrysanthème,* the dashing French officer returns and finds her biting the coins he had left her, testing them. He was shocked by this. I wasn't. Given his attitude, she would have been a fool to have done anything else. No Mrs. Pinkerton, she would have recognized a bad tourist when she saw one.

And this is what Loti became in Japan. Toward the end of his book he wrote, "The chief occupation in this Japanese country seems to be a perpetual hunt after curios." And shopping was what he did. He took back enough to outfit a whole "Japanese" room in his Rochefort mansion. Okiku was just another *souvenir d'un voyage,* one he did not take home.

The bad tourist, always imperialistic, does not wish to learn or to experience. The aim, rather, is to acquire as much as cheaply as possible, then to return home with the loot. This is what Loti did.

In 1919 Ryunosuke Akutagawa wrote a short story called *The Ball.* In it, a woman remembered that 1885 Rokumeikan ball and a poetic young Frenchman with whom she spoke. Asked if she recalled the name, she replied, "Indeed, I do. His name was Julien Viaud." "Then," said her interlocutor, "he was Loti, the author of *Madame Chrysanthème.*" "Not at all," said the woman. "His name was not Loti. It was Julien Viaud."

But her interlocutor was correct. Whatever the young Viaud was like, all was obscured by the needs of Pierre Loti.

Chishu Ryu

It was 1958 and Chishu Ryu had been asked by *Kinema Jumpo*, the big film magazine, to write something about Yasujiro Ozu, the director, his mentor. *Equinox Flower*, Ozu's latest, was about to open.

But he did not know how to begin. Usually when he talked about Ozu, people said: There you go, off on Ozu again. And it was true, he often talked about him. But how could he talk about himself without mentioning Ozu? It was the director who had formed him, turned him into an actor.

How to begin, that was the problem. And I can imagine him looking puzzled, that boyish pursing of the lips, so like the fifty-two-year-old actor on the screen, so like Ozu.

They had been together almost from the first, director and actor; in fact, he claimed to have appeared in all but two of Ozu's fifty-odd films. And then in 1930, despite his youth and inexperience, Ozu gave him one of the leads in *I Flunked, But . . .*

Ryu had no idea how to begin there, either. Ozu helped him, gave him something to do, indicated where hands, feet, eyes should be. But he never once told him what the character was like.

—I remember one time, he wrote later, when I was playing the father, the leading role in *There Was a Father* (1942). And there was this difficult scene. And I didn't know how to start. So Ozu told me to stare at the end of my chopsticks, then stare at my hand, and then speak to my child. The simple act of doing these

From **Different People**, *1987*

things would convey a certain feeling, an atmosphere. But Ozu never explained what the feeling was. The actions came first. Ozu merely told me what to do and then let me discover how it felt. That can be very difficult. I remember once, in one scene, I tried to follow his precise instructions up to twenty times and each time I failed. So I finally gave up.

Ozu arranged the look of his cast just as he arranged the look of his set. They did what he said, and it usually worked—the Ozu atmosphere being founded on the simple premise that if the outside is all right the inside will take care of itself.

Ryu's outside was perfect. Later on, critics were to say that without him the Ozu atmosphere could not exist. And Ryu was aware at a very early stage that he was the Ozu persona, nothing else.

—I was so awkward, so raw and untrained at the beginning. Ozu showed me everything. He gave me absolute support, as long as I followed his directions.

—Since everyone in the studio knew that I wasn't very good, the whole staff used to take a break when the time came for me to do a big scene. They just walked out and left Ozu and me alone. It was then that we rehearsed, endlessly, he giving me all sorts of advice, showing me just how he wanted it. This went on until somehow I managed to get it right.

—Then at the first screening of the film I would see what I'd done and I was always surprised to find my performance so much better than I'd expected.

Whoever Ryu had been before Ozu, he now became an Ozu character. He felt, he said later, as if he were one of his colors, one of the colors with which he was painting his picture.

—There was this 1936 film called *College Is a Nice Place* and I played a student. In one scene I had to take my new suit to the pawnshop. Then, when I received the money, just two bills, I was

to look sorry for what I'd done. I had no idea how to do it. So Ozu told me that when I got the money I should look first at one of the bills, then look at the other, and then look up.

And there it is, up there on the screen—sorrow. In the midst of a comedy we have these poignant few seconds, where the fact that the eyes have looked at the bills at all means surprise or concern or disappointment, and the fact that the actor then looks up implies knowledge, comprehension, and the fact that the two are joined to what we know of the story results in sorrow.

—There was another film, made in 1947, *The Record of a Tenement Gentleman.* I was supposed to be reading someone's palm and was drawing the lines of the hand on a piece of paper, one by one, with brush and ink. Every time I pressed the brush I bent my head forward. Ozu stepped in and stopped me.

—When I saw the film I realized why. My bent head would have ruined the unity of the composition. At the same time, the fact that I did *not* bend my head, as one would normally have done, lent the character a kind of comic charm, which is just what Ozu, must have wanted. At least that's what we got on the screen when the picture was released.

Then, in 1963, on his own birthday, Ozu died. And shortly after that, on a train returning from Osaka, I happened to meet Ryu again. He was fifty-seven at the time, about the age of the father he had played in *Tokyo Story* some ten years before. We spoke about the dead director.

—Ozu used to tell me, you know—and not just me, told everyone—that Ryu wasn't a very good actor. And that's why I use him, he would say. And it's true. I can't think of myself without thinking of him.

I wonder now if that death seemed like a betrayal. Deaths often do. There is a dreadful sense of being left behind. For who was Ryu now that Ozu was dead?

The bullet train raced on and we sat in silence

and thought about Ozu. And, though I said nothing, I wondered about Ryu's future.

But his future was assured. He later appeared in picture after picture and with director after director, and he was always good, a fine actor, and he always played the Ozu character.

I have seen monster-films in which the scientist is the Ozu character, teen-age singing star films in which the schoolteacher is the Ozu character, lurid murder-mysteries in which the inspector is the Ozu character. Always the same person, whether mad scientist or wily police officer—and always Ryu.

It was 1985 and I had just seen Juzo Itami's comedy, *The Funeral,* and there, playing the Buddhist priest, was Ryu. He mumbled the sutras gorgeously and played with his tassel and averted his eyes when the money appeared, and then extracted a present from the head of the mourning family. It was a perfect performance, one straight out of Ozu—a posthumous Ozu comedy.

Ryu was at the party afterward. He was now about eighty. He had that old man's way of blinking his eyes as though in constant surprise, that

blinking which he so brilliantly showed us when he was only in his late forties, in *Tokyo Story.*

Is it because he is eighty that he blinks like a man eighty years old, I wondered, or because he knows from experience that this is how men of eighty should blink?

And there, amid the beer and the orange juice, the strips of dried squid and the peanuts, the posters for the film and, someone having thought to bring it, the picture of Ozu—amid all this I suddenly remembered what the director had told one of his actresses who, baffled, had asked him what she was supposed to be feeling.

His answer was: You are not supposed to feel, you are supposed to do.

And I looked at Ryu, that wonderfully skilled unskillful actor. He was raising his glass. We were drinking to his health. And soon he would begin a little speech. It would be the one he always gives.

—I don't know quite how to begin. When I talk people say, there you go, off on Ozu again. And it's true, I often talk about him. But how could I talk about myself without mentioning Ozu?

From The Honorable Visitors, *1994*   *The Foreigners*

It is difficult to guess how concerned Cocteau actually was about this "massacre of pretty, waxen faces." Certainly it was sentimental in that the famous French writer was going to do absolutely nothing about it. What emotion occurred was of that easy variety which exclaims, professes, and then turns away.

But something more is involved. This empty concern,

common among thinking visitors, seems to imply that the "real," that goal of the serious traveler, has been achieved, that the attractive and doomed faces in the whorehouse contain an actuality that less persevering and attentive foreigners fail to see.

Such a belief predicates the existence of a "little people" who are somehow more real than larger people of some

importance in whichever exotic society one is visiting. This interesting predilection sits upon firm racist presumptions, and even in our relatively sophisticated times is seen the traveler who locates a devoted maid who cries when he leaves, or—even—discovers that perfectly marvelous little restaurant, much loved by the natives, but which other travelers do not know about and will not find.

Toshiro Mifune

I look again at Mifune. He is sixty-five now. Yet he remains much as he was at twenty-five. The face has changed but the person is the same.

His laugh, for example. The lips curve but the eyes remain serious. It is a polite laugh, one intended to bridge silences. It is also a social laugh, one intended to prevent misunderstandings. In addition it expresses agreement, concern, unease—all qualities other than humor.

Mifune's humor consists of belittlement—of himself. He learned early on, perhaps, that making light of himself, or seeming to, was a way of earning regard. When speaking of himself he adopts that reasoned, fair, but guarded tone that some men use when speaking of their sons. He will spread his fingers and raise his eyebrows when he mentions his career, then sigh—as though it were not his own. This is charming—something he perhaps discovered long ago.

The laugh is part of the charm: it indicates that he is not taken in by himself, that he is not vain, not proud, regards his accomplishments (whatever they are, he seems to suggest) seriously but not too seriously, and is quite willing to consider himself as just another person, someone on the same level as—well, you and me.

His manner has its uses. When a famous man, and Mifune is now world-famous, projects what is called a low profile, then the result is likability. If the actor is also a businessman, as Mifune is,

From Different People, *1987*

owning his own production company, the result is also productive—he is a man to be trusted.

Yet one should not consider this a veneer, a front, something he deliberately uses. The self we present is no less real because we choose to present it; it is something we come to embody. Mifune is an actor, but in this sense we are all actors. And the qualities he embodies—hardworking, scrupulous, trustworthy, *nesshin* (doing his very best)—are real enough.

But sometimes these fall short. Just when he is being his most reasonable and straightforward, the gaze will withdraw, the laugh will sound empty. One guesses that these distractions are personal. One feels that they are permanent.

Mifune has had his problems: his company and its ups and downs; his divorce proceedings,

messy ones; his friend—twenty-five years younger—and the child she bore him; the uproar when he took her to a 1974 state dinner attended by

. . . he remains much as he was at twenty-five. The face has changed but the person is the same.

Gerald Ford and the emperor, and the actor was accused in the press of an act of *lèse majesté*, of flaunting his mistress in the imperial presence. All this and then the break with Kurosawa.

From A Hundred Things Japanese, *1975*   *The Body*

Fundoshi.
A loincloth, a waistcloth, a breechcloth.
Whatever its presumed old-fashioned impracticality, and consequent present unpopularity, the *fundoshi* remains an article of clothing eminently suited to human needs and aspirations.

It covers the sex with decency but is not prudish; the tightly tied *rokushaku fundoshi* displays as much as it covers and well reflects traditional male pride. Further, it always gives support. Even the shorter *etchu fundoshi*—an invention of the economy-minded Japanese Army during the Meiji period (1868–1912)—is designed to support. Further, the supporting function

of the fundoshi is flexible. While relaxing or amusing himself the wearer may loosen the garment; on the other hand (and traces of this remain in the phrase *fundoshi o shimenaosu,* meaning to gird one's loins) when going into battle or other exacting action, the wearer can tighten his pouch and prepare himself. The fundoshi is thus indicative of a certain attitude, that of the whole man who rightly considers his sex a part of himself and neither hides nor flaunts it.

How different the apparent attitude of the contemporary wearers of the Western-style *buriifu* or *panti.* When new its supporting function is limited to too tight; after several washings, however, this article ceases to

give any support whatever. Its decorative function is nil and it is an encumbrance to all natural functions. The sex of these wearers must seem comparative strangers, to be met with only furtively in bathroom or in bed.

And yet this impractical foreign garment now boasts a far greater number of Japanese wearers than does the fundoshi. That traditional article is a legacy of the South Seas, of Southeast Asia, areas where men unselfconsciously think of themselves as whole and natural. Japan once had this quality. The striking lack of the fundoshi on the contemporary scene is one of several indications that this is no longer so.

Yet, since he has not changed in the last forty years, since the withdrawn eyes and the empty laugh were there when he was twenty-five, the problems—if that is what they are—must be deeper, more complicated.

Perhaps only a man as self-effacing, as thoroughly nice, as Mifune could have put up for so long with all that it takes to be an object of attention to Kurosawa. The object is, naturally, never seen for what it is, only for what it is capable of. Like any good director Kurosawa sees people in terms of how they can be useful to his project—his current film.

One of Mifune's problems is that he wants to do the right thing in a world that is plainly wrong. I know nothing about the reasons for the divorce but I think it possible he might have infuriated his wife by trying to be good, by trying to do right, by being so eternally such a nice guy.

The world does not like nice guys. Not really. They always come in last, says Western wisdom. And Eastern wisdom acts as if they do. They are charming, fun to be with, absolutely trustworthy, and so what? So says the world.

Mifune has been cheated in his business dealings, has been a victim of fraud and misrepresentation, and, finally, has been misunderstood in the most important emotional relationship he ever had—that with Kurosawa.

In Mifune Kurosawa found his ideal actor, one so open and so intelligent that he understood at once, instantly embodied the director's intentions. Kurosawa in his autobiography mentions this: If I say one thing to him, he understands ten. I decided to turn him loose.

And he may have thought he did. But it was always Kurosawa himself who was molding the performance.

Mifune has appeared in almost a hundred and twenty movies by now and yet only in the sixteen Kurosawa films is he a fine actor. It was unpleasant Kurosawa who drew from pleasant Mifune these performances—Kikuchiyo in *Seven Samurai*, Nakajima in *Record of a Living Being*, Sutekichi in *The Lower Depths*, Sanjuro in *Yojimbo* and *Sanjuro*. If we do not recognize the Mifune before us in these shadows on the screen it is because he does not either—and Kurosawa did.

Perhaps only a man as self-effacing, as thoroughly nice, as Mifune could have put up for so long with all that it takes to be an object of attention to Kurosawa. The object is, naturally, never seen for what it is, only for what it is capable of. Like any good director Kurosawa sees people in terms of how they can be useful to his project—his current film.

The break between director and actor is commonly thought to have begun with *Red Beard*. Mifune, in his own beard for over two years, was unable to take on any other work—yet unable to work on this film because Kurosawa kept delaying—in debt, worried, yet, with all of this, behaving well.

There were, however, words. And when Kurosawa, like many directors, senses defection of any kind, he will then push until an open break is achieved. In this he was successful. The last time I spoke to him about using Mifune again—now that the director was making *Ran* and Mifune was the right age for the part—Kurosawa said brusquely that he wouldn't have anything to do with actors who appeared in the likes of *Shogun*.

That Mifune more and more appears in the likes of *Shogun* is because he needs the money. Also, he needs to be working, like any actor. And he knows this feudal warrior role so well that he can do it easily. Moreover, he is a very nice man who finds it very difficult to say no.

Perhaps that is the permanent worry behind the absent gaze and the empty laugh. It is the look of a person who is doing his best to be good in a world that is not. Mifune has no drive for perfection, he has a drive for virtue.

How otherwise transparent the man is. His office has plaques on the walls, trophies. It is the room of any Japanese business executive. One expects golf clubs or racing-car pictures. His living room has lots of beaded lampshades, an onyx coffee table on gilt legs, an overstuffed chair like a throne, embossed wallpaper, diamond-patterned carpet, ludicrous crystal chandelier. It is all in the ordinary taste (or lack of it) of the newly rich in Japan, but there is nothing in it of Mifune.

He is not concerned with office and house. Someone else designed, chose, bought for him. He is interested only in how well he does, how true he is, how understanding he can be.

The devotion to virtue is a terrible thing. It also accounts for Mifune's being no different from what he once was. Being good is the ambition of a certain kind of child—the child who graduated from being bad but who never went on to being both, the usual definition of maturity.

His distracted gaze, his laugh, his concern that the conversation continue on its meaningless way, his acquiescence, his understanding, distant but there. Being all good seems to be as difficult as being all bad.

Being all anything is hard. As I look at him and again he laughs, briefly, looking down at the table, I seem to hear his parents saying what a good boy Toshi-bo is. And I can see Kurosawa, that bad parent, turning away from this good son who loved him.

Then Mifune suddenly smiles. Not laughs. Smiles. The smile is something else. His face lights up, his gaze returns. He looks at you as though he sees you and is amused—by you, by himself, by life. The smile is many things—it is also a sign that for a short time Mifune has forgotten about Mifune.

From Partial Views, *"Notes for a Study on Shohei Imamura,"* 1983

The Japanese

One of the first inferences to make is that there are actually two Japans. One is the "official" version, the often beautiful world of the Noh and the tea ceremony, the subservient kimono-clad woman, the feudality of exquisitely graded degrees of social standing, and such approved virtues as fidelity, loyalty, devotion—in short anything which the outside world knows of Japan. This is the "official" version because it is also the exported version and it is this world which is shown the visitor. At the same time, however, it is truly "official" in that it is approved by society. This is the way that Japanese society likes to see itself, whether or not it actually happens to be like this.

The other Japan might, judging from Imamura's films, be called the "real" version. His people, it has been often noted, do not behave like "Japanese" because none of the rules of order and decorum insisted upon by the official version apply. These people, always from the so-called lower classes, do not know the meaning of fidelity or loyalty. They are completely natural and are to that extent "uncivilized" if civilization means (as it does) a removal from the natural. They are selfish, lusty, amoral, innocent, natural and all of the vitality of Japan comes from their numbers.

Shozo Kuroda

Old Mr. Kuroda—Shozo his nicely old-fashioned given name, a neighbor—blinks. Old men blink like babies, as though not yet used to their eyes. His eyes widen, contract, then blink, each sight as though astonishing. He stares at me, stunned.

I stare back. Old people are faintly disreputable. We may feel sorry for them but at the same time we condemn, as if being this old, lasting this long, were somehow a social fault, a breach of etiquette.

His daughter sighs and wipes his chin, as she would that of a small child. And what is it now? she asks, turning, hearing his yammering: Oh, I see. That's nice. Then she looks away. She is speaking to him as he must have spoken to her when she was very young.

Later, while he is lying down, taking his childlike afternoon nap, she says that he has no *darashi*. Strong words: *darashi ga nai*. I know perfectly well what it means, but am not sure what it specifies.

Let me look it up in the dictionary. There. Slovenly, untidy, sloppy, disheveled, unkempt, slipshod, etc.—a list of attributes ending with, oddly: a loose fish. What could that be? One always learns something about one's own language from the Japanese-English dictionary.

And we have no comparable phrase in the West, where sloppiness is considered less of a sin and can even be seen as attractive, a sign, in young people, of naturalness, spontaneity, freedom from conservative restraint.

From **Different People**, *1987*

No virtue here, however, even—or particularly—among the young. No, certainly *not* attractive, here where everyone must pull his own weight, where nothing too different is tolerated for too long, where appearances are so much more important than truths.

Strong words, but she smiled as she said them, as one might when speaking of a child, someone you understand, forgive, love. And—she continued—he wet his bed the other night again. Talk about *darashi ga nai koto.* And who had to get up and change the bedding so that he wouldn't be lying in it the whole night long? Another sigh—a fat forty, hopes blasted.

A situation reminiscent of an Ozu film—*Late Spring,* perhaps. But there the daughter still has her life before her. And there he is still a fine figure of a man. Ozu, being an artist, knew where to stop. No point in showing Setsuko

Hara blowsy; no point in revealing Chishu Ryu drooling and incontinent. We already know. We sense the years ahead. Ozu need show us nothing more.

With Shozo, however, the disaster has already occurred. He has become disreputable, the way that accident victims appear. I remember an ex-landlady idly turning over the pages of a photography book and discovering a picture of survivors from the *Hindenburg,* dazed, clothes burned away. How horrid, she said, then, peering more closely: And what a way to appear in public!

A snort, a gurgle from the next room. Miss Kuroda knows all these signs as though they were a language. Oh, dear, she says: He's woken up. And here I was hoping he would sleep for an hour.

A shuffling sound. Then he reappears, kimono disheveled, sash dragging. A loose fish. Is

---

From A Lateral View, "Gesture as Language," 1980

The Japanese

Japanese gestures are thus rich in opportunities for mistake. There is the famous example of the Japanese smile. The West had long been taught that the smile means pleasure, amusement or happiness. It is consequently there used accordingly.

But, as Lafcadio Hearn long ago observed, the Japanese smile is not only such spontaneous expression. It is also a form of etiquette and the Japanese child is still taught, usually through example, to smile as a social duty. Other countries, of course, also know of this usage, but there it is externalized and called the social-smile. In Japan the utility of the smile has been

internalized. It has become, at least, a semi-conscious gesture and is to be observed even when the smiling person thinks he is unobserved. He races for the subway door, let us say. It closes in his face. His reaction to this disappointment is almost invariably a smile.

This smile does not mean happiness. No one is happy to have missed a subway. It does, however, mean cheerful acceptance. From an early age, the Japanese is taught to express no emotion, which might disturb a sometimes precarious social harmony. Though scowls or even temper tantrums in the subway would not, in fact, upset

society's equilibrium, this beautiful smile blooming in the teeth of disappointment does indicate that many taught gestures can become pseudo-involuntary, if social pressure is strong enough.

In Japan, indeed, this special gestural use of the smile can be extreme. Smiles at the death of a loved one are still to be witnessed. The message, properly read, is not that the dead are not mourned. Rather, the smiler is implying that bereft though I be, larger social concerns are more important and I am determined not to cause bother by making an emotional display upon this sad occasion.

surprised to see me. Blinks. Thinks I come every day. Is told it is the same day. Oh.

—Not long for this world. (This she says in front of him, and his trembling makes it seem that he is nodding in shocked agreement. Actually, he appears not to hear.)

I look at him and think of the brave days of Meiji when he was probably a fine figure of a man.

—Now, Father, do sit down. Don't just stand there. You'll tire yourself. See? Mr. Donald has brought us these nice pears. I'll peel you one.

Mono no aware, the pathos of things. You accept it, you even in a small way celebrate it, this evanescence. You are to observe what is happening, and be content that things are proceeding as they must, and therefore should. Very traditional this, and quite a nice idea.

She sets to work, her strong, manly fingers expert, the peel unwinding in one long strip. He waits, the corners of his mouth moist.

Of what does he remind me? A baby watching candy being unwrapped? A dog watching its dinner being made? Me, under the Christmas tree, watching tissue paper being removed—or me at a later age watching clothes being taken off?

—There now, isn't that nice?

Prettily quartered, the pear is set before him. His hand hesitates, then conveys a chunk to his mouth. His eyes close. He seems to smile.

—Juicy, she says, wiping his lips with her handkerchief. Then she straightens his kimono, reties his sash, makes him presentable.

He blinks, gums the fruit, smiles at me. Thanking me—with his mouth, not his eyes. They are far away, looking at things long past, the blank eyes of someone who has seen everything and still continues to look.

The view is suitably autumnal, with a bright blue sky, the red of the ripe persimmon, and the light yellow of bleached grass. The pears are the very last of the season. And I remember the view half a year ago, the pale sky of summer and the deep green of the grass.

She had sat there, on the same cushion. We had been gossiping about a younger woman in the neighborhood who had lost her patron—apoplexy. She laughed lightly, then suddenly frowned.

—And what will happen to me once he goes? she wondered.

I misunderstood, thinking she might be referring to too little money, too much freedom. But this wasn't what she meant.

—What shall I do? *Nani o shimashoka?* (Precisely—and she could as well have asked: Who shall I be?)

Old Mr. Kuroda slowly swallows, staring at 1900. His daughter looks at her hands, spreads her fat fingers. And I gaze at them both, caught for an instant in the sunshine of a late autumn.

Mono no aware, the pathos of things. You accept it, you even in a small way celebrate it, this evanescence. You are to observe what is happening, and be content that things are proceeding as they must, and therefore should. Very traditional this, and quite a nice idea. I wonder if it was ever anything more.

Old Shozo Kuroda looks into the sun, his eyes blinking, his lips still working, his mouth curved as though in a smile. There is no simple cut to "The End," no surge of music to indicate a final cadence. Life, not being art, knows no such conventions.

Hisako Shiraishi

Round face, neat gray bun, hands clutching purse, she looked like any ordinary old woman. And her sighs, her wan smiles, her complaints, these too were those of an ordinary old woman left to herself.

I had noticed her at the vegetable shop, staring at the cabbages, pinching the strawberries, and remarking on the prices. I saw her too at the local variety store—which advertised itself in English, perhaps misunderstanding the term, as the Chic Commode. She was asking for a discount on washing powder because she bought so much.

—I keep a clean house, I heard her say, as though she were being accused of not doing so. And I remember thinking that here was an old lady who did not have anything to keep her occupied. Little did I realize that I was to become that occupation.

She was a neighbor, with rooms directly beneath mine in the twelve-story apartment house (it called itself a "mansion") where we both lived. It was from other neighbors, those on either side, that I learned more about her.

Children, one or two of them, but neglectful they were. This from the piano teacher on my left. Not that she blamed them. Also a husband, long since dead. Probably from having to live with her. This with a snicker from the retired postal worker on my right—at which his wife pinched him and looked disapproving.

Hisako Shiraishi, her name on door and postbox, was not popular. She didn't mean any harm, I was told, but she was a

From Different People, *1987*

complainer and she tried to take advantage. Apparently she brought "disharmony" into the meetings of the Shuwa Mansion Residents' Association.

—She's always complaining, said the retired postal worker, encountered in the elevator, away from his wife: We just hate to see her at the meetings. The trouble is she's got nothing else to do.

And I remember thinking that here was an old lady who did not have anything to keep her occupied.

So it was that I, quite innocently, volunteered. I began to say good morning to Mrs. Shiraishi. This startled her and she aimed a suspicious eye at me before returning my greetings in a guarded manner. Determined to be pleasant I smiled whenever we met, and held open the lobby door. She would scurry past, then turn to stare accusingly from the safety of the elevator.

Seeing unfriendliness, I ought to have retreated. Instead, I responded as though it were some sort of challenge. I will be nice, I will, I told myself. Whether I was actually concerned about bringing a ray of sunshine into the old woman's life is doubtful. I suppose I simply believed that everyone ought to get along with everybody else. Otherwise I can't explain my presenting myself at her door with a ripe watermelon.

The door opened a crack. A dark eye looked out.

—What do you want? she asked suspiciously.

—I happen to have this watermelon, I said: And I thought you might like it.

—Why? she asked—an instant response, like the snap of a trap.

—Well . . . it's the first of the season, I said, unable to think of another reason.

The door opened a bit wider. She stood there, staring at me. Then: I hope you don't think that this makes up for it.

—Makes up for what?

—It's been terrible, she said, her voice a whine: When you shake out your rugs from your balcony, all that dirt comes right in my windows.

I, feeling absurdly guilty, apologized, promised to take care, and was backing away when a small, strong hand reached out, captured the watermelon, drew it in, and slammed the door. I stood there with that awful prescient feeling that I had done something irremediable.

Sometime afterward I left the city for a week or so, and when I returned—was just through the door—there was a telephone call from her.

—I'm calling to complain. I couldn't get a wink of sleep last week because of the noise you were making. Every night, on and on. I don't know what to do. I must have my sleep, I'm an old lady. It's too cruel.

I said I would come down. She was waiting just behind the door, and pushed it open as soon as I rang. This time she invited me in, as far at least as the entryway. I looked into her neat kitchen and she, seeing this, at once slid shut the sliding door. Then she told me at length what a horrible week she had had.

I guessed what had happened. I had given my friend Fumio the key and told him to use the place if he wanted. He had had friends in. Youngsters all, they had probably made a fair amount of noise. So I apologized to her, bowed, said that it would certainly not happen again, backed out, and decided to talk to Fumio about this.

Yes, they had had a party, until midnight maybe, and one of the girls *was* rather heavy, and, yes, they had danced a bit. But only once, only that Saturday night, certainly not *every* night. What he said, I knew, was true. I also realized that I was beginning to discern the outlines of the vast problem Mrs. Shiraishi would become.

Not for a time, however. Yet even then I noticed that I was actually trying to be quiet in my own apartment. I was trying to walk more lightly, was closing doors more quietly. This I thoroughly resented. It was as though the neurasthenic old woman had come to live with me, as though she were there, in the closet, peering out with dark and beady eye.

Then, quite late one night, a telephone call: I wonder if I could ask you to make a little less noise. It's late. People are trying to sleep—me, for instance. I've not had a wink in the past few days because of all the noise. I need my sleep. I'm an old lady. Do try, please, to walk less heavily. And could you flush your toilet less often? It makes such a noise and it always startles me.

I said I would and the next day went to see my neighbors. How did that old woman get my telephone number, I wondered. Oh, that was easy enough. The Shuwa Mansion Residents' Association would have given it to her. The real problem, continued the retired postal worker, was that she was terrible when she had a grudge. I ought to be careful—just put up with it.

When I told the piano teacher, she expressed a token interest but suggested that, since we did after all have to live here together, perhaps I should be a bit quieter. I stared at her—a woman whose pupils' *Für Elise* I had been enduring daily for some time.

After that there was quiet for a while until one evening a knock came on the door and outside stood a uniformed policeman. He inquired as to my identity and then told me that my downstairs neighbor had lodged a complaint about the racket I was making, had demanded assistance, which was why he was here and just what had I been doing?

I invited him in, showed him my quiet apartment, and told him the history of my relations with Mrs. Shiraishi. He did not seem surprised, merely nodded and said that he would remember this next time she called—if he was on duty, that is. If he wasn't, I might have to explain it to

---

From The Inland Sea, 1971　　*The Foreigners*

And I realized that my quest was over—at least part of it. Sitting in the sunny Hiroshima station, a freshly bought paperback *Persuasion* in my pocket, I understood what I had guessed earlier: that the voyage had not been to find them, but to find myself, and that—to an extent—I now had.

In the train, looking at the flat, bright coast, traveling to the ferry station, I suddenly, and for no apparent reason, thought of Lafcadio Hearn dying and penning a few last bitter pages.

The book was called *Japan: An Interpretation*, but he, like all of us who come to this land—attractive, mysterious, and impenetrable as a mirror—was writing about himself; the tender, myopic, beauty-loving Lafcadio was being, finally, interpreted.

I mingled with the others who left the train, waited for the gates of the ferry to open. This disillusioned end I would be spared, I thought, I hoped. I would never find them, the real Japanese, because they were always around me, and they were always real, but I might at last decide what my own real self was, and hence create it.

But it was too nice a day just to sit and ponder. So, for the first time in my life, I was able to achieve the feat I had so long admired in the Japanese: I shook my head and put aside perplexing thoughts. Then I turned with a smile to the waiting, open day, and—along with all the others—boarded the boat.

a good many patrolmen before they all understood.

—But this is unfair. I'm doing nothing and she calls the police.

—I know, he said, a young cop, a bit uncomfortable but smiling: Still, Japan's a small country. We all have to get on peacefully together somehow.

When he had left I went downstairs, bearing no gifts this time. The door opened a crack. Inside the eye lurked.

—What do you want? asked that hated, whining voice.

—I want to know why you called the police when I wasn't making any noise.

—You were. You were dancing.

—I was alone.

—I heard dancing.

—I was not dancing.

—That's what you say. But someone was. I heard it. I must have my sleep. I've had no sleep for nights. I'm an old lady. I need my sleep.

—Mrs. Shiraishi! I am going to bring this up at a meeting of the Shuwa Mansion Residents' Association.

—I already have. The meeting was yesterday.

In the morning I went to my neighbors. Neither of them had gone to the meeting, but even if a complaint had been lodged, the husband told me, no one would take it seriously.

—The police do. A cop actually came to my door.

—He was only doing his duty, he explained: Come on, now, this happens to all of us occasionally. We all have to live together peacefully. Japan's a small country. You've just got to learn to put up with it.

—But I'm not guilty, I said, upset, using somewhat dramatic language.

At this point his wife came and pulled him away. Though she whispered, I heard quite plainly what she said: Now you stop—we don't want to get involved.

A short period of peaceful coexistence followed. Then one night, very late, there was a great pounding at my door. I was asleep but I knew who it was. Rushing to the door, barefoot, in shorts, I caught the scurrying Mrs. Shiraishi before she reached the stairs.

—Look, I said, holding on to her, speaking softly, carefully, as though to an upset child, or an excited animal: Look, just come and see for yourself. There is no one here. I am alone. I was asleep. No one was making any noise.

She allowed me to pull her to the door. I turned on the light. She seemed to be searching for signs of a party, but I also saw that curiously greedy look which solitary people have when peering into others' homes.

—They're all on the balcony.

I turned and stared, realizing that she did not believe what she was saying. She merely did not want to be in the wrong.

—Then come over here, I said, crossing the room and opening the balcony door.

She peered into the dark.

—They climbed down.

—Mrs. Shiraishi. This is the eighth floor. There's no way to climb down. You've been hearing things.

—I know what I heard, she said—a round ball of a woman with eyes like knives.

—Look, I replied, seeking to understand what was making her behave in this fashion: This apartment is old. Sometimes I too hear things. They seem to come from just above. But they don't. They're coming from some other apartment. So maybe someone really is having a party and it sounds as if it might be here, but it's not. It's somewhere else.

I was hoping not only to give her some kind of reason for having mistakenly bothered me, but even perhaps to send her out to pound on other doors.

But she stood there in her nightwear, small, compact, her gray hair a helmet: I heard what I heard, she recited, and I know what I know.

In the morning I woke up the head of the Shuwa Mansion Residents' Association and told him what had happened. Clutching his robe about him, shifting on his bare feet, he said: Oh, Mrs. Shiraishi. We know about her.

—Well, if you know about her then can't you stop her banging at doors and waking up members of your association?

It was not until this was said that I realized I had done the same to him, woken him out of a sound sleep to complain. He seemed unaware of this, however:

—The fact is that when we've got a country as crowded as this, one has to learn to get along. Now, I know that Mrs. Shiraishi can be a nuisance. But, even so, the woman has had a pretty hard life. Though it isn't generally known, actually, her husband killed himself.

—I'm not at all surprised.

The head of the residents' association looked at me sadly, as though my attitude was one of the things the matter with this otherwise peaceable world.

—Look, I said, deepening this impression: I can call the police too, you know.

He shook his head: Oh, we wouldn't really want that.

—Well, I didn't really want that old woman banging on my door in the middle of the night either, you know.

Back in my apartment I slammed the door and let my own suspicions have their way. Oh, I knew why this was happening to me. I certainly wouldn't be treated like this if I wasn't foreign. It was because I was a foreigner that this crazy old woman had unleashed her paranoia on me. And it was because I was a foreigner that I was being fobbed off with talk of how tiny Japan was and how we all ought to be living cheerfully together. And this from the man who by rights ought to have been protecting me.

I told the piano teacher as much. She nod-

ded in a sympathetic way, then remarked: But it's true, what he said. Don't you think you could put up with it, a little thing like this?

—A little thing! I cried: That crazy woman pounding on my door in the middle of the night! Is that a little thing?

It's late. People are trying to sleep—me, for instance. I've not had a wink in the past few days because of all the noise. I need my sleep. I'm an old lady. Do try, please, to walk less heavily. And could you flush your toilet less often?

—But if she thinks you are making all that noise . . . not, of course, that you actually are.

—Look. You live next to me. Have you ever heard any of my wild all night parties?

—No, I haven't. But you must remember that these apartments have very thin walls and so one can hear a lot. Perhaps it's just the usual everyday noises that she's complaining about.

—Perhaps you're right, I said, now confirmed in my own paranoia: Because I can certainly hear all *yours*!

After that I talked to the retired postal worker:

—And the head of the residents' association will do nothing at all about her. Nothing. She's a menace!

—I know, he said, looking very unhappy: But we're all in the same boat. We've all got to make the best of it.

—Oh? Well, why then do *I* have to make the best of it and *she* doesn't—if indeed I am making all that racket every night?

I knew why, all right: it was because I was foreign and she wasn't; because I was an interloper and she wasn't. This I did not say, perhaps only because I had no opportunity—for at that moment his wife called out (*Anata!*) and with a show of helplessness he closed the door.

I stormed back to my room, and heard the telephone ring. It was, of course, Mrs. Shiraishi. This time, however, she was not complaining. She said, surprisingly: *Naka yoshi ni narimasho*—Let's be friends.

—The fact is that when we've got a country as crowded as this, one has to learn to get along.

At once I was at her door, anxious indeed to be friends. She stood there, small, round, neat, and invited me into the kitchen. I stared about me, eager to see what kind of lair the monster had.

And there I was introduced to her daughter, a person about my own age, with rimless glasses, cold as ice, staring at me with open belligerence.

—I asked her to come all the way down from Gumma, I was in such a state, no sleep, every night those horrible noises, and she said that if we became friends maybe you would somehow be more quiet and I could get at least a little sleep. Here.

And she put a small glass of plum brandy into my hand.

—All right, Mrs. Shiraishi, I promise not to make any noise and you must promise not to telephone me or call the police or come banging at my door.

—But the noise, the noise.

—Look, Mrs. Shiraishi. There is no noise. It's in your head. You think you hear it.

I turned to her daughter for some kind of understanding. Surely she must know how crazy the old woman was—she was her own child. I met with none, however, merely a cold and rimless stare.

—Oh, I saw Mrs. Watanabe on the street, cried Mrs. Shiraishi: And she said you're getting neurotic, Mrs. Shiraishi, and I said to her yes I certainly was, and why not, me without a wink for weeks because of all the noise going on every night. So as a last resort Mariko here said we should try to become friends.

Despite my earlier eagerness, I did not in fact want to become friends with her or her rimless daughter. I wanted never to see either of them again. And yet I wanted to stop tiptoeing about my own apartment and wincing when I flushed the toilet. I wanted to take back from this old witch the power that I had given her.

Did she herself believe any of this business? I still wonder about that. Perhaps it isn't even a relevant question. She had merely found something, finally, to which to devote her life: me and my noisy ways. Her paranoia had found a perfect object.

And so, I now see, had mine. Mad Mrs. Shiraishi, her chilly child, the piano teacher, the postal worker and his spouse, the head of our ineffectual little organization, even the cop on the beat—all were united in this great plot against me, whose only sin, after all, was that of being a foreigner. This would not have happened to me, was my belief, if I had been Japanese.

As indeed, I realize now, it wouldn't have. For then I would have behaved quite differently. For one thing I would have taken no watermelons to crazed and dangerous neighbors, and even had I done so, I imagine I would then have moved skillfully through the association and among the neighbors until enough social pressure had accumulated to crush the old hag.

As it was, I finally did the thing that Japanese do when they fail. I gave up. When the phone calls began again with tearful pleas for me not to flush my toilet with quite such vehemence, when a new cop appeared and had to be informed, when the postal worker was out whenever I asked, then I did what any ordinary citizen would have done. I moved.

My apartment had become as though haunted. I was creeping silently about in it, sliding doors open and shut ever so carefully, and actually refraining from pulling the chain except when absolutely necessary.

The place is probably haunted still. Whoever was unfortunate enough to move into it probably received visitations from the same old body with her hair in a bun. And if they are fully and successfully Japanese they are probably putting up with it.

For that is the true difference. The problem is not simply whether one is foreign or not, but rather whether one can grin and bear it—whatever "it" is. This is what counts. That foreigners notoriously cannot do so makes the matter seem more fraught with prejudice than it perhaps is.

Now moved elsewhere, with nice quiet neighbors in the apartment below, I sometimes think of Mrs. Shiraishi. Old, alone, with only that cold child to call her own and relations not too good there either, shunted off into an apartment, forgotten—is she not symptomatic, in her way, of these times, of this society?

Well, maybe, but I am not interested in that. Mrs. Shiraishi remains for me a real person, not some representative of her people. A real person who in several and highly uncomfortable ways resembles me. We both cause disharmony. Perhaps that is the real reason why I could not put up with her, why I could not somehow manage to live peacefully with my neighbor in this small country.

From The Temples of Kyoto, 1995   *The Body*

There are many portraits at Ninna-ji. One looks at those faces as they gaze back from scroll and screen: plump, bottom-heavy faces with mild melonseed eyes and sometimes the decorative topiary of a mustache or a beard.

The outline is known. It is the Heian beau-ideal, the heavy face which reflects good eating, supported below by a girth found attractive in a culture where weight meant wealth.

But this emperor, that bishop, this shogun—did these men look like this? As in China, portraiture in Japan was so late in developing that even now the formula face is the preferred. And back then portraits were lay figures with labels attached.

There was an official beauty for the male from Heian times on. It was agreed upon and the sum of its details meant respectability. What we might find virile, and even physically beautiful, to them repelled. Sei Shonagan watched with disgust ordinary carpenters eating and the Lady Murasaki turned with aversion from the bodies of naked grooms surprised by a palace fire—unforgettably horrible, without the slightest charm, she found the nude body.

For women, however, the beau-ideal was not so carefully composed. Indeed, it was created through subtraction: what she should not have. Her eyebrows were shaved and replaced higher on a surprised forehead, her teeth were blackened, the mouth a dark hole denoting beauty. From the earliest days she was composed—a blank surface upon which men painted.

Furthermore, the creature was invisible: living in shadows bundled into twelve concealing layers, her essence so negative that the nocturnal lover was often not entirely certain that he had the right person.

Hanako Watanabe

Down the subway stairs hurried the tofu man's wife, her face serious, intent. She had perhaps heard the downtown train pull in—bells, shouts, whistles—and was hurrying to make it.

In this station, mine for many years now, there is a long flight of stairs leading to the lower level where the downtown train passes. I, coming from uptown on my way home, had just got out of the car and was walking along the platform when I saw Mrs. Watanabe hurrying down.

Seeing the train about to draw out, she broke into a run. But the doors were closing, the whistle was blown, the train began to move.

Mrs. Watanabe stopped short in front of the closed doors now sliding past and smiled. At a moment when we of the West would have turned our mouths down, she turned hers up. It was not an ironic grimace, common enough, nor was it mock despair for the benefit of those looking on. The smile was innocent and natural enough to seem instinctive.

But what kind of instinct could create this expression of delight, I wondered. And what assumptions must lie behind it? This was not the first such smile I had seen. I saw it daily, on the faces of those apparently pleased to have missed the train. The tofu man's wife was simply the latest in a long line of disappointed grinners.

For surely, I thought, disappointment must be the paramount emotion attending this experience. To then smile was, by my standards, unnatural. What person in his or her proper senses would register pleasure at the prospect of inconvenience?

From Different People, 1987

Well, I reasoned, standing there, pretending to read a poster, it would have to be someone who entertained priorities higher than personal convenience, higher than missing a subway train.

I tried to fit things together. The smile that informed the face of the racing Mrs. Watanabe, and all those other hundreds and thousands I had observed over the years, began to develop only when it seemed obvious that the train would not, after all, be caught. This expression was not then the result of any hope that one might, after all, be on time.

Indeed, as I had seen often enough, if there was time and no uncertainty, the expression was the ordinary, blank subway face, the same the world over. Only when hope was slipping away did the smile blossom.

Confronted with the closed subway doors, the train already in motion, the smile was wide and forbearing, with only a trace of self-consciousness or embarrassment. It was as if the small fact of having missed the subway was already subsumed into the many other uncertainties of life.

Moreover, if Mrs. Watanabe had said anything at that point (I was still pretending to examine the poster and she had not yet seen me), it would

probably have been: *Shikata ga nai*—It can't be helped. This comment is heard at least a million times a day on these islands. It is to Japan as "Have a nice day" is to America—something one says without thinking, says even when *shikata ga aru,* when it *can* be helped.

Yet here perhaps, I decided next, lay a clue to these higher priorities. For behind it was the idea (common enough here but revolutionary-sounding where I come from) that acceptance ranks over irritation, that accord is more important than discord, that the positive is more valuable than the negative.

This is to American ears an astonishing assumption. And its reverberations linger on, suggesting thoughts unwelcome: that the communal is more important than the individual, for example. Nevertheless, it is just such notions surely that produced the smile at the foot of the subway stairs.

Still standing there, I tried to imagine the system of social training that was responsible for this phenomenon: whole centuries of it during which all the Mrs. Watanabes and their husbands and children were taught that a display of personal irritation or indignation was not,

From Where Are the Victors?, 1956   *The Foreigners*

There she was, standing next to the tall student who was going to marry her. Michael stared at them both. Another culture, another race—they might have come from the other side of the moon. Yet Haruko was all |he had ever wanted, and the student beside her was an alien—strange, a bit forbidding, always incomprehensible. He wondered how he could think of them each so differently. Or was it that Haruko was just as alien, just as strange, just as fantastically different from him? And was it then that Haruko and others like her would always prefer other Japanese? And that Michael and others like him would always have—what?—others like Gloria?

Michael looked at the floor and then at his own white hands.

For the first time he realized that he never would be able to understand what he loved, and that that might well be the reason he loved it so. His earlier disillusion fell from him. Again he loved Haruko, and he loved her because he would never understand her, nor the student by whom she stood, nor the fatuous Mr. Ohara, nor those other Japanese near them.

by and large, socially productive. Rather, as a member of the social body, one ought to uphold its standards. The personal (by definition, often negative) reaction should be subdued, so that the coherent whole could continue in an atmosphere of harmony.

And I also thought how easy to control these generations consequently were, and are. With a populace who believed this, the process of ruling was considerably simplified. Brainwashing, oppression, totalitarianism—these terms occurred to me, a person really interested only in his *own* atmosphere of harmony, one devoid of any larger social implications.

But I felt sure there were larger implications. It was certainly true that this kind of self-abnegation in the face of personal disappointment can be politically manipulated; it can also result in quite mindless acceptance of a social norm. But there was something else, something of deeper value.

So I turned again to look at Mrs. Watanabe. Though she had long ceased smiling and was staring off into space with that universal subway face, I remembered the form her smile had taken. Yes, it certainly suggested forbearance . . . but also—for want of any better words—a kind of affirmation.

The poster I'd been staring at reminded one not to leave one's umbrella on the subway. This was a pragmatic race, intensely so. It was one that believed in the "rightness" of things, and rejoiced in it. It saw that reality, neither malign nor benign, is all we have; that what *is* exists quite outside the limitations of our personal convenience; and this should be accepted, made much of.

The more I thought about it the more familiar the idea became. I considered the attitude of the haiku master; the attitude of my favorite film director, Ozu. I thought of what the *suiboku* brush-and-ink master puts in and leaves out, and how the true Zen *roshi* approaches the real and instant now. In all these examples that now came

flooding to my mind a personal predilection is sacrificed (too strong a term?) in the interests of something else. And that is the appreciation of reality. Not a higher one, merely reality itself; a small celebration of its qualities. It is the attitude of the older Japanese who looks in the mirror, sees one more gray hair, one more wrinkle, and is pleased because things are going as they must. And things going this way are fitting, proper—in a word, good.

I glanced at Mrs. Watanabe waiting for her train. Would she, I wondered—she of the beautiful, indulgent smile—also grin at her wrinkles and gray hairs, affirming the impermanence of life? It seemed unlikely as she stood there rocking slightly in her neat housedress, staring ahead. Yet it didn't seem impossible, for I remembered her expression, common but mysterious, when she realized she would miss her train. I knew that what her smile represented had contributed to and been exploited by centuries of feudal rule; at the same time, I saw in it a token of another scale of values, an affirmation that went far beyond the ordinary concern with positive and negative.

At which point Mrs. Watanabe first noticed my own universal subway face and gave me a friendly smile: *Ara,* is that you, Mr. Donald? Going downtown?

—No, I just got off.

—That was ten minutes ago—just missed it myself. What have you been doing?

—Oh . . . nothing much, just standing around.

—At your age, she said with a smile: Me, I'm off to my sister's for the afternoon. Husband's looking after the shop. And about time, too.

She went on in this fashion until the subway train arrived and she got in. Then I climbed the stairs, still thinking. Whatever its historical associations, I couldn't but approve of that smile of Mrs. Watanabe's, find it admirable in its implications, and envy her its unthinking, assured possession.

JAPAN
Fiction

A View from the Chuo Line

There was this part on the Chuo Line when you're coming from Shinjuku and just before you get to Ochanomizu Station where just as the train makes this jog, if you're sitting the first car on the right hand side facing front, all the scenery seems to come together—the trees on both sides slide in and those new buildings slide out and it is suddenly like a forest and the train track is like a streetcar's and everything gets small and natural and it looks just like it must have looked a hundred years ago.

Minoru took a big breath. That had been a long sentence. Then, since Katsuhiro didn't answer, he added: Like an old photograph.

His friend, Walkman whispering in his lap, finally asked: Well, how long does it last?

—Oh, it's over by the time you notice it.

—Well, I never heard about it, said Katsuhiro, fingering the earphones.

Never saw anything on TV about it.

—I don't think anyone ever noticed it before, said Minoru.

—You mean it's not famous?

—Well, we could talk about it and make it famous, said Minoru, smiling, then looked down at the Walkman.

Katsuhiro was silent for a time, then said: But we're going in the wrong direction.

—Yes, but being on the Chuo Line made me think of it.

He looked of the window—Yotsuya Station.

—Could you photograph it? asked Katsuhiro.

From A View from the Chuo Line and Other Stories, *1990–95*

—Maybe, but then it would just look like a lot of trees around Ochanomizu.

—What's so special then?

—It's the effect, said Minoru. The way everything moves in and for just one second it's as though it's a hundred years ago.

—One second? Just one second?

—Or two, maybe.

—Well, I don't think anything that short is going to command a lot of attention, said Minoru's friend, picking up the earphones.

—Well, it doesn't. That's why no one has noticed it.

Katsuhiro looked at him as though he already had the earphones on and then said: You ought to notice more practical things if you're going to notice things. Something you could take a picture of.

Then, getting interested: Or, better yet, a movie. We could get it on TV maybe. We'd get the tape recorder going and just when it moves in like you say we could freeze-frame it.

Minoru looked out of the window—Shinanomachi Station—then said: I think you have to see it for yourself.

—But why? asked Katsuhiro, now interested. If you can see it you can photograph it. Right? That's what the Fuji Film ad says. And it's true. Our eyes are only lenses, you know. We're just like cameras that way. So we would make this tape and then show it to Dentsu or somebody. If it's so interesting as all that maybe we could even sell it.

Minoru looked out of the window at the distant towers of Shinjuku. Then, since he didn't answer, his friend finally said: Well, you brought it up. Then he carefully put the Walkman earphones into his ears. The whispering almost stopped.

Minoru looked at his friend nodding his head, moving his lips to unheard music. Then he said: I got this deaf friend and he was always bashful about wearing his hearing aid because people always used to look at him in the trains, but now since everyone is wearing what looks like hearing aids no one pays any attention to him anymore.

As the train raced into Shinjuku Station he continued gazing at the nodding, unhearing profile of his friend.

The Gods

From A Lateral View, *"Japan: A Description,"* 1984

Universal principles make up nature, but nature does not reveal these principles, in Japan, until one has observed nature by shaping it oneself. The garden is not natural until everything in it has been shifted. And flowers are not natural either until so arranged to be. God, man, earth—these are the traditional strata in the flower arrangement, but it is man that is operative, acting as the medium through which earth and heaven meet.

And the arrangement is not only in the branches, the leaves, the flowers. It is also in the spaces in between. Negative space is calculated, too—in the architecture, in the gardens, in the etiquette, in the language itself. The Japanese observes the spaces in between the branches, the pillars; he knows too when to leave out pronouns and when to be silent. Negative space has its own weight, and it is through knowing both negative and positive (yin and yang), the specific gravity of each, that one may understand the completed whole, that seamless garment that is life. There are, one sees, no opposites. The ancient Greek Heraclitus knew this, but we in the Western world forgot and are only now remembering. Asia never forgot; Japan always remembered.

Commuting

Akira caught the eight-fifteen express every morning for the half-hour's commute into the city. This left him fifteen minutes to go from the station to his office, buy a pack of cigarettes, and be at his desk at nine when his section head walked in.

Catching the eight-fifteen, however, meant travelling when the train was most full. He rarely got a seat and so stood for the thirty minutes, looking out of the window since it was too crowded for him to read the morning paper.

Having nothing else to do he looked at the familiar suburbs or at the other passengers as they too, pressed together, stared past each other. One at whom he particularly looked was a young woman who got on at his station every morning, always the same place on the platform, and tried to stand at the end of the seats next to the door so that she would be protected from the crush of bodies.

One day he was pushed against her and there was no moving away. They were face to face and she looked past him, he past her. This was common etiquette in crowded commuter trains. People ignored each other.

But though he looked over the crowded heads as though into the distance, he could not ignore her. He had seen her for some time now, had admired her appearance, and now he was pressed against her, so closely that he could smell the light scent she used and, under it, her perspiration in the closed car.

Face to face they stood, pressed by the people around them. He felt her breasts against his chest, and her thighs against his.

From A View from the Chuo Line and Other Stories, *1990–95*

When the train rounded a curve they swayed as though they were dancing. He raised his head and read the advertisements overheard. She stood and, he thought, endured him.

When the terminal was reached and the crowd shifted, she turned and disappeared without a glance, just as if she were not bearing, for a time, his imprint. Just as though he were not carrying her scent all the way up to his office.

That evening, going back on the seven-thirty express, sitting in the half empty car, reading his evening paper, he thought of her, closed his eyes, breathed deeply. But the scent was gone.

* * *

The next morning Akira looked for her and there she was, standing where she always stood. When the crowded train slid to a stop, she waited until the others had forced their way on and then tried to slip into her place at the end of the seats. Knowing that this was what she would do, he

turned, deflected two men trying to push their way on, and let her slip under his arm into her place. Then he moved in and took his, pressed against her.

The scent was the same as the day before, today even stronger he thought, or perhaps he thought so because he had been expecting it. He closed his eyes and breathed deeply as her odor became his. Then he looked briefly at her face, slightly below his. Their eyes did not meet and if she recognized him she gave no sign of it.

Standing as still as he could in the moving train he concentrated on her breasts. His chest felt them, as though it were his hands. And his thighs measured hers and the cavity between them.

The city was reached and with a sudden turn, like a fish liberated from a bowl, she was out and into the flow of the crowd, bobbing down the platform.

He could follow her down the street, find out where she worked, learn her name. But he did not,

The Gods   *From* The Erotic Gods, 1966

Sometimes the sight alone is enough to rout evil. At Takatsuji in Kyoto there was a May festival that began at ten in the evening and lasted all night. It was dedicated to a certain Hanjo-sha (perhaps a local form of the goddess Benten) who was so ugly that she tried to come between young lovers and the festival was to quiet her. At ten her palanquin was made ready and the young men of the district gathered to carry it. At a signal, the leader of the procession would shout 'mawashi o tori nasare ya' ('take off your loin-cloths'). This accomplished, clad only in short coats, penes plainly visible, the

young men would jog their way through the streets, carrying the unfortunate spirit back home but rendering her contented for another year.

Showing the deity the penis quite often had a calming effect. In Bingo there was the custom of quieting the kitchen god by giving a glimpse. If the rice pot bubbled too much it would make bad rice and one could tell by the sound when it was in such a temper. At such times the man of the house would rise, go over, lift his kimono or open his fly, and expose himself. After the deity of the cooking pot had had a good look, it usually quieted

down. If, however, it happened to glimpse the charms of the wife (a not unlikely occurrence since she had to squat to fan the fire) the result was always a fiercely bubbling pot and spoiled rice. Though the god of the kitchen is Kojin, who is male, the pot-deity was apparently female.

The preventative and/or benevolent virtues of the penis are apparently many and a number of *matsuri* and New Year's customs retain these. On Miyake Island at the entrance to Tokyo Bay there is a January festival where the young men of the village carry through the streets a long rope from which

he had just fifteen minutes to buy a pack of cigarettes and get to his desk. But before he fell asleep at home that night he wondered if she would be standing at the same place on the platform.

She was, and she seemed different. Perhaps a different dress or a different way of doing her hair. He tried to remember what she had worn the day before and could not. I am the same, he thought. I am not different. And, as though to indicate this he performed the same maneuver as the day before and she slipped into place as though following his lead and joined him, face to face.

She must remember, thought Akira. She must know. No matter how unconscious she seems, she is conscious of me. This could not be a coincidence. She knows what I am doing. And she did not wait on another section of the platform, she did not refuse this place of hers.

Riding to the city it was as though there had been an understanding. She knows that I know and I know that she knows. It's like a date, he thought.

He lowered his gaze from the advertisements and looked at her. She was gazing over his left shoulder, her face impassive, her expression neutral, and he began to wonder. Perhaps she knew nothing, truly paid no attention. People were like that. They had to be when they did things like commute in these crowded trains. Maybe she was unaware of him.

And as he thought this he felt a disappointment that was almost comically disproportionate. But no, she had to know. After all, girls knew what went on in those crowded morning expresses. He had read comic books about it, seen movies about it. Girls knew about it and tried to avoid it.

Or, in the comics and the movies, they welcomed it. Akira thought about what he had seen. The hand holding the paper skillfully, as though innocent, rubbing against a breast—or a cunning finger tracing a slow pattern on a thigh, moving ever higher as the woman colored and breathed more rapidly.

carved phalluses hang. They attempt to swing the rope so that these objects strike the girls along the way, and the idea is that the young ladies will have good luck the entire year round. At Hasedera (Hatono-mura, Choshu, Yamaguchi Prefecture) there is a March *haru o-me* (spring male-female) *matsuri*. A large phallus is offered to the deity and is later used to chase the girls with. If the girls don't come to the festival, they won't have a chance to marry that year. In Shizuoka there is a January festival where a large wooden phallus is carried into the homes of newly-weds and the bride is struck lightly both before and behind. In Tokyo's Kawasaki the New Year's pine-tree decorations are fashioned into an enormous penis, which is then used to strike at the fleeting girls. In Nagoya at Shichisho Jinja in January the boys carry anything of the proper shape (pestles, umbrellas) and the lucky prodded girl will have no misfortune that year. At Matsuimura there is a *dosojin* festival in January where the children swarm into the streets to beat their mothers and other passing ladies with straw phalli; and in Akita during January the children build themselves snow houses out of which they rush to strike women with switches, meanwhile shouting a verse the purport of which is they must bear more boy-babies. Also in January, in the Yusa district of Yamagata, there is a *yome-tsugi*, or bride-abusing day, where groups of boys carry a large phallus into the bride's home. She must appear, properly dressed, and lift the object respectfully to her forehead three times. If she does not, the boys—appointed messengers of the gods—are certain to do some small damage, kicking in a *shoji* or tearing up a garden-fence. A much less explicit festival remains popular in the resort town of Ito where, for three days during the month of October, young men are encouraged to pinch the behinds of the girls, the favored ladies to run away screaming, laughing, and fortunate for the entire year to come.

His own hands felt heavy, immobile as he lay against the girl and remembered every curve from the day before and the day before that. And she, was she remembering his flat chest, his straight loins—he thought of this and wondered.

If so she gave him no such indication. She was not attempting to move away but then she would have had no way of doing so. She was not turning her face from his stare, but then she couldn't. They were held together as though by passion. Today maybe there would be a sudden sharp glance of connivance as she turned.

But there wasn't.

* * *

As the days and weeks passed they daily met at the same place, same time. These meetings troubled him, delighted him, excited him, saddened him. She must be really stupid, he thought, not to notice. But the next day he decided that she must be of the most noble and trusting nature, wise in her refusal to acknowledge their growing love.

That must be what it was—love. And he respected her, which is why he always kept his hands to himself. This made her respect him as well. He was a mature, understanding person, perhaps someone with whom she wished to entrust her whole being.

This is how Akira thought in the crowded train but in his solitary bed she became a temptress, flaunting full breasts and offering spread thighs with an open smile that he had never seen on her face.

Washing his own face in cold water in the morning he thought of her and realized that he was living for this morning commute to the city. It was the most important part of his day. He thought about it while eating breakfast, while walking to the station. And he thought about it afterwards, sitting at his desk. And in the evenings the empty train home was lonelier than he would have thought possible.

It was as though he was truly alive for just thirty minutes every day, from eight fifteen to eight forty-five. During this half-hour all of his senses were acute—he saw, heard, smelled and felt as, it seemed, he never had before.

The way her hair curled off her forehead, the soft sound of her steady breath, moving just past his ear, the smell of scent and, beneath it, body, the cool layers of her dress, her under-clothing, her skin—and beneath that her warm muscles, herself.

And half an hour was no longer enough. One spring day, when she turned and slipped away as though escaping, he followed her, glimpsing her in the crowd ahead. When she turned, he turned; when she stopped to buy a newspaper, he stopped. It was as though they were moving in tandem, together at a distance.

At nine, when he should have been at his desk, standing, bowing to his section chief, he was on the other side of the station watching her enter an elevator. He did not have the courage to join her. The connection broke and he arrived at his own office fifteen minutes late and lied about a train breakdown.

But now he knew where she worked and so, as soon as he decently could, he left his office and ran to her building where he loitered about the lobby, watching the elevators disgorge. And when she did not appear, he went to the station and hung around the platform, looking. But he did not know what time she went home. It was probably nothing so prompt as her morning commutes into the city. She was out with someone. Her girl friends. Or her boy friend.

Alone at night he thought that he was her boy friend and that she was his girl friend—the girl of his dreams.

* * *

As the days passed and they met every morning and rode to the city together he decided that she was simply waiting for him to say something, to do something. After all, she was a proper person—not at all like some of the girls in the comic magazines who suddenly began caressing the men in front of them. She could properly respond only to his own declaration.

But after all these mornings a trust had been built and a caress would be vulgar and a sudden remark would be stupid. Standing there, face to face, torsos as though one, he decided what he would do.

That night he went back home early and spent several hours writing a letter, then rewriting, then copying it again, making it small enough to fit into the palm of his hand.

Holding it, he stood beside her on the platform and then turned and held the door open, leaving room for her to slip under his arm and into her place. Once face to face, however, he wondered how he could give it to her.

There was a pocket in her blouse, but he could not simply put it there, under her nose as it were. He could press it into her hand, hanging there in the dark by his. But she would certainly misinterpret and think she had been mistaken in him. Her belt, but it might fall out. Perhaps her purse.

It was always the same one, small, with a clasp and a handle, and she carried it on her wrist. If he could somehow open it and put the letter inside then she would find it—perhaps at her own office.

He imagined her surprise, the puzzled expression when she saw the square of paper. Then the curiosity on her face as she unfolded it, and then the smile as she read it.

For in it he told her of his growing love and his concern and respect for her. And he signed it and gave her his address as though offering her his heart.

But now it sat wet in his sweating palm, in the crush of the car, and he ached to put it in her purse and did not.

That night he recopied it and then sat at his bedroom desk looking at it. I know her for only thirty minutes a day. The rest of her life, what

went before, what came afterward, I know nothing of. Either end of her life is a mystery, I know only this small middle segment.

And she, is she thinking of me as well, wondering about the other two parts of my life? He thought she was, yes, he was certain that she was. She wondered why he was not braver. Tomorrow he would be.

And tomorrow he was. With the smile of an old friend he held the door to let her in under his arm, and facing her he felt already like a husband. Full of bravery, as well as regard and trust he almost playfully unclasped her bag and was going to slip in the letter.

But she pushed him violently in the chest and began to call for help. Those around her could not ignore the cries and several other office workers shifted in the crowded car and she told them that this man was a thief and they lunged at him and held him until the next station, then they were all shoved out.

The other office workers held fast and the girl told the station attendant who called the police. At this small suburban station where Akira had never been before, she glared at him as though she hated him and said that he must be a professional thief because he always stood near her every day and she had thought nothing of it until today but now she knew he had been planning to rob her. Then she began to cry.

Looking at her wet face, he thought of the letter. That would explain everything. She would read it and would forgive him and the police would realize that it was merely a lover's quarrel and the two other office workers would slap him on the back and she would be so surprised she would forget to cry and then slowly she would begin to blush and she would lower her eyes and beg his pardon.

But the letter was no longer in his hand nor was it in her open purse. It must be on the floor of the commuter train, just about now, eight forty-five, pulling into the terminal.

Magic Show

—And he was never the same after that, she said.

—In just what way? had asked Miss Tanaka, the child's teacher.

—Really? had said her friend, Kimiko.

—Now, just don't start that again, her husband, Hiroshi had shouted.

But Akiko knew what she knew. Her Kenji had just never been the same after that.

It was his idea, being taken to the magic show. He'd read about it in the paper, then friends at school had gone and told him about it. He just kept after her, as only a ten year-old could. She hadn't wanted to take him but she finally did.

—So you see, it was all his own idea. I'm not one of those mothers always hauling her child off to this or that. I'm not an education-minded person.

—And it was expensive too, she added, because it was a foreign show and the magician was a foreigner and his girl assistants were foreigners too.

—Oh, it was interesting enough. Had a good view because Kenji of course insisted on sitting in the front row.

There were rabbits coming out of hats and bouquets out of empty hands, and pigeons fluttering up out of nowhere. And Kenji had just sat there with his mouth open.

This big box was brought out by those blonde assistants. It was sort of like a wardrobe, had a door on it, and the magician

From A View from the Chuo Line and Other Stories, 1990–95

smiled and showed his teeth and took his stick and tapped it inside and out to show it was solid. Then he asked for a volunteer.

There weren't any, of course. But he leaned over and waved his stick and Kenji just stood up and climbed onto the stage.

—It was hypnotism, of course. My Kenji was a well-mannered, bashful child. He would never have done a thing like that. And it was so sudden. First there he was beside me and the next minute he was up on the stage like a little celebrity. That foreigner, he just leaned over and hypnotized my child.

Then he had made Kenji step into the big box and closed the door and made some passes with his wand while the blonde women smiled and marched around on their high heels. He then opened the door. The box was empty and Kenji was gone.

—Just imagine how I felt, said Akiko, and Kimiko nodded, having already heard the story. There I was, a mother, and my child had vanished before my eyes.

But she had been brave, had not given way to hysterics, had simply sat there, hands gripped so tightly that her knuckles, she noticed, turned white.

Then a few more passes and the door was again opened and there he stood, Kenji, blinking in the bright lights. Everyone applauded and the magician bowed and the blonde women bowed and Kenji bowed.

—Right then I knew something had happened, said Akiko. Kenji would never have bowed. He just couldn't have. He wasn't that kind of child. He was well bred, bashful. But this little boy up there bowed and smiled like some kind of actor.

—Yet, I still didn't realize right away. I was so happy to get him back that I just didn't notice— not at first.

But then, at McDonald's over the Cokes and french fries, she saw how different he was. He was smiling, looking around, talking away, so pleased with himself. Her Kenji had much better manners, such a nice, quiet little boy.

Yet, it wasn't until the middle of the night that she was certain. Suddenly, for no reason, her eyes opened. Something about Kenji, she thought. Silently she crossed the corridor, opened the door.

There in the light from the hall she saw him asleep. Only it wasn't Kenji. It was someone else.

He had been changed. Just how, she could not say, but a mother knows.

The next minute he was up on the stage like a little celebrity. That foreigner, he just leaned over and hypnotized my child.

So back in the room she shook her husband awake and told him what she knew. He told her to go back to sleep, told her she had had a bad dream.

—And so I had, she said during the many times she later told her story. But my dream was true. This is something my husband cannot understand. And Miss Tanaka, Kenji's teacher, is no help either. But I know what I know.

—And so I started watching this boy. Everything he did I had my eye on. And sure enough, he was acting differently. I don't know, but like he was self-conscious. Like someone playing a part, like an actor, like he was impersonating my son.

When Akiko gets to this part of the story she always sighs: He took him away, the magician. And he left me this. Oh, I don't think he exchanged bodies or anything like that. But I know that he changed my little boy. Kenji was never the same after that.

Tanabata

The rain stopped two weeks later. After fourteen days of steady downpour, a soft, sudden, summer wind blew the remaining clouds away, tinkled the windbells, and scattered drops from leaves and stalks. On the evening of Tanabata, the festival of the stars, the sky was clear. As it grew darker, stars appeared, and Sumiko, after finishing the dinner dishes, was putting the final touches to the decoration that she had intended hanging all day long but had not found time to.

She was cutting star shapes from magazine covers, and Setsu had said, smiling, that this was very childish of her. She used mostly movie magazines, of which she had a number, because their covers were heaviest, glossiest, and brightest. On the opposite side of the red star was a part of Troy Donahue, an eye, an ear; on the reverse of the blue was a section of Ann-Margret, the middle.

These she tied, like balls and tinsel on a fir, to a branch of bamboo, cut that morning and kept in water. There was also a glass windbell, no longer of use now that the clapper had fallen out, and strands of paper, this time from pages of the weekly magazines.

Thinking that the decorations still looked bare—because the strips and strands were supposed to be red, yellow, green, and white instead of the color used in the magazine, black—she tore more movie magazines apart, looking for brighter colors, and this took until the stars were fully out. Then she went out to set up the decorated bamboo.

From Companions of the Holiday, 1968

Looking up at the bright stars, she smiled, glad that the clouds were gone, because if it continued to rain on this day, the celestial lovers would be kept from meeting and they would have to wait for an entire year before the magpies could bridge the lovely weaving maiden across the milk river separating the heavens and allow her, for one night, to enjoy the company of her herdboy lover.

She climbed the wooden stairs, black beneath her, to the landing built against the lower roof of the house, where on sunny days she hung the shirts and sheets. Days ago she had decided that the laundry platform was the proper place to put her decoration. There, in one corner, she wedged the decorated bamboo branch, and then she leaned against the railing, enjoying the black against the stars, blacker than the sky itself, illuminated occasionally by the flash of summer fireworks far away. She looked up to find the Weaver Star—that was the girl—and continued to do so for some time, unsuccessfully, until she heard heavy steps on the gravel beneath and someone saying that he had brought the bacon.

Hearing this, she was silent for a few seconds and then, more loudly than she had intended, said: "Which one is the Weaver Star?"

There were more heavy steps, this time uncertainly approaching the stairs, followed by: "Good evening."

"Which one is the Weaver Star?"

"What?" and a scuffling in the gravel as though something had been tripped over.

"Today is Tanabata, you know. Where is the star?"

"Oh," from below, "Tanabata."

"Do you know which one it is?"

"No." And the footsteps came to the stairs.

There was silence, which Sumiko broke. "Well, you can't see much down there. Come up here and look."

"Is it all right?" The voice sounded cautious.

"Of course it's all right."

The laundry platform shook, feet stamping step by step, then a white undershirt loomed from below; the rest—arms, legs, face, feet—was black under the stars.

"Good evening," said Saburo, and the undershirt bent.

"I can't find it," complained Sumiko, not looking at him, looking up into the air, into the sky.

"I don't wonder. Just look at them all."

"Is it supposed to be bright, I wonder."

Saburo paused and then said: "That one is very bright, that red one over there."

"That's the light on the Akasaka television tower, silly."

Another pause, then: "I *knew* that. It was a joke!"

Saburo, his head thrown back, was very close, and Sumiko, turning, could see his open mouth, filled with stars, his neck stretched, and the great manly lump on his throat cut against the sky. She could smell him too, the strong male smell he always had, even fresh from the bath; and the smell of the meatshop, which was rather nice; and that other odor she could not recognize but which made her think of hair.

"Oh, look at that," said Saburo, turning his head.

"I made it this evening."

"It's pretty. What's the matter with the bell?"

"The tongue fell out."

"Oh, when?" Saburo seemed concerned.

"A long time ago. I found it in the storeroom."

"Oh, well, then." He seemed reassured.

Overhead there was a buzzing, as of an insect. Sumiko looked up and saw, not nearly so bright as the stars, the lower lights flashing red and green. "Oh, that may be it," she said, smiling.

"Maybe so," said Saburo absently, turning and looking in an entirely different direction.

"No, *there*." Adding: "It was a joke."

"I knew *that*," said Saburo and was silent.

Sumiko smelled Saburo close and felt him

almost against her, blotting out the stars; yet all the time she knew he was a good distance away, a white undershirt leaning against the rail. The windbell rang noiselessly and the paper streamers stirred in the breeze while the stars revolved.

We should talk, she thought to herself. But she did not feel like talking, and Saburo apparently had decided not to, since he was silent as the minutes grew and the breeze failed.

Finally the undershirt moved. "We should not be here at all," he said darkly.

"And why not?"

"You know why."

"No, I don't."

"Miss Setsu," he said, almost whispering, moving closer.

"She's asleep. She always goes to bed early now that she's not feeling well," said Sumiko, and then realized that she too was whispering, that the two of them were murmuring under the stars while the celestial lovers crossed the milky river dividing the heavens.

"Still, if she knew . . ." said Saburo, still whispering, still moving closer.

"If she knew, then she'd make me come in; that's all."

"That is not all. She'd make me go home; I'm not supposed to be here anyway. They'll wonder where I am as it is; I'm supposed to clean up when I get back."

"Do you care?" asked Sumiko, boldly, turning so that her back rested on the rail and she could face Saburo, did she so desire, by merely turning her head.

"Well, that *is* where I work, you know," he said, and the white undershirt was cut in half: he had crossed his arms over his chest, as though cold.

"What are you going to do, Saburo? Eventually I mean."

"I don't know . . . I guess," he said, apparently thinking. "But I've got a plan. I want a place of my own. And they would help me, I think. After I get to know enough. But I don't know half yet."

"Do they let you cut?"

"Only heart and liver and things like that. Steak sometimes if we are busy and they don't like the customer very much." The undershirt

The Gods
From **The Erotic Gods,** *1966*

A belief in phallicism implies a belief in the magic resulting in fertility; therefore, though the organs are powerful, their conjunction is even more so. Copulation becomes a ritual that ensures a good crop. In Japan, even now, this observance is said to continue. In a section of Tohoku, a farmer and his wife make love in a field while the seed is being sown into the waiting earth; in Akita, after the silk worms are set to spin in their attic rooms, a couple is selected to spend the night there; also in Akita the men and women who plant the rice shoots sleep together afterwards; during some planting seasons, however, particularly during the Niinamesai festival-season, wives refuse their husbands so as to be ready to receive the soil-deity. The magic that these couples practice is sympathetic: they serve as exemplars for nature.

They are also all that remain of one of the most interesting and most mysterious of early Japanese religious customs, the *utagaki.* This was a festival that included dancing and concluded with copulation. It occurred at set places—Ibaragi's famous male-female mountain, Tsukuba; Mt. Hie near Kyoto; Takachiho; and the beaches of Suminoe and Takasago—and at set times. We should probably call it an orgy, but only because we do not have a word that insists that it was also sacred.

The opening dance was important—and its remains are seen

was again complete in the starlight and seemed closer as the breeze sprang up. The streamers rustled and the stars spun. "She hates me," he added.

"No," said Sumiko, knowing he was speaking again of Setsu.

"She wants you here," he said, sounding despondent.

"She says I'm too young," said Sumiko and was at once surprised by what she had said. She and Saburo had never said anything to each other before, and here she was, talking quite openly with him. It was not proper, and was certainly not at all like the romantic meeting on the laundry platform that she had occasionally thought of, but it was nice to be able to speak, even in this way, of what she often thought of now—what she would do when Setsu had gone.

"Would you ever leave here?" he asked suddenly.

"What a question," she said, evasively.

But Saburo, recognizing the tone of her refusing to take him seriously, said: "No, I'm being serious now. Have you ever thought of leaving?"

Have I thought of anything else? Sumiko asked herself. Then she said, honestly: "I wouldn't know where to go," and felt his elbow by her own. She also suddenly recognized the smell: it was the odor of pomade.

"Have you already been to the bath, Saburo?"

The elbow was removed. "Why?" he asked, sounding suspicious.

"You're wearing pomade."

"I always wear pomade. Keeps my hair down."

"Well, it smells good."

The elbow was replaced, and Sumiko, her back against the rail, lifted her face and looked at the stars. There was a sudden convulsed movement. The undershirt quite disappeared and Sumiko felt Saburo's mouth wet against hers, his head outlined against the stars, his smells surrounding her, his arms around her, his legs against her, his eyes reflecting the skies as he stared.

I'm being kissed, she thought.

Then he backed off, so suddenly that their mouths seemed scarcely to have touched. He

in the various *matsuri* or folk festivals so common and so popular in Japan—because dance is, for man as for beast (the porcupine, the heron, the pheasant), an eroticant, and the Japanese are, more than some peoples, in need of such: not only are they sexually slow, but the male organ is not noteworthy for its size or potency (hence the degree of compensation, often fantastic, seen in statues or in latter-day erotic prints) and a degree of psychological preparation seems necessary. After the dance and the sake, and the generally heightened atmosphere

caused by the presence of the god, the heated populace (presumably in couples—one cannot imagine the Japanese copulating in mass) retired to various places in the forest, on the beach or mountain, and did not return until dawn.

There was another and perhaps more basic reason for the *utagaki*. Among the poor—and this is where such festivals occurred—sexual restraint is usually impossible because sex is the only available emotional outlet. Phallicism has never had much attraction for the monied; its attractions

are reserved for the uses of the poor. The extent of the attractions are seen in a birth rate that is usually three times higher than that of the rich, who have other things to do. When the poor are offered an alternative, the birth rate drops. After the war, rural Kyushu was fully electrified. This meant that one no longer went to bed with the sun, one could work, or read, or look at television and the birth rate was cut by half in the first year. Nevertheless, the spirit of the *utagaki* survives.

stood looking at her, warily. She was breathing with her mouth open. Then suddenly she began fixing her hair.

Finally, she asked: "Where did you learn how to do that, Saburo?"

The undershirt made indecisive movements. "I don't know. I . . . saw it in the movies."

"Well, I go to the movies too, and I never saw anyone kiss like that."

"That's just the way they do it."

Sumiko turned away and smiled in the dark. "It is not. All wet like that. I can't imagine that they do it that way in the movies."

"They do," said Saburo. "You've seen it as well as I have. Just like that."

Sumiko shook her head, indicating that she could not imagine Troy Donahue doing that to Ann-Margret. I have been kissed, she thought.

But she turned, smile hidden, and said: "Saburo, that was your first time!"

"Well, what if it was? It was yours too. You know so much more about it?" He sounded angry. "You don't know how to at all. Just standing there. You don't know any more about it than I do."

"But that's what women do. They stand still and get kissed."

"They're supposed to help. No, I don't know how they're supposed to. You can never see that well. But they are supposed to put their arms around you, and they are supposed to like it." He sounded very angry.

"But I did like it, Saburo."

He did not move, black against the stars, while the fireworks on the horizon crowned him. "You did?" He sounded surprised.

"Yes, of course, I did."

"You did?"

Then both leaned on the railing and looked at the stars while the paper streamers whispered and Troy Donahue's ear struck softly at Ann-Margret's ribs and the clapperless bell swung to and fro. I was kissed, thought Sumiko.

"We have a color television at our place," Saburo suddenly offered.

"Really? We only have an old black-and-white one of the master's, but no one looks at it. It's broken," she explained. "And Miss Setsu hates it anyway," she added.

"Maybe you'd like to come and see it sometimes. I know how to work it. It's very bright," he added, tempting.

"It's green and purple mainly," said Sumiko. "I saw it in the department store."

"That's because they didn't know how to work it. I do. It comes out very natural—sometimes," he added honestly.

He's asking me for a date, she realized. She imagined them in the dark at the back of the meatshop, gazing, arms around each other, at the green and purple images.

"Sumiko," he said, "did they say anything about me to you?"

Sumiko considered. "Hiroshi says you smell." Since he did not answer, she hastened on: "Though I like the smell myself."

"I don't mean things like that," he said, softly.

"Well, Miss Oharu just can't forget about you. Talks about you all the time."

"I mean things like that."

"She teases me terribly."

"She teases me too."

There was silence until he added: "She thinks we ought to get married."

Sumiko was so quiet that he continued: "At least, that's what she says. It wasn't my idea, though; from the first it was Miss Oharu's."

"Then you don't like the idea?"

"I didn't say that. I said it was so sudden."

She turned to look at him. "And what do you think that *I* should say? After all, it's your responsibility."

"What is?"

"Oh, stupid. The girl can't say anything. You know that. Look at the movies you learn so much from. The girl never says anything, no matter what she's feeling, and then the man talks to her and he finally asks her, and then she answers. It goes like that."

"I don't know about things like that," said Saburo, sober and proud.

"You don't know anything about anything," was her opinion.

The undershirt moved, hesitant in the dark. "Where are you going, Sumiko?"

"Well, if you'd be kind enough to move out of the way, I'm going down to bed."

"But it's still early."

"I have to work tomorrow."

"But so do I."

"Then I would suggest that you also go home and go to bed."

"Sumiko!"

"Well, what do you want? To stand up here and practice your kissing technique? Believe me, Saburo, you need a lot of practice."

"I thought we could just talk."

"I think we already have. Good night." And Sumiko, a contented smile hidden by the dark, took the first step down, then stopped: "And be quiet too. If Miss Setsu heard, it'd be terrible."

"What would she do?" asked Saburo.

"Don't shout. It would be terrible."

"She'd only make you come in and me go home. You said so yourself."

"You're not even supposed to be here."

"I told *you* that."

"Well, it's the truth." And she went down another step.

"Sumiko?"

"What now?" And she simulated a sign of impatience.

"Do you come up here often?"

"Every day—to hang out the wash."

"Not daytime. I mean at night."

"Oh, sometimes; sometimes not. I never know."

"It's nice here. It is romantic."

"It's what?"

"Romantic."

She counterfeited a scornful laugh. "Now wherever did you learn a word like that? The movies?"

"All right, go on down, I don't care!"

"Saburo," she hissed, "you're shouting."

"I don't care!"

And he rudely pushed her against the stair rail and went down ahead, his white undershirt indignant and angular, his feet heavy in anger, shaking the laundry platform. The hedge snapped as he slapped at it, his sandals rang on the flagstones, and the bamboo-lattice door screeched.

For minutes after, she could hear his progress as the furious sandals clattered through the silent streets.

And she waited until, blocks away, the heavy noises failed and further progress was silenced. Then, descending slowly to the squatting, waiting house, she looked once more into the air, at the brilliant stars set near, just out of hand's reach, and smiled to herself, her hand caressing the railing.

At the bottom she turned and, as though from a well, saw the decorated bamboo and, black against the sky, its bell, its streamers, its stars framed by angles of the roof, and behind it, the river of stars separating the heavens.

She smiled into the dark and then shut her eyes, remembering. Not once did she think of any older, kind, and moustached gentleman; she thought only of the smell of pomade and the sight of the white undershirt and the way the stars had been reflected in his open eyes, and that she had for the first time in her life been kissed.

She smiled again, hugged herself. Then with a grunt of effort she climbed into the kitchen, padded down the darkened hall, softly slid open the door, heard Setsu groan once and turn, heard also the first few large drops of the returning rains, laid aside her outer clothes, crept onto her pallet, laid her head on the hard pillow, sighed, smiled, closed her eyes, and was asleep.

Five Zen Inklings

The Monkey Mind: A Sermon

The mind is as active, inquisitive, willful, and impatient as a monkey. It leaps from thought to thought, examining this curiosity or that, always losing interest and springing off again on some new and aimless quest.

Natural, typical, even attractive as such simian behavior is, few of us would choose to act in such a manner. Yet all of us have monkey minds, for it is in just such a fashion that the unattended mind occupies itself. Few of us would choose a monkey as a lifetime companion, yet we all choose to live with our monkey minds. Thus, we are like unwilling owners of gibbons, forever straining at the leash—or of gorillas, who simply pick up a person and carry him along.

Yet, though all of us have monkey minds, few of us notice that we do. It is perhaps only at night, when we are trying to sleep, that we become aware of the aimless currying with which the mind indulges itself. All would be well, of course, if we were ourselves monkeys. But, though very close relatives, we are not monkeys. Nonetheless we must, it would seem, share our lives with them. No matter where we go nor who we become, the mind faithfully accompanies us.

From Zen Inklings, 1982

If one lived with a real monkey what would one do? After it had been admired, played with, after attempts to communicate with it had been made, then it would have to be disciplined. We would cage it, or train it. No matter how highly we approved of it in its natural state, or how we regretted our attempts to fetter nature, we would eventually, forced to live with it every second of our lives, apply some discipline. Otherwise our own lives would become unendurable.

This being so, it is strange that so few people have attempted to discipline their monkey minds. This mind is no less tractable than is the animal itself. Both can be taught. Perhaps the reason is that we are not comfortable when aware of our minds. We prefer to be unconscious of them.

Yet, little by little, awareness grows. We, imperfect, are not one with our minds. So we are unlike our monkey cousins, all unaware. Happy, integrated they; unhappy, fragmented us. We would not become aware of our minds if we could help it. Eventually, however, we cannot help it.

We become aware and know that our minds are not entirely, only, us; that we are not wholly, merely, our minds. The monkey appears, chattering and restless. We are forced to train it.

The training is simple. Do not let it fling itself about, forbid it its fruitless quests, make it concentrate. Easier said than done, you say, but to say it is to do it. Simply tell it to stop. It will listen—for a moment or two. But, the minute you relax, off it goes again. Drag it back. Again order it to stop. Do not allow it to wander away. Attach it to something.

Imagine a cage and do not allow it outside. When it springs out, pull it back. As often as it wanders off, make it return. This will happen many times, and you will yourself become very tired. Bringing back the monkey mind is, in fact, a good recipe for putting yourself to sleep. But if we do not wish to spend our lives sleeping, we

must find a way of controlling the mind without ourselves nodding off.

Therefore, train it by day as well as by night. Do not let it go off gamboling, attractive as it— and you—may find such vain pursuits. Pull it firmly along, put it to work, make it truly think. Give it a problem—a puzzle, a conundrum—or merely make it count.

It will grow more quiet. It will also grow more sly. As you concentrate upon it, it will take the very subject of your concentration and build a story or a probability upon it. Before you are aware, monkey mind firmly in mind, you will find yourself again racing through the treetops.

Bring it back again. Resist its efforts to make you think about it. Ignore it and concentrate upon the cage. Then it cannot escape until you open the door by relaxing. Which, of course, you will want to do. Not only for the sake of the monkey mind, which, after all, by its own nature likes to flit about, but also for the sake of yourself, since a life of intense concentration is scarcely more worth living than is a life of aimless and transient interest.

If you persist, however, you will discover that the mind becomes docile. Finally, it will come when you call it and sit with you. Perhaps not for long, but for a time. When this occurs the monkey mind has finally become aware of itself. It has wakened. And to wake your mind is the first step toward wakening yourself. The way toward one mind lies ahead.

The Bones of Buddha

Long ago there lived in the old capital a Zen master named Tanka. One cold winter day, when the boughs creaked and a dog's bark could be heard all the way across the city, Tanka went to Eirin-ji to call on the priest.

He found him out. Walking about the large,

freezing hall, his breath hanging before him and his hands tucked into his armpits, Tanka waited. Still, the priest did not return.

It was so cold that the flowers at the altar remained open, as though in ice, so cold that the boards squeaked by themselves. And still the priest did not return.

Finally Tanka went into the temple kitchen and found a hatchet. Then he returned to the main hall and began chopping at the large statue of the Buddha on the main altar.

When he had enough kindling he sent an astonished acolyte out for some coals and soon had a bonfire going. To it he would from time to time add a hand from the statue, or a piece of robe, or a foot.

The resident priest returned and stood amazed and outraged, looking at the fire in the middle of his hall. Then he began to shout and to remonstrate. Tanka, who had been warming his backside, stared at him. What, shouted the priest, did he mean by this extraordinary and sacrilegious behavior?

—What do I mean? I am simply attempting to gather the *sarira* of the Buddha.

Upon saying this he calmly fed more wood into the fire.

This action did not calm the priest. It further enflamed him.

—Sarira is the bones and ashes of a cremated saint, old man. How do you expect to find sarira in a wooden Buddha?

—Oh, well then, said Tanka. If they have no sarira, then we might as well burn the others too.

So saying, he began to chop up the two statues attendant to the main Buddha. Finally the altar was bare, and the main hall was nicely warm.

This occurrence caused a scandal among the priests, but when Tanka's old roshi, Baso, heard of it he was pleased. He gave his old pupil a new name. It was Tennen, which means "natural," or "spontaneous," or "inherent."

Manjusri

There was a monk who, despite all of his efforts, remained unawakened. Every day, all day long, he sat with the others, his mind empty. And every evening he remained as he had been.

His roshi told him that this was a matter of no importance. Do not, he said, become attached to anything, including any ideas of satori. Simply sit; practice zazen. This the monk attempted, yet he knew that he was pressing, pursuing.

At sanzen with the roshi he sat silent.

Then one day the master asked him if he had been paying daily reverence to Manjusri.

This is the bodhisattva who represents wisdom. Often he is shown on the Buddha's left. In one hand he holds a sutra. In the other he holds a sword. It is called the sword of wisdom because it cuts through all delusions.

—This sword also cuts thought, since all thought is also delusion, said the roshi. You should emulate him.

In the *zendo*, on the left side of the statue of the Buddha was a statue of Manjusri. The monk knelt before it. The face was serene, and the sword was sharp.

Every day the monk knelt before the statue, but his delusions remained secure, and thoughts fell upon him. Finally, one day, he decided.

Either he would attain insight or he would kill himself. He would not return to past mindlessness, and he could not penetrate into the mindlessness beyond.

On that day he did not go into the zendo with the others. He stayed behind in his cell and faced the blank wall. Nor did he fold his hands in his lap. Rather, in one hand he held a lighted stick of incense, and in the other he held a sharp knife. I am enlightened by the time this incense has burned, or I am dead.

As he sat, the sunlight glinting from one hand, the smoke rising from the other, he found himself thinking. He was thinking of the mere pain of death.

Mortified, he cast the thought away. Surely, after all these months of discipline he should not be entertaining such a puerile fear. Yet, the thought returned. It stood there, interfering with what he took to be the most important passage of his life.

He concentrated, emptied his mind. It returned.

Stay then, stay. And it stayed. His imagination awoke, and he saw himself writhing, his throat cut, and he felt already the searing pain.

But that, he considered, will at least, at last, unify me. This pain will be so intense that I will no longer think. I will be—finally. And dead I will be one with myself.

Having thought this, he no longer attempted not to think. His mind filled with all the many images he had so long repulsed. He stood to one side as they rioted and waited for the rout to end, knowing that in this life he could not attain what he had so sought.

Time passed. One hand was of iron, the other of fire. He sat and waited, no longer concerned, because he no longer hoped. The knife glinted, and the incense burned lower and lower.

Several things then occurred.

The incense burned his hand, the glowing stub having reached his flesh.

He dropped the knife.

He then dropped the incense.

Then, like a fish turning over, everything moved. The world, himself—everything shifted. It was a single movement, at once over. And at that moment he knew.

He opened his eyes and snatched the burning stub from the mat before it had even been singed. He stood up and looked at his hand. The burning incense had left a line of red down the finger and up the thumb.

It was the pain, the pain he had feared, that made him know. But it was not the pain he had expected, not the pain of the knife. It was the pain in the other hand that had awakened him.

The monk walked swiftly to the room of his master, stopping once only to bow before the statue of Manjusri.

The Holy Demon

There was once a demon who desired to become a priest. His reason was that being evil—the nature of demons—was too difficult. Being good might be easier. Thus it was that he desired to take his vows.

This is one version of the story. Another is that he saw the badness of his ways and was contrite. Yet another was that he had been living on a diet of bad people and wanted to taste some good, hence his desire to enter a temple. For all these differences, the stories do agree that one

From The Temples of Kyoto, 1995   *The Japanese*

Apprehended in the midst of his aesthetic appreciation, he was with his young son condemned to be boiled in oil in the bed of the nearby Kamo River. During this, the father held the child over his head before, himself no longer to endure the torture, purposefully and mercifully dashed his off- spring into the bubbling liquid, then himself collapsed into it. This example of parental concern is still approvingly spoken of.

day he presented himself at the temple gate.

The abbot, worldly man that he was, heard the request without surprise and said that he would bring up the matter at the next council. Until that time, then, the demon might again retire to his lair. Also, he might want to do something about his talons. They would certainly render handling the prayer beads difficult and, in any event, would probably catch in the long sleeves of the priestly habit.

The demon saw the reasons for this, went home, took a knife, and pared his talons. This hurt, and his paws were still aching when a week later, neatly bandaged, he presented himself.

The board was sitting on the matter, the abbot informed him, noting with a small smile

the absence of claws. Would he please be so good as to return in a week? And, in the meantime, he might want to do something about his horns. They would interfere with ecclesiastical head-dresses, were he ever to rise above mere monk, and, in any event, did not go well with priestly garb.

The demon agreed with this, went home, and began paring his horns—a long, difficult, and painful process. He finally had to burn the stubs, an experience not at all comfortable. Then he presented himself at the temple, two depressions where the horns had been.

The abbot complimented him on their absence; then he smiled regretfully and said that all of the members of the board were not as yet

The Gods

From The Inland Sea, *1971*

The shrine lay in the path of the declining sun. The shadows were beginning to lengthen, the light was growing horizontal. The open-mouthed shadow of the stone torii that marked the approach to the shrine stretched into the dark of the trees at the base of the hill. The sand of the beach was still gold, but inside, beyond the gateway, all was a mass of thick black trees and bushes. On the beach, it was still day; inside the grove, it was already night.

Many Shinto shrines lie on heights. One goes up and up and up to worship. The steps lead straight into the sky and are always steep. It is work to reach such a shrine. The faithful must arrive puffing, gasping, senses reeling. This is as it should be.

One arrives as though newborn, helpless, vulnerable. One's panting sounds in the ears because a shrine is very quiet, quieter than a church. A church is hushed because one is made to be quiet; a shrine is simply quiet. It is so far away that noise does not reach.

You yourself may be as noisy as you please. Gasps for breath, eventual shouts and laughter, are quickly swallowed up. You speak in a normal voice as you walk about, investigating every-thing, peering behind this door, into that box. The reverent, the hushed, the awed—these have small place in a shrine. If there is any restraint, it comes from nature itself. You may lower your voice, just as you naturally lower your voice in a grove or

a gorge. If you feel like it, you impose a willing silence upon yourself.

Shrine prayer is not com-munal prayer. It is solitary and spontaneous. No one says when to begin or when to stop. You choose your own time. You speak to the gods in the way you might greet your hosts at a party. It is a discreet, friendly, happy, polite prayer.

Apparently no one came to pray any more in this small shrine. The stone steps had been forced apart in places by roots of trees grown large after the shrine was built. The only motion in this tangle of bushes and weeds were the large red crabs that, looking already cooked, refused to move, menaced with waving

entirely of one accord. Could he not come back the following week? And, in the meantime, he might think of what to do about his fangs. These would interfere with his eating the simple monkish fare and, in addition, somewhat detracted from an otherwise attractive smile.

The demon understood the wisdom of this, returned home, and with many a howl of pain and some tears put his teeth to the grindstone and ground them down to the gums. Smiling in agony, he then, a week later, again presented himself at the temple, showing two great gaps where the fangs had been.

The abbot, affable, received him at once, noting with pleasure the holes in the demon's smile. He then imparted the best of news. The board had finally agreed. It had decided that it would be a signal honor to have a demon monk. Also, a consideration not imparted to the penitent, the propaganda value of a demon brought to Buddha would be great.

The demon attempted to look pleased but seemed somehow less zealous than before. Upon inquiry, the abbot learned that this was because the demon was feeling poorly. Though he had originally come in earnestness and good health, the excision of talons, horns, and fangs had, it appeared, not only tired him but actually made him ill. His paws were bleeding, his forehead was infected, his gums were suppurating, and he had a fever.

The abbot showed his sympathy but remarked

---

cleft claws, and denied being afraid.

At the top one is ready for the god. One is reeling, fainting, panting. And there, as though for reward, spread out like a banquet, is a view of the other side of the bay, the sea, the distant farther islands, all gleaming in the setting sun, as though cast from bronze and floating on lacquer.

Here at the top it was still day, though below, back toward the village, the sea was clouded and the beach was darkening. The shrine, seen through a line of trees, gleamed a rich yellow, the color of cut wood in sunlight. It was silent. I heard the cicadas the moment they ceased.

Walking through the clinging weeds I crossed to the shrine and stood before the votive box. The god was just inside the closed doors in front of me. I pulled the rope of the god-summoning rattle. The sound was like that of a dry husk shaken. These gods have no bells—the only sound they know is this dusty sound of dried reeds shaken by the winds.

Shinto is nature. Perhaps animism—and Shinto is the only formal animistic religion left—is the true religion. It has roots deep in all of us. One recognizes this. It is the only religion that can inspire the feeling children know when the wind or a rock is made god for a week or a day. Its essence is unknown and unknowable, yet this unknown does not exclude us because we too are unknown. This religion speaks to us, to something in us, which is deep and permanent.

Once I had sounded the rattle, once its rasping cry, like the quiver of a cicada, had died, once the god was looking from his trellised doorway, I was afraid not to give. The votive box looked hungry, its slats like teeth.

The Shinto gods are near us. They prefer money. I dropped a coin; then, not knowing what else to do, shook the rattle again. A dark shape stood for a second against the sky, whirled about me, was a speck of black in the darkening sky, was gone. It was a bat.

The sun was sinking behind the farther mountains behind me. Its final rays fell on the shrine as the distant shadows began climbing nearer, toward me. The farther sea was a sheet of gold, which, as I watched, faded at the edges, the deeper blue becoming black while the sky, still azure at zenith, faded slowly and a single star appeared, quite suddenly, opposite the disappearing sun.

that, after all, the good life is the strenuous one. Only those with strength, both outer and inner, should consider embarking upon it. The demon was left to extract from this what he could.

In the meantime, continued the abbot, it would be best for him to regain his health before joining their community. The demon understood all this, went back, and became very ill indeed.

The fever raged, paws throbbed, head knocked, and his mouth was nothing but aches. Since he could no longer claw, butt, and consume sinners he also grew thinner and thinner. If being good is this difficult, he thought, I had better not attempt a virtuous life.

Finally, feeling near death, the demon went again to the temple. There he told the abbot that, though he no longer had the strength to become a priest, he would like to die in the embrace of the true religion.

The abbot agreed at once. The bishop would be much pleased. A repentant demon would have been a good thing, but a dying demon, surrendering to the church, would be a sensation. So the abbot at once invited the sick demon into the temple, gave him a room to himself, and assigned two acolytes to nurse him.

Every day the sick demon sank further. He took to the prayer beads but they hurt his paws, tried to eat his rice gruel but it hurt his jaws, even tried on the hat of the dead but it hurt his head. Being good is frightfully difficult, he decided, much more difficult than being merely evil.

But he did not die, and little by little the pain left him. This event was viewed with some displeasure by the abbot. There would, apparently, be no sensation. He would have to content himself with a good thing—a repentant demon. Well, he was big enough, at least, to do most of the heavy work around the temple.

At this point in the story the various versions again diverge. In one, the demon, maimed though he is, finds happiness in being good—

preparing the bath, cleaning the attic, lugging the rice bales. In another, he suffers a final, fatal relapse and expires amid clouds of incense and much evidence of Buddha's benevolence.

In yet another, however, the demon fully recovered. Every day he felt better and better, and this troubled him because the innocent creature did not know what was occurring. Being good cannot be this simple, he thought. Then he discovered the reason. His talons, horns, and fangs were growing. He was again becoming an evil demon. Only he did not phrase it in this way. He was filled with delight because he was again becoming himself.

So, when no one was around, he practiced his grimaces and felt with joy the evil wrinkles again forming around his mouth. He gnashed his fresh fangs with pleasure and playfully dug holes in the matting of his room with his new horns. When the acolytes were around, however, he was careful to look innocent and keep his eyes round. He also rarely smiled, lest they see the sharp new fangs.

I have tried to be good and I have failed, he told himself. But he felt no regret. To return to his own self caused too much happiness for that.

He also reverted to his old habits. One day, feeling particularly joyful, he sprang from his pallet and gobbled up both of the acolytes. They tasted very good after so many weeks of nothing but gruel. He snapped their bones and got at the marrow with the innocent and earnest zeal that was naturally his.

Then he crouched in wait in the corridor and ate up all the other priests and finally, as he was coming around a corner, the abbot himself. Then the demon stretched himself, roared, and galloped off into the forest.

It was, as the late abbot had prophesied, a sensation indeed. Whole generations were frightened into proper behavior with the tale, no one ventured near the place, and both cobwebs and legends formed around the deserted temple.

All agreed that a terrible thing had occurred. All except one. He was a holy man, an old monk who lived in a hut in the mountains. He said it was the most natural thing in the world.

It is all very well for a demon to become holy, he said, but he must become holy as a demon, not as some mutilated creature no longer itself. And, in any event, who was to say that this demon was not, as he had always been, in some way, his own way, holy?

As for the temple—well, one must pay for one's mistakes. And, all in all, the good life is the strenuous one. As for the demon, he had attempted to become what he wasn't, and this, said the mountain holy man, had almost killed him. Impelled by a longing for ease, always a bad counselor, he had wandered far from his natural path. Fortunately for him he had returned to it.

Perhaps, after his adventure, he had returned with a new purpose, with a fresh insight. He now knew how difficult goodness is and could compare his old lazy badness with his new and understood evil. One must die in order to be reborn, and whether the result is good or bad is beside anyone's point.

Then he delivered the moral that always comes after the text. There is, whether we like it or not, room for all of us in this world, priests and demons alike. To awake to one's own true nature is the aim of all.

This version of the tale is not popular and is not often heard.

The Sage

Shigeko, a woman of middle years, sat on the veranda and looked at the stones, seven of them in the garden before her, in the summer their northern sides covered with moss.

From The Erotic Gods, 1966

The Gods

In Kyushu's Oita Prefecture (at Nakayama in Ono-gun) there is an autumn festival at the local Hachiman Shrine, called the *kadake-matsuri,* where the boys are supposed to *seri-ni-iku* or, 'go and push' the girls. This is a mock ritual rape: the boys try to push the girls into the dark and the girls give a few token screams. It stops there but did not always. In the same prefecture (at Usuki in Kaita-kaibegun) there was, until the last century, an August festival where every woman, whether married or not, was supposed to enjoy three men before return-

ing home. If she did not, it was an offense against the deity. This attitude is still seen in Oita (Yoake-mura, Hida-gun), where any girl who does not show up for the annual and very innocent-appearing tug-of-war between the sexes in the middle of July is said to be physically abnormal in her parts and hence unwilling to participate.

That women must make themselves available was a definite part of these *utagaki* like festivals. In Ehime (Kamiukiana-gun), at a shrine commonly known as the Bobo Hachiman (*bobo* being an explicit dialect-word for the

act of making love), there was a biannual *uno-toki-mairi* festival where the woman wore a towel over her shoulder and any man pulling it off might have her. In the middle of August at Okawa-chi-mura in Yamanashi Prefecture, the same custom was observed with the difference that the woman also carried a rice-straw mat, both to disguise herself and to serve as ground covering. If she came back with towel and mat still in place, the husband is said to have been furious at having such a demonstrably unattractive wife.

She had lived in the house since a child and grown older with the stones. Watching the days pass, she was unaware of the years. Unlike the stones, but like most of us, she lived in the future.

Looking at the stones in the summer garden, hearing the sound of the wind-bell hung overhead, Shigeko was already in her mind living the next day.

She could do this because she believed that she possessed a real self. This was someone who lived inside of her and who was authentic. Consequently what she, the Shigeko on the veranda looking and listening, did and said and thought was not really real. It was only the outside.

The real Shigeko inside knew this, but one of its properties was that it could not communicate with the false Shigeko outside. The reason was that the real inside self was always, vaguely, for the future and never, somehow, for the present. Someday this real and beautiful person would be released but always not quite yet.

This belief was in no way extraordinary. It had nothing to do with religion or with any sense of wonder. It was much more comfortable—this feeling of reality hidden away inside, inaccessible but surely there. It is how most of us feel.

No one else believed in this real and authentic being inside of her. They saw only the usual contradictory Shigeko who did this or that, actions they could find good or bad. This outside person being all they saw, that was all they believed in.

She likewise returned this lack of faith and never believed that others were any different from the way they acted. That others might also believe that they each had a real self hidden away never occurred to her. At the same time she did not find this odd and yet continued to cherish this real self of hers as though it were an unborn child.

The summer deepened, and Shigeko sat daily on the mat. The cicada was heard over the wind-bell, and the garden turned a darker green. As always, she gazed at the seven stones, but now a feeling of sadness made itself felt. It stilled thoughts of tomorrow. It insisted upon the

The Gods

From The Erotic Gods, *1966*

The Japanese, even now an animistic people and in that sense seemingly areligious to followers of the more complicated faiths, are among the most death conscious of all peoples. They continue to practice a necrolatry that is practically Egyptian in its intensity; one sees it in the *o-bon* festivals, in what is called 'ancestor worship,' in the sense of the elegiac which so pervades the culture, in the Noh drama, in the highly developed historical sense. It is precisely because of this extraordinary consciousness of death that the Japanese have created a religion that directly worships life. Shinto and those earlier and continuing beliefs (phallicism among them) upon which it is based, affirm life and are silent on death. Buddhism, on the other hand, a relatively late arrival in Japan, is almost garrulous on the subject, and dismisses this world in which we live as of no importance whatever compared to the possible next one. Perhaps this is the reason why Shinto and Buddhism have become so happily wedded in Japan—in the words of an old saying. ". . . when things are going well, one goes to the shrine; when trouble comes, one goes to the temple."

One of the earliest forms of life worship, and one to be observed in the histories of all countries, though usually not observed so well nor so recently as in Japan, is phallicism. It is not—or at least only in later and more sophisticated forms—a worship of the sex organ itself. Rather it is, through

pathos of today. Shigeko began to weep, viewing the rocks as though through rain.

Her consolation was that soon, tomorrow perhaps, her real nature would rescue her. As the sad days passed, however, the real Shigeko refused to come forth. The false woman on the veranda waited and waited, but she remained only herself, as the rocks remained only themselves.

After a time, the cicada dead, the garden cold, Shigeko finally began to doubt that there was a tomorrow person hidden away under the layers of daily habit. Rather, the daily person sitting there appeared the only real Shigeko.

But that was impossible. This common self is as changeable as the weather. It is driven by aimless hopes and desires. It has no more substance than the wind-ruffled surface of a pond. Surely, under this, in its depths, must lurk authenticity.

The cold winds of autumn brushed her as she sat on her mat on the veranda, and the sun disappeared. If it were true that there was no other self, no salvation for tomorrow, how then, she thought, could she hold herself together, could she rationalize herself, could she become the solid object she had always envisioned herself to be?

She looked at the bare rocks, no longer mossy. They were themselves, only that. They were solid rock all the way through. And she—she was incorporeal, as fluid as water, or as air. They were there, now. She could not be said to exist at all.

Afraid to move, she sat very still. No longer able to look, she closed her eyes. She tried to calm herself by breathing deeply. She refused to think of the now-terrifying tomorrow. She willed to calm her mind.

Though she did not know it, she was meditating. One of the natures of meditation is to sit still though in terror, to breathe deeply though the heart is racing, to remain silent though the cry is on the lips.

She had come to meditation from a path entirely different from the ecclesiastics and mystics, but she joined them on the road of necessity. They may think it leads to salvation; Shigeko thought it led to madness.

the organ, a worship of life. The penis is a being attached to man, a second self; life palpably flows from it, so the bearer is god-like; it not only represents, it *is* fertility, procreation, generative power, and because of this it has the strongest of all magical prophylactic powers, the power to protect and the strength to ward off evil.

There are many remains of this belief in the world. Even now in Arab countries a holy promise is concluded with the one promising placing his hand on or near the organ of the one promised; St. Greluchon at Bourg-Dieu near Bourges, St. Giles in Britanny, St. René in Anjou, St. Regnaud, St. Arnaud, St. Foutain are all phallic deities, and in the church at Embrun the stone penis of the saint is dyed a deep red from the consecrated wine poured over by local women praying to be relieved of barrenness.

In India there are the Hindu lingam temples near Calcutta; in Greece one still sees the *hermae,* those upright stones that indicate boundaries but whose origins and uses are phallic; and in Japan one finds even now an abundance of phallic stones—in a 1953 count there were 420 in Nagano Prefecture and 14 in the one city of Tokyo alone.

The logical connection between phallicism and stones is observed in most countries, but certainly no longer to the extent that it remains visible in Japan. One of the reasons is that Japan has more stones than most countries—it is a country composed almost entirely of mountains. Another is that litholatry was the earliest of all Japanese religions, and that later animism and its still later codification into Shinto continued to observe the spirit either in or of the oddly shaped rock.

Sitting, eyes closed, under the weak winter sun, Shigeko became more and more troubled, but, at the same time, she became more and more certain. It was a strange combination of feelings, doubt and faith mingled, both absurd. Why should she sit when she so wanted to flee? Why should she flee when she could, for at least a bit longer, sit?

The days passed, and the weeks. She slept and ate and sat and slept again, always feeling deep inside of herself, not that comforting reality she had once known, but only the hole it seemed to have left.

Yet, as time passed, it was thoughts such as these that she gradually learned to refuse herself. This she found the strength to do, because she now thought of herself as insane, harmless perhaps but quite mad. She found this strength because she had come to like sitting, a day spent largely in the darkness behind her closed eyes.

Blind in the darkness she slowly detected content. It was like a growing light. This was understanding. There was now no question of a real self. The real self sat on the mat.

It sat there every day and refused to look, refused to think. And that was all there was. Time had stopped. There was only now, this very instant—the eternal now of the snow-covered garden.

One day, months later, the hole inside Shigeko was no longer there. Having been no real self it could have left no hole. She was a body in space, whole, entire, displacing so much air, weighing so much, solid.

There she sat, palpable, herself, an object like the stones. Slowly she opened her eyes. There was the garden, brown, sere. There were the stones, still wearing the late snow, but in no way different from themselves in summer.

From that day she began to know peace. It was not that she had found answers to her doubts. It was that her doubts had ceased to

have importance, even meaning, for her. To worry over real self, false self; to wonder over sanity, madness—this now seemed something that had happened long ago, in childhood. And who was she? If anyone had asked so limited a question, she would have said that she was a woman sitting.

And now that it no longer mattered, she could look into herself, though she no longer had any sense of peering into something hidden or secret. Rather, it was as though she had turned her head to view another part of the garden.

There she found nothing—precisely nothing. But it was not a hole, a void. It was the natural nothing of which all things are composed. It was the nothing of simplicity, the nothing that all things share and in which she too could share—this beautiful and lambent quality of nothing.

She looked at the rocks, now covered with the lightest green of new moss. Could she remember when this nothing, this very quality, had so frightened her? Yes, naturally, she could, but it was like being asked so obtuse a question that there could be no answer. The remembrance itself, real enough, was irrelevant.

And so she continued her life. The summer deepened, the greens grew strong, and the windbell chimed. It was precisely as it had been a year before. Nothing had changed, for there is no tomorrow. Shigeko herself had not changed, for she had always been what she now found herself to be.

Others, friends, relatives, knowing of the months in eye-closed darkness, were avid for a change, any change, in others, in themselves. But they found little. She was only perhaps more easily satisfied, more quickly pleased.

They asked if this was, perhaps, satori.

Shigeko laughed and said, oh, no, it was nothing like that.

She was right.

It was nothing like that.

It was something else.

Tokyo Nights

Twenty-two

"Speaking of cocks, I saw Ken Takakura's."

"Wherever."

"At the gym. I go there every day to work out. Not dressed like this, of course. He was in the shower."

"How was it?"

"Oh, nice. They have it all fixed up. Private units, sting-spray—"

"No, no. The cock."

"Well, normal, of course."

"Then what's all the fuss," asked the bartender who had been listening. "Why are you talking about it?"

"But, I've seen him so often in the cinema," was the answer. "And it is very interesting to see someone's cock after you have seen him so often in the cinema."

Hiroshi, who had also been listening, turned away from the two with a grimace. He apparently did not enjoy being in the Lovely Boy though it was, everyone was saying, one of its better nights. Friday, payday, a warm clear night, AIDS (for the time being perhaps) forgotten. And in any event, the Lovely Boy had a plaque on the door firmly repulsing foreigners. 'No Foreigners!' it said.

From Tokyo Nights, *1988*

Though unclean infections from abroad was only one of the reasons, Saburo had already confided. "We're sort of like a club here," he had said. "And a new face barging in, a different colored one at that—it sort of shreds the social fabric, as it were."

"And then he took me to this wonderful place, all flowers, where the boys kneel at you, and real TV stars sometimes come in, though none happened to be there then."

The social fabric was at present all of a piece. Boys, lovely and not, pressed (among others) against Hiroshi sitting sullen on his stool, and men more or less his own age, company lapel-pins in their pockets, were pressing back. Judy Garland on the hi-fi sang her heart out.

The bartender bowed and Saburo slid onto the stool beside Hiroshi's. "Sorry," he said, "just checking the week's receipts."

"Satisfactory I would say, judging from all the activity," said Hiroshi dryly.

"Yes, can't complain. Things are looking up. Course it's payday. Anyway, since we get all our money on turnover, the more the better."

"Actually, I wanted to talk to you," said Hiroshi.

"Talk away then," said Saburo with a smile.

"Here?"

"Well, it's good business to show my face here once in a while. Makes them feel at home to see the owner about. Hi, there, long time no see!" And he smiled and winked at someone behind Hiroshi.

"Got a pretty good mix here now if I do say so. These kids all have this liking for middle-aged guys. And these middle-aged guys all like kids. It seems to work. Funny tastes people have. Good-looking boys just out of high school and they take a liking to someone short and forty or so with a little pot belly and a receding hairline."

As he said this a good-looking boy, seemingly just out of high school, leaned over several people, looked Hiroshi straight in the eyes, smiled, and asked if he would pass the toothpicks.

Hiroshi glared, passed the toothpicks and Saburo chuckled. Barbra Streisand took over.

"Well, what did you want to talk about, old friend?" asked Saburo leaning back against the bar, regarding the busy clientele.

"Look, did Mariko say anything about Mitsuko?"

"Nothing, not a thing, not at all," lied his old friend.

"I'm a bit worried, you see. And you seem to be seeing her more than I am these days."

"Lovely person, Mariko. Always a pleasure."

"She is threatening things if I don't stop seeing Mitsuko," said Hiroshi, emotionally.

"Now, now," said his old classmate.

"I do think that's common," said a voice beside them: "Why do those kind always use girl's names. Mitsuko, indeed. If they feel like that about their boy friends they ought to put them in drag too."

"Now just you look here!" said Hiroshi, roused.

"That's all right, that's all right," said Saburo. "No offense meant nor taken, I'm sure. And you, old pal, you better behave."

"What about that faggot there? He just called me a faggot!"

Voices rose about that of Barbra Streisand. Well, get her, was among the comments and Saburo with many a smile and chuckle made peace.

"Look, old buddy," he said with a smile straight into Hiroshi's ear, "this is my bread-and-butter. *I* know you're not queer and that should be enough."

Hiroshi looked around. Posters of Dietrich in pants, Dean in jeans; pictures of pre-teen boy singers with dimples; guests with small bangles and swiveling eyes; high laughter and the steady clang of the old-fashioned American cash register.

Hiroshi shook his head. Perhaps he was disapproving of the clientele, or perhaps he was wondering how Saburo, from the same graduating class after all, had come to this. Probably the latter for he now suddenly said: "Hear about Shimizu? He's with the dog pound now."

"Ichiro Shimizu? Our classmate?"

"The same."

"Why, whatever?" Saburo seemed unduly shocked—unduly for the master of the Lovely Boy.

"That's the way it goes nowadays. Can't count on anything in this world."

This Buddhist observation was nodded over by Saburo who then said: "How much does the dog pound pay, I wonder."

"Less than the Lovely Boy," said Hiroshi with no irony at all.

So they talked on and finally Hiroshi came to, perhaps, the point: "So, you see, since it's inadvisable for me to see Mitsuko myself at this time—she's come to expect too much and then there is Mariko to watch out for—I was wondering if you would, well, take her out from time to time."

"Me?" asked Saburo with what appeared to be genuine surprise.

"Yes. You could let her know that I am going to have to back off for a little while, until things cool down, you might say. And you could sort of get her out of the idea too that I am going to get her her own place, if you don't mind."

"*I'm* certainly not," said Saburo, "getting her her own place, I mean."

"I know, I know. It's just to keep her occupied, your seeing her, I mean."

"Well, I don't know about that," said Saburo with what appeared reluctance.

"Please, for my sake," said Hiroshi emotionally.

More heads turned, more glances shot. The bartender beamed, apparently approving of what he perhaps took for middle-aged love.

There was a murmur of appreciation also among the nearby clientele, and then the suspended conversation was continued: "Talking about famous cocks, did I ever tell you what this older friend of mine told me about Mishima's?"

But this conversation went unheard by Hiroshi. He and Saburo were busy planning together how to arrange the meeting, how to make it seem casual, natural, normal.

Twenty-three

"*Wa*! Tanaka-*san,* it's been a long time, imagine meeting you here of all places. Now you just sit down with us for a bit. This is my old friend, Saburo Tanaka, and this is Mitsuko Koyama, and, well, it certainly has been a long time."

Saburo smiled his boyish best, excused himself, sat down at their table, just as though the meeting were accidental and had not been rehearsed at least several times by the two men involved. In the background 'Don't Get Around Much Anymore' was again heard.

"Funny thing, I was just talking to Mitsuko here about you, what a good friend you've been to me, Old Classmate, and there you appeared."

"Like a ghost," said Mitsuko, smiling.

"Like a devil," said Hiroshi, snickering. Then: "Didn't know you came here much."

"Don't get around much anymore," said Saburo with a lazy smile at Mitsuko. "But I still manage the old Starlight Lounge."

"I love it here," she proffered: "Just like a foreign land."

"It never changes in this world of change,"

said Hiroshi seriously. "And that is one of the things to appreciate about it."

The two went on eating their chicken à la king while Saburo had a brandy and Hiroshi continued with: "Like the cuisine."

"Umm, delicious," was the opinion of Mitsuko: "Just like a foreign land."

Then Hiroshi held a finger in the air as though testing the wind and, on cue, the headwaiter glided over and whispered into his ear, and Hiroshi assumed an expression of surprise, wondered who on earth could have known he was here, and went off to answer what was assumed to be the telephone.

During the interval, Saburo deployed himself to be as charming as possible and Hiroshi returned to find the two in laughter. "Oh, your friend," she gasped: "He is so humorous."

Hiroshi nodded, as though preoccupied, then said: "Look, there is no apologizing for this. Head office. Emergency. I've got to run. Mitsuko, shall I take you home? Not that I have time to. No. I have an idea. It is very rude of me but might I ask my friend Saburo here to take you out a bit. You don't mind, do you? I thought not. And, Mitsuko-*san,* I'll be in touch. *Un-ja!*" And he raced from the Starlight Lounge while Satch (Happy) Suzuki looked after him with what appeared to be disappointment.

"Well," said Mitsuko. "Just like that!"

"Yes," said Saburo easily. "He always was a bit strange, even in school."

"Impossible to imagine him as a schoolboy," was her opinion.

"Should think not," he said, smiling: "You're still quite a schoolgirl yourself."

"I am eighteen," she said, as though this was a virtue.

Then: "Head office," she said. "Hmph! President Mariko I should imagine."

"She is an unusual woman," was his opinion.

"Isn't she though," said Mitsuko. "I understand she is a friend of yours as well."

"Yes, family friend as it were, old friend of Hiroshi-*san*'s that she is, you see."

"I see," said Mitsuko, staring, as though she saw nothing. Then: "She seems to take very good care of him, possessive, you might say."

"Yes, you might say that," he said reasonably. Then: "You see, his is the type of personality that seems to demand that. There is something child-like about him, don't you think?"

"Yes," she said, turning and looking, smiling as though she were finally with a real adult: "I do think so. Now that you mention it."

They talked on, to the strains of 'Chattanooga Choo-choo' and the coffee and apple pie and brandy were all finished at the same time. Then Saburo produced the money Hiroshi had forced on him, paid the bill, tipped the headwaiter, and handed a small bank note to the happy Satch (Happy) Suzuki as they left.

Twenty-four

"And then he took me to this wonderful place, all flowers, where the boys kneel at you, and real TV stars sometimes come in, though none happened to be there then."

"And did he kiss you?" Sumire wanted to know.

"No, not yet, they're classmates after all," Mitsuko answered, dodging the swinging leather jacket of a large, ugly, adult, shaved-head male, with a knife scar showing who had just entered and was swaggering past. "My Pussy is getting very tough," she observed.

"Police came in day before yesterday, arrested," offered Sumire, making faces at her Johnny Walker over Lady Borden.

"Were you here?"

"No, but I heard, TV. Anyway, go on."

"Well, anyway," said Mitsuko reverting: "Not that I would mind at all."

"I should think not. Being kissed by a stranger, imagine. I've only been kissed by my relatives so far."

"Would not have minded at all," repeated Mitsuko. "But he was too much of a gentleman to even attempt. Put me in a taxi with that boyish little smile of his, that little nod of the head. Oh."

"Is he really so dreamy?"

"Dreamy."

"More so than Hiroshi Watanabe?"

"Oh, him. He's not dreamy at all."

"But aren't they of an age?" asked Sumire.

"Age is not all that matters," said Mitsuko mysteriously, then dodged again as two young males, one drunk, crashed into the next table, collapsed, breaking a gin bottle. Outside motor bikes revved endlessly and all of Harajuku swaggered past.

"My Pussy is getting dangerous," observed Sumire.

"Yes, we probably shouldn't come anymore."

"It can't last," was Mitsuko's friend's opinion. "Not when it gets as open as this. The police will tolerate anything but openness. They'll be doing drugs here next, you know."

The big, drunk youth at the next table produced a bottle of pills, poured them down his throat, and then drank water from a pitcher, one with a cute little mother cat and her cute little babies on it, relic from the days of My Kitty.

"See?" Then: "Well, you going to let him take you out again?"

"I might," said Mitsuko. "If he asks. What

From Japan Journals, 1947   *The Japanese*

The poor Japanese are torn with the most conflicting desires. I first became aware of this when I more closely examined their landscape. They are highly self-conscious of the beauty they have plowed from their soil and are quite aware that it appears pleasing to the eye, used to a vast chaos, of the Westerner. In this way the Japanese know the word "cute" only as a term of the highest approbation. Thus, also, one finds them arranging vistas, manufacturing pagodas, and insisting that a 20th-century piece of junk has a true 10th-century "spirit." But, at the same time that they assert their quaintness, they also feel it necessary to appear progressive and up-to-date in the Western meaning of the terms. So after a time one is no longer surprised to see a really 10th-century garden completely obscured by a shining steel-enforced suspension bridge which is, in every way, a replica of that one, so vastly large, that extends across the Bay of San Francisco or to find just outside the exquisite Kannon temple at Kamakura, a beer-garden the electric and neon sign of which, stretching across the facade of the temple itself, reads, "Kannon Kuntry Klub." Since the people have discovered that both endeavors, their practice of being themselves and cashing-in on their culture and also their progressive habits of copying precisely the casings of Ronson lighters, bring them the kind of adulation and regard which they require, feeling themselves, indeed the poor cousins of the vastly superior Western world, they are in a quandary because, unfortunately, these two endeavors are practically mutually incompatible. This leads to comments like one from a Japanese friend who was upon all other occasions a most sensitive and perspicacious young man, who said, upon learning that the Horyuji murals at Nara had been destroyed by fire, "Oh, well, they were pretty but they never attracted many tourists. Anyhow, we in Japan have quite enough already left of the old artifacts, don't you think so?"

with Hiroshi-*san* permanently out of the picture and all."

"Permanently?" small eyes bright, asked Sumire as though this news had a special interest for her.

"Take him, take him," said Mitsuko easily. "But, really, he's more trouble than he's worth."

"Isn't it Madame Mariko who's the real trouble?"

"Yes, he is just her slave."

"Slave," repeated Sumire, marveling.

"You two girls into that?" asked the acned waiter, now crewcut and tattooed, sweeping away their plates. "Why don't you let me introduce you to someone I happen to know?"

"Why don't you mind your own business?" said Mitsuko. Then, to her friend: "This place is really losing its tone."

"Isn't it just? Go on."

"Well, as I say, seeing as how Hiroshi-*san* is neglecting me, I just don't see any reason why I can't go out with Saburo-*san*. If he should happen to ask me, that is."

"Is he a company president too?"

"No, he's not."

"What does he do then?"

"Well, then—promise not to laugh—he's the sole owner and proprietor of this very successful bar."

"Why should I laugh about that?"

"Well, you see, one of the reasons it is so successful is that it is for men—only."

"Oh, no," Sumire, laughing.

"You promised not to laugh," said Mitsuko.

"Not another gay bar. Really, Mitsuko-*san*, you seem to collect them, and you work in one of them."

"That's a lesbian bar."

"Same thing," was her friend's opinion.

"Saburo's is a cut well above the others and as I say he is in it only for the money. Homosexuality is one of Japan's major growth industries he said."

"Oh, really?" asked Sumire, perhaps impressed.

Then, as though remembering: "Speaking of which, did Madame Mariko go tell The Mistress about you and Hiroshi-*san*, like you were afraid she'd done?"

"It is difficult to say," said Mitsuko. "Probably not. The Mistress has been more friendly lately. Frankly, I am a little disturbed. She cries now. Makes these scenes in the kitchen. Calls me stone-hearted."

"Really? I feel sorry for her," said the soft-hearted Sumire. "There's this scene in *A Mother's Heart*—"

"Sorry? For her? Better be sorry for a gila monster," said Mitsuko. Then: "Oh, it's awful. You know, she's got this thing about the ocean, always got Charles Trenet's *'La Mer'* on. Says it calls her, will claim her yet. And so when she feels this way now she starts talking about a watery death and then goes and locks herself in the bathroom."

"Down the drain," laughed Sumire, merrily, then, remembering to be sorry: "Poor thing."

"You know, I wouldn't mind putting up with her, frankly, if it were only for bed once in a while, but it is this awful possession I don't like. I think that jealousy is a very vulgar emotion."

"Like Madame Mariko's for poor Hiroshi-*san*," said Sumire quickly.

Mitsuko looked her approval: "Precisely." Then: "Look at me, I don't feel possessive of poor Hiroshi-*san*."

"No, not when you have someone as interesting as your Saburo-*san*," said Sumire with what appeared to be envy.

"Well, we will just have to wait and see," said Mitsuko with apparent satisfaction.

Then the tattooed youth put down a bottle of vodka and four glasses and said that it was compliments of the gentlemen, looking at the next table where two big ugly boys, one with shaved head, one with open mouth, sat and stared, and Mitsuko pulled Sumire to her feet and together the two fled My Pussy and ran out into the hot, humid, July night.

High School Girls

The sun slowly disappeared, hidden behind a late-summer haze. I turned away from the silent village with its single old man sorting squid, and walked along the deserted black-sand beach, following the course of the ship, looking out at it until the last trace of its smoke had disappeared from the horizon. I felt left behind, though the choice to stay here had been my own. I felt lonely.

Several schoolboys were digging away in front of me, busy with sticks and shovels. They were uncommunicative because they were digging sandworms for night fishing and this was serious business indeed.

I turned from them. Above the beach, standing in a grove of pines, looking out to sea as though they too had been following the vanished ship, was a group of girls. They stood holding the handlebars of their bicycles. They were about fifteen or sixteen years old and wore school uniforms—navy-blue, white-piped sailor collar, buttoned cuffs, ankle hose. Their hair was either in pigtails or worn long and straight and held by a ribbon.

I looked up at them, then walked slowly past.

One turned to the other and I heard her ask: "You think he can speak?"

I stopped, looked up at them, and said that I could.

Smiling at one another, they walked slowly out of the grove and down to the beach, trundling their bicycles, hands on handlebars. They looked like girls being led by animals, hands on horns. We began walking along the beach.

From The Inland Sea, *1971*

153

They were at the age where they were both children and adults. From time to time one would chase another as though they were five-year-olds; at other times, they walked as straight and solemn as if they were twenty-five. They walked beside me but apart. I would turn from time to time to watch them. Sometimes they screamed with laughter and dropped their bicycles. Sometimes they walked straight, looking ahead as though deaf. The tires left long snake-like tracks in the sand ending at the now distant stand of pine and the almost invisible group of little worm-digging boys.

If all girls of this age are shy, then Japanese girls are sometimes more shy than is normal. I did not speak, not wanting to lose them. It was nice walking with them on a beach where I had never been, my footprints separate from theirs and their tire tracks.

Finally, one spoke. I must find it strange that they should be wearing their school uniforms when school had not yet begun. Well, the reason for this was that the uniforms had been in mothballs all summer long but now autumn was almost here, and they were airing them by wearing them.

"We smell very strange," said the smallest of the girls.

"We smell like mothballs," said another, giggling.

I turned to the girl walking next to me, a beautiful girl with long hair and fine eyes set wide apart, and asked what they did all during the long summer when there was no school.

Oh, they loafed, she said, using the Tokyo slang phrase *bura-bura*—they loafed around and didn't do much. They certainly didn't study. There would be enough study all winter long.

Did they help their mothers?

But this was talking down to them. For a second or two there was no answer, then the girl at my side turned—graciously, she was no child, not at this moment at any rate—and said, yes, sometimes. She must have looked much like her mother just then, she was suddenly a young lady. At the same time two of her friends ran their bikes into each other and collapsed, screaming with laughter, like little children.

Yet talking with the girls was easy. They used simple words, accommodating themselves to my grammar and vocabulary, using the standard language of Tokyo, though among themselves they occasionally murmured in the island tongue, which sounded somewhat Osaka-like but was still incomprehensible to me.

At the very end of the long sand beach we sat and rested on a group of rocks. We also stopped talking. When you sit down, you become a group, and if you do not know each other well, there is silence. There was no rushing to fill it with meaningless conversation. They waited until it was naturally over. They looked idly for shells, or spread their skirts on either side of them on the rocks. They looked at the sea or the sky or me—all with a natural grace rare in city girls.

None of them were beautiful except the girl nearest me, but they all seemed beautiful. Their silence, their calm waiting for the talk to begin again, their acceptance of things as they were—this made them beautiful.

They had the dignity of being fifteen. This natural dignity, as though they were already mature, seems to last longer in the country.

All during the latter part of our walk the girls had talked freely, had asked questions and answered them. They seemed never to have heard of that horrid ideal—the well-brought-up Japanese maiden. This creature must gaze with downcast eyes at your feet. She must answer only with faint murmur or, better, insulting giggle; must be vague in all matters, including her name and age; must appear to do everything with the greatest reluctance; and should, as often as possible, appear almost disagreeably pensive. But these country girls were natural, charming, candid.

The silence grew, stretched, then waned.

When it was time, the girl next to me asked me to tell them about Tokyo. I started with stories of traffic jams and other disagreeable aspects of city life.

"No, I don't mean things like that. I mean, what is it like? Do—well, do people stay up all night?"

I supposed that a few probably did but that most were asleep by midnight. New York, now, on the other hand—

She was not interested in New York. "Midnight," she said, wonderingly. "Here, on this island, everyone is asleep by nine."

They went to bed early because they rose early, about five in the morning, when the fishermen went out, when the farmers left for the fields. Her father was a farmer and she had never in her life slept past seven in the morning except once, and that was only because there had been a funeral and the whole family had gone, but she had been sick and hadn't gone, had stayed at home alone.

She smiled at her sloth. She wanted to sleep, just once, until eight in the morning, just for the thrill of it. But she never had and she guessed she probably never would.

The other girls sighed. They felt the same way. I said that I was certain that, after they had grown up, sleeping until eight in the morning would be a common occurrence. The others smiled at this, smoothed their skirts, poked fingers at roving crabs.

The girl sitting next to me did not smile. She looked out to sea. The possibility of being in bed until eight in the morning seemed unlikely. Growing up seemed unlikely. She looked like some lady in exile, past despair; she turned her eyes to the horizon, but expected no sail.

"What will you do when you grow up?"

She turned and gently smiled. "Oh, I will get married and have children."

"Here?"

She nodded.

"But that is such a long time away."

She smiled again. "Not really. I leave school in two years." Then: "Did you see the boy at the store, the son of the owner?"

I had not.

"Well, he is seventeen now, just out of school. I will marry him."

I smiled, thinking this some last childhood dream. Perhaps not even that, perhaps it was

From The Inland Sea, 1971 *The Foreigners*

There is never enough to do when you travel.

This must be one of the reasons why travelers the world over are known for their attempts to pick other people up. It is not that they want sex so much as it is that they want something to fill the emptiness that their very freedom has created. And what else can you do after the coffee shops, the zoos, the museums, and the libraries are rifled?

Too—another factor in favor of seeking sex—there is no more personal undertaking. Naked, lying down, one is resolutely oneself, the person one otherwise left at home. The freedom to lose yourself, one of the great attractions of the sexual encounter, is based, after all, upon the assumption that

you have first found yourself.

At the same time—tips for the traveler—there are few better ways of learning the language, of taking the temperature of the land, of measuring the inner states of its inhabitants. Also, there are few more attractive memories to take home with one. Sex makes, in its way, the ideal souvenir.

some ambition she was confiding; perhaps he did not know of her feelings; perhaps her only assurance was that of hope. I said it sounded romantic.

"No, it isn't romantic. It was decided last year. His father came to see my father. It didn't take even fifteen minutes. Girls marry early on this island."

"But do you like him?"

She nodded, looking out at the sea. "He is a nice boy—he works hard."

The other girls seemed not to be listening, but they were very quiet. The sea lapped against the rocks. A bird called. An invisible boat hooted. The girl with long hair looked at the sea.

In another ten years she would look like her mother and would have had several children. She would no longer be what she was now.

At fifteen there is an awakening. A girl begins to know who she is. And she is not only a wife or a mother. She is more. But eventually she will be forced to forget. She will be the honored *oku-sama,* the person inside, or the person-around-in-the-back, however you translate it. Her husband will do whatever he likes. So will her children, if they are boys. She will think that this is somehow right. And that it is also somehow right that she never gets to do anything she herself wants, and never again meets the person she is now.

"I'll marry him," she says. "I will stay on the island. I will have children here." She seems to have abdicated already. Just now she has begun to discover what kind a person she is. And just now she is turning away.

She has abdicated but she has not yet forgotten. She sits on the rock, a schoolgirl, her bicycle lying in front of her. She is still whole. She still belongs to herself. Soon she will make herself forget what it was like to be fifteen with the whole world inviting.

* * *

The other girls had raced off down the beach like children, screaming and laughing. The conversation had not been very interesting, not to them. Now freed from the restraint of the occasion, they raced away, their hair flying behind them, their sailor collars stiff in the breeze. The beautiful girl with whom I had been talking stayed. She was returning to town and so was I.

It was late afternoon but a summer haze had settled and it seemed like dusk. The way back was long and the beach was darkened. We talked about my country and her country.

"Don't you get lonely?" she asked.

"Sometimes I do."

"But being away from your country and your people. I cannot imagine being away from mine."

"You would be if you went to Tokyo."

"Yes, I suppose so. I'd like to go. Just once, just to see it."

"Maybe on your honeymoon."

She smiled. "I know. But we don't have honeymoons here, you know. We have a big party and almost everyone drinks too much and then we all get up and go back to work the next day."

"Are you going to have children?" I asked, delicately. She was fifteen and should know about things. At the same time I felt hesitant. She was still a child.

She was not hesitant. Yes, she was going to have a number, she decided, but not too many. Besides, they would be busy working. And, besides that, the island had been electrified several years before.

I stopped, thinking I had misunderstood.

I hadn't, however. She went on to explain. Last year, she had read, a remote part of the southern island of Kyushu had finally been electrified. And this year's birth rate was just a fraction of what it had been the year before. You see—if there are no lights, then people go to bed before they are ready and they can't sleep. And if you can't sleep, then there are only a few things you can do and making babies is one of them. Did I understand?

I nodded. At the same time I was surprised. No fifteen-year-old Japanese girl I had ever met had ever said anything like that. I glanced at her as she walked beside me, her profile against the pines. It was bland, unreflective, innocent.

We were nearing town. We passed the general store. I looked at her again to see if she would look in to see her future husband. She did not. We walked on.

"There's the inn," she said. "If you're going to stay, that's the only place. And you will stay, I think. There are no more boats." I thanked her. "I will help you," she said.

She did. Introduced me to the innkeeper, a fat woman, took me up to my room, inspected it, complained about the view, sat down when I asked her to, had tea with me after the woman had padded away, floor creaking.

We leaned against the low sill, looking out of the window at the sea, now dark. The light was gray, pearly, the cloudless haze-covered sky was like half an oyster shell lowered over us. I looked at her arm, lying next to mine on the unpainted wood of the sill.

Her skin was beautiful. Perhaps nowhere on earth is there more beautiful skin than in Japan. Usually hairless, it is not like a mere covering. It is as though the entire body, all the way through, were composed of this soft, smooth lustrousness. I touched her arm. She looked at me, her eyes dark under the darkened sky.

*   *   *

I had made a mistake. To me it had seemed natural. Our being together. My loneliness. And then—for this is the way we think—the frankness about Kyushu when it was still dark. And then her not looking for her boy-husband, nor being ashamed of being seen with me, even though engaged. Then this extraordinary business with the inn and her sitting close to me and the fat woman regarding this all impartially as if

it were usual. Perhaps, I had been thinking, this was some lovely island custom of which I had been unaware. All of this led me to my mistake.

She did not understand. She allowed me to stroke her arm—soft, full, with that translucent skin; let me turn her hand over as though it were some marine animal we were both examining, and hold it; did not object to my putting a hesitant arm around her waist; and was completely and genuinely surprised when I tried to kiss, touch checks, rub noses—whatever it was I had on my lonely mind.

I did not speak, not wanting to lose them. It was nice walking with them on a beach where I had never been, my footprints separate from theirs and their tire tracks.

How often does this happen in Japan, I wonder—daily, hundreds of times, I should guess. A Japanese would have known that it was impossible; a Westerner always hopes that it won't be.

The foreigner who gets excited in the mixed bath, that classic comic character. I often enough make fun of him; I often enough become him. This is because of what we feel in Japan—the promise, the lure of the place, the mirage of pleasure, the distant vista of—uh—happiness.

It is never quite where you are but it is always just around the corner. The people are so agreeable, so permissive. They are, after all, very different, and you are, after all, very different from them. Why not?—since it seems to be offered, why not just take what you want, what you need?

You can, I suppose. Certainly a part of my quest is devoted to seducing the natives—a travel adjunct observed by traveling foreigner and traveling native alike. But in the case of fifteen-year-old girls you would be wise not to. If you are like me, you want to seduce rather than corrupt, and you attempt to maintain the fuzzy line separating the two. I want to take without hurting, I tell myself. This is not, however, true. I don't want to take. I want to be given. And this is what the friendly Japanese always seem on the verge of doing—giving. And sometimes they do, though I should add that it is easier to make friends with boys than with girls.

The light was gray, pearly,
the cloudless haze-covered sky
was like half an oyster shell
lowered over us. I looked at
her arm, lying next to mine
on the unpainted wood
of the sill.

And I, innocent despite experience, go around hoping to be seduced and consequently read such unlikely intentions into the thoughts of this little girl who has kindly helped me find a room, into even those of the fat woman who has, of course, seen nothing unusual. They must have many such helpful children on the island.

I did not, I was happy to observe, feel guilty. My years here have taught me at least this much. But I did feel—Japanese feeling—ashamed, and—universal feeling—put out.

Nor did I share any of this wisdom with the suddenly sober little fifteen-year-old who, I had managed to convince myself, had been making

advances to me. Instead, I sat back, smiled, and looked out of the window again. So did she. Then she giggled and began prattling again, smelling of mothballs and, under this pervading odor, of her own soft skin, that delicious rice-powder smell that makes one think hungrily of bread freshly baked.

I sat there, at least enjoying some of the feeling of the shame upon which I insisted. Ashamed of being big and lumbering and stupid. This is how the foreigner traditionally feels in the small, fragile Japanese house. There he sits all hands and feet, afraid of sticking an elbow through a *shoji* pane.

He never gets over it, even after many years. He may, however, refine the feeling, as I have done: I no longer feel clumsy around their houses; I feel clumsy around their feelings.

My major feeling, however—I have no idea what hers was, if she had any—was petulance. I had been, somewhat obscurely it must have seemed, offended. Now cross, querulous, I sat glumly, and she finally, perhaps sensing a lessening of welcome, stood up to take her leave.

She had short legs; she looked dumpy in her school uniform; her eyes were too far apart, making her look bovine.

Could she and her little friends come and call in the evening and talk some more?

No, they could not, I answered, adding churlishness to my other faults.

I went to bed early. It is perhaps true that the best way to get to know a people is to sleep with them, but this is complicated in Japan. Innocence always gets in the way, just the kind of innocence that I—like everyone else—want to go to bed with. I occupied an indulgent half-hour or so with thoughts of what I should have done, what I now decided (safely alone in bed) I had really wanted to do: torn schoolgirl uniform, thighs immodestly up in the air, cries for mercy, etc. Eventually, however, I grew bored and fell into a deep and satisfactory sleep.

The Stone Cat

Kitagijima is a quarry island. The little town is attractive. It has a broad basin of a harbor with steps at one end, steps leading directly into the water like those of Benares or of Adriatic ports. There is a shiny stone torii and a row of stonecutters' shops. The town is covered with stone dust, as if with volcanic ash.

And everyone in it is dead. The apprentices lie covered with stone dust, looking like fallen statuary, sound asleep. In the general store a woman lies in her lair, a half-eaten watermelon in front of her; in the tiny government office, men in clean white shirts lie amid abacuses and telephones; a young boatman sprawls in the bottom of his boat.

The people are asleep. This is the Mediterranean of Japan, the only place where the siesta is observed. Inside this small town women are flat on their backs, arms and legs extended, a sheet pulled across the stomach because it makes you ill to sleep with your middle exposed. Men are on their sides or asleep in chairs, displaying that surprising ability the Japanese have for falling asleep just anywhere. Children are asleep in the grass. Babies are lying spread like starfish.

This occurs after the noon meal. It is very natural; it is undoubtedly good for you. At one time perhaps all Japanese fell soundly asleep after eating, as people do now in Greece and Italy and Yugoslavia. Now only in far off and forgotten places such as these islands do the Japanese allow themselves this pleasant custom. In Tokyo at this hour the city people have gulped

From **The Inland Sea,** *1971*

down a bowl of noodles, taken an aspirin, and are on their way back to their offices. Here on the islands they sleep.

The siesta is so rare in industrious Japan that my first thought is that a pestilence, some kind of sleeping sickness, has attacked the place, felling people as they worked. But in these quiet islands, where nothing ever happens, the siesta comes naturally. Waiting, I sit on the pier.

And everyone in it is dead. The apprentices lie covered with stone dust, looking like fallen statuary, sound asleep. In the general store a woman lies in her lair, a half-eaten watermelon in front of her; in the tiny government office, men in clean white shirts lie amid abacuses and telephones; a young boatman sprawls in the bottom of his boat.

Finally the young man in the bottom of the boat stirs, turns over, sits up, yawns, and looks at me.

"I came to see the place where the cat was thrown away," I say, to show myself not unacquainted with native customs.

"What cat?" he asks, rubbing his eyes.

"The cat that was thrown away."

"Who threw it away?"

"I don't know, but it was a long time ago I suppose."

"What?" He sat up, stared at me, his face heavy with sleep.

"They threw a cat away some place around here, you see. If you go there you can see it."

"If someone threw a cat away, it wouldn't still be there, would it? Where did they throw it away?"

"I don't know. Into the sea, I imagine."

"If you throw a cat into the sea, then it would die. It wouldn't be there now. Was it your cat?"

"No. This happened a long time ago."

"My friend's cat got lost last year," he told me, trying to help.

"No, this was perhaps hundreds of years ago."

He looked at me and finally said: "Well, if it was hundreds of years ago, you wouldn't find it around here now. Cats don't live that long, you know."

"I know, I know," I said impatiently. "It's a—it's a . . ."

I suddenly could not remember the word for "statue." So I said: "It's a stone cat."

He looked at me, no longer sleepy, eyes slightly narrowing. He got up, began tinkering with the boat, turning to say: "Why don't you ask at the town office?"

He turned his back to me, baited a line, and began to fish.

The officials were stretching, yawning, waking up. A girl was making them tea. I presented myself at the counter and asked about the cat.

"A lost cat," said one official, turning to another who was yawning and rubbing his back. He produced a form and asked my name, my age, my nationality.

"No, no," I said. "This is a cat that was thrown away."

But the word for "to throw away" is *suteru*, which sounds much like *shiteru*, an inflected form of the more common verb meaning "to know." Consequently the first official raised his eyes, looked at the second, and said: "It is a cat he says he knows."

Then, to me: "You know this cat?"

"No, no," I said. "I said it was a cat that

was thrown away," pronouncing the word very distinctly.

"A thrown-away cat," said the official as though correcting me. Then they both looked at me. An abandoned cat, perhaps? A valuable animal? A lost or strayed cat of some significance to me?

"No, it was thrown away some time ago."

"How long ago?"

"Maybe hundreds of years."

They looked at each other, then at me, then said they had no records that went that far back. I thanked them and said I would look around.

Outside the office I suddenly remembered the word for stone statue—*sekizo*—but I did not want to go back to the town office; so I asked a girl sitting in front of the empty beauty parlor. Her hair was up in clips and Scotch tape.

"Where, please, is the stone statue?"

"What statue?"

"The statue of the cat."

"What cat?"

"The thrown-away cat."

"Is there a thrown-away cat?"

"There was. But that was hundreds of years ago."

"Oh, really?" she said, picking up a magazine. She looked at it intently, biting her underlip with one tooth. She did not look up again, eyes on magazine, so I thanked her and went away.

When I looked back at her she was staring at me, eyes wide under a forest of hair clips. My next glance caught her racing next door with the news.

The watermelon-lady didn't even answer. She was busy finishing her fruit. The muscled and stone-dusted boys were making such a racket with their hammers that they couldn't hear me. I sat on the pier and watched two little boys watch me.

Finally, hopelessly, I asked: "Where is the cat?"

"Out there," said one, pointing to a distant promontory.

"The stone cat?"

He nodded.

"The one that looks at you so as to make your blood chill?"

He nodded, pointed, and turned to the other little boy for corroboration. Then both turned toward me and nodded again.

"If I could walk there, how long would it take?"

There was some doubt. Well, was it far? This was a matter of such disagreement between them that no answer was given. Well, did it take a long time? This they did not even hear, being busy arguing.

I walked over to the young boatman. He was still fishing, his back to me. Across the inlet, the two officials were hanging from the window staring at me.

"I found the cat," I said.

From The Japanese Garden, 1972

The Gods

In Zen Buddhism one does not seek to analyze the truth. Rather, one grasps the truth as a whole. "Not logically, but intuitively," goes the phrase, "does one seek the truth." This spiritual ideal presumes an awareness and acceptance of the entire universe. The dry garden with its sand and stones is a kind of Zen lesson. It is a garden abstracted, a world created in all of its diversity, yet unified. It is not realistic because it is real. It goes one step beyond the expected and moves toward the ideal. Each element in it is natural, yet this combination of elements is an embodiment of Zen philosophy, a model of Zen thought.

He turned and looked at me, then said: "That's nice."

"It's out there." I pointed to the promontory in the distance. "Is it far?" I asked politely.

He looked, measuring it with his eyes, then equally politely agreed. "Yes, it looks far."

"I should like to go there."

"Is that where your cat is?"

They were visible from the village because of their extreme size. It took an hour, moving slowly over the clear blue water, through the motes of the afternoon sun, the bottom of the sea lost in the blackness beneath. As we eventually neared the rocks, he shut off the motor. We floated in sudden quiet. He looked over first one side, then the other, as though he expected to find the animal struggling to the surface.

"Oh, it's not my cat. It's a stone statue."

"It's a what?"

"It's a . . . stone cat."

"Oh, a stone-cat," he said, pronouncing the words as he might have Angora-cat, Persian-cat, Maltese-cat. Then: "Well, cats like fish." This was to serve as transition between my cat and his going back to his baited line.

We were silent for a time, his back to me.

"Will you take me in your boat?" I asked.

He turned around and looked at me. "You want to go out there and search for the cat in my boat?"

"Yes, please."

"And you think you'll find it?"

"I hope so."

He looked at his fishing line, then sighed and drew it in over the gunwale. "Very well, we'll go out and search for your cat in those rocks way over there."

"Thank you very much."

"Don't mention it."

The rocks were enormous and a great distance away. They were visible from the village because of their extreme size. It took an hour, moving slowly over the clear blue water, through the motes of the afternoon sun, the bottom of the sea lost in the blackness beneath. As we eventually neared the rocks, he shut off the motor. We floated in sudden quiet. He looked over first one side, then the other, as though he expected to find the animal struggling to the surface.

The rocks were high blocks, piled one upon another. I could not imagine what kind of storm could have balanced such enormous weights. The boat drifted among them. I looked at the rocks while the helpful boatman searched the waves.

"I think one of the men of Heike must have brought the cat here and then his leader or someone made him throw it away," I said.

"One of the men of what?"

"The Taira clan. You know, Heike and Genji."

"Oh, them."

"The cat is of that period."

"Oh," He stopped searching the waves and was just getting out his fishing line again when I saw the cat. It was so near and so huge that I hadn't seen it. The top block, big as a small house, was the head. The rest was the body, and a cleft was one of the ears. The hole was the eye that turned the blood of passing sailors chill.

"There it is! there it is!" I shouted.

He put away his fishing line. "I don't see it."

"It's made out of stone. There. See its head, and its ear? And that hole is its eye."

"Oh," he said, beginning to understand, "so *that's* what you wanted to see." Then, suddenly the earnest mentor, he explained that I should have asked for the *neko no katachi o shita ishi* ("stones in the form of a cat"), that *sekizo* meant a man-made statue. Not, he added, that it made much difference. He had never heard of it before, and he doubted that those little boys had either. In any event, he concluded, it didn't look much like a cat to him. Nor did it to me, though there was something vaguely animal-like about the shape.

"It looks more like a dog," he decided. Then: "Maybe it was a dog they threw away."

"Well, perhaps. But they told me it was a cat."

"And you came all the way from Tokyo to see this then?"

"Well, not only this. But I came to this island to see this."

He looked at me closely. "Do you like it?"

"It doesn't look much like a cat. But now I've seen it at any rate."

"Do you want to go closer? Do you want to climb on it or something?"

"No—no thank you. This is fine. I've—well, I've seen it now."

"Are you happy?"

"Yes, yes, very happy."

"I see. You are happy that you finally saw it. Is that it?"

"Yes, that's it."

"I see."

He sat in the boat and looked at me. I suggested that we might as well return, and as he bent over the engine, he said that, yes, one might as well, now that one had seen the cat, now that one was happy.

There was not much conversation on the way back.

At the pier I wanted to pay him for his time and trouble. Oh, no, that wasn't necessary—it wasn't far.

Nonetheless, he had been very kind to take me.

"No, that's all right," he said.

Several people had stopped, at a safe distance, to watch us. Now all the employees hung from the windows of the town office.

"I don't feel right about not paying," I said.

"Oh, no," he said. "Besides, it was educational. Now I'll know where the cat is next time someone asks me."

Until the next boat came, hours later, I sat on the pier. Passing schoolchildren whispered audibly about cats. The beauty-shop girl, now coifed, clattered about on her clogs and with many looks and urgent nods spread the next chapter of her remarkable tale. The office windows remained full of white-shirted, attentive officials. Little work was done on the island that day.

* * *

The next boat carried me around the tip of the island, right past my stone cat. I could have viewed it with comfort and equanimity had I stayed on the other boat, though whether I would have recognized it is not so certain. We passed quite close, however, and then turned into a small port on the other side of the island.

Four little boys were playing by the otherwise deserted pier, casting their shadows after them in the afternoon sun. I leaned over the rail. They saw me and stopped playing, conferred among themselves, and then approached, all in a bunch, to test their English.

"Hello," said the first, to which I responded.

"Good-bye," said the second and I answered.

"I love you," called out the third.

Then, just as the boat was pulling out, the last little boy shouted:

"Who are you today?" And I continued island hopping: Shiraishijima, Takajima, Konojima, and beyond, to the Honshu mainland

The Silicate Filter

I do not, however, leave immediately. Perhaps it is that I am feeling the mixed revulsion and fascination at finally going to Hiroshima that must afflict all Americans. I explain to myself, however, that it is because I want to do some shopping.

I cannot find what I want. I never can; it always infuriates. At present I am searching for a silicate filter for my cigarette holder. Until last month they were readily available. Now, however, a new kind of cigarette holder has appeared that requires another kind of filter. The manufacturers have, with great foresight, seen that the tobacco stands carry now only the kind of filter useless to my holder. At the same time they cunningly display the new holder in order to tempt me. But I am firmly attached to my old. Impossible to find silicate filters in Tokyo, I agree—but surely here in the country . . .

Not at all. The giant hand of enterprise covers the land. The tobacco stands of Kure are as naked of the desired filter as are those of Ginza. And all of this overnight. Two months ago kiosks all over Japan were stacked with my kind of filter.

The same is true of everything else. I keep photo albums and have for years used a certain kind. Last year I suddenly found that no one had them any more. They were no longer being made. Shortly it developed that the kind of album in which you paste the pictures was likewise unavailable. Now only the new kind—sticky silver paper covered with thin veneer—is available. It is new, therefore it is good—supposed to save you time or something.

From The Inland Sea, *1971*

More seriously, when a Japanese publisher issues a translation of a Western book he prints only a certain number of copies and no more. Second printings are almost unheard of, no matter the continuing demand. If the edition sells out in a week or in ten years, it is all the same to him. It takes a monumental demand—*Gone With the Wind, Lady Chatterley's Lover*—for him to consider further printings. The same is true of phonograph records—and the same, naturally, is true of shops that sell books and records. They order one of everything, and when it is gone it is as though it never existed. There may be talk of having to order it from the publisher, but this does not mean that such will indeed occur, it is merely a phrase indicative of the impossibility of your project.

One detects a paradox here. Japan, the land that loves time, has a dizzying rate of turnover in small things like photograph albums and cigarette filters, the life expectancy of each model of which must be measured in mere months; Japan, land where tradition is respected, cannot even keep its books and records in print. But I know perfectly well that footwear (*geta*) in use since the Middle Ages are still sold on every street; that kimono in almost no way differs from styles five hundred years ago are still to be bought; that, indeed, the only kind of saw you can buy (one that cuts when pulled rather than pushed) is one perfected in the mists of antiquity.

Then it strikes me that naturally this would be so. *Geta* and kimono are Japanese; cigarette filters and photograph albums are not. Though I dare say there are many more people using my kind of filter than there are using *geta* at this late date, nonetheless, the mystique holds—things Japanese, no matter how useless, are important; things foreign, no matter how useful, are not, not really, that is.

And if I want to find a book or a record it had better be Japanese. I had been looking for Jane Bathori singing Satie, had been trying to find for a friend the superb Japanese translation of the *Memoirs of Hadrian.* If I had been looking for everything ever written by some local Kenneth Roberts—Eiji Yoshikawa, for example, author of *Musashi Miyamoto* and other claptrap—or all the recorded songs of Kokichi Takada, croaking ladies' favorites of decades back, purveyor of *ryukoka*, ersatz folk-flavored "popular" tunes of a nearly violent insipidity, these would have been there, hundreds of copies of them.

. . . hair barrettes in the shapes of Mickey and Minnie Mouse, and bracelets on which are imprinted, in English, such harmless if redundant phrases as I AM A GIRL.

There are areas, however, where some things foreign remain. One wonders at this, and then realizes that a subtle change has taken place in the objects, that they have been japanified, and that some fancied resemblance to something already in the culture has proved their unhappy saving, and—finally—that they have not been saved so much as preserved, like flies in amber or, more fitting simile, like the mammoth in the ice.

An example is to be found in any department store. There is a section, rather near what is called the young-miss corner, where what appear to be cakes are being sold. But these are not cakes. Rather they are quaint little clocks in the shape of snow-covered chalets or vermilion-turreted castles, music boxes built to look like windmills and waterwheels, wooden letter-holders that appear to be mailboxes or dog houses. Nearby are flounced French-flapper dolls to decorate the virginal bed, a variety of cute accessories including

hair barrettes in the shapes of Mickey and Minnie Mouse, and bracelets on which are imprinted, in English, such harmless if redundant phrases as I AM A GIRL.

There is no generic name for this assemblage, unfortunately, but it is at once apparent that the objects are all for young ladies. Further, for young ladies of some means if little discernment. They are for the *ojosan,* the young lady of good family who may be exposed to things foreign but never in their possibly dangerous and original form, who must, on the other hand, be continually reassured that such are, after all, despite their charming novelty, really, somehow, Japanese.

Take the clocks and music boxes. They are always in the Swiss style, such being thought of as the safest since the least exceptional—the Swiss being moderate, hard working, and not overgiven to innovation. At the same time, the style of carving is quite Japanese—it is of the variety known as *Kamakura-bori.* And though the music box may be in the form of the exotic windmill (the Netherlands is another safe choice, it is the most unexceptional country in Europe, think the Japanese, next to lovely Switzerland), it will sound, if wound, that beautiful old Japanese favorite "Moon on Ruined Castle."

Such objects now belong to the Japanese *ojosan* and exist no place other than in her world. Her life is one of exclaiming with delight at the more gooey desserts and crying with innocent if nonetheless Lesbian pleasure at performances of the Takarazuka—the all-girl "opera" that manages to preserve all the amenities of the old-style Shubert Brothers musical (glimpsed by a Japanese director in the 1920s and never forgotten) with most of the originality and wit of production numbers of American films from the 1930s.

It is she who presumably rushes through the stacks of charming frocks to sate herself with Mickey Mouse barrettes and cunning Bavaria-inspired weather forecasters in which the pretty couple safely wear kimono. Without a thought

in her charming head, she hovers, hummingbird-like, over the arrayed treasures and finally makes a choice that her chairman-of-the-board father or flower arranging-teacher mother will happily pay for. All of these girls are virginal, all of them are as pretty as flowers, and all of them have vegetable intelligences.

Of perhaps more import, however, is the fact that Mickey and Minnie are thus, and in typical Japanese fashion, saved for the ages. Long after their celluloid originals have turned to dust, long after every reference in Western literature is free of their names, they will remain in Japan, Mickey and Minnie together, and though possibly no longer to be recognized as mice, they will have taken on an autonomous existence simply because they have endured and will confront us from watch-face or hairpin with that implacable air of mystery which we now find in pre-Columbian sculpture or the artifacts of Etruria.

Wandering through the varied cultures of Japan or—better choice—climbing about among the different strata of civilizations on this island plateau, one comes across such fossils as this continually. This one—made of chalets and French-flapper dolls—is still soft to the touch as it were, but the one containing, say, T'ang music and dancing is hard as rock.

There is none, however, for cigarette filters. These remain foreign, intransigent. I ask at one last kiosk. No, the old lady knows what I mean but they stopped selling them last month. "But how about this?" And, with the air of unveiling the latest invention, she reveals a tray of brass pipes, long, attractive if filterless. These are those traditional pipes, once smoked by men and women alike, each holding a pinch of tobacco that went out after one puff, with which lovers of the Kabuki are quite familiar, which have been in evidence for the last two centuries, and which, though I have not seen one used for years, are still quite available. It is because they are Japanese, you see.

JAPAN *Later*

The "Real" Disneyland

Looking at Tokyo one sometimes wonders why the Japanese went to all the trouble of franchising a Disneyland in the suburbs when the capital itself is so superior a version.

Disneyland, and the other lands it has spawned, is based upon the happy thought of geographical convenience: all the interesting localities on earth located at one spot. Thus, there are African rivers and Swiss mountains and Caribbean islands and American towns. One feels one is seeing the world in miniature and, indeed, "it's a small world" is the slogan of one of the concessions.

Compare this now to Tokyo. There are hundreds of American fast-food stands with matching mock-Colonial architecture, there is a plaster Fontana di Trevi and a state guest house modeled after Versailles; there are dozens of red lacquered Chinese restaurants and equal numbers of white stuccoed Italian; there are thousands of boutiques with famous foreign names (Gucci, Dior, Yves St. Laurent, Arnold Palmer) printed all over them; there is an imitation Baker Street straight from London; the Museum of Western Art in Ueno has Rodin castings all over the front yard; and there is even an onion-domed Russian Orthodox cathedral. All of this, and much more, in a glorious architectural confusion of Corinthian columns and chromium pylons, dormer windows and curved escalators, half-timber, plain red brick, sheet steel, textured Lucite.

In this architectural stew (something from every place on earth) even the authentically Japanese takes on the pleasant flavor

From A Lateral View, *1985*

of ersatz novelty. Thus the old Toshogu Shrine in Ueno or the Awashimado (1618) in Asakusa appear in Tokyo's Disneyland context just as pleasingly synthetic as the new Japanese modern-style restaurant gotten up almost right as a French bistro.

It is evident that the Japanese claim to prior Disneyfication is a very strong one. No other country has brought the principle of the microcosm—ikebana, bonsai, chanoyu, *gardens—to such profuse perfection. No other has managed to turn so much into something else.*

In the face of this massive transplantation of everywhere else right into the heart of the capital, the Disney enterprises would seem to face the stiffest of competition. Tokyo is a mammoth Disneyland with an area of nearly 2,500-sq. km., and a working staff of almost 12 million. Yet not only Tokyo but all of Japan seems always to have the time (and the money) for the little imported Disneyland perched on reclaimed land in the outskirts.

One of the reasons would be that Japan is the real home of all such concepts as Disneyland has come to exemplify. To go there is, in a way, to come home. It was in Japan, after all, that the concept of the microcosm has been most fully elaborated, from its beginnings right down to Walkman-type baby loudspeakers for the ears, the wristwatch TV, and the smallest and fastest silicon chip yet.

Japan, too, has also displayed a fondness for the geographical microcosm, the bringing together of famous places into a single locality. Look at the number of little towns in Japan that sport a Ginza, plainly a replica of what was once Tokyo's most famous shopping street. And look at the number of gardens that have a little Mount Fuji, small but climbable, included among their attractions.

Indeed the classical Japanese garden gives ready indication of how dear the microcosmic impulse has long been to the Japanese heart, and how early the Japanese had perfected these small visitable worlds.

Take, for example, the Korakuen in Tokyo—an Edo-period garden. One climbs a small hill, which calls itself Mount Lusha in China, and finds oneself at a replica of the Togetsu bridge from Kyoto's Arashiyama district. But the view is not the river but Hangzhou's famous lake—we are back in China again. Not for long, however; climb another hill and here is Kyoto once more, the veranda platform of the Kiyomizu Temple, one of the famous sights of the city.

Some Edo gardens are even more Disneyland-like. For example Tokyo's Rikugien in Komagome. Here, in one place, arranged somewhat like a miniature golf course, are all of the 88 classical sites, all tiny, and all with noticeboards explaining the Chinese or Japanese association.

Lest it be thought that all of this is just big-city Tokyo and late Edo commercialism, Japan's claim to early Disneyfication must be defended. Did you know that the garden of the elegant Katsura Villa is itself a miniaturization of famous scenic attractions from elsewhere—that there is the Sumiyoshi pine, and the Tsutsumi waterfall, and the Oigawa river, and the famous wooded spit on the other side of Japan, Ama no Hashidate? And that even the elegant moss-garden, that of Saihoji, contains—if one knows how to find them—scenes from ten famous places, reproductions of ten famous things (rocks, etc.), ten poetic references, and ten famous pine trees—all reproductions, fancied though they be, of something somewhere else?

Even Ryoan-ji's famous rock garden has its Disney attributes. Those rocks—what are they, besides being just rocks? Well, they are various things. They are manifestations of the infinite, or they are islands in the ocean, a section of the famous Inland Sea. Or (a very Disney touch, this) they are a mother tiger and her frolicking cubs.

Even earlier, the avatar of Walt Disney was alive and well in Japan. He would have loved the Byodo-in, replica of a Chinese water pavilion, with imitation Chinese swan-boats (phoenixes, actually) being poled and pushed about. And he would have noted with pleasure that in gardens of the period everything was always something else—something from far away. One way of arranging garden rocks in inland Kyoto was *suhama* (graveled seashore) and another was *ariso* (rocky beaches).

Earlier yet, Japanese gardens were displaying the vision that later made Disneyland famous. Here in the first gardens what do we find? Why, things from far away indeed. The garden was a representation of Sukhavati, the Western Paradise of the Buddha Amitabha. And those rocks in the water were the three islands of the blessed—Horai, Hojo and Eishu. And that big rock in the middle—that is Mount Sumera itself.

The date of this kind of garden is 1000. Just think—almost 1000 years ago Japanese vision and technique had in Sumera made the first Space Mountain!

It is evident that the Japanese claim to prior Disneyfication is a very strong one. No other country has brought the principle of the microcosm—ikebana, bonsai, *chanoyu*, gardens—to such profuse perfection. No other has managed to turn so much into something else.

So, when one wonders why Japan, such a Disneyland itself, needed a real Disneyland, one must conclude that it found here something in which a true fellow-feeling was discovered. And also, perhaps, because in Disneyland it recognized as well one of its own enduring qualities.

This is a passion amounting to near genius for kitsch. If kitsch is defined as primarily something pretending to be something else—wood acting like marble, plastic acting like flowers, Anaheim, California acting like the Mississippi—then Japan has a long history, a celebrated expertise and a strong claim to mastery in just this very thing. In fact, Japan often enough has been called "the home of kitsch."

If this is true then, with understandable enthusiasm Japan embraced the biggest piece of kitsch in the West. Did so, then broke off a chunk and brought it home to add to its collection.

From Tokyo, 1999 The Japanese

The Japanese are, more than most, a module people. The language, the thought itself tends to modular forms: the cliché is respected, the ritual is observed; most of the arts—Japanese dance, the martial arts—are taught in the form of modules called *kata*. One wonders at the origin of this. Is it perhaps the pragmatic advantage of form? Invariable observations oil the machinery of human relations; modular construction lowers unit cost. What is now true of computer parts was once true of tatami sizes and remains true of seasonal complements. And each unit is, within the confines of its genre, complete.

Walking in Tokyo

One walks for various reasons. Often it is to get somewhere. Occasionally it is to enjoy the walk. The street leads someplace. Usually it is seen as a stretch connecting one place with another. Sometimes it is seen as itself. Different cities have different streets. The differences depend upon how the street is used and how it is seen. That is, walking in Marrakech is different from walking in, say, Chicago.

And walking in Tokyo is different from either. Streets here have their mundane and ostensible uses but they also have something more. The Japanese street remains Asian, and it is still, in a number of senses, an area of display.

As, to be sure, are the streets of other cities. One thinks of the *plaza,* the town square, the café-lined avenue. But there are differences. In Europe, one is part of the display—to see and be seen, to look and be looked at. The street is a stage. How different Japan. There are no European-style cafés, few American-style malls. And usually no place to sit down. You, the walker, are not an actor.

Rather, you are an active spectator. The display is not you and the others about you. The display is the street itself. The direction is not from you to it but from it to you.

Shops line the street, open up, spill out. Clothes on racks and sides of beef alike are shoved onto sidewalks. The fish shop's scaly glitter is right there, still gasping. Baby televisions piled high blink at you, eye to eye. Not here the closed transactions of the super-

From A Lateral View, *1986*

market. Rather, on the Tokyo street, there is the raw profusion of consumption itself.

And even in the more sedate avenues, such as the Ginza, where goods stay indoors, the display continues. Signs and flags proclaim; *kanji* (Chinese ideographs) grab and neon points. Signs, signs everywhere, all of them shouting, a semiotic babble, signifiers galore, all reaching out to the walker, the person going past.

This is what is very Asian about the Japanese street. This we would recognize if the units were mangoes or rice cakes. But here they are calculators and microwave ovens, instant cameras and word processors. The content startles.

Yet the form reassures. This is, even yet, the Japanese street we see in Hokusai and read about in Saikaku. In old Edo the main street was called the *noren-gai.* The better shops advertised themselves with their *noren,* those entry curtains marked with the shop crest. The noren-gai was the better stretch where worth and probity were the standards.

The concept remains. The noren may be facade-high neon or a mile-long laser beam, but the *gai* (district) is still marked as the place of display. From Ginza's store-window showcases to the piles of silicon chips out on the sidewalk—like exotic nuts—in Akihabara, the display continues, a year-round drama in which all the actors are for sale.

The Japanese street is, in a way, the ideal to which all other streets must aspire. It is the ultimate in unrestrained display. Other streets in other countries are handicapped by zoning laws and citizen's associations and the like. Not so Tokyo, or not to that extent. The Japanese street is very public.

Conversely, the Japanese home is very private. In Edo all the houses had high fences. In Tokyo, though suburbia must content itself with merely a token hedge, privacy remains much respected. The house and the garden (if there is one) are private property in the most closed and restrict-

ed sense. In a city as crowded as Tokyo—Edo, too, for that matter—privacy is a luxury almost as expensive as space. What is acquired at great expense is zealously guarded.

What is enclosed is, thus, private property. And what is open is not—it is public. So it is with most Western cities as well. But in Japan the difference is that the public space appears to belong to no one; it seems to be no one's responsibility. As a consequence, there are few effective zoning laws, very little civic endeavor, almost no city planning, and while housing is subject to scrutiny, the surrounding streets are not.

And so, the streets of Tokyo are allowed an organic life of their own. They grow, proliferate; on all sides street life takes on unrestricted natural forms.

Tokyo is a warren, a twisted tangle of streets and alleys and lanes. Though there are some grid-patterned streets where civic endeavor has in the past attempted some order, this enormous city is a comfortable rat's nest, the streets having grown as need and inclination directed. Opportunities to remake the city were resisted not only after the various Edo disasters, but after the 1923 earthquake and the 1945 firebombing as well.

The reason was, of course, that the warren was preferred. It was seen (better, felt) to be the proper human environment. The Japanese, like the English, prefer the cozy, and consequently the streets of Tokyo are as crooked and twisting as those of London. There is a corresponding sense of belonging as well. The cozy warren is just for us, not for those outside.

Which is what one might expect from a people who make so much of what is private (ours) and so little of what is public (theirs). For such folk the neighborhood is of primary importance (and Tokyo is a collection of village-size neighborhoods), and its public aspect attains intimacy only when incorporated into the well known.

For example, sections of old, twisted Tokyo

are being torn down. Not because of any civic planning, but so that the most expensive land in the world may be more profitably used. And the new buildings are often built foursquare, with straight streets. Not from any notions of urban efficiency, however; it is merely that buildings are most cheaply constructed if they are squarish and right-angled.

So, the old tangle is torn down. And it is rebuilt, incorporated within the basement of the high-rise that took its place. There again are the bars, the little restaurants, the warren reborn.

The significance of public areas belonging to no one is not that they belong to everyone but that they can be used by just anyone. This means that the owners or lessees of private land in public places can be as idiosyncratic as they like.

Take modern Tokyo architecture. Visitors are astonished by its variety, given what they may have heard of the Japanese character. Instead of the expected conformity, they are presented with the wildest diversity.

The glass-and-concrete box (cosmetics) is next to the traditional tile-roofed restaurant (sukiyaki and *shabu-shabu*), which is next to a high-tech, open-girder construction (boutiques), which is next to a pastel-plastered French provincial farmhouse (designer clothes).

The architecturally odd is there to attract attention. Thus Tokyo mainstreet architecture has much the same function as the signs and banners that decorate it. To stand out is to sell something better. (As for conformity, there is plenty of that, but it is found in nothing so superficial as architecture.) Though profit may be a motive for eccentric architecture, it is not its only result. Among others, the stroller is presented with an extraordinary walking experience.

With space used in this distinctive fashion, one naturally wonders about the uses to which time is put. These are, as one might have expected, equally noteworthy. It is not so much that one can time-travel in Tokyo (and can do it even better in Kyoto), go from the seventeenth to the twentieth to the eighteenth century by walking around a block. One can, after all, do that in many European cities, which have more old buildings than Tokyo. Rather it is that Tokyo provides a fantastic rate of temporal change. In Europe a building was built for a century. In Tokyo a building, it often seems, is built but for a season.

 *The Japanese*

From A Taste of Japan, 1984

Whoever said Japanese cuisine was all presentation and no food was, of course, quite wrong, but one can at the same time understand how such a statement came to be made, particularly if one comes from a country where it is simply enough that food looks decent and tastes all right.

Actually, the presentational ethos so much a part of the Japanese cuisine continues right into the mouth. Is there any other cuisine, I wonder, which makes so much of texture, as divorced from taste? The West, of course, likes texture, but only when it is appropriate and never when it is tasteless. Consequently, the feel of the steak in the mouth, the touch of the clam on the tongue are part of the Western eating experience, but they are not enjoyed for their own sakes. Rather these sensations are enjoyed as harbingers of taste.

Japan, is again, quite different.

There are, in fact, not a few foods that are used for texture alone. *Konnyaku* (devil's tongue jelly) has no taste to speak of though it has an unforgettable texture. *Tororo* (grated mountain yam) again has much more feel than flavor. *Udo* looks like and feels much like celery but it tastes of almost nothing at all. *Fu,* a form of wheat gluten, has no taste, except the flavor of whatever surrounds it. Yet all are prized Japanese foods.

They go up and come down at an almost alarming rate. In the Shinjuku and Ikebukuro sections, if you miss a month, you might well next time get lost, so fast and frequent are the metamorphoses. What you remembered has now become something else. And the hole in the street, the vacant lot, now holds the current architectural icon, a glittering chrome-and-glass structure like a giant lipstick or a mammoth lighter.

Old Edo had its construction-destruction compulsions as well, but they were different in that, first, there were so many fires that the reconstruction came to be seen as repair; and second, the new structures were not extreme because there were sumptuary laws and because the Edoite had only wood, tile and stone.

Now there are certainly no laws against display, and the Japanese architect has steel, glass, concrete and plastic, all of which can be forced into any shape desired.

The temporal dislocation in Tokyo is so extreme that the capital is, consequently, never finished. It is in a permanent state of construction. Like life it is always in flux. It is an illustration of itself—a metaphor for continual change.

The display of the Tokyo street, the Tokyo park, the Tokyo garden is thus a varied and a complicated thing. Walking becomes a variegated experience with many a surprise.

This is not perhaps unique to Tokyo, but is certainly not typical of the world's major cities. There—Washington, D.C., Beijing, Moscow— one is presented with a view and the view is the experience. Once you have glanced at it you have comprehended and no amount of strolling about will add anything. There is nothing left to discover after the view of the Capital, the Temple of Heaven or the Kremlin.

Obviously, human variety was not in the minds of these architects; rather, it was human similarity that was being both courted and celebrated. And Tokyo, too, has its monolithic views—but it only has two of them: the Imperial Palace and the Diet Building.

Otherwise, there are no views at all. Everywhere you look it is a chaos, but what a fascinating chaos it is. It is a mosaic city, a melange city. It has no center. It has no outside. It even seems to lack the structural supports we know from other cities.

One of these we know from the early medieval

The reason is that the Japanese appreciate texture almost as much as they appreciate taste. The feel of the food, like its appearance, is of prime importance. The West, on the other hand, does not like extreme textures. Those few Westerners who do not like sushi or *sashimi* never say that it does not taste good. Rather, it is the texture they cannot stand—the very feel of the food.

Not only do the Japanese like textures, they have turned their consideration into one more aesthetic system governing the cuisine. Textures, runs the unwritten rule, ought to be opposite, complementary. The hard and the soft, the crisp and the mealy, the resilient and the pliable. These all make good and interesting combinations and these, too, have their place within this presentational cuisine.

There are other aesthetic considerations as well but this is a good place to stop and take stock of what we have so far observed. For review let us take a very simple dish, a kind of elemental snack, something to eat while drinking, a Japanese canapé. Let us see how it contrives to satisfy the aesthetic demands of Japanese cuisine.

The dish is *morokyu*, baby cucumber with *miso* (bean paste), usually consumed with sake, more often nowadays with beer. Let us look at its qualities. First, the colors are right; fresh green and darkish red is considered a proper combination. Second, the portions are small enough so that their patterns can be appreciated—the dish consists of just one small cucumber cut up into sticks and a small mound of *miso*.

city and from its modern descendant, the Islamic city. This is the division into trade towns. Streets of the goldsmiths, area of the camel drivers, pits of the dyers—that sort of thing. Such remains are visible in all major cities: the West Side of New York, for example.

Tokyo has something of this, things bunched together from the old days before there was public transportation: Otemachi, where the banks' headquarters are; Sudacho, where the wholesale cloth merchants are; Akihabara, down the street, where the cut-rate appliance people are.

But this grid cannot be used to comprehend the city because it is not operative. It is simply left over. Operative is a micro-grid that finds a bank, a cloth merchant, an appliance store in every neighborhood. And there are hundreds of neighborhoods in each district, and dozens of districts in each section, and tens of sections in this enormous city.

Duplication, therefore, becomes one of the features of a Tokyo walk. When you reach another public bath you are in a different neighborhood. And each neighborhood is a small town, which has its laundromat, its egg store, its hairdressing parlor, its coffee shop.

Looking at the inner structure of Tokyo one is reminded of the inner structure of the traditional Japanese house. The sizes of the *tatami, fusuma* and *shoji* are invariable. The construction is by modular unit. City construction is likewise modular—the laundromat in Asakusa and the laundromat in Shinjuku are identical.

We of the West, used to large swaths of activity, do not know what to think of the filigree of Tokyo, its fine embroidery of human endeavor.

But we of the West know what to *feel*. Walking on the streets of Tokyo we are aware of a sense of human proportion that we might not have known in the city from whence we came. To walk in Tokyo is to wear a coat that fits exceptionally well.

The proportions (except where mania has taken over—the towers of west Shinjuku, for example) are all resolutely human. We raise our eyes to see buildings; we do not crane our necks. And the streets are narrow—all too narrow if it is one where cars are permitted. And there are little alleys just wide enough for a person. And there are things to look at.

Things to look at! Tokyo is a cornucopia held upside down. One does not know where to

---

Third, the arrangement and plate complement each other. The round mound of *miso* (*yamamori*) is considered operative, so the dish is served on a long, flat, narrow plate, thus emphasizing the very roundness of the bean paste. The length of the cucumber—and it is always cut along its length, never its width—stretches away from the *miso* and emphasizes the emptiness and again, by contrast, the fullness of the food. Fourth, the dish should be redolent of summer, since *morokyu* is mainly eaten in warm weather. So the dish should be untextured, unornamented, of a light color—white, pale blue, or a faint celadon green—thus emphasizing the seasonal nature of *morokyu* itself. Fifth, the textures are found to blend. The cool crispness of the cucumber complements perfectly the mealy, soft, and pungent *miso*.

Let's see, is there anything else? Oh, yes, almost forgot— the taste. Well, *morokyu* tastes very good indeed, the firm salty *miso* fitting and complementing the bland and watery flavor of the cucumber. But it is perhaps telling that, with so much going on in this most presentational of cuisines, it is the taste that one considers last. Perhaps it is also fitting. The taste of this cuisine lingers.

Naturally, one cannot compare the taste of a few slices of fresh fish and almost raw vegetables with, let us say, one of the great machines of the French cuisine, all sauces and flavors. And yet, because it is made of so little, because there is so little on the plate, because what there is is so distinctly itself, Japanese cuisine makes an impression

look first. If people say, and they do, that Tokyo makes them feel a child again, this is because it makes them all curiosity, all enthusiasm, all eyes.

This then is the display of Tokyo. It perhaps may be mercantile but its appeal goes far beyond the financial. Things become, in this plethora of sensation, detached from their utilitarian aspects. They exist for themselves: the cascades of kanji, the plastic food replicas in the restaurant windows, the façade, stories high, made entirely of TV sets.

One then remembers the woodcuts of Hokusai and Hiroshige—views of Edo—and sees the similarities. All of that detail, all of those particulars, all that decoration, the sheer movement of it—it is real and it is all here now.

Especially on Sundays—the day (along with national holidays) when Tokyo turns itself again into Edo. The main streets in the major sections (Ginza, Shinjuku, Shibuya, Ikebukuro, Ueno) become malls. Motor traffic is forbidden (from 1 to 6 PM) and, as in olden times, people swarm into the streets. Unlike weekdays, when they rush about in the modern manner, on Sundays they stroll in the old-fashioned way. In Edo style they take their time, look at the stores, stop for a snack and saunter on.

Here, one thinks, looking at the leisured throng, Edo lives on. Despite the new backdrop of TV and computer games, the true human activity is the same, now as then. To leave the house and enjoy the display, to gaze at the latest and perhaps purchase a bit—this is what old Edo did and what new Tokyo does.

The new merchants, conservative as always, greatly feared for trade when the carless Sundays went into effect several years ago. They thought no one would come if they could not park their wheels. They were ruined, they wept in large advertisements. Not at all. They had not reckoned on the Edo spirit. Now the merchants look forward to Sunday and even department stores spill out onto the crowded streets. They have more customers on Sundays than they do on any other day of the week. Now smiling management gives out free balloons and plastic flowers to the passing crowd, while overhead kanji dances and neon glows in the sunlight.

All of Tokyo is out walking, sauntering through the streets, enjoying that amazing display which is Tokyo.

that is just as distinct as that of the French.

This is because the taste is so fresh, because the taste is that of the food itself and not the taste of what has been done to it. The sudden freshness of Japanese cuisine captures attention as does a whisper in the midst of shouts. One detects, in presentation and in flavor, authenticity. Things are introduced and eaten in varying degrees of rawness, nothing is overcooked; one feels near the food in its natural state. Indeed, one *is* often very near it because so much Japanese food (cut bite-sized in the kitchen and arranged on plates before being brought out) is cooked or otherwise prepared at the table, right in front of you.

Japanese cuisine is, finally, unique in its *attitude* toward food. This ritual, presentational cuisine, which so insists upon freshness and naturalness, rests upon a set of assumptions concerning food and its place in life. Eventually, the cuisine itself depends upon the Japanese attitude toward the environment, toward nature itself.

These assumptions are many.

First, one will have noticed that the insistence upon naturalness implies a somewhat greater respect for the food than is common in other cuisines. At the same time, however, it is also apparent that respect consists of doing something to *present* naturalness. In other words, in food as in landscape gardens and flower arrangements, the emphasis is on a presentation of the natural rather than the natural itself. It is not what nature has wrought that excites admiration but what man has wrought with what nature has wrought.

The Street: Notes on Construction

TOKYO: Form and Spirit

Theme I: Walking

The Street

Notes on the Physical Construction

RULES perhaps to be observed:

- The Street will TURN whenever possible; there will be (unless unavoidable) no long straight stretches extending across an entire gallery.

- The Street, as it meanders about the entire museum, will follow one of the patterns of the Edo Stroll Garden. That is, whenever possible there will be vistas (windows, holes in the walls) showing both where we have been and where we are going. Further (in the Sen no Rikyu style) these window/ holes will frame something pertinent. For example, in a wall containing nothing but pachinko machines, all working, a blank hole in the middle will show us a section we have been through, will perfectly frame the Contemplative Buddha.

- The Street will obviously have its own SPATIAL form, which will be both varied and unified. At the same time another dimension should be observed. This is the TEMPORAL. The street will do more than carry you along: it will conceptually indicate. At the same time the street should not be chronological because Japan is not. Like Tokyo itself there should be

For the Walker Art Museum exhibition, "Tokyo: Form and Spirit," unpublished, 1986

178

time strata but the general under-drift should be vaguely chronological. Computers should not come at the beginning of the street; *torii* should.

- Nothing should be discrete yet everything should be in units. There should be a module feeling about the construction itself. As though many of the parts are interchangeable. As though the floor might be the ceiling, and that the experience YOU are having is what everyone else is but is not the ONLY one.

The Construction of the Street and an indication of its progression might follow the general pattern indicated below

1. Entry into the street is through massed orange wooden *torii* (as at the Fushimi Shrine), a corridor made of them, turning slightly so that end is not at first seen. Between them, however, one can see flashing neon of other section, hear cascading pachinko balls, other indications of modernity.

2. From Shinto directly into Buddhism. From the *torii* lane a sharp turn into a dark space and there, hanging, a Section of the Buddha—perhaps half the head (enormous), perhaps a single hanging hand (huge) in the *mudra* for LEARNING. About one, the sound of chants and bells, the smell of incense. But right over Buddha's head/hand, the roseate glow of neon from another section of the street.

3. A section of the Street turned into The Room. The side, ceiling and floors all made of *shoji*. Roland Barthes' desirably Japanese room which can be turned upside-down with no one noticing. One is enclosed in the milky light. On the left one *shoji* door is very slightly open. The passerby peers and catches his/her breath. There in the several inch view (only for those who notice), a perfect Japanese garden (real looking but really a back-lighted Kodachrome).

4. Street of Crafts. All helter-skelter, all piling out of small "shop" doors (and all nailed down so that the patrons don't walk off with

---

From The Temples of Kyoto, 1995   *The Gods*

Buddhism as a religion also had need of its places of refuge, areas of retreat. Prayer is essentially private—this is something that Shingon knows. The altar is black until the candles are lit. The most important ceremonies are early in the morning, in the last dark before the sun rises. The worshipper kneels alone and contemplates both darkness and self.

Temples cultivate shadows. Very few Japanese things traditionally were made to be seen in the bright light which now illuminates them. Electrified Kabuki looks flimsy and garish because it was meant to be viewed only by massed candlelight; black lacquer seems mottled and dull because it was made to be seen in dimness, its surface reflecting only ambient light. The Great Buddha at Todai-ji in Nara with its giant lotuses and attendant bodhisattva looks like backstage at *Lakmé* because all of this detail was never meant to be so plainly viewed. Turn off the lights and the statue again assumes its dim presence. This can be comforting. The Yakushi Nyorai waits in the medieval cold, the invisible Kannon remains in her chamber.

Yoshida Kenko (1283-1350), a retired court officer, would later write in his *Tsurezuregusa,* known as *Essays in Idleness,* that visits to temples are best made by night. Very true—and here in the civilized shadows of Ishiyama-dera one again remembers that darkness is a friend to religion.

the show)—*geta* and *zori* and kimono and carpenters' tools and pots and pans, an entire fantasy of work and wear. The sound is the babble of humanity, but all in Japanese.

5. Ending on an enamel tunnel and a moving walkway which carries one into a wonderland of food. All natural, all Japanese (and all plastic). The tunnel narrows so that the brilliantly lighted cases on all sides, ceiling as well, are quite near. The sound of the fish markets, the vegetable markets, old street cries.

6. Swirling into a small rotunda where (if you want, but I don't) come the Hokusai, Hiroshige graphics, all blown up (but still looking like Sony ads, I think). Perhaps redeemed by color, flags, banners, etc.

7. Others might include:

A passage made entirely of small TV sets, like mosaic, and all showing the same thing. A portion of the Street we have seen before. Us milling about in it. The TV sets cover floor and ceiling as well and have a bend in the middle of the street so that at one point you are surrounded by these tiny sets, like the facets of a great eye.

Japan the Toy Store. All the mechanical toys (monsters, rabbits, turtles, robots) in Japan, all lined up and all GOING at the same time.

It is probably impossible, but how elegant to have everyone take off his shoes, or at least put something over them.

Little Akihabara—turn a corner and wham! All the electronic junk in the country, blinking, howling, whining, flashing—talking robots croaking out greetings in four interchangeable languages.

Much use throughout to be made of *kanji*. No one there will be able to read it. But there

they will be—Barthes' signs—the signifier without the signified.

Ludus Japonicus should be represented, i.e., Sport. Perhaps a baseball throwing machine, or a bank of them. Or the sumo champ you put a coin into and he arm wrestles with you.

The *kata* of judo or kendo shown one by one and put in some artful juxtaposition to the module units of Japanese architecture to show that they are the same. The idea of *kata* as a learning process incorporated into the structure of the street itself.

As the Street continues it gets brighter and more frenetic and noisier but, at the end, some pool of quiet brilliance. The street ends—a noisy waterfall suddenly entering a quiet pool. Something darkish and warmish and "consoling" at the end. We are all One Together. We Are All *Nakama*.

The Center itself should have a kind of *genkan* for getting into the shoes. If you cannot leave your shoes, at least you should somehow be persuaded to leave something of yourself behind so that you will be different throughout the experience.

So, at the end, there should be an anti-*genkan* when you get back (sadly, regretfully) into the ordinary you. You should get something back, or perhaps receive something.

During The Street you ought to be given things. Everyone should get something. Tiny paper umbrellas, single silicon chip. Something free. Slips of paper with lucky number. Your FORTUNE perhaps at the beginning of the Street and then you tie it to the posts at the end of the Street so you are still there and you too have given.

Hiroshima

Hiroshima. The historical fact of the city lives only in the imagination. "There!" one thinks. It was right there—the great fireball, the terrible wind, that high cloud, mushroom of death. Right there—the skeleton of the Industry Promotion Hall, the only solid building that survived, rising above the plateau of this delta city of bridges and waterways—right there it was dropped.

I stand in Peace Park, on the balcony of the museum, and look at the spot where massive death was. This is where concrete crumpled like paper, where iron smoked and twisted, where annihilated humans left their shadows etched in concrete.

Trying to visualize, trying to imagine, as though I had myself been there, I fail. The immensity is impossible to reconstruct and consequently to comprehend. It was chaos and our minds are too orderly to comprehend this.

Hiroshima itself has not retained the experience. The park, the museum, the paper cranes, the memorial statuary, the ruined promotion hall—they are there. But the city is, after all, the largest in southern Honshu. It is too important to be merely museum and memorial. It is many things to many people now, and few indeed must be those to whom it is just the city where the Americans dropped the first atomic bomb a quarter of a century ago. Life, as the typically Japanese phrase has it, goes on.

This is also one of the facts of death—that one forgets it. One may disapprove of oneself for forgetting, may have wanted to keep the fact green, tended like a grave. It is impossible. Life is

From The Inland Sea, *1971*

too strong. Death loses on every occasion except the last.

And Hiroshima has other things to think of. The people find their city neither a place of past horror nor a shrine, just as the Romans—who have had to live with the Vatican in their midst—do not find their city particularly holy. Besides, only twenty persons remain out of each original wartime one hundred. The rest were either killed or have moved away. With house gone, family gone, city gone, there was no reason for survivors to remain.

New people came in. They were, as was to be expected, people with few former roots in the city. They were also, to an extent, profiteers and speculators. That was over two decades ago. Now they are respected; some are councilmen, others run the city government. Not so long ago the local Chamber of Commerce wanted to tear down the ruined industry promotion hall because it was not good for the image of their bustling, up-and-coming city. All those dead memories of death and destruction—they were bad for business. That this was not allowed was the doing of the country, not the city. The national government would not permit it; the local government was all for it.

The bomb is not spoken of except by those in the tourist industry and, presumably, among those very few wounded survivors who remain alive. These few are hidden away, are not spoken of. They linger unseen in homes or hospitals; they are relegated to the slums of the city, then disregarded. The bomb has become tiresome, except as a propaganda weapon. Consequently, its victims are no longer interesting. Recently one of these survivors—a man with keloid scars, a beggar—was run off the streets and no longer appears on the bridges and street corners in the city where he was once, perhaps, a happy and respected citizen.

This indicates one of the most terrible facts of being human. The unfortunate are, try as we will not to do so, further degraded by us. We take from survivors what humanity they have managed to retain. Though we look with conventional horror at pictures from the German concentration camps, a part of the horror that we feel should lie in the fact that we certainly think, and just as certainly refuse to acknowledge, that these unfortunates are somehow no longer human and that this makes it all, somehow, not as bad as it might be. The man who divorces his innocent wife after she has been raped by someone is behaving in an all-too-human manner.

The bomb is therefore forgotten except when useful. Otherwise, it is old-fashioned, a serious defect in modern-minded Japan. It is unfashionable. This does not show itself in cynicism as it might in a worldly city, but in apathy. It is understood that the period is over, that it is now history and that history is not interesting.

 The Japanese   *From* A Lateral View, *"Tokyo, the Impermanent Capital," 1979*

The Western social structure which a city such as Tokyo most resembles is the single "city" which the West erects with full knowledge that it is not supposed to last. This is the exposition. Massive buildings are thrown up, streets are made, vast crowds are accommodated, but only for a season. The assumption is that all this will be pulled down. Consequently, building only for now, architects are traditionally encouraged to be both contemporary and extreme. Thus Tokyo is like an international exposition which has remained standing. If city structure in Japan remains "primitive," then these extremely contemporary-looking structures are like the tents of the nomads—with the difference that the Japanese move not in space but in time.

I Like Myself Here

"What do you think of Japan?" This is the first, the salient question that one is asked. Every acquaintance, every friendship, every love affair is begun with: *Nihon wa do omoimasu ka?*

How to respond? I think the most honest answer is: I like myself here. There are places—Calcutta is one—where you can come to loathe yourself. I never knew I would be ready to kick children from my path, to strike out at cripples, to compose a face apparently contemptuous at the sight of misery so great it seemed almost theatrical. And all because of sheer terror.

I, along with most of my richer Western brothers, had believed that such qualities as disinterested politeness, trust, friendship, even love are necessities. It had never occurred to me that they are luxuries until India showed me that this is so. Such attributes—the pride of Western man—are but accouterments, like well-cut clothes. They are removable. One can go naked and miserable. No, not *one* could—*I* could.

Japan, at times suffering as great a misery as India, found another solution. Going naked was not enough for the Japanese. They developed a civilization that partially conceals the more ferocious facts of life. Floods, typhoons, earthquakes, grave financial debacles—these are not to be hidden and they are therefore treated as imponderables, acts of God. It was in this way that the Japanese, originally at any rate, regarded the bombing of Hiroshima and Nagasaki; it is this feeling for the unexpected evil that accounts for that pessimistic-seeming phrase forever on all Jap-

From The Inland Sea, *1971*

183

anese lips, *Shikata ga nai,* "It can't be helped." Seemingly pessimistic, it is actually quite hopeful. This, perhaps, indeed can't be helped, but at least one's mind is cleared, and it is understood that whatever comes next will not be so bad.

The Japanese keep up appearances. Even the poorer are relatively well dressed. The best suit or dress is worn every day. The West in its more hypocritical moments has condemned this. Keeping up appearances is hypocritical. But to believe this is to disregard a great truth that all of Asia knows: appearances are the only reality. To wear your best suit daily implies a degree of self-respect but, more important, it also defines a reality that one chooses for oneself. If one looks like and acts like a certain kind of person—then one *is* that kind of person.

This truth, so simple, so basic, has evaded the West for centuries. Both church and psychiatry—not often so perfectly aligned—have mutually condemned it, the one finding in it the seeds

of freedom, the other discovering in it the seeds of anarchy. Yet common sense—which is about all the Japanese have in way of transcendental values—indicates the truth. The only way to get prosperous is to look and behave in a prosperous manner; the only way to get out of an emotional funk is to shake your head and think of something else. You become, as near as possible, what you think you ought to and would like to become.

The Japanese is thus freed from his own history. Simply because he was a certain kind of person does not mean that he must continue to be. Perhaps it is just this freedom that allows the Japanese to make so much of history, to learn from it, to play with it, since it has no power otherwise to control his actions or to hold him back from whatever he might want to do.

In the same way he does not have to hide completely from himself the more horrid of the facts of life. They are there—suicide, murder,

The Foreigners   From an unpublished work, 1963

Foreign Thoughts on Watching the Passing of a Matsuri Procession.
The foreigner watching the matsuri is delighted and excited. He senses something familiar, but something he cannot quite name. At the same time he is vaguely disturbed. Something seems not quite fitting. Looking about, he decides that this is because the matsuri is being held in front of modern buildings, in the midst of ordinary traffic, beneath the electric wires of the contemporary city.

Omikoshi and naked men in hanten are mixed with the

everyday activities of everyone else. This somehow disturbs the foreigner, particularly if he is trying to take pictures. He finds himself searching for angles that do not include buildings, signs, electric wires. He realizes that he wants to separate the traditional matsuri from its contemporary background.

Failing in this, the photographing foreigner notices that the many Japanese who are also taking pictures of the matsuri are not concerned by what he thinks of as the intrusion of contemporary life into a traditional spectacle. Seeing this,

the foreigner stops and thinks.
Why, he wonders, was it so important to him to take pictures, which would capture the matsuri but would give no hint of the contemporary life in the middle of which it takes place? Then he realizes that he was thinking of the matsuri as something different from everyday, modern life. And he saw that the Japanese do not.

Then he understands the reason why. It is because the matsuri is a part of everyday life, no matter if the omikoshi is brought out only once a year and that the young people

insanity, death in all its hundreds of forms—but they are no more insisted upon than they are denied. Japan seems to be the ideal compromise between India's undressed open wound and the West's open wound suppurating behind a bandage. The Japanese disclaims nothing and, at the same time, really hides little.

For this reason, the Japanese mind has always reminded me of the Japanese garden, which is a place that nature plainly made but which man has just as plainly ordered. The insipidity of nature tamed, as seen in the Western garden, is missing, but so is the awesomeness of the jungle. It is a wilderness but not a chaos. There are many paths, and if they turn and double in a curious manner quite different from the grand promenades of the Western park, it is because the Japanese observes and preserves the natural lay of the land.

It is this quality, then, that makes one like oneself here. One is close to nature in all ways,

and nature is also one's own nature. At the same time, one is not lost in the natural of which one is only a part. Japan is a good place for the foreigner to live.

Not for all, however. You either love Japan or you loathe it. Like Lafcadio Hearn, you gasp and press it to you heart, for a time at any rate, or else, like Bernard Shaw, the place rubs you so wrong that you even forget your manners, refuse to take off your shoes while treading tatami mats. Writers like Somerset Maugham or James Michener like it: writers such as Aldous Huxley and Christopher Isherwood do not care for it.

And it is also true that Japan has seldom appealed to the exceptional Western mind. It is perhaps too comfortable a land for that, given to few of the extremes with which greatness is associated. At the same time, it is natural that an original mind would not find the place attractive. Not only is it, in its way, too reassuring, it is also a country that has found means to call a

wear fundoshi and hanten on no other day. A matsuri is not something dead, to be seen in a folk arts museum; it is something alive, to be seen every year on the streets of Japan.

Other countries, he remembers, have their seasonal matsuri—solemn processions, most of them historical, often quiet, usually staid. But to see a typical Japanese city matsuri—the Asakusa Sanja, the Shinagawa Kappa, or the Kanda Myojin festivals—is to realize the difference. Though Japan does have some festivals as thoroughly dead as most foreign festivals— the jidai matsuri would be one of them—the ordinary Japanese festival is full of life.

There is shouting and pushing, there is exertion and exhaustion, there is a packed, disorderly throng, and there is nudity, flesh against flesh—a sure sign of life and health. The Japanese matsuri is so entirely different from the staid processions of Europe and America that here, the pondering foreigner realizes, is something important and vital which has, somehow, survived directly into his own times.

The gods in the Western processions are carried slowly and reverently, like corpses. The god in the omikoshi, however, is bounced up and down like an infant. The baby god of the matsuri, like all babies, likes to be tossed into the air. He is no

corpse; he is an infant deity, full of life and promise. And this, the foreigner decides, is fitting because the matsuri signalizes not only spring, the birth of the New Year, but also the birth of religion itself.

Those in the Western procession proceed with solemn step; they are self-important, a part of a social civic occasion. Those in the Japanese matsuri weave as though drunk under their burden and there are no individuals. Each member is moulded into the mass, that many legged and armed creature carrying the god. Each individual willingly submerges himself, happily becomes another pair of arms, another pair of legs. He is no longer himself.

truce, if not a halt, to the great war between aspirations and actuality—and it is just this disparity that has always sent great writers off to glorious battle.

This could be one of the reasons why the Japanese do not have a particularly vivid or even meaningful literature—at least, not if you think of literature as composed of Shakespeare, Cervantes, Tolstoy, Dostoevski, Conrad, Melville, the great searchers of the soul.

But I am not of that mind. I prefer Fielding and Jane Austen, Turgenev and Chekhov. And I also like Natsume Soseki and Tanizaki, Nagai Kafu and Kawabata. It is not so much their civilization that appeals to me in these writers, it is their wisdom and—perhaps more important— their way of imparting it. They know that only in appearances lies the true reality. Jane Austen was quite right to leave out the Napoleonic Wars. They were not her reality because they made small appearance where she was. Consequently

perhaps, she, and the others with whom I have grouped her, do not need to tell. They are content to show. The natural life they lead and write of is so much a part of them that, whether they approve of it or not, it allows them the freedom of tact and irony.

This said, one would hope that the Japanese would admire Jane Austen above all others and honor their own masters as well. This is, however, not true. The heavier Russians (not Turgenev) are admired above all, as is whatever they understand of Shakespeare, though Cervantes is regarded only from the safe distance of *Man of La Mancha*. That the Japanese have spiritual inclinations is not to be doubted. I doubt very much, however, that such inclinations have ever come to anything.

The commonest Japanese way of exercising these inclinations is to read *The Idiot* or to go far away all alone or to climb a convenient mountain by oneself. The Japanese is too pragmatic,

---

He is outside himself—one with the others, one with the god.

The matsuri is no civic occasion. It is an eruption of raw, chaotic life into the measured, restricted, lifeless city existence. The watching foreigner feels a vitality, a nearness to nature and to natural man, which his own country seems long to have forgotten, except in its uglier manifestations—gangs, mobs, war.

He also senses an important paradox, one that perhaps only Japan still displays. Just as this ancient and traditional matsuri occurs naturally in front of a modern and contemporary background, so the mystery of religion, its ultimate concern with death and life, is embodied

by the mundane health and high spirits of the omikoshi carriers. It is a ceremony where the common and the vulgar become the vehicle for the obscure and the profound. It is the yearly mating of the transient human with the abstract eternal.

The thoughtful foreigner suddenly remembers something he once read. "And within the thick white and scarlet ropes, within the guard rails of black lacquer and gold, behind those fast-shut doors of gold leaf, there is a four-foot cube of pitch-blackness." It is a "cube of empty night." The author—who was it?—was writing of the omikoshi and noticing the strange calm. The black and empty weight seemed to stabi-

lize the motion. The shouting, heaving men were like waves. Over them rode, serene, the empty home of the god.

The foreigner suddenly remembers. It was Yukio Mishima, of course—in Kamen no kokuhaku. At the same time the foreigner again recalls the feeling he himself had—that this matsuri was somehow familiar to him. Then he recalls. It reminds him of his own childhood, that time when one does not yet know of civilization, of social order. The omikoshi is empty because the god is reborn every year.

The foreigner ponders the paradoxes. A traditional festival still so alive that it can take place right in the middle of

nessman intent on giving him a good time at Enoshima, the geisha who is called in, etc. This hilarious mini-*Rashomon* exposes the foibles of everyone, foreign and Japanese alike, and ends in a still astonishing chapter where the book is turned upside-down and what we had been laughing at is revealed as tragedy—a very Japanese construction.

The theme is revealed in the *nom-de-plume* used by the author (try phrasing it as a question in Japanese) and its implications, the seduction of Japan by the West are shortly reversed. The book is a minor masterpiece and as revealing now as it was then.

Mirror, Sword and Jewel. By Kurt Singer. Kodansha, Int., reprint of the original 1973 edition.

This extraordinary book, which consists of observations made in Japan from 1931 to 1939,

was written in finished form after WWII and then misplaced upon the death of the author. In 1971 the late Richard Storry, the eminent historian, received the manuscript, edited it and got it published.

The book is filled with insights such as: "Let (the foreigner) experimentally but unreservedly behave according to Japanese custom, and he will instantly feel what a cell endowed with . . . human sensibility must be supposed to feel in a well-coordinated body." And, "the most drastic proof of the existence of a specific Japanese civilization is perhaps the impossibility for any typical Chinese or Westerner to live in this medium without feeling slightly oppressed, even when charmed, subtly excluded even if allowed to participate."

The Kimono Mind. By Bernard Rudofsky. Tuttle reprint of the original 1965 edition.

lakes of the Shiretoko Peninsula in northeast Hokkaido. There is the last frontier, where these exquisite ponds lie unmolested along the top of a precipice, which drops straight to the Sea of Ohkotsk. The waters team with trout, foxes come out to watch you pass, and the forest is as it has always been. A new and narrow path encircles these enchanted miniature lakes (course time: one hour) and each turn reveals a wonderful new vista.

Tokyo Story. The single work of art which says almost everything about Japan and makes it universal in the saying. This 1953 film by Yasujiro Ozu is so deep, despite its domestic surface, that it plunges you through the par-

ticular and into an eternal where gratification and disappointment, life and death, are completely and wonderfully accepted. The uniqueness of being Japanese is disregarded, seen through, in the radiance of the uniqueness of being human.

Ibusuki Jungle Baths. I hear that this romantic wonder has been dismantled and the whole turned into something for the moneyed newly married, yet during its time (1950–80) it was a marvel. It was the new Eden— a great glass palace with a forest inside, and a mountain, a river and a lake, and dozens of different pools for the bathers. At night it was illuminated only by tiny star lamps and that distant naked strolling couple

became the new Adam and Eve.

D.X. Gekijo. Not long for this world but still visible as I write is that wondrous chain (Toji, Shinjuku, Funabashi) of theaters where the facts of love are displayed on stage and the mysteries of sex are approached with trepidation and flashlight. It is not often that a civilization so plainly shows our common roots as here in this womblike replica of the original cave, where the paying customer takes his choice, and where the polymorphous perverse of the very young in all of us is allowed a return to the wondrous innocence of childhood.

A notorious book: wildly unfair, packed with error, and glorious. This last quality is the result of the author's affectionate exasperation, which cuts through all the cant otherwise written about Japan (volume after volume) and presents the confrontation with heartfelt drama.

On women's *geta*: "These pedestals serve a double purpose—to elevate the wearer symbolically and to unbalance her physically. And on the *obi*: "(It) would seem indeed a senselessly vicious construction were it not for the extenuating fact that men derive infinite pleasure from watching hobbled women."

Basil Chamberlain is Dr. Johnson in Japan—rude, opinionated, sensitive, learned, and fair.

He also dares to call the Ministry of Transportation "the Japanese counterpart of Duncan Hines," and to attack the image of Japan presented in the JTB *Official Guide*: ". . . although it lists the addresses of every Tax Administration Office and District Court, it never mentions, say, the existence, past or present, of Yoshiwara or Shimabara."

Like all good writers Rudofsky is appreciative: "A Japanese room is as chaste as a seashell, so much so indeed that we have come to look at it as the quintessence of austerity . . . yet in the Orient one finds austerity perfectly compatible with voluptuousness." And "it is not just in utilitarian principles that the Japanese excel—they have a knack for infusing poetry, even magic, into routine performances and routine situations . . . the bath is one of them and sleep is another."

Empire of Signs. By Roland Barthes. Hill and Wang, N.Y., 1982. A translation (by Richard Howard) of the 1970 French edition.

Barthes came to Japan in the mid-1960s, knew nothing about it and set out, unprejudiced by any general theories about "the Japanese," to describe the country and its people.

He was from the first captured by the rhetoric of the country, its signs and what they meant, or didn't. Tokyo "offers this precious paradox: it does possess a center, but this center is empty." *Pachinko* "reproduces . . . on a mechanical level, precisely the principle of painting *alla prima,* which insists that the line be drawn in a single movement, once and for all. . . ." And on packaging: "It is as if, then, the box were the object of the gift, not what it contains. . . . Thus the box acts as the sign: as envelope, screen, mask, it is *worth* what it conceals, protects, and yet designates."

Barthes's is a provocative and startling book—one, which sees through its own grid and finds a real people, and a real author.

* * *

This is not the end of the list of "best books" but it is all I have room for. The reader will have noticed that none of them are from among the accepted *nihonjinron.* This is because I do not like *nihonjinron,* find them limited, pretentious and arrogant, prescriptive rather than descriptive, and much more concerned with their theories (*giri/ninjo, honne/tatemae,*) than with their presumed subject.

For those who would like to be inoculated against their influence I can suggest two recent good books: *The Myth of Japanese Uniqueness* by Peter Dale (Croom Helm, 1987) and *Images of Japanese Society* by Ross Mouer and Yoshio Sugimoto (KPI Ltd., London). Also Ian Buruma's *A Japanese Mirror,* a splendid antidote, is now locally available in the Penguin edition. Good reading!

The Sex Market: The Commercialization of a Commodity

I take it as understood that all societies have to an extent discovered in the sex lives of their citizens a powerful incentive to commerce. Even left to itself, sex tends toward commercialization—how much more useful then if this lucrative urge can be channeled to more effective mercantile use.

This idea is one, which occurs to any businessman, and my here discussing Japan's achievements in the field should not be seen as finding the Japanese phenomenon in any way unique. Rather, as always, Japan's way is the common one—but made more efficient, more effective, and much more visible. Japan's highly successful example is here then presented as the model for emulation. No one has better than Japan shown how a natural instinct may be turned into a well-run business.

In order to discuss this complicated topic in a responsible fashion, I am going to divide my subject into several sections: first, the love hotel as an example of Japanese business know-how, the right product for the right public; second, venues of commerce as an example of business adaptation; third, the specialty markets; and, fourth, new means of marketing.

* * *

Japan's sex industry has been estimated as a ¥4 trillion business. Just how this figure was arrived at and how it compares with

From Partial Views, 1994

those of other countries is not apparent, but it is very large—indeed is almost equivalent to the national defense budget.

And one-fourth of this amount, also a large sum, is from the revenue of the so-called love hotels. It is these I wish first to examine, seeing in them a paradigm of the business acumen, which has so effectively sustained and to an extent created Japan's sex market. For while all societies have commercialized sex itself, only a few have marketed the venue, and none to the extent that has Japan.

There are over 35,000 thousand such hotels, 3,000 in Tokyo alone. The rooms range in price from ¥5,000 on up. This is for what is called in the parlance of the trade a "short time." A longer time, like all night, costs more. Here the price climbs to the height of a certain all-night suite for ¥200,000 where—to be sure—you are allowed to occupy what is billed as a "million dollar" "rococo" bed.

Prices differ for services offered. There are beds that rotate, or go up and down; mirror-lined rooms; two-level suites with a glass bottomed bathtub intended to be viewed from below; a "space-shuttle" bed for simulated take-offs and, for the ultimate in safe sex, an S/M chamber. In addition, many hotels serve breakfast, often including that popular item, broiled eel, and most rooms contain what is called a Romance Box, which holds whiskey, soap, and a vibrator.

There is also the latest in TV electronics. Each room has a television set with closed-circuit soft-core porno, and many have self-operated cameras which relay the performance onto the tube—and it is said into the main office as well, where a further profit might then be made.

With such a variety of attractions it is not surprising that love hotels outrival Disneyland in popularity. The main reason for this popularity is, of course, the lack of venue anywhere else.

The Gods

From The Erotic Gods, 1966

Benten (Sarasvat or Lakshmi) was originally the daughter of Sagara, a Hindu dragon-king, and was herself goddess of streams and seas. Her earliest manifestations showed her as half-fish or serpent, and when she became 'canonized' in Japan (in the tenth century it would appear) she retained her liking for the ocean and settled mainly on islands. One of these was Miyajima (originally Itsukushima) near Hiroshima, where the main shrine is said to have been inspired by the sea-king's underwater abode and where, even now, the tide rushes beneath its crimson pillars and

is reflected on its lacquered ceilings. This island was sacred and, as in Delos, it was forbidden to die there and women were until fairly recently not allowed to give birth in the precincts. This must have pleased Benten, whose insatiability for men was equaled only by her aversion for her own sex.

She was also fond of another island. This was Enoshima, only a few hours from Tokyo, and she probably first stayed there during the thirteenth century when the capital of the country was located at Kamakura, just around the corner of the bay. She was extremely popular

there and, further, the island had (and has) a large cave that must have reminded her of her serpent ancestry. There exist many statues and talismans of Benten in her snake form and she was perhaps the original of *byaku-fujin*, or the white-snake lady, of Chinese folklore. In any event she was, like the lubricous reptile she occasionally became, unusually promiscuous. Even now her temple on the island of Shinobazu Pond in Ueno has the reputation of being a lovers' tryst, and the most famous remaining phallic-stone still standing in Tokyo is directly on

Japanese dwellings are crowded and couples are correspondingly cramped. Japanese business, in taking advantage of this sociological fact, has, as usual, given the customer the latest technology combined with the most recent "image."

Since it has been ascertained through careful appraisal of the market that it is women who often choose which hotel to go to, the image has been sent up-market. Indeed the term love hotel is no longer much heard. Rather, one speaks of the "fashion hotel" or the "leisure hotel" and while love hotels had such names as "Empire" and "Metro" and "Rex," names with masculine associations, the fashion hotels have names such as "Chez Nous," "Petite Elegance," and the popular "Once More."

In addition, the better leisure hotels are arranged so that from parking the car to paying the bill, the couple is never directly viewed. Entry is electronically controlled, as is payment, privacy is assured, and no one sees the happy pair—unless, of course, they unwisely elect to commemorate their performance on tape.

Also, the new leisure hotel is fully automated. Mr. Masao Chokki, president of the Hotel White City in Tokyo, has said that "our staff can clean a room in just seven minutes." And he adds: "The love hotel industry is something you can really put your heart into and be proud of."

Such sentiments are understandable when one comprehends the degree of business acumen, which has gone into making such an outstanding financial success of purveying to customer needs. Here, as elsewhere, then, Japan leads the world.

* * *

I turn now to an outstanding example of adaptation in the world of Japanese business. Though the Japanese businessman is often accused of rigidity (not adapting to circumstances, not accommodating, not opening up markets) we can see here just the opposite—an example of

the shore. It is perhaps a portrait of one of her later lovers, the famous mountain-dweller and magician Enno Shokaku—certainly the face of the rock plainly shows such a gentleman, but when viewed from the rear it becomes one of the most explicit of stone penes.

She had an enormous number of lovers, many of them human. At Seimei-ji in Toyokawa-cho in Aichi there is a Benten festival that celebrates her predilection for handsome horse-drivers. She took one away with her and that was the last that was heard of him—hence this festival that features charms in the shape of well-endowed horses. Somewhat more fortunate was a samurai of the Tanuma family (as recorded in the story collection *Chimmon Kishu*) who fell in love with the statue of her at the shrine on Enoshima and slept with her (or her statue) every night, with no known misfortune befalling him. Equally lucky was the Kamakura general, Hojo Tokimasa (whose story is told in the *Taiheiki*). He went to pray to her daily, and on the final and thirty-seventh day the beautiful and unclothed goddess appeared before him, answered his prayers, turned herself into a big snake, and was swallowed up by the sea. She also liked demi-gods—her connections with the *nio-sama*, those muscular heroes which guard temple gates, are well-known, but she liked almost any man and consequently there are some who cannot now be identified.

She also had a husband. Just as lovely Venus was united with the lame and otherwise disfavored Vulcan, so Benten was wed to Bishamon who, though being god of both war and wealth, was incredibly ugly. This might have accounted for her promiscuity; certainly it suggests a reason for her otherwise mysterious aversion to other people's happiness. Her enmity toward young couples is notorious; if they pray at her shrines she will surely break them up, though—given the example of her Ueno sanctuary—the grounds around them are safe enough.

adaptation, which has resulted in yet greater sales.

The problem appeared back in 1984, and it was one, which struck at the heart of the industry—the commodity itself. What occurred was that a Turkish diplomat complained that those baths—which had become the principal purveyor of the commodity after the passing of the postwar anti-prostitution laws—were called Turkish. Indeed *toruko* had become the most common term of reference.

Always sensitive to the feelings of others, the Tokyo-to Tokushu Yokujo Kyokai (Tokyo Special Bathhouses Association) met and then announced that the over one hundred affiliated bathhouses were amenable and would change their designation.

But to what? In order to determine this, a democratic method was devised. The public,

appealed to, responded with numerous suggestions—more than two thousand postcards arrived. Among the contenders were Romanburo, Colt (that is, Koruto, a backward rendering of toruko) and Rabuyu (a felicitous combination of "love bath" and "love you") but the winner, hands down, was Sopurando, or Soapland.

Note the simplicity of the construction: a suggestion of cleanliness—soap; and a proposal of pleasure—Disneyland. This masterly construction (so typical of Japanese accommodation when called upon) was an instant success. When the term was officially adopted, Mr. Ilhan Oguz of the Turkish Embassy shook hands all around and said: "I think that the Association has found a good, clean name for its establishment."

The Japanese public, as is its wont (one of the qualities which makes sweeping mercantile

The Gods

From The Erotic Gods, *1966*

In this happy land the Japanese lives in a very close group, which occasional fits of xenophobia still indicate. His idea of perfection is worldly and social. He has never had a profound or a troubled relationship to the cosmos because his is made entirely of the nature he finds around him. Since his heaven is on earth, so is his god. In this way he remains entirely theanthropic, both protected and nurtured by his environment.

One of the results of this is that he is guiltless. There is no tribune larger than the group from which he comes; there is no god looking over his shoul-

der from on high; consequently, there is no conscience. The deterrent to evil is the chance that he might get caught for then his society would certainly punish him. He may feel ashamed, but he cannot feel guilty.

Even now violations of various kinds are not properly considered misdemeanors unless there is a complaint. And it follows that punishment is not for the good of the soul but for the good of the community. If the culprit is caught he is punished by the temporal authorities; if he is not caught there is no need for punishment because there are no divine authorities.

Neither is there such a thing as original sin. The Japanese is born into the most perfect of all countries, it fits him as he fits it, he conceives of his death as a part of his life, and the greater part of his life is spent celebrating his own existence through work and procreation. Japanese life is, to be sure, no longer quite this simple, but it is a pattern of this simplicity upon which it rests, and it is only through reference to this basic pattern and how it evolved that one can understand the Japanese attitude—then and now—toward the simple and profound necessity of sex, which

decisions so invariably successful), went right along with the decision and Soapland the toruko became. There was some grumbling among those who now had to go to the expense of altering their neon displays but progressive opinion prevailed.

Prices then rose to match the level of dignity of the new title and more efficient moneymaking methods were employed. Calling out an attendant by name now cost a bit more; there appeared an unexplained but dignified *atobarai,* unspecified charges when you checked out; and the categories of service, special service, double service, extra special service, and full course (the latter being what we might call making love) were more strictly insisted upon; but there were perks as well—for example the new "fashion massage," a service which formerly the patron had been forced to practice upon himself.

So, it will be seen that once again Japanese business practices have demonstrated just how adaptive they can be. With evidence such as this there should be less complaint about not opening up markets.

* * *

We turn now to the specialty venues. Here progress varies but there are some examples of enterprise. Take for example the *nozoki-beya.* These, as the name indicates, are establishments where the clientele look through peepholes at the main attraction (usually billed as a "schoolgirl") performing within. A thousand-yen bill is inserted to open the small hole and—at the more enterprising establishments—another bill opens a hand-sized window somewhat below waist level.

These have been steady sellers for years, voy-

---

we find so weighty, portentous, and unwieldy.

To the Japanese (as to the Greek) an appetite is an appetite. When he is hungry he eats, when he is drowsy he sleeps. Meals often do but need not correspond with the hours set aside for them, and the Japanese are probably the world's most adept in catching catnaps. Sex, just another appetite, is satisfied wherever possible though there are social rules regarding fitting and untimely hours and places. When all of these appetites are functioning normally, the Japanese is as healthy as any human being ever is. One might call this his Shinto phase—that time when he is free of misfortune, when he wears his body and his

aspirations like a well-cut suit of clothes.

There is also, however, another phase. This is when illness, misfortune, or death enters, and interrupts or cancels the appetites. This is the Buddhist phase. Throughout Japanese history one discovers that when the life force is flowing and all is well, the prevailing sentiment is Shinto; when death and disaster strike, it is Buddhist. Perhaps this is because, as Percival Lowell has stated: "Shinto regards the dead as spiritually living; . . . Buddhism regards the living as spiritually dead." That is, when all is well death is acknowledged by being ignored and the dead are somehow or other still with us; when all is not well, when this life is

revealed as less than perfection, when one's attention is forcibly drawn to the certainty of death, this world is abandoned and some faint hope is entertained for another.

Most Japanese are both Shinto and Buddhist and find no difficulties in a double religion. The enthusiasm with which Buddhism was originally accepted in Japan, indeed, argues for some prior need or disposition. The two religions are complementary, the *yin* and *yang* of belief: they are opposite but one. And both accommodate themselves to those phallic beliefs underlying all religions, that act as the muscles of theology, and that are even now plainly visible under the skin of modern civilization.

eurism having been heavily marketed in movies and *manga* alike. But then the market had stabilized itself and even shown signs of falling off. Particularly, the charms of that lower window were found to be limited.

As though in answer, an innovation—from one of the enthusiastic workers herself—just recently sprang into view. The customer had put in his customary bill and, instead of the window, the door opened. And there, before the surprised patron, stood the girl herself. "But you are supposed to be inside," he is quoted as having said. "It's just too much trouble," was her response as she pulled him to her.

Thus do institutions change their shapes and what is voyeurism's loss is business's gain. She also pulled her patron into the much more lucrative mainstream and her independent action might be seen as just what the entrepreneur is capable of in a growth industry.

It is indicative that in this case the innovator was a woman because it has become increasingly evident that the female market is the one most clamoring for attention. With the largest disposable income now in the handbags of unmarried women, the Japanese sex business is being transformed from a females-for-males service industry into a more level playing field. As social critic Joseph Lapenta has stated: "More money and more free time have thus impacted a previously male-oriented industry."

There were earlier signs of this: the proliferating and highly lucrative host clubs, for one. Now, however, there are a growing number of male strip shows for women. The strippers are at present still all foreign, usually white or black, but it seems just a matter of time before the potential for part-time work among Japanese males is realized as well.

The sight of excited customers stuffing bills into the posing straps of the happy *gaijin* strippers is one which would warm the hearts of businessmen everywhere. This is particularly so in Japan where such activity indicates just the tip of the iceberg, as it were.

Not all, however, has been growth and profit and, within these specialty markets, it would not do to paint too rosy a picture. Though the various S/M establishments within the country have shown a healthy gain, other markets have not. Particularly disappointing has been that sober venue so misleadingly called the "gay scene."

The Body   *From* A Hundred Things Japanese, 1975

Tachishoben.
To urinate (lit. "while standing") in a public place.
Tachishoben, the act of urinating in public, is typically Japanese only in that it is performed so much more openly and freely than in most other countries. Though there are occasionally enforced laws against the practice, it is still commonly encountered and had best be regarded as a typical part of the Japanese scene.

Typical, certainly, is the process of reasoning, which permits tachishoben. Traditionally, the Japanese entertain a strong dichotomy between yours and mine—or, more precisely, ours and theirs. Thus private politeness and public rudeness, and the other seeming paradoxes which have long been observed by the apprehensive foreigner. The fact that no one practices tachishoben within the private garden but everyone does on the public street on the other side of the wall, is just another example of the dichotomy at work.

The garden belongs to us, or to people we know, and must therefore be respected. The street, on the other hand, since it belongs to everybody belongs to no one and need not be respected at all. Also, the

Here it is a matter of concern that little development is occurring. Rising profit remains basic to any drinking establishment yet most of the male homosexual bars have, scandalously, not raised their prices in the last five years. Drinks, unbelievably in modern Japan, still cost a mere ¥500 and one is allowed, unaccountably, to nurse a single drink most of the evening. A note of hope, however, is that the female homosexual bars are among the most expensive in the city and snacks are served whether wanted or not—a sure sign that a sane business sense is prevailing. In general, however, the so-called gay scene exhibits only economic degeneracy. There are no racks of theme T-shirts, no guided tours, no Gayland concept at all. If ever an area needed development it is this one.

Leaving this depressing subject, it is a pleasure to turn to more forward-looking developments. One of the very latest to hit the scene took advantage of the new technology in a highly dramatic form. There are still some bugs in the system but the signs are all there.

There recently opened in Shinjuku the "Kabuki-cho Virtual Sex Salon." While it did not last long enough to catch on with the general popula-tion, it was nonetheless written up in the popular press, though in such terms that it is difficult to ascertain precisely of what it consisted.

Apparently in addition to the helmet and glove of the more conventional virtual-reality wear, there was a digitalized codpiece. Though this itself contained a sales flaw, depriving the franchise holder of the lucrative female market, the other flaws in the apparatus were such that this slight miscalculation went unremarked.

What occurred is subject to some speculation but there was an apparent electrical failure. One young patron experienced, in the words of the reporting daily, a *gyaku funsha koka*—literally, a "reverse jet-fountain effect." Though otherwise uninjured, the patron refused a free trial run to take the place of the aborted experience and this led eventually to official inquiry and the closure of the Kabuki-cho Virtual Sex Salon, an establishment which had, after all, billed itself as "The Ultimate in Safe Sex."

But bugs in systems eventually get ironed out and where there is hardware, software will follow. It would be unwise to dismiss virtual sex as a merely bad idea—rather, one should think of it as a bad idea whose time has not yet come.

viewers of the tachishoben are either complaisant friends or else nameless strangers and, in either case, if for entirely different reasons, censure is not to be expected.

There is another reason for this indulgence. Urban Japanese still cling to their rustic origins and are fond of calling even Tokyo a village, albeit an overgrown one. They secretly yearn for the rural life of a former age and admire behavior among their fellows, which they feel to be natural, just as they admire a life which is natural, i.e., in tune with nature. To them the modern urban scene is not welcome, but only tolerated. No one would take a farmer to task for urinating in a stream or at a roadside while working in the paddies, and citified Japanese, recognizing the farmer in themselves, look upon those under the influence or nonchalantly relieving themselves in the street not entirely without approval, recalling perhaps a village life that once was, a life closer to nature and to the natural instincts of man.

Tachishoben thus joins a host of like manifestations (rowdy drunkenness in public, knocking people about in crowded trains and subways, public vomiting, breaking of queue lines, etc.) which insist that the civic ideal does not exist even though private politesse does.

In this way tachishoben enjoys a tenuous if polar link with the tea ceremony. Both, at extreme positions, are a part of the spectrum of the Japanese way.

After such setbacks it is indeed a pleasure to turn to the most innovative and most successful of the recent forays into the sex market, one which has indeed milked its idea of its full potential. This is the video box.

Like all great business concepts, the idea is simplicity itself: a large room in which stand a number of large boxes; the customer enters one of them and locks the door; this activates the TV into which he inserts his thousand-yen bill; the roman-porno film begins . . . and the only other accoutrements are an open box of tissue and a wastepaper basket.

Voila. The beauty of the idea becomes apparent. Japanese business know-how has harnessed one of nature's most universal urges and has persuaded the patron to pay for a pleasure hitherto wastefully free. I cannot think of another nation which has had the vision, the sheer imagination, to take such successful advantage of such an enormous market.

I do not think, after this success story, we need look at others of the specialty markets. Rather, I would like to turn to another section of this burgeoning business scene and end my presentation with yet another instance of successfully pragmatic Japanese business know-how.

* * *

New merchandise and new means of marketing offer the brightest insight into the enterprising world of the sex business in Japan. This is the eternal new product, the *shinhatsubai,* which keeps the profits rolling in.

Here one of the most successful means has been the vending machine. Not only do these purvey alcohol, tobacco, soft drinks and hot lunches, they now do their bit to satisfy an increasingly open demand.

There is, for example, the lucrative condom industry in this age of AIDS. Though for the up-market buyer there are now rubber boutiques such as the extremely successful Condomania in

that heartland of the young, Harajuku, there is no doubt that the greatest number of prophylactics are sold by the privacy-insuring coin-operated machines.

And now in a bold new step these same machines are vending porn-video. No longer need the patron make the sometimes-embarrassing visit to his corner shop. He (or she) can in perfect anonymity purchase porn for as little as ¥2,000 ($20) a title. This is to be certain soft-core porn and until now the enterprising businessman remains unable to open up his market to anything more firm.

To obtain what is known as "the real stuff" the corner shop must still be visited a number of times until mutual trust between owner and patron is built to the point where the area under the counter is displayed. This is a wasteful and a time-consuming procedure and some of the best business minds are at present working on a solution.

The problem is that, since Japan has no censorship laws as such, there is a problem when it comes to defining what is obscene and what is not. Explicit lovemaking was obscene, but what of photos and foldouts? For a time a useful line was drawn at pubic hair. Any nude photos or films with it were obscene, anything without it was not. This led to a number of anomalies, shaved models among them, but it at least defined the field.

Magazines and books entering the country were routinely cleaned of hirsute details by squads of housewives working part-time and equipped with special equipment, which scraped the areas free of any image, whatever.

Now, however, it is apparent that the pubic-hair line is not holding. Recent photo anthologies, indeed, have breached it. There was some retaliation—the printer of the Japanese edition of the Madonna coffee-table book *Sex* was fined—but before long enterprising Japanese photographers were following this bold lead. Though there were occasional attempts at appeasement (hair gel for example in the pictures of Nobuyoshi Araki), on the whole Japanese photographers have met the challenge of repressive thinking.

As always, a healthy business sense prevailed and it became apparent that an enormous and unrealized market existed. With money to be made on all fronts there are now many less pornography crackdowns. To be sure, however, mercantile vision must still do battle since attitudes repressive to this free trade still exist.

For example, probably the greatest growth potential is among the young and yet Mr. Masaru Morimoto, chairman of the Osaka City Youth Leaders' Council, can say that: "Excessive commercialism by adults is destroying a healthy environment for the young."

Well, one might ask Mr. Morimoto to examine the results in the dollars and cents of the recently found fact that porno *manga* are read by sixty percent of all middle school and high school students. And these, we would remind him, are the future mothers and fathers of Japan.

Yet, the battle against the business continues. Just recently one of the most inventive of shin-hatsubai in the sex industry has been questioned. This is the marketing of used schoolgirl underwear in vending machines.

Its mercantile effectiveness is unquestioned: bought for as little as ¥100 a unit, it was sold for as much as ¥500. In just a month an enterprising trio of men made over ¥17 million. Obviously a public was out there, just waiting to be fingered. Equally, there was an abundant source. The newly rich schoolgirls working hard to use their underwear, playfully referred to their new employment as *H-baito,* the *baito* coming from *arubaito,* a common loan-word for part-time work, the H from the romanization of *hentai,* which means "perversion."

Yet enterprise always has its enemies. The Education Ministry took an interest and finally decided that these entrepreneurs may have bro-

ken the Antique Dealings Act. The result was a closure of business.

One could go on and describe further the obstacles, which have been put in the way of enterprise. For example, the necessary flyers for sexual services which so colorfully decorate so many of our phone boxes—brightly-colored flyers that are ruthlessly destroyed by shortsighted authorities despite the cost. It was recently estimated that it cost Osaka ¥30 million in 1993 to clear away all the *pinku bira,* as these sticky bits of paper are affectionately called.

But mercantile enterprise thrives on adversity. Resourceful business minds, put to work, have responded. Now NTT has reported that sex service advertisements are being stamped with indelible ink on the box itself.

The future beckons as more and more business outlets are being discovered. NTT itself and the other communications giants might well avail themselves of the many sex-service lines, both professional and amateur, which now stretch across the country, catering to any appetite and creating not a few. Or the interested investor might consider stock in Gainex, a concern marketing explicit computer games: though the current model features only a mild striptease more, much more, is promised.

And the business-minded may take heart in that the authorities have now named some 55,000 individual videos, books and other items as harmful to the young. If that is not success, I ask you, what is?

These then, are some examples of this highly successful commercialization of a commodity in Japan—one which, despite setbacks, has gone to heights which might well render the foreign businessman impotently envious, limp with shame.

Enterprise, imagination, application, and sheer single-mindedness have in Japan turned an instinct into an industry, have carved an empire from an urge.

TV: The Presentational Image

Television presents only itself and it presents itself as only television. The convention of theater, of film, is that something else is being presented—life itself. And this is also the convention of certain elements of television—the drama, the movie—but the format of the media, that of a daylong, nightlong variety show, prevents its pretending to be anything other than what it is. This being so, presentation in television is direct. The person doing the talking looks directly at us, the watchers. There is no convention to insist that we are looking at something other than what we are. The only reality is the ostensible—someone in front of the TV camera talking to us.

If we are being addressed this directly by commentator or by salesman, we are, in a way, also addressing them. These people are doing it *for* us, the watchers, and our opinion of them is for various reasons valuable. They want to appear at their best both because they wish to sell us something or influence us in some other way and because, since they are in the public eye, they want in more general terms our good opinion. Various are the ways in which they attempt to obtain this.

We are all familiar with many of the means—carefully chosen words, an implied flattery, the attempt to create enthusiasm, a certain ingratiating unnatural naturalness. We are not so familiar (nor are they) with less conscious means: those through which they, perhaps unknowingly, imply and we, often equally unknowingly, infer; those through which we consciously deduce. These

From A Lateral View, *1980*

would include what they say without using words—the speech of the face, the hands, the stance; it would also include their ideas on the medium and how to use it, ideas we deduce from viewing TV as an entirety; it would also include their true, rather than their merely stated opinion of us.

Naturally this varies in various countries since assumptions upon which this behavior rests vary conspicuously from one culture to another. This being so, something is revealed about assumptions, beliefs, and generally agreed upon ideas, when these varying positions are regarded. Those to be seen in Japan are common to that country and there are a great many of them.

So many that it is difficult to know where to begin. Let us start with one which is, so far as I know, unique. This consists of the commentator at one side of the small screen and an assistant at the other. The commentator is always male and usually middle-aged. The assistant is always female, usually young and often pretty. He comments on the news or upon the subject of whatever the program is, and she assists.

But her assistance is so minimal that, to our eyes, she might as well not be there at all. Not for her the "equal" participation of the American "anchor person." She nods soberly at the camera when he makes his various pronouncements; she says *So, desu ne?* (Isn't that just true though?) when he makes a cogent point; and she will sometimes add a bit of information of her own which, upon examination, turns out to be a rephrasing of what he himself has just said.

To people of other cultures watching these two the effect is unsettling. We are certainly used to double commentators but usually each commentator really comments. In this format—and it is very common on Japanese television—the pretty girl is not only redundant, she seems absolutely unnecessary. Precisely, we fail to comprehend her function. Yet she has a very important one.

A commentator is, by definition, giving his opinion. In the West this is quite enough. One man's opinion is as good as another's, etc. In Japan, however, to give an opinion is to appear opinionated, and this is a fault in a society where dissenting opinion is at least officially unvoiced, and where a consensus of opinion is the invariable goal. These two qualities are hopefully ensured by this near-mute, if attractive, young lady. Her nods and monosyllables of agreement indicate that he is not alone in his opinion and that therefore he is not merely opinionated. Rather, he is stating a truth, since more than one person agrees upon what he says. At the same time she introduces harmony—it would be unthinkable of her to disagree with him or even to offer a conflicting opinion of her own—by indicating that we *all* (and it is *us* she is so earnestly nodding at) agree and the wished-for consensus has, indeed, already been reached.

One can trace this strange duo back to radio, where they are still to be heard, his voice supported from time to time by her syllables of assent. One can perceive its principles in even earlier forms of entertainment. In the Bunraku doll-drama, the various voices of characters and commentator (all spoken and sung by a single man) are mutually supportive; in the Noh drama, the chorus affirms and comments upon the dialogue. I can think of no instance where the commentary is not supportive, which means that I can think of no example where irony or any other "deeper" meaning is even suggested. Nor should it be, since the intention is a straight presentation within a context which seeks to make us regard the ostensible and only that as the real. This is as true, in Japan, of ancient drama as it is of modern television. It is, however, only radio and television which has made the assenting voice female, thereby plainly implying that women in Japan have a male-supportive role—and no other.

That women are somehow the weaker sex and are therefore naturally subservient is a typically

Japanese message and appears in many forms through many different media. In television this major burden is carried by the commercials where, by implication, the woman is only daughter, wife, homemaker, and mother. In these roles she is identified almost entirely as a consumer: when young she eats chocolates and tries new face creams on camera; married, she is careful about underarm odor and the kind of menstrual napkin she wears; about the house she smiles over the virtues of detergents, air-conditioners, vacuum sweepers, and as a mother she forces various foods on her surprised and delighted spouse and children.

In this, of course, Japanese television is little different from television in any consumer society. The difference is the directness with which this is done. In ostensibly democratic and egalitarian America the commentator's helper would be laughed (if somewhat nervously) off the screen; and any such overt suggestion (there are covert suggestions aplenty) that woman's place is in the home would no longer help sell the product. As always in Japan, however, the intention is

so open, so unveiled, so unmarred by any irony or duplicity, that the messages emerge with an often-startling clarity.

Take, for example, the "togetherness" that is being pushed by TV commercials now that the "prime selling target" has moved from wife and children, and become the family as a unit. In Japan, it should be understood, to be a family man is a very progressive social stance to take. It means that one is unwilling to sacrifice one's family (and, by extension, oneself) to the all-powerful employer. One's private concerns now come before one's social responsibilities. This mini-revolution is actually meaningless because, in practice, it means that the husband merely devotes more leisure time to his family and may, occasionally, attempt to avoid working at the company on Sundays. But the idea of such a revolution is very attractive. One of the symptoms is the wide use of the English "my" in various slogans: ("My Car/My Family"). It is symptomatic of the symptom that it is the English, "my" which is used, and not the Japanese *watakushi no*. The one, being a foreign word is as yet free from

The Gods   From The Japanese Garden, 1972

Nearly all the makers of these gardens were, as one might expect, also tea-ceremony masters. These men, whether samurai, priests, or tradesmen, shared a series of presumptions about nature and consequently about gardens. The aesthetic is contained in one of the more famous anecdotes about Rikyu. Having once carefully swept his tea-garden and raked all the fallen leaves out of the way, he went to the tree and shook it. Several leaves fell. These he

left as they were. It was these leaves which made his garden natural.

One arranged nature but only to an extent, and that extent was gauged by an extremely refined aesthetic sensibility. It was not a question of contrivance; it was a question of control. This control extended in the same direction in which nature itself extended. The desired end was to reduce and hence heighten effect. Flowers were never used in the garden

because, since flower arrangements were used within the tea-house itself, blossoms in the garden would detract from the blossoms inside. One makes an effect by reducing; less always means more; a whisper captures attention when a shout cannot. The technique for this was called *sashiai* (literally, 'mutual interference'), and its understanding is central to any comprehension of Japanese aesthetics.

In this regard, one comes upon

the unwelcome egotistical nuances, which surround the Japanese.

Another symptom is the "happy family" which now finds its way into TV commercials. Here father, mother and kids are all gathered at the family table or, more rarely, on the family *tatami* while mother introduces them to this or that new product. Their glee is so extreme that even father is carried away by it. He compliments his wife on her buying prowess. *Sasuga* ("Isn't that just like her") he says, smacking his lips and beaming. She simpers her pleasure and the children grimace and look at each other knowingly—everything is OK with Mom and Dad.

Messages are rife in this small vignette. Among things suggested are: buying the right things is the true secret of a happy home life, at the same time the wife's role as mere shopper has been subtly reinforced because she is after all fulfilling herself in this role, just look at the smiles on those kids' faces, and just look at the playful hug her husband is giving her—things are going to be OK in bed tonight too.

There are some perhaps unintended messages

as well. The one, which strikes me most strongly, is the apparent lunacy of the family. They behave like manic-depressives in the upward swing—all those roguish smiles and frenetic laughs over what is, after all, only a new breakfast food or laundry soap. It is the behavior of the mouse family or the rabbit family in the animated cartoons. There is something quite inhuman about these excesses.

Abroad, the TV watcher is, naturally, already familiar with this type of crazy family. He is so familiar with it that he is prepared to read the message with a certain cynicism. When sponsors discovered this, the family was promptly removed—the substitute was another family shifted a few millimeters nearer reality. In Japan, however, the viewer is usually immune to cynicism—being Japanese—and the family is taken at face value. These people are happy with their new product: this is the only message read.

(That the sell is very hard indeed is apparent. But in Japan there is only hard sell—no soft. The reason is that, in a culture where the ostensible

---

two words, one of which we met earlier: *sabi* and *wabi*. The former, which was translated as 'patina,' indicates that kind of elegance created by time alone. The elegance of wabi is somewhat different. The wabi quality makes much, indeed, everything, of very little or nothing at all. Its apparent poverty is its salient attribute. Another Rikyu anecdote illustrates the point.

He had a garden in which were growing a large number of marvelous morning-glories. It was arranged that a party come to view them. They arrived early but discovered not one. All had

been uprooted and the area was nothing but sand and pebbles. Inside the teahouse, however, arranged in the small alcove, set in a ,plain holder, was one single, perfect morning-glory. Just as the whole of the garden, the whole nature of all morning-glories everywhere, was contained in that single flower, so, wabi insists, the entire world is found in but one of its varied aspects.

Thus the architecture of the tea-house and the design of the garden itself were purposely rustic, deliberately unostentatious. Man's most 'natural'

architecture, that which derived most visibly from nature itself, was considered proper for the house, the environment it sought to create, and the attached garden. Here, beauty was discovered, surprised as it were—a concept called *mitate*, literally, the discovery of a new way of viewing.

To insist upon the perfection of a few fallen leaves, or a single common flower—this led to mitate. Forced to look, led to observe, one suddenly sees, as though with new eyes, a world of beauty in the most ordinary things.

is always the real, any attempt at soft sell—and there have been some—results in an unfortunate side-effect: the sponsor doesn't really believe in his product; he is sneaky and shifty in its presentation; if it is good enough to buy why doesn't he just say so?)

More important than this simple reading, however, is what the reading affirms. In being happy with the new product the family has reached yet further agreement, yet higher harmony. No dissent, no confrontation will rend this happy group. And by behaving like a demented mouse-family this social unit has, furthermore, shown that they are unexceptional, that they are Mr. and Mrs. Status Quo with all their little Quos—that they are, in fact, no threat.

I am no threat. This message is so clear and so incessant on Japanese television, and so accounts for the tone of the medium, that one must examine the phenomenon in some detail.

One might begin by noticing that the adults in TV commercials are all really children. They cock their heads like precocious youngsters, they use the gestures of the school child, they smile and laugh in the most uninhibited manner (and one markedly in contrast to the smiles and laughter of true Japanese adults), and cajole in a way truly typical of the spoiled Japanese child. Further, the disembodied voices in these commercials (those we listen to while looking at the products) are plainly adults imitating children. Further yet, the music accompanying all this is reminiscent of the jaunty marches associated, in Japan at any rate, with kindergarten.

Perhaps behind all of this is some urge to return to the golden age of undisciplined, permissive, Japanese childhood, but the implication (to the extent that any is acknowledged) would seem to be that we are all as harmless as children. Look at us: we make fools of ourselves, we invite you to laugh at us, we are fatuous to a degree—and yet, since we are so harmless, your laughter cannot but be indulgent, your hand cannot but reach into your pocket, your fingers cannot but open

 *The Foreigners*   *From* The Honorable Visitors, *1994*

Reports of this unknown land now proved so unlikely that, back in England, Oscar Wilde remarked that "the whole of Japan is a pure invention." To be sure, "the actual people who live in Japan are not unlike the general run of the English people." It was what we might now call the media-picture of the place that made it seem so unlikely, so—well—picturesque.

This was what Japan was discovered to be—picturesque. It was almost impossible that something this old and this distant not be so found. The pictur-esqueness of the place and its people was much observed and a consequence was the number of vogues for things Japanese to be seen in the Western capitals.

There is more to the picturesque than its artistic quality, however. A picturesque people is, by definition, an underdeveloped one, and a picturesque land is also one just lying there awaiting the developer. The picturesque, among its other qualities, offers promise of financial gain.

Newly opened Japan must have had an abundance of this quality because, even now that Japan has been distinctly overdeveloped, one still hears native seller and tourist buyer alike dilating on the picturesque charms of the place.

At the same time that the people were found to be picturesque, they were also discovered to be childlike. This was because the Japanese were so new to the Westerner, all ignorant of their history and their ways, and because they were newly born into the modern world. Consequently,

up the billfold. And if you don't want to—then no harm done because, you see, we have really asked for nothing.

In a way this is soft sell with a vengeance. These monstrous children are, in a truly childlike manner, having it both ways at once. It is in this manner that their message reaches the consumer who, not having been really, truly asked, can feel all the more free to do just what has been suggested. The happy family has merely offered him an example of unexceptionable, non-threatening togetherness.

Look how unexceptionable I am: this is a message which demotes the threat of another person looking into your living room, and if the actors in TV commercials purposely imitate children, those non-pros on the talk-shows, the amateur hours, the endless "personal" interviews, indicate that the childplay is based upon something very real.

Notice the hands of the ordinary citizen when he appears on television—and bear in mind that in Japan the ordinary citizen is brought to appear on the tube with a frequency greater, I would guess, than in any other country. Where are the hands? They are folded in front of him, one gripping the other, in the lap if he is sitting, at the crotch if he is standing. This is the "good" position.

On foreign TV, particularly American, the non-pro often seeks to make something of his personality by waving his hands about more than he ordinarily would. They suddenly become "expressive" of him. Likewise, his stance—if he is standing—is not that of the ordinary Japanese facing the TV camera. He will assume a "natural" stance, in which the pelvis is expressively tilted— just a hint of aggression. If he stood as does his opposite Japanese number, feet together, hands safely in front, something like the schoolboy at attention, Americans would read the image as indication of embarrassment, would see someone who is immature, and, at any rate, someone without "an outgoing personality."

But in Japan, conversely, the gesticulating for-

Japan was found to be juvenile and its natives were discovered to be, like delightful children, "quaint" and "droll."

As with the picturesque, the juvenile indicates not only charm but also promise. These childlike folk should be taught the ways of the adult world. Like infants, they ought to be trained for their own good. Like teenagers they must be taught to behave. Colonial control usually finds a need for childlike natives. They make, among other things, good customers.

These the Japanese were proving to be—buying everything necessary for this new country they were creating. And they thankfully had little to sell. Artistic goods, mostly. These had been praised by a few Western authorities, the expatriate American artist James McNeill Whistler among them, but the Japanese did not need to be taken seriously on what really counted—the economic front.

Still, the artistic items sold rather well. And the country was filled with pretty things— bronzes, lacquer, cloisonné, pottery—all waiting to be acquired by the Western tourist for very little. It made for something of a trade imbalance—the Japanese importing steam engines and telegraphic equipment while exporting pots and paper parasols—but no one worried about that back then. That the day would come when Japan would be exporting automobiles and transistors and importing such foreign handicrafts as McDonald's and Coca-Cola was not envisioned.

And so the great metamorphosis of Japan began, and these earlier visitors to Japan had laid before them one of the most astonishing spectacles in history: one country deliberately changing itself into the semblance of another; a cross-cultural collision the like of which the world had never seen.

eigner is seen as egotistical (a bad thing), ill mannered, and quite capable of disturbing an implied social harmony by his individualistic gesturing. On the other hand, the Japanese are all standing in well-mannered identical positions (well-mannered, to an extent, because they *are* identical), no one calling any undue attention to himself, all possible areas of danger (the hands, the pelvis) under firm control, all individualistic tendencies properly sacrificed to attain a goal of unexceptionable "good manners"—how well brought-up, how proper they indeed are.

(Apparent contradictions to these observations are, I think, only apparent. That Japanese TV dramas, differentiated from the commercials, are filled with the utmost anti-social violence does not indicate that such a display is to be condoned. Rather, it indicates a concern for the natural violence which hands firmly in the lap keep successfully under control. It is part titillation and part horrible example—in any event those exhibiting this degree of individuality are always reformed, put into prison, or killed. In the same way, the fact that in the home-dramas the happy housewife is revealed to be a mass of suffering, given to multiple love affairs, abortions, ungrateful children and a high degree of suicide, indicates no further degree of reality about real Japanese housewives. Rather, it represents an opposite extreme—both ends being equally far from middle: the real Japanese woman. In any event, both violence and tear-jerking are illustrations of fantasies entertained by sponsors and TV producers, if not by the audience.)

The pervading juvenility of Japanese TV is the result of its conciliatory intentions. The complete fatuity of all Japanese programming except the dramas (where the fatuousness is of a different degree), its bland, inane foolishness, is a small price to pay when the result of something as grand as complete uniformity and utter consistency. Still, to the foreign viewer, Japanese

television brings to mind Douglas MacArthur's famous (and much resented) description of the Japanese as a nation of twelve-year-olds. It also makes one think that the general missed the age by at least a decade.

I am not saying that the Japanese are really like this. I am saying that the image they project on television, the image they choose to present is precisely this. One sees it in other situations. (Japanese formal behavior—so relentlessly conciliatory—remains absurd to foreigners who do not understand its reasons.) These are always those where a degree of presentation is called for. We are unexceptionable, we are no threat, we are—just look—nice and good. An evening of Japanese TV—in which this single intention is tirelessly presented and represented—makes one wonder just how the myth of Japanese inscrutability ever got started: could anything be simpler, or more simple-minded, than this open, naked display?

What we are seeing, however, is only that which has been selected. People on the tube—pro and amateur alike, both the newscasters and those who design the commercial—select (telling word) their "image." Just as the Americans choose to present a type which is more individual, more argumentative, more "vital," than anyone you are apt to find on an American street corner, so the Japanese have chosen an image carefully lacking in any obvious individuality, given whole-heartedly to assent, but equally "vital" in that the goal of the presentation is a uniform front. That safety would be identified with childishness, and security with inanity are natural consequences of the presentational aim. Here too, as in the dramas, we are dealing in part with hopeful fantasy—since no people could ever be as bland nor as unexceptional as those on Japanese TV. Unlike the fantasy in the dramas, however, this is accepted as "real." One presents this image as into a reflecting mirror. And that mirror is the audience.

Epilogue

The Nourishing Void
Japan: A Half Century of Change
New Year's 1999

The Nourishing Void

In Tokyo for the first time, semanticist Roland Barthes looked toward the empty Imperial plaza, the invisible palace and the woodlands beyond, and wrote that while Tokyo does possess a center, this center is empty.

This was observed with an air of surprise. Where he came from, centers were never empty. But he could see why Tokyo's was, and he could understand its functions. This empty center was an evaporated notion, subsisting here not in order to radiate power, but to give to the entire urban movement the support of its central emptiness.

The idea of emptiness supporting something is not commonly encountered in the West. But it has long been known in Asia, and once remarked upon is seen everywhere—both in the old scroll painting and the modern advertisement. What is all that empty space doing there? Why isn't it filled in?

It is not filled in because it is already filled in with itself. It is a structural support. The emptiness of the scroll defines the tiny person crossing the minuscule bridge. In the advertisement it defines that important small print running across the bottom of the page. In both cases, emptiness plays a positive role. It has its own weight, its own specific gravity: its own presence.

To see the full in the empty can be defined, I think, as a creative act. From nothing, something is created. And Japan has traditionally been elevated by the invention of the fullness, which invests the empty. Examples spin out from this central

From Partial Views, *1992*

idea. Lots of mud and no money? Then create, like the Chinese and the Koreans, superb pottery. Lots of room and no furniture? Then make an aesthetic of space itself and invent the concept of *ma* to account for it. Lots of time for unemployed samurai? Then elevate manner into a ritual and create a space where temporal routine is so heightened that it becomes transparent—invent the tea ceremony, where guests with time on their hands sit and savor the emptiness.

From the tea ceremony came an entire celebration of the empty as reflected in the carefully shabby, the ostentatiously poverty-stricken, the expensively *maigre*. Wabi, sabi—things made of very little, of a striking simplicity: the cracked pot holding a field flower.

Such invention, no matter its resultant chic, is created from want. From nothing, something is created because it is necessary. The Japanese woodworker created in his box an artful disclosing of the very grain of his materials—that was his aesthetic. The Japanese gardener, with only stones and trees at hand, honed out of this emptiness something ideal, which he necessarily called nature.

Emptiness can also be a virtue in other ways. What else is the Zen koan but a riddle constructed to be empty? It is up to you to fill it. As Barthes further noted: Zen wages a war against the prevarication of meaning.

It does so because meaning fixes fully and for all time just one single meaning. All those overtones that so resounded before this naming are stilled. Meaning closes. Emptiness, on the other hand, leaves open, all options still hanging. Meaning, wanting to fill this fruitful emptiness, prevaricates because it opts for the single rather than for the fruitful multiple.

Emptiness can also be celebrated. Look at the movies—specifically, watch the movies of Yasujiro Ozu. His world is created of very little indeed: the frames of domestic architecture; a single camera position, low; one form of punctuation only, the straight cut; no plot—simply layered stories of simple, haiku-like cause and effect. Often his scenes are empty. People have not yet entered, or have already left. The camera gazes in an empty half-dark room at a common vase. And we fill this vessel with the emotions we have been holding, emotions generated by the film. We fill the empty scene with meanings just as we fill the empty koan with insight.

Meanings flow, and disappear as the film fades, as the guests bow at the end of the tea ceremony and go home. Here is the temporal equivalent of a nutritious emptiness: an immortal perishability, an eternal transience. Examples abound: the carefully mended tea bowl, the cherished tarnish of the silver caddy, the haiku that freezes forever a single moment. These are things created from the stuff of time itself.

Even now, much is made of the cherry blossom—not in full bloom *mankai* but when the petals begin to flutter down. The transient moment thus symbolized is seized upon and visible perishability is prized. Thus transience is traditionally celebrated, just as emptiness is traditionally commemorated. Finding nourishment in the void is thus truly creative. But you have to have the void before you can find the nourishment. And what if this fruitful void fills up?

Something like this is occurring in modern Japan. As I write, emptiness is draining away. A civilization traditionally predicated upon the virtues of being empty is becoming full. The ideals of poverty have been superseded by the ideals of wealth. Since the conclusion of World War II, this traditionally poverty-stricken country has become progressively richer—that is, the government, not the people themselves. But the people have been easy to lead away from the void of poverty when shown the mountain of things for them to buy.

The empty room is no longer filled with the richest of emptiness. Instead it now contains the television set, the videotape recorder, the cassette deck, the deep-freeze, the answering machine, the microwave, and much more. It is crammed.

There is a glut of time, too—a democratic distribution for everyone. Stretches of time are no longer creative voids to be filled with contemplation. Time is now to be killed and taxidermized with pachinko, or with brand-name shopping, or with *karaoke*. A nation of creators has become a nation of consumers.

This consumerism is the result of a kind of demoralization. Imagine a nation, the culture of which was predicated on the creative use of want. Now remove the want. If the void no longer nourishes, it is because it is no longer there; nor are the master carpenters or the artist masons, and the tea ceremony and the art of arranging flowers have both been transformed from celebrations of emptiness into big businesses.

As to why this should have occurred in a country famed for wringing nourishment from emptiness, I think that the reason—or one of

the reasons—is that Japanese culture, perhaps because of its long competitive bias, is one of the most pragmatic.

Everything is for use, hardly anything exists for its own intrinsic self. Nature becomes the garden and flowers become the ikebana. This urge to create is extremely strong. When there is little to create with, and scant material upon which the searching, pragmatic spirit can exercise itself, *ma* and the tea ceremony come into being. When more material comes to hand, as at present, there is a natural swing toward the methods of consumption—a much lesser goal.

As the empty world implodes in the midst of excess, it carries away with it a certain necessary creativity—a special and precious ability that in large part brought into being that fast-receding culture recognized as traditionally Japanese.

The empty center is still there, but it supports less and less. Its immaculate transparency turns opaque. A new Barthes, in Japan for the first time, might not even notice it. And as the emptiness vanishes, a kind of creation vanishes with it.

From The Temples of Kyoto, 1995

The Gods

In the Komponchu-do, rebuilt in 1642, the Yakushi Nyorai is said still to stand and so it may—it is impossible to tell in the darkness. Across bare, cold, red-lacquered floors now long rubbed pink, the barefoot visitor slides into the shadows of the great central hall and there, between the further pillars, opens a gulf.

Ten feet below, faintly illuminated by candles stands the personage. Seen as though across the moat of darkness, it is perhaps the statue carved by

Shicho many centuries ago. Near it is that perpetual lamp said lit by the founding monk. Though it was in fact put out by Nobunaga when he began his depredations, this fact is ignored and it burns as though it has always. Yet it reveals nothing—the figure before it remains in the darkness.

The muffling scent of incense hangs in cold air and there remains something of the militant blackness of the huge, brooding, vanished complex. The

heavy roofs weigh in the cold mountain air, the great cryptomeria stand black over the still temples, and still flags hang from the high eaves—yellow, green, red—speaking of old China and beyond, to ancient, cold Tibet.

In the dark of a winter afternoon the great icy Komponchu-do seems—as do all frozen things—to be waiting. The single lamp, cold as the gulf in which it burns suspended, is the only sign of life—the sign of a life to come.

Japan: A Half Century of Change

When I came to Japan in a cold January in 1947, the first thing that I noticed was change. It was dramatic. Tokyo, like most Japanese cities, had been nearly destroyed during World War II. People were living in the subway tunnels, there was not enough food, and yet already on this burned plane of black ash was rising the lemon yellow of all the new buildings as the odor of burned wood gave way to the smell of fresh-cut lumber. Change was already upon the land. Every day I saw roads being made, canals being filled, as the new city burgeoned.

And watching the carpenters at work—sawing through the new wood—I saw that their tools cut as they were pulled, not pushed, as they were back in the United States. I noticed this with understanding—this was something I recognized, having long heard that Japan was a kind of topsy-turvy land where everything was done backward. This had indeed been among the earliest accountings of the country—a model created by and for early visitors. So here was something I could relate to: a paradigm for Japan, a model through which I could grasp the metamorphosing place.

Seemingly different, always changing, Japan famously demands a working model for comprehension, as though the place needed an articulated map, or a working metaphor. Here I was, brand-new, twenty-one years old, and already searching around for one.

Topsy-turvy land fitted my needs, if not those of the Japa-

From Partial Views, *1994*

nese. So when fellow Occupiers looked at the carpenters and smiled and said: "These people got a long way to go," I agreed. That was because these backward people were by definition trying to catch up with the West. They had been at this for some time now, nearly a century, and taken many a wrong turning. But now, thanks to us, they were finally on the right track.

This is what I thought as I stood at the Ginza crossing looking at the kimono and old army uniforms, hearing the *geta* and watching Hokusai's Mount Fuji being blocked out by all the new buildings. They might lose a view, I philosophized, but they were gaining a city.

This was something we Occupiers could understand. The old Japanese military model had proved faulty and the new American economic model seemed to work a lot better. Finding something familiar in an attitude which estimated everything solely by its practical bearing on current interests, we Occupiers worked hard to help put these reversed folks right. There was land reform, the big business cartels were broken up, democracy was introduced and individuality was being governmentally promoted.

And as I looked at the city of Tokyo growing taller around me, at the Japanese around growing healthier, wealthier every day I saw that my topsy-turvy paradigm was itself upside down. I had found them reversed only because I came from the other side of the earth. But if you thought about it, at this very instant, the people of the U.S.A. were standing on their heads. And, as for my belief that They were catching up with Me: They already had.

* * *

I left Japan in 1949 to go back to school at Columbia University and when I returned to Japan in 1954, the Occupation was three years in the past. Land reform was over, the big business cartels were more or less back in place, democ-

racy was being digested away: I saw so much had changed that I did not recognize the place.

What I saw as new was now even more interestingly mingled with what wasn't. Old Shinto shrines on the top of new high-rises, white-robed acolytes on motorbikes, and ancient *zaibatsu* executives reclining in their new steel and glass headquarters.

On the streets I still saw some kimono but this traditional dress was overpowered by copies of Dior's New Look. Geta were still seen and heard but shoes predominated, getting ready for the Gucci tsunami to come. And standing on the Ginza crossing I saw that Fuji-san had now entirely disappeared, covered by layer after layer of new buildings. And I remembered my earlier model, the now vanished topsy-turvy land, as I gazed at the backward people who were rapidly becoming forward.

Looking about, I discovered a new model: Japan, land of contrasts, a place where the new and the old lived equitably together. Under the modern veneer, this ageless core lived on.

I found supportive paradigms everywhere. My neighborhood, little Tansumachi, had its named changed to Roppongi 4-chome, and was then flattened to make room for a new high-rise. There went the egg-lady and the chicken-man, there went the fruit-shop boys. And yet when the high-rise was completed, I found that the fruit boys had a new shop in its depths, one now named Boutique des Fruits.

Change within continuity—that is what my new model of the country allowed and accounted for. That there had also been a loss in quality did not disturb me, in part because I optimistically looked about at the changed country and thought that my having Occupied it might have had something to do with its present prosperity.

Nor was I alone in my self-congratulatory fits. Ten years after the Occupation was over, the U.S. was gazing across the Pacific like a fond parent

(continues on page 219)

A Display of Innocence

The entrance to Onomichi's night-town is marked by a neon arch. Outside, the city is already dark. Inside, the lights begin at once—lines of bars with names such as Jun (Purity) and Midori (Green, but also a girl's name) formed from bent neon tubing or in illuminated letters on glass tinted purple (a color presumed to be erotic); big cabarets covered with blinking lights spelling out such names as Shin Sekai (New World) or Kopa (after the well-known Copacabana); large and expensive nightclubs, with hostesses lined up in the entryway because the evening is still young, named Gessuimei (Moonlight Water), Buruu Shato (Blue Chateau), or the like.

It is very hot: here in this labyrinth no breezes blow and the heat of the day lingers on. The lined-up hostesses favor evening gowns of georgette and velveteen, not the coolest of materials. Already their makeup has started to run and they keep touching their perspiring faces with handkerchiefs rolled up and held in the fist. One is having difficulty with a rhinestone-studded slipper. Another is drinking a glass of water with small bird-like gulps while keeping an eye on the passersby and smiling between sips.

Men walk up and down the streets. The only women are those standing in the doorways of bars or lined up just inside the nightclubs and cabarets. Most of the men seem to be sailors, but all of them are dressed up and, though they may wear clogs on bare feet, they also wear neckties around their tanned necks.

I wander on, peering into the side streets, where the neon and electric lights stretch into the distance. The bars become smaller and there is an occasional large red-paper lantern marking a plebeian *nomiya,* the Japanese-style drinking place, usually with counter and stools, where sake is more ordered than whisky and where such presumed delicacies as *oden* (vegetables and eggs stewed in a vinegar mixture) are served. I am in that valley which separates all night-towns, divides the "purely" Western from the purely Japanese.

Soon the first willow tree makes its appearance and I hear the twang of the samisen. After a few more blocks I spot plastic cherry blossoms and see the first kimono. I also suddenly smell the sea and, between the houses, see the tall illuminated masts of cargo ships. I am now in the Japanese quarter of this Japanese night-town and soon reach the small creek with its invariable rustic bridge, its grouped willows, its pink and blue lanterns.

Here the customers are fewer, and, this early in the evening, these small streets seem almost deserted. A child rushes past me, late for supper; there is the sudden sound of women laughing together from one of the houses surrounding me; in the distance a phonograph is playing the "Gunkan March" and I smell squid being roasted.

At the crossroads, where I stand, there is a small bar on one corner, new, its unpainted wood almost white, and a small theater on the other. A sign proclaims it to be the sole home in this area of the zen *sutorippu;* The latter word is, of course, "strip," and the former certainly has no Buddhist connotations, being one of the words for "complete" or, perhaps, "utter." In this small and attractive theater one may gaze upon the stripper who strips all. This art is now but rarely practiced in the larger cities. Tokyo, for example, has completely forbidden it, though *han sutorippu* is permitted, the *han* (half) referring to the upper portions of the performer.

Two old men in kimono come out smiling; I go in.

It is a very small theater with five or six rows of seats and a tiny proscenium with pink cotton curtains. Among the other patrons is a pimpled adolescent sitting directly in the middle of the first row. He stares straight ahead, eyes glazed. He has, I guess, sat through at least several performances.

I rest in the pleasant half-darkness smelling that not unattractive odor of mildew, urine, rotting wood, and DDT that these places always exude.

Presently the scratch of a phonograph needle introduces the first strains of a samisen melody and the curtains sway in the breeze as though someone has opened a door backstage. The adolescent—in a white coat and round white cap, an errant *sushi-boy*, I suspect—leans forward, resting his chin on the stage itself, and the curtains slowly open to disclose a middle-aged Japanese lady in full kimono, sweat flecking her neck and forehead, ready to begin her dance.

It is a classical dance and she dances very well indeed. There is that firmness in her movements, that precision, just soft enough to be human, which classical dance calls for and without which it becomes a series of postures. Her performance is more complicated, however, in that, in addition to the classical choreography, she must also gradually unloosen the many garments that bind her, dropping first one obi, then the other, turning to allow us to admire the back of her neck, a renowned beauty-spot in Japan; then she must let her outer kimono slide from her shoulders, then her inner kimono.

She performs extremely well and her slight overripeness, her impassive and matronly face, brings something attractively perverse with it, heightening the obvious fact that she is, after all and essentially, only performing a striptease. Her performance is extremely personal, is, in fact, artistic, and without this quality the erotic can never exist.

First one nude shoulder appears, then another, as she takes off her *hadajuban*, a half-kimono that covers the breasts. One breast appears, and then the other. Now she is standing only in her *koshimaki*, a red-silk slip wrapped around her from waist to knees. This she slowly opens, still moving to the sound of the samisen, faithfully performing a classical dance intended to be done fully clothed. Perhaps the adolescent does not, but certainly I experience a slight feeling of disappointment. Those charms imagined or hinted at are so much more potent than those—no matter how well formed—exposed.

Finally, as the last notes of the samisen fade, replaced by the scratch of the record, she fully opens the red silk and we see, as the advertisement promised, "everything." She stands perfectly still, sweat running, the local Benten, a provincial Ishtar, and the curtains rustle closed.

It was a fine performance, up to a point, but at the end she faltered because the dance she had learned did not, after all, include the opening of the *koshimaki*. Indeed, the original dance was designed so you could imagine that magical moment, perhaps, but never directly view it. All Japanese art—perhaps all art—lives only through suggestion.

Thus considering. I was startled by the strains of "Gunkan March." To its lively military beat stepped onto the now open stage three very young girls, two in kimono and one in a kind of drum-majorette costume, with a tall, furry, tasseled hat but no baton. While the others made vague hand motions—left, right, left, right—she bounded about the stage, kicking and clapping her hands together beneath alternately upraised thighs.

She lost no time divesting herself of her uniform, flinging it about with simulated abandon, while the other two decorously bared their shoulders. Soon she had divested herself of her short skirt and was prancing about in gold-spangled panties, her epaulets hanging loose, while the other two hiked up their kimono to show thick legs, and the march pounded on.

The number reminded me in its enthusiastic artlessness of the private shows one could once see in Tokyo—and can still occasionally glimpse in places farther from the capital. There, on the bare tatami of someone's living room (for these shows were always held in someone's house), cramped between the wife's sewing machine and the childrens' toy-box, one witnessed all kinds of lovemaking going on just a few feet away.

One of the nicest, funniest, and most typical of these exhibitions that I ever witnessed featured a pleasant young country girl who came on naked, bowed, beckoned to her female friend, who entered somewhat more bashfully, sat down, pulled her friend on top of her, and at once went into visible ecstasies. They crawled all over each other, patting and licking, then a double-headed instrument was produced which they used with greatly evident enjoyment. Then the second girl stood up, bowed, left, and was succeeded by a young man, who bowed and at once fell on top of the waiting original girl. Nothing came of this, however, because the man suffered an attack of stage fright. Under her skillful administrations, however, he eventually recovered his self-possession and treated us to perhaps all of the forty-eight classical positions. Then, after the heights of ecstasy had been sufficiently simulated with cries and groans and arched backs, he stood up, bowed, and again the girl was left alone upon the mats.

She then promptly produced a number of objects: a banana, a full beer bottle, a length of string. With no more preamble than a small smile, she peeled the banana with her fingers, inserted it, and bit off great chunks. When it was consumed, she deftly removed it and put the mess daintily on a square of tissues. Then she bowed. Next she inserted the beer bottle and after some effort managed to pull off the cap (doubtless previously loosened). She put the full bottle to one side and bowed again. Then she tied one end of the string to a small square of paper and inserted it. Next, she held the loose end out to one of the guests and invited him to pull. He attempted, and several others after him, but she always won the resulting tug-of-war. Bowing, she removed the paper, squatted, and asked for small change, ten-yen coins. After receiving a number, she inserted them all and then asked the assembled guests to name certain amounts. Forty yen, ten yen—she never made a mistake,

depositing the called for amount in her own hand and exhibiting her mathematical prowess. Then, like a proper housewife returning borrowed dishes, she offered to return the coins to their original owners, smiling only slightly when repayment was declined by all.

Then she made a low and formal bow, stood and with two hands hid those charms the talents of which we had so fully viewed, smiled a most charming smile and—the reason I remember this girl with such affection—said: "*Domo, shitsurei itashimashita*," a common polite phrase that might be translated as "I have been very rude." All of this was accomplished without the least suspicion of irony because there was no irony, and none was necessary. This is what you say when you must leave, when you have stayed perhaps a bit too long, when you wish to reassure and at the same time show an attractive degree of gentility.

It was only I who found this degree of the incongruous irresistible. None of Japanese in the audience thought it funny; they did not smile and try to hide their laughter. They were busy finding their coats and, one after the other, bumping into the sharp edge of the sewing machine on their way out. Innocent themselves, they did not appreciate a display of innocence as extreme as this, at least not as much as I did.

Try as one may—at least in my case—it is impossible to find anything sordid in Japan and,

consequently, one is oneself a bit freer of this mental color, this psychological taint. The girl busy with her bananas and her small change was not dirty. She was doing her work, and doing it well.

And so was the younger girl now up on the stage. The march was thundering to a climax, the gold-spangled panties had been thrown aside and there, glimpsed between kicks, was the small and furry opening that attracts all eyes.

It particularly attracted the now bloodshot eyes of the *sushi*-boy, who, mouth hanging open, moved his chin slowly across the stage floor until the edge hit his throat and prevented further progress. The kicking stopped, though the music continued, and the girl, smiling—perhaps the boy *had* remained through several performances—and with the best will in the world, spread her thighs and knelt directly in front of him. His eyes rolled up, his head lying on the stage as though severed. Then she made a small movement and brought herself within inches of his nose. He emitted a rattling sigh that I could hear above the deafening march, and she was at once on her feet again, kicking and prancing, smiling, sweat falling like rain, her two companions, also nude, writhing in some kind of imitation snake dance and the curtains closed. The performance—all half-hour of it—was over.

When I left I glanced back; the *sushi*-boy was still there, sitting back in his seat now but unable, apparently, to move farther.

leaning over a crib. That infant economic nimbleness that is now being so deplored in what is left of the trade talks, was originally approved of by the proud parents.

This pragmatism, this going for what worked regardless of all other considerations, was, we thought, an American gene happily at work in fecund Japan. The country was our younger sibling, a smart kid with growing pains.

And, for so long as it worked, Japan took to the kid-brother role. It fit and it was also economical for the country. The money saved on national defense alone was considerable. Also, it was thus a better role than that of big brother—for Japan well remembered (even if it didn't much talk about) just where treating the rest of Asia as little brown brothers had gotten *it*.

Dependent, this sibling looked up to its protectors. This perceived difference we all, having gotten used to it in the Occupation, enjoyed. I liked being apparently looked up to, rarely contradicted to my face, and accorded what I thought was special treatment. That I was also being marginalized as well did not occur to me. After all, even though that Golden Age of Opportunity, the Allied Occupation of Japan, was over, not a few foreigners still managed to get ahead in the country entirely because of their nationality and their color.

White was the shade of preference. What would have happened to us in friendly Japan if we had been yellow or brown or black did not occur to many. Nor did we ponder the reasons for our being so singled out. Yet it was only because we were the people from whom lessons could still be learned. We were the obvious pragmatic choice for a model, we had after all won the war, and our favored status would last just as long as did our usefulness.

In 1968 I again left Japan, this time to take up a position in New York. If I had stayed in Ohio I would perhaps have been a salesman at the local Sill's Shoe Store, but I had come to Japan and so I was returning to my country as Curator of Film at the New York Museum of Modern Art.

* * *

I saw upon my return to Japan in 1974 that so much further change had taken place that any earlier ideas on the grand role of living tradition in Japan seemed now inadequate. Tradition apparently covered much less territory than I had originally thought. ´

An example occurred when I went house hunting. During my first stay the rule had been that the rooms were all Japanese—that is, all tatami-matted, except for one Western (hardfloor) room. During my second, the rule was: all Western except for one Japanese room. And now, in my third stay, all Western, no tatami—and in one place I saw that the hot-water heater had been put in the *tokonoma,* traditional alcove for flower arrangement.

Also, further indication of change, it was difficult to find anyone to rent to me. I had to have a sponsor, had to put down a sizable amount as deposit. It became apparent that I, though a very white American, was no longer looked up to.

Perhaps it had been already noticed that the U.S. model was not as successful as originally hoped. And as more and more poor white foreigners came to work in rich Japan—as L.A. girls came to serve in the clubs, as Ohio boys came to labor as doormen—it became impossible to slide by simply by being white. Of a consequence we, native Occupier and newcomer alike, found Japan changed. The Japanese, we said, were becoming arrogant.

An interesting choice of word because it indicates a change from what was perceived as tractable and compliant. Independence is always viewed as arrogance by those being replaced, and though the postwar U.S. had not actually intended an open colonization of Japan, it still did not like the idea of the natives getting uppity.

And as for change, it was all very well we thought, so long as it proceeded along the lines of the approved model: surface changeable, the core inviolate. But now—in the Seventies and to grow increasingly more apparent in the decades to come—a new model was becoming necessary.

Among the attractive newer metaphors was one which invoked stratification. Japanese culture was composed of successive layers in which the new was merely piled on top of the old. The Shinkansen Bullet Train now ran faster than all other trains but the carpenters still pulled their saws. People named their girl children Aya and Misaki and thought the common Hanako unspeakably old-fashioned—yet somewhere in the provinces a new Hanako existed.

Another model was a complicated structural affair in which the country was seen through such polarities as *uchi* and *soto* (inside vs. outside), *ninjo* and *giri* (one's own feelings vs. society's). This theory made Japan appear a place unique and was consequently a popular model with the Japanese themselves as well as the interested foreigner. It was, however, impervious to change.

Perhaps for that reason I never found much use for this model. It could not prepare us for what was happening. It lived in the past and as became more apparent, as the economy bubbled, Japan lived in an eternal present.

I, who sort of believed in ancestor worship, even if the Japanese didn't, was thus surprised when I saw the Shiba Tokugawa tombs razed to make way for the Prince Hotel. And I, who thought that a cozy symbiotic relationship existed between Japan and nature, reacted with alarm when I saw the coastline being concreted over, forests cut down to accommodate golf courses, and national parkland given over to developers.

More was to come. Later on I saw that lifetime employment, a Japanese tradition if there ever was one, was there no longer; that the upward-bound escalator—just stay on, don't bother to work, and you will be safely carried to the top of your bureaucratic profession—had stopped; and that the national diet had changed: coffee and toast became the easy-to-make national breakfast with difficult *gohan* and *miso* soup reserved for

The Foreigners From Japan Journals, 1992

November 22, 1992. A gathering of *gaijin*. Some of them new here, some not, and yet all share the same delusion. The Japanese are a singlefaced, single-minded unit. They are all clones of each other. They are "them." That I who have lived here nearly half a century should know better is not surprising. What is surprising is that anyone who has been here a day should not know better. And yet the cant continues:

"You got to understand them, you can get around them this way, if you do this you can bet that they'll do that." All of them? In mass? And yet were I to tell them that "the Japanese" were just as different, just as varied as, well, as *they* are, I would not be believed.

I try it. No, I am not believed and I am aware of something more. I am not liked. I am looked upon as having spoiled the party,

as though I am the single one not to comprehend, the one, hence, to rend that great warm accord that they were feeling when they were talking about "them." One girl with harlequin glasses says she feels forever the outsider. I do not ask if we don't all feel outside, particularly now, in the U.S.A. Instead I listen as a man with longish hair enthusiastically agrees and says he has a theory about that. He tells

Sunday, maybe. And finger-licking-good American junk for in between.

And that wasn't all. My former models had all made room for the idea of defenseless little Japan inundated by ruthless Western imports. These poured into the country and thus diluted tradition—that was how my paradigm worked. Now, I saw that it was not that way at all.

Japan reached out and dragged in. Anything it wanted it got; anything it didn't got kept out. A discerning shopper, the country willingly opened itself to what was useful, and snapped shut in the face of what was not. Well, so did Ohio, I supposed, but with nothing like the scale, the openness, the panache.

This simplified bivalve exemplar of the country did not have the elegance of former miniatures but it seemed to have the virtue of accuracy, at least for the present. It explained a lot: for example, the true use of English in the country. For decades now the Japanese had been getting it all wrong. We had chuckled over it ("We Play for General MacArthur's Erection"), and "these people still have a long way to go" seemed the comforting message.

Then it occurred to me that this misuse of my language was not funny and further did not, as I then believed, show a contempt for English by ignoring the integrity of the original. No contempt was involved, and no ignorance either. Writings in ads, on signs, on T-shirts, on shopping bags alike, were not intended to be English. They were Japanese-English, and this was not a subdivision of English but a subdivision of Japanese. It was a language directed only toward an uncritical audience for whom meaning had no importance, though the significance of the newly acquired did.

Tradition was judged by the same rule. If it could be turned into the pragmatically useful it remained. This usually meant becoming a new product. Kimono and geta had all but disappeared, yet some remained as new signifiers: a girl in a kimono meant Traditional Type, going about her ikebana or her koto lesson. A boy in geta meant either Traditional Tradesman or Traditional Student Rightist. And the despised Hanako was revived as the trendy and self-mocking title for a new magazine, which told all the young people what to buy.

her the theory. We are always outside, they are always inside. I know the theory. I have voiced it myself often enough. And I am aware of that nice full feeling that comes with it—the feeling that I have understood something, that something is certain—that in this floating world I have found a small but stable rock.

And yet I know that foreigners are not branded outsiders. I think of how many inside positions I myself have. And I do not think that everyone who is Japanese is also therefore inside, since I know many who are not. How much more complicated the world is than this.

But it is just this dumb and symmetrical simplicity that so appeals—to me along with everyone else. There is so much of this now, so much more than there used to be. I thought it had to do with Japanese wealth and consequent unpopularity. But now I think there is more to it. Looking around the fragmented world I realized that simplicities are everywhere searched for—and found. Models are being made of reality, and then judged as though they were real. And the reason is that simplicity is easier to control than complication.

If the world has a movement now it is to the right. Back to the easy simplicities of skinheads and neo-Nazis, of Serbs, of Islam, of Jew-baiting and Japan-bashing. It presages a new Baroque, an age of totalitarian power, of willful stupidity, of studied simplicity, of fatuous and fundamental "happiness."

The kimono itself was subsumed in the wrappings of Issey Miyake; the architectural tradition turned into the eclectic Japanesque of Arita Izozaki; Edo *mura* became a local tourist draw, and the Japan Travel Bureau began urging trips to Kyoto as time-travel to the picturesque Orient, while I sat and watched my traditional Japan turn into Japanland.

"Established in 1988" one read, carved in stone, in 1989. "Trad but mod" said a slogan of the Eighties and it said this about the new. From abroad poured in the products Japan thought Japan wanted as the traditional retained was being sliced into bite-sized pieces.

I felt I was living in a museum that was being swiftly destroyed. The wreckers were at work and—oh, there goes a room I thought never would; oh, there goes a whole wing of what I had thought was the permanent display.

And there I was in the shambles without a map, minus even a model because eventually my two-cylinder paradigm could not begin to cope with change this great.

* * *

Then I remembered something that fine scholar and good friend Edward Seidensticker had once written: "The relationship between tradition and change in Japan has always been complicated by the fact that change is itself a tradition."

I had, of course, long been aware of Japanese consciousness of change. For example, the fuss made about the seasons. And even now in contemporary Japan with its vast hydroponic farms and its enormous distribution circuits, flowers and food in season were still made something of and this seemed so because it gave some excuse for celebrating transience.

Certainly the annual cherry-viewing orgies all over the country were such. Particularly, I was told, evanescence is celebrated when the petals are floating to the ground and change was at its most palpable—the death of the blossom. There was even an exclamation for appreciation of natural change: *a-a aware.*

And I remembered my classical readings. For example the famous opening line of Kamo no Chomei's *Record of a Ten-Foot Square Hut (Hojoki,* here given in Burton Watson's translation): "The river flows unceasingly on, but the water is never the same water as before." I had thought that in looking at the stream Kamo was affirming the reassuring fact that the body of water was, after all, permanent. But now I saw that what he was indicating was, instead, the fact that the water itself changed, was always different.

And I remembered the shrine at Ise. This single wooden edifice is replaced every twenty years. It is torn down and an identical replica is constructed. This has been going on for centuries. And it had seemed to me obvious that this exemplary structure celebrated tradition. It was the core holding.

But now I was not so certain. Ise surely satisfied the claims as of eternity and the hopes of immortality—though in a way quite different from that of, say, the pyramids. But at the same time it celebrated transience. It accepted change and it did so by accommodating it, by building evanescence into the structure of the Ise Shrine itself.

Looking at the shining towers of Shinjuku, Hokusai's Mount Fuji long vanished, I tinkered away at my homemade model. Every culture copes with change but how many, I wondered, had made it a moving part. Lots of nostalgia for the good old days to be sure, lots of bad-mouthing the new bad ones, just like everywhere else, but in addition to that, an accommodation to the evanescent, an acceptance of this fact of life.

Shikata ga nai (it can't be helped), that bleat which so irritates the foreign resident, could now be seen as a graceful acquiescence to the great principle of change itself. After all, there is nothing one can do about it means: let us rather get on with life.

Change is in Japan put to use, in the most pragmatic of manners. It alone is permanent and hence a steady source of power. It is perpetual motion, the dream of the physicists come true. And I saw that during my nearly fifty years in the country Japan had not changed in its attitude toward change. It was always hands-on and still was.

For example, any respect for the integrity of any original becomes beside the point when it is change itself that is being accommodated. The traditional landscape gardener moved this rock over a couple of feet, that bamboo grove back a yard or two, and swiped the view of the mountain in the process. The result was the natural garden, a product of change. Ikebana, classical flower arrangement, changes venue and placement, and only then calls itself "living flowers" though they are of course no longer quite that, being cut.

The difference that I thought I had noticed in Japan's attitude toward nature was then but one of degree. When the daimyo built himself a landscape garden his need was aesthetic because such labor-intensive work as this would otherwise not have been so ostentatiously indicative of his degree.

When it is money itself, rather than aesthetics, which satisfies the demands of social standing, then forests are cut down for golf courses and ancestral tombs are trashed for hotels. But the difference is only in degree—now, famously, money must make more money. The demand is no longer aesthetic—it is economic. Yet the mechanism is the same. Everything changes. Though there may be amber-like blocks of permanence within this moving magma, they remain only because they are useful for the time being.

What is important, and what is eventually defining, I decided, is this genius for the harnessing of change. Having decided this I looked at my new, small, metaphor of the country. It lay there in my palm, a whirling gyroscope. This might become a model, a system of thought—one I noticed nearly fifty years ago—which welcomes and celebrates that very change which so transforms us and our world; which accepts death as well. For if there is no mortality there is no life, let alone aesthetics.

And over the hum of my gyroscope I heard the words of the priest Kenko who now nearly seven hundred years ago wrote: "What if man lingered on. . . how things would then fail to move us. The finest thing in life is its uncertainty."

From The Honorable Visitors, 1994   *The Foreigners*

And I think of [Marguerite Yourcenar] as the last of the line, as the final—and in many ways the finest—visitor. Japan continues, but the "Japan" that I have here been concerning myself with does not. Future visitors now see something else: a vast, dynamic, technologically superior land, one where the traditional remains are gentrified, where the past has become a theme park.

For some time now, I have felt that I live in a vast museum that is being dismantled. "Oh, there goes that room and I had thought it would last forever. Oh, there goes the whole wing."

Such destruction is but natural since it is also creation, but a new kind of visitor is now called for. The collision of cultures, the spectacle of the century, one country evolving from its past into its future—this is over. Now something else will happen. And other visitors will come to watch it.

New Year's 1999

January 3, 1999. Cold—even the morning crows are silent in the chill. I look from my window at the park below and the only living thing is a solitary crane, white in weak sun, standing amid the withered lotus. No sign of the homeless. I do not know where they go.

How empty winter makes everything. The space outside my window is now enormous, with the sky half of it, empty of clouds, empty of birds. In summer the leaves crowd the season, details are filled in, people are wandering spots of color, sound is muffled. But now all of this is dismantled and a sound, a barking dog, is heard for miles.

I turn from the window—it makes the fourth, the north wall of my home. Opposite it are bookshelves holding my books on film, on Japan, and the chest where I keep my shirts and socks and underwear. To the east are my closets, which also contain my CDs and bedding when people come. To the west, another window, this one shaded from the outside and beneath it the hi-fi set, the TV unit, and books on photography and art, and all my scores. That is one room. The next contains the corner where this machine sits and on which I type, a dark corner protecting me from the distractions of the view. Behind me the kitchen, beside me the door to the bathroom.

It is small by Western standards, though large by Japanese— two whole eight-mat rooms, if they had mats. It is just right for me. Snug, small enough to keep clean, my space—nothing

From Japan Journals, *1999*

further away than a couple of paces. And it has heating. My big room heater is on now and here where I work my small foot heater as well. And over my lap that coverlet that my mother knitted, how many years ago now?

January 6, 1999. I go to see the Ozu exhibition again this afternoon but not having read the notice properly find it closed. Since I am already on the enormous campus of Tokyo University I decide to look around, having never been there.

What I find as I walk and walk and walk is a whole city with its own bus system, its stores, its monuments and buildings. Though right in the middle of Tokyo it is suburban and there are trees everywhere, even a park within this park, a glen with a lake. Sanshiro's Lake, I read. This must refer to the Natsume Soseki hero who came up from the country to go to what was then Tokyo Imperial University.

It looks like a city too because all the architecture is the same style—yellow, brown, beige, ochre brick with iron doorframes, window lattices, fittings. The style is late Thirties—art deco. And as I look at this prewar city I remember Tokyo in 1947 when everything—everything that was left—looked like Todai does now.

From The Japanese Garden, 1972   *The Gods*

From the first gardens to these last gardens, down to the modern gardens of our own age, the Japanese attitude toward nature is revealed as the continuous endeavor to extract the essence of a stone, a tree, a view. In order to do so one recognizes the nature of each, insists upon it, allows this nature to display itself.

The original stone or tree is never natural enough for the Japanese. Rather than working against nature, however, clipping the tree or squaring the stone, the Japanese gardener has from the beginning worked with nature, worked along its grain, as it were. There is pruning and placing but this results in the revealing of a line which nature itself created and then obscured in its own plentitude.

That the Japanese idealize is true enough, but the method of idealization is, as has been indicated, to perceive and then to free that which already exists.

The assumption of this act, as we have seen during the course of this book, is that nature and man are one. By its acceptance of the transitory it emphasizes both the timeless and the instant which is now. By discovering unity in variety, it discovers the forever unique.

In Japan one clearly sees the passing of this philosophy from one generation to another, from one age to the next. It is more than a tradition. It is living thought. And, being alive, it is also variously interpreted.

As the great poet Matsuo Basho said, centuries ago: one should never imitate that which has been inherited from one's forebears; one should, instead, strive after that for which one's forebears strove.

He was speaking of *haiku*, but he could have been speaking of many things, so common is the attitude expressed. He could have been speaking of gardens, for, no matter the form—paradise garden, tour garden, water garden, sand garden, island garden—behind each is the same attitude toward nature. It is one which remains the same despite its changing forms.

The modern gardener, living in this age of express highways and jet travel, continues to 'strive after that for which one's forebears strove.' It is a belief in the identity of man and nature, one which humbles in its insistence upon the transitory nature of the merely human, but which, at the same time, dignifies by its equal insistence that we are all a part of something larger than ourselves.

The low winter sky, the small declining sun, the bare ginkgo trees—the feeling of fifty years ago is so strong that I seem to smell charcoal burning, chestnuts roasting, The few students I pass look scruffy as they did back then and I expect the odor of the camellia oil they used to wear on their hair.

I look up at the windows and find that, just as in postwar Tokyo, those working there have piled their boxes, their files, their bookcases against them. Windows are not for looking out. Windows are for clutter. Travelling in space, somewhere right in my neighborhood where I have never been, somewhere immense, another country, I am also travelling in time—half a century swallowed.

Wandering around, I find the bookstore and there on a shelf I discover my own kyogen, published decades ago, long out of print, to be found nowhere on earth probably except right here on this shelf where it has been waiting for twenty-five years. I buy it. It is still the original price—five hundred yen, a sum that would barely buy a cup of coffee now.

My past in my pocket I walk in what I think is the direction of Ueno and in so doing find the back gate, the Ikenohata Mon. It is right behind that awful Sophitel Hotel which so ruins the view from my balcony. I have passed every other day and never knew that the entrance to this lost world lay right in back of it, right next, I find, to Benkei's Well. The plaque says that in 1945 it saved the local populace during the fire raids by giving fresh, clean water. There is a pump there now. It still works. There is a large damp spot on the old concrete under its spout.

Now I know where I am and there, across the lake is my apartment house. I walk home, the sun setting at four-thirty, the reeds silvered, back-lighted, haloed, the ducks settling, the cormorants already asleep, black statues of themselves. The homeless, ten or twelve, sit by the shore that still holds the light, looking at the last of the sun and the coming of night.

Bibliographical Note

This bibliographical note has no pretension to being complete—which would make a volume in itself—instead it will be selective and personal (and fairly thorough for all but the researcher). A somewhat more conventional bibliography and (complete) filmography, including many uncollected essays as well as interviews and privately published works, are to be found in the German volume *Ricecar für Donald Richie*, listed below in the next-to-last entry.

Essential Reading

The Inland Sea. Tokyo: Weatherhill, 1971. Ostensibly an account of a single journey to a little-seen area of Japan, this book is Richie's masterpiece. Published at about the midpoint of his five-decade stay in Japan, the book presents his by-now fully matured view of the Japanese. (Of course, one must acknowledge his detestation of such generalizations; a blurb for a paperback edition called it "an intimate view of the 'real' Japan.") This book portrays an honest but discreet laying bare of Richie's character, with the breakup of his marriage lingering in the background of the narrative and with the writing acknowledging the double-subject mirror of self and Japan. Tender, funny, always compelling, compiled from a variety of sources and in fact many journeys to

by Arturo Silva

227

the Inland Sea, this book is one that Richie himself lists under his works of fiction.

Ozu. Berkeley: University of California Press, 1974. This book is another masterpiece; one of the best explications ever devoted to a film director (Richie worked on it for ten years). The subject is Yasujiro Ozu, master of the "transcendental" (and real) style of cinema—and one of Richie's few real (and transcendent) masters. While the writing is ostensibly a piece of film criticism, because its subject is "the most Japanese of Japanese film directors" it is also one of the best books ever written on Japan. *Ozu* is really a meditation on one of the supreme and unique artists of the century and cannot be praised too highly.

A Lateral View: Essays on Contemporary Japan. Tokyo: Japan Times, 1987. This is a collection of twenty-three of Richie's best essays, composed between 1963 and 1995, divided into six sections offering broad views of Japan, Tokyo, Japanese semiotic systems (fashion, gestures), theater, film, and popular culture.

Different People: Pictures of Some Japanese. Tokyo: Kodansha International, 1987. A collection of forty-eight sketches—"pen portraits" as they used to be called—it depicts various Japanese Richie has known. It is modeled on a nineteenth-century Japanese book. To anyone who thinks that Richie harbors generalizations about the "Japanese character," these individuals provide an immediate antidote. These portraits are brief and often exquisite studies, epiphanic aspects of character that are delineated and rarely go "deep." Subjects range from Yasunari Kawabata, Yukio Mishima, and Tetsuko Kuroyanagi, to a woman barber and a tattooed sushi chef (she doesn't fit in, he does), and the woman who smiles when she misses her train (included here). A second printing was titled *Geisha, Gangster, Neighbor, Nun* (1991), and a third, the one currently available, *Public People, Private People* (1996) with a new arrangement and added chapters. (Richie has voiced regret over the title changes.)

Tokyo: A View of the City. London: Reaktion Books, 1999. This book is essential reading for anyone interested in what fascinates people with the great capital—and what has kept Richie there for fifty years. (For the Tokyophile, the book provides the necessary passionate element to accompany Edward G. Seidensticker's two volumes on Tokyo's history—*Tokyo* is dedicated to Seidensticker—and Paul Waley's historical guide.) *Tokyo* is more an imaginative meditation on the city, and thus again an antidote to those far too many Tokyo books with agendas.

Two other favorite books should also be mentioned here. They may not be "essential," but where else to put such delights?

Tokyo Nights. London: Olive Press, 1988. This work is as much a rigorously ordered avant-gardist novel as it is a twentieth-century Restoration romp. Richie mentions that *Tokyo Nights* takes Henry Green's *Doting* as a model. When all the "Japan As Number One" and "Japan Inc." books are long forgotten, this will endure as *the* book for a (hilarious) understanding of what living in Japan in the bountiful 1980s was really like.

Zen Inklings: Some Stories, Fables, Parables, and Sermons. Tokyo: Weatherhill, 1982. First conceived in the wake of his psychoanalysis, which ended in 1971, but not composed until the early 1980s, this volume came at two crossroads in Richie's life (see the introduction). Surprising and unexpected, the book is also about personal and artistic freedom. Richie "studied" Zen during his initial stay in Japan with Daisetsu Suzuki, only to leave having learned that he did not have the wherewithal to sit *zazen* style in hope of attaining *satori*. What he did learn, however, turned out to be far more fruitful: simply, that he must be true to his nature. (A fuller account can be found in the "Note" at the back of the volume and a portrait of Suzuki in *Different People*.) But a Zen approach is present in much of Richie's work. (Did he learn as much from Ozu's films as from Suzuki?) This volume contains charming retellings of Zen legends and sermons (Richie does have the occasional desire to want to impart a lesson). Perhaps Richie did not gain enlightenment, but, ringing so true, this is as good an introduction to Zen as any. Who would not want it on their short shelf of books on Zen?

Books on Japan

(Included in this group should also be *The Inland Sea, A Lateral View,* and *Different People,* just discussed above.)

Lafcadio Hearn's Japan: An Anthology of His Writings on the Coun-

try and Its People. Tokyo: Tuttle, 1997. This work can be read in conjunction with *The Honorable Visitors* (described below). Having taken care of those "lesser" Japan commentators in *Visitors*, it is no wonder that Richie would, in a volume published only two years later, deal with his major predecessor, Lafcadio Hearn. As mentioned earlier, I know I am not the first person to believe that where for the twentieth century most people (travelers or no, consciously or not) approached Japan via Hearn's ghost-tale/romantic lens, the next century of the "Japan view" will—or ought to be—Richie's. Accordingly, he has had to lay the Hearn ghost to rest. The most important part of this volume (actually, not the most wide-ranging anthology available) is, of course, Richie's introduction.

The Temples of Kyoto. Tokyo: Tuttle, 1995. The curious origin of this book goes back to the 1960s, when the photographer Alexander Georges took photos of various Kyoto temples. These remained unpublished until an enterprising editor came upon them and thought they might make an attractive coffee-table book. Richie was asked to compose the text. The result was a book devoted to those twenty-one pre-selected temples (not gardens, the reader should know). Richie's writing turns the book not only into a history of each temple but, in fact, into his own potted history (nonprofessional, illuminating, and entertaining) of Kyoto from Heian times to Edo. (Its extensive bibliography reveals the depths of study he undertook for the project.)

Partial Views: Essays on Contemporary Japan. Tokyo: Japan Times, 1995. This second collection of essays, twenty-three in all and written between 1962 and 1987, is neatly divided into four sections: "Some Opinions," "Some Descriptions," "Some Places," and "Some People." Some of the best essays include "Intimacy and Distance: On Being a Foreigner in Japan" and "Japan: A Half Century of Change" (both reprinted here), "The Japanese Way of Seeing," "Sketches for a Portrait of Yukio Mishima," and the long "Notes for a Study on Shohei Imamura," which had previously been published as a book for the Australia Film Institute in 1983.

The Honorable Visitors. Tokyo: Tuttle, 1994. The portraits in the book are a fascinating view of twelve Westerners (mostly writers) who visited Japan from the Meiji period on to the near present. The book can be read as a sort of companion piece to *Different*

People, as well as a passing commentary on what it means to travel and write one's travels. For all his journeys, it is a wonder that Richie has not written more travel literature besides *The Inland Sea* and the pieces in *Partial Views*. There have been a few occasional writings, the last important one being a trip to Bhutan and published in the *Japan Times* (February 18, 1998). While I think that a certain autobiographical element appears in almost all of Richie's work, even where least evident, nowhere is it more complicated than here. Indeed, *The Honorable Visitors* can almost be read as an example of literary critic Harold Bloom's controversial "anxiety of influence" thesis. While his subjects stayed in Japan only a few short weeks or months, not the decades Richie has, the book does seem to read as if he were confronting his noted forebears, approvingly and otherwise. So, the book begins with Isabella Byrd, whom he likes for her intrepidness at wandering off the beaten tourist track (à la Richie). The heart of the short chapter on Ulysses S. Grant focuses on his famously encouraging appeal to his hosts to preserve the Noh. Would one be unjustified in reading here an indirect self-reference to the Richie persona in *Different People* who urges an official at Toho Studios to prepare export prints of Ozu's films? When the prints were done, Richie brought them to the 1963 Berlin Film Festival, thus almost single-handedly introducing to the Western world the very filmmaker that the Japanese thought least exportable (as they'd also regarded the Noh) and who has subsequently become the most universal.

The subjects proceed. The chapter on Pierre Loti (printed in this volume) reads almost like a "there but for heaven go I" cautionary tale. Both authors approach the country as a sexual wonderland: one is somewhat disappointed, or only temporarily fulfilled, and the other is satisfied, permanently so. Too, the chapter on Henry Adams—the point being that he missed the rare opportunity of seeing the country in a great period of historic change—can be read as Richie proclaiming, "I didn't!" (i.e., Richie in the immediate postwar period). Without overextending this comment, I am convinced that each subsequent chapter can be read similarly. Tellingly, the book concludes with a tour taken by Marguerite Yourcenar (one of Richie's most revered authors), and she being guided by no less than Richie himself.

An anxiety of influence? Perhaps. But not without reason. There is an old adage that if one wants to "understand Japan" then one must stay either two weeks or twenty years. In *The Honorable Visitors,* he deals with the former and sees where they either got it wrong or right. (Lafcadio Hearn seems to have gotten it both ways.) If this small and charming book were not about other, historical subjects, I would place it among the essential readings.

A Taste of Japan: Food, Fact, and Fable; What the People Eat; Customs and Etiquette. Tokyo: Kodansha International, 1984. This is a delightful (and recipeless) tour through the Japanese kitchen. Sushi and tempura, yes, but also soba, tonkatsu, and sake.

The Japanese Tattoo. Tokyo: Weatherhill, 1980, with photographs by Ian Buruma. The book, again, is as much passionate anthropology as it is art criticism. It is also about the Japanese attitude toward the body—and obviously written before the more recent Western tattooing and piercing craze.

The Japanese Garden: An Approach to Nature. New Haven, Connecticut: Yale University Press, 1972. This volume was published under the name of Teiji Itoh, a well-known scholar of Japanese gardens and aesthetics who was ostensibly to write it but for some reason could not—so Richie did. The second edition acknowledges his authorship. Lavishly photographed, the book provides a chronological tour through six styles of gardens. Chapters are brief, to the point, and contain some of Richie's best writing on the Japanese relationship to nature, as well as displaying his aesthetician-historian-manqué mode.

The Erotic Gods: Phallicism in Japan. Tokyo: Zufushinsha, 1966, with Kenkichi Ito. This illustrated quasi-anthropological book (specifically, it is about the phallic stones that once were to be seen throughout the country; there is one last one in Tokyo's Ueno Park that Richie often lovingly visits and mentions in his *Journals*) is a fascinating study of its subject. It has long been out of print.

Introducing Japan (1978) and *Introducing Tokyo* (1987). Tokyo: Kodansha International. These are more "commercially" inclined, thin, large-format, illustrated gift books bearing the Richie signature. While light reads, they are good presents to bring home to one's loved ones.

Books on Japanese Film

The Films of Akira Kurosawa. Berkeley: University of California Press, 1965. In addition to his book on Ozu, Richie has written the definitive study of Akira Kurosawa, composed in an *onsen*— hot springs resort—in Kagoshima Prefecture in less than four weeks. The second (1984) edition's chapters on the films *Dode-sukaden* and *Dersu Uzala* were written by Joan Mellon. The third (1996) edition was "expanded and updated" by Richie, except for Mellon's chapters. The book was reissued in 1998, following Kurosawa's death, with a new epilogue.

* * *

Richie has also written a number of books dealing with the whole of Japanese film; created at various times, they reflect differing critical perspectives. The first is a thorough film history, written under the then-prevailing Kracauerian/Bazinian view of film as a "redemption of reality." This is *The Japanese Film: Art and Indus-try* (Tokyo: Tuttle, 1959, and later, Princeton: Princeton University Press, 1982), by Richie and Joseph L. Anderson. Other books include *The Japanese Movie: An Illustrated History* (Tokyo: Kodansha International, 1965); *Japanese Cinema: Film Style and National Character* (New York: Doubleday, 1971); and the small and concise *Japanese Cinema: An Introduction* (Oxford: Oxford University Press, 1990). These last volumes are only briefly noted because, as of this writing, Richie has recently finished a final, thorough volume of the history and aesthetics of Japanese film, *A Hundred Years of Japanese Film: A Concise History, with a Selective Guide to Videos and DVDs* (Tokyo: Kodansha International).

Richie has also edited *Rashomon* for the Rutgers University Press series of screenplays and commentaries (1990), as well as *Focus on Rashomon* (New York: Prentice-Hall, 1971). He also edited the screenplay of *Seven Samurai* (New York: Simon and Schuster, 1971). His translations of Ozu's *Tokyo Story* (with Eric Klestadt) and of Kurosawa's *Ikiru* appear in *Contemporary Japanese Literature*, edited by Howard Hibbett (New York: Knopf, 1977). Critical essays on Yasujiro Ozu, Kenji Mizoguchi, and Mikio Naruse appear in *Cinema, A Critical Dictionary: The Major Filmmakers*, edited by Richard Roud (London: Secker and War-burg, 1980). Richie can also be heard on the Voyager laser disc edition of Mizoguchi's *Ugetsu* (1993).

Fiction

Memoirs of the Warrior Kumagai: A Historical Novel. Tokyo: Tuttle, 1999. Begun in 1985 (though conceived in 1960), Richie continued to work on the manuscript over the next thirteen years. The name of the title character is forever linked in the Japanese imagination with the young, beautiful samurai Atsumori, slain in battle by Kumagai, who, in remorse, takes the tonsure. In this historical novel, portraying a brilliant recreation of the end of aristocratic rule and the rise of the shogunate, we get Kumagai's side of the story. It becomes, in the end, a variation of John Ford's *Liberty Valance* thesis, "print the legend."

Companions of the Holiday. Tokyo: Tuttle, 1968. An affectionate and romantic-comic view of Japanese life seen through the lens of the servants of wealthy foreigners, this book's description and dialogue are exquisite. One can easily read the influence of Ozu here (or Henry Green's *Loving*), but a more significant one might be Thomas Raucat's (1928) *The Honorable Picnic.* The book is also somewhat autobiographical in that it evokes the house Richie lived in in Roppongi in the 1960s.

Where Are the Victors? Tokyo: Tuttle, 1956. Initially published under the "safe" (and meaningless) title *This Scorching Earth*, besides being Richie's first published book, it is also his semiautobiographical view of the Occupation. Critical of the "victors," its perspective is, naturally, very sympathetic to the "indigenous personnel." The narrative is somewhat cinematic, one scene leading to another while presenting an array of characters, Japanese and American, in just a single day in 1949. It is a bravura performance.

Autobiography

In addition to the *Japan Journals*, which will appear posthumously, Richie has also written some memoirs, called *Watching Myself,* and another called *Sections of a Child.* (The first section appears in this volume under the same title, first published in *Contemporary Authors: Autobiography Series* 20 [Detroit: Gale Group, 1994] as "Prose of Departure"—a title taken from a poetry and prose composition by his friend James Merrill and dedicated to Richie.)

While the memoirs cover his early years to just about before his arrival in Japan, the *Journals* are somewhat incomplete and do not really become an almost day-by-day account until the 1980s. But that gives us two entire decades. When published, they will reveal an extraordinarily complex and curious personality, and certainly put an end to Richie being regarded only through the single lens of Japan.

Miscellanea

In what one is tempted to call yet another case of an "anxiety of influence," Richie edited the two volumes *A Hundred Things Japanese* and *A Hundred More Things Japanese* (Japan Culture Institute, 1975 and 1980, respectively; later republished as *Discover Japan*, volumes 1 and 2, Tokyo: Kodansha International, 1983). The two hundred subjects range from bonsai and origami to mothers and department stores. Contributors range from a number of renowned "Japan experts" to Angela Carter and Richie himself. The anxiety-inducing volume in this case would be Basil Hall Chamberlain's perennial classic *Things Japanese* (1927). While that book is still worth reading, these two are more fun and eccentric.

Richie is also a music critic manqué. Since the mid-1990s, this side of him has been gratified by writing brief reviews for the bilingual magazine *In Tune* (San Francisco and Tokyo). He has also written liner notes for the CD edition of *The Film Music of Toru Takemitsu* (Nonesuch #79404, 1997). He also wrote music criticism in the 1950s for various Japanese magazines, including what he has called his "neglected masterpiece," "Paul Hindemith's Mathis der Mahler," appearing in *Ongaku no Tomo*, Spring, 1964.

Reproductions of some of Richie's artworks (prints) can be found in *Zen Inklings*. In 1996, Alex Kerr edited *Nudes*, a slim pamphlet (paintings; Chiiori Ltd., Kyoto).

Richie has also "appeared" in three works of fiction: in a novel by his former wife, Mary Richie, *A Romantic Education* (New York: McCall, 1970); in Joan Mellon's novel *Natural Tendencies* (New York: Dial, 1981); and as the hero (or villain) of a Francis King story called "The Goat." Finally, for a one-paragraph view of what it felt like to have Donald Richie as a tour guide in Japan, see the chapter "Nipponese Journal" in Duke Ellington's autobiography, *Music is My Mistress* (New York: Doubleday, 1973).

Richie served as editor of *Words, Ideas, and Ambiguities: Four Perspectives on Translating from the Japanese* (Chicago: Imprint Publications, 2000). This is the transcript of a 1998 colloquium on translating moderated by Richie. The participants include the noted translators Howard Hibbett, Edwin McClellan, John Nathan, and Edward Seidensticker.

Films

Between 1949 and 1953, Richie made ten short films in America. In Japan, between 1953 and 1968, he directed another twenty-five. In 1975, he made a TV documentary on Kurosawa. Though he was well known to aficionados of experimental film, no serious study of Richie's films has yet appeared (in English at least; in Japanese, Yukio Mishima, Shuji Terayama, and Nagisa Oshima have commented). In spring 2001, Image Forum in Tokyo presented a retrospective of Richie's films and released a handsome catalog (in Japanese) with essays by Oshima and Tadanori Yokoo, among others, as well as a video collection of four of Richie's films: *Atami Blues, Boy with Cat, Dead Youth, Wargames*. Some of Richie's films are available from the Museum of Modern Art, New York. A complete filmography with short annotations is in the German volume listed below, *Ricecar für Donald Richie*. In 2001, a documentary film on Richie's life in Japan and his involvement with film was being made by PRINZGAU/podgorschek of Vienna.

Richie has also appeared in three films. In *Rikyu* (1989), about the fifteenth-century tea master and directed by the contemporary tea master and filmmaker Hiroshi Teshigahara, Richie appears as the head of a Jesuit mission to the court of warlord Hideyoshi. He plays a GI in *Tokyo-1958* in a collective film by Teshigahara, Susumu Hani, and Zenso Matsuyama. And he narrates and appears at the end of the film *The Inland Sea* (1991), a beautiful one-hour adaptation of his travel classic directed by Lucille Carra.

Non-Japan Writings

An essay called "The Moral Code of Luis Buñuel" can be found in *The World of Luis Buñuel* (edited by Joan Mellon, Oxford:

Oxford University Press, 1978). The moving "Bresson and Music" appears in *Robert Bresson* (Cinémathèque Ontario, 1998). And a book commissioned by the Museum of Modern Art, New York, *George Stevens: An American Romantic*, appeared in 1970. An intense essay on voyeurism, "The Gloriole," appeared in *Margin* (London, 1986).

Occasional Writings

Richie wrote film reviews for the *Pacific Stars and Stripes* from 1947 to 1949 and then for the *Japan Times* from 1954 to 1969. Since 1972 he has written a weekly book review for the *Japan Times* and occasional travel pieces and film criticism. He also regularly writes for the *International Herald Tribune, Time, Newsweek*, and other newspapers and magazines.

Collected, these writings must measure in the hundreds, if not thousands, and would provide a gold mine for an intrepid researcher. Think of it: to watch the development of a sensibility during the late 1940s and middle 1950s as he comes to awareness of Japanese culture and film! To have been at the premieres of films by Ozu, Mizoguchi, Naruse, and Kurosawa!

Unpublished Writings

There are a number of unpublished writings by Richie, including at least two of his most heartfelt works. The first is a short novel about a boy coming to sexual awareness called *A Divided View*. The second is his *Japan Journals, 1947–99* (with some considerable gaps, most occurring because he was either in New York [1969–72] or plundered them for his published works). These have been edited by Leza Lowitz and are to be published posthumously. There are also a number of short story collections, the best of which is *A View from the Chuo Line and Other Stories* (three of which appear in this volume). In 1999, Richie began work on an autobiographical novella/romance, *Other Islands*. One hopes that someday it too will find publication.

On Donald Richie

The first book of its type on Donald Richie is a pamphlet (75 pages), *Ricecar für Donald Richie*, published in German by the Japanisches Kulturinstitut Köln in 1997. It includes numerous selections of his work (among them, one brief composition, *Rikyu Rounds*, and three short poems), as well as four essays on Richie and a bibliography and filmography.

Richie has also been the subject of numerous interviews, the most extensive of which was conducted by Janet Pocorobba and appeared in *Kyoto Journal*, number 41, 1998. An interview conducted by Trevor Carolan appears in the *Bloomsbury Review*, volume 21, issue 2, March/April 2001. (More interviews are listed in the German volume.)

Archive

The "Donald Richie Collection" of papers (unpublished works, journals, uncollected essays, and fugitive pieces) is on deposit at the Mulgar Memorial Library, Boston University. His collected film criticism (including the early work for *Pacific Stars and Stripes* and the *Japan Times*) is in the Museum of Modern Art Film Study Center, New York.